2016 Annual Competitiveness Analysis and Growth Slowdown Analysis for ASEAN-10

NUS National University of Singapore

Lee Kuan Yew School of Public Policy
ASIA COMPETITIVENESS INSTITUTE

In 2016 and 2017, ACI was ranked 13th globally, 2nd in Asia and 1st in Singapore amongst 90 think tanks worldwide under the "Best University Affiliated Think Tank" category by the Think Tanks and Civil Societies Program at the University of Pennsylvania, USA.

About ACI

The Asia Competitiveness Institute (ACI) was established in August 2006 as a research centre at the Lee Kuan Yew School of Public Policy (LKYSPP), National University of Singapore (NUS). It aims to build the intellectual leadership and network for understanding and developing competitiveness in the Asia region. ACI seeks to contribute to the enhancement of inclusive growth, living standards and institutional governance through competitiveness research on sub-national economies in Asia. It identifies mitigating issues and challenges for potential public policy interventions through close collaboration with regional governments, business corporations, policy think-tanks and academics. ACI's three key research pillars include (i) sub-national economies level competitiveness analysis and city-level liveability analysis, (ii) firm-level competitiveness analysis in 16 Asia economies, and (iii) Singapore's long-term growth strategies and public policy analysis.

ACI's value propositions may be encapsulated in its acronym:
Analytical inputs to initiate policies for policy-makers and business leaders in Asia
Capacity building to enable others through improvement in productivity and efficiency
Intellectual leadership to create pragmatic models of competitiveness and inclusive growth

The institute's core research competencies can also be encapsulated in this acronym describing our evidence-based assessments conducted on public policies for **A**SEAN in the context of the rise of **C**hina and **I**ndia.

Vision and Mission

- ACI's over-arching vision is to build up its research credibility with policy impact, contributing as a professional, world-class think-tank.
- ACI's mission is to establish our niche as a leading policy think-tank by identifying competitiveness trends, opportunities and challenges, as well as promoting competition and synergising complementarities amongst Asian economies and business corporations.
- ACI endeavours to articulate sound recommendations, entice discourse, and shape agenda in the arena of public policy amongst Asian governments.
- ACI undertakes evidence-based analysis of public policy issues and decisions, in order to provide assessment of their effectiveness as well as economic and societal impact.

Research Initiatives and Collaborations

I. Identify trends of competitiveness and policy analysis on trade and investment of ASEAN, within the regional context of competition and complementarities with China and India.

II. Identify competitive strengths and conduct policy analysis on Singapore within the context of regional economies with international benchmarking.

III. We are regularly releasing three indices on liveability ranking including 64 Global Cities, 100 Greater China Cities and 17 Shandong Cities.

IV. We have established an Ease of Doing Business Index on Attractiveness to Investors, Business Friendliness and Competitive Policies for 21 sub-national economies of India and 33 sub-national economies of Indonesia.

V. We have signed Memoranda of Understanding with The World Bank (2015), SPRING Singapore (2014) and European Central Bank (2014). The Memorandum of Understanding between The World Bank and National University of Singapore, coordinated through ACI, was signed in 2016.

VI. We have signed Memoranda of Understanding with various institutions in Greater China economies, including Shanghai Academy of Social Sciences (2016), Shandong Academy of Social Sciences (2015), Chongqing Municipal People's Government (2015), China Institute for Reform and Development, Haikou (2015), Counsellors' Office of the People's Government of Guangdong Province (LOI, 2014) and Chung-Hua Institution for Economic Research, Taiwan (2015).

VII. We have signed Memoranda of Understanding with six Chief Ministers' Offices in Andhra Pradesh (2015), Bihar (2015), Chhattisgarh (2015), Madhya Pradesh (2015), Odisha (2015) and Punjab (2015).

VIII. We have signed Memoranda of Understanding with Committee for Acceleration of Priority Infrastructure Delivery at Coordinating Ministry for Economic Affairs, Indonesia (2016), Indonesia Investment Coordinating Board (2014), Indonesian Agency for Agricultural Research and Development at Ministry of Agriculture (2014), Indonesian President's Delivery Unit for Developing Monitoring and Oversight (2013) and Employer's Association of Indonesia (2013).

IX. We have signed Memoranda of Understanding with ASEAN think-tanks and institutions, including Vietnam Chamber of Commerce and Industry (2016), Centre for Strategic and International Studies, Indonesia (2015), Institute of Strategic & International Studies, Malaysia (2015), Philippine Institute for Development Studies (2015), Thailand Development Research Institute (2015) and Central Institute for Economic Management, Vietnam (2015).

About ACI's Research Pillars

ACI has consciously engaged in economic research that has significant relevance to Singapore and the Asian region. Over the years, ACI has focused on our expertise in quantitative competitiveness analysis and simulation, spinning off volumes of research output in the applications of our methodology and regional insight. At this stage, ACI has identified three core research pillars that will guide and define its research efforts moving forward. The three research pillars are as follows:

Pillar I. Sub-national Economies Competitiveness Analysis

ACI engages in systematic and methodical competitiveness analyses of the *sub-national economies* by using an evidence-based, empirical approach involving a comprehensive list of relevant indicators, which are categorised under multiple layers called the 'environments'. A number of our projects, including competitiveness analyses of Greater China, ASEAN-10, India, and Indonesia, as well as other thematic research projects, were conducted by adopting this common methodology, with potential variations in the specific environments and indicators. ACI's competitiveness analysis of Asian economies goes beyond the usual ranking to offer constructive policy recommendations on how individual member states can improve their rankings vis-à-vis their sub-national or regional peers through the application of the 'what-if' simulation, which provides the projected improvements of each state's ranking whereby the bottom one-fifth of its indicators are enhanced.

Pillar II. Micro-based Firm Level Competitiveness Analysis

Micro-based firm level competitiveness analysis is ACI's second research pillar that has been developed in view of the intrinsic importance of firm-level competitiveness in terms of productivity, efficiency, and governance. In the context of globalisation, mobility of economic activities, and blurring of borders, an understanding of the determinants and dynamics of firm-level competitiveness is paramount, in order for policy makers to make adjustments and prepare their industries for an increasingly competitive economic landscape. To this end, ACI has partnered with the European Central Bank to carry out research in this area, possessing a solid foundation in firm-level productivity research in the form of European Competitiveness Network database and methodology. ACI envisaged the expansion of CompNet into Asia, thereby pioneering the Asia CompNet research network encompassing 16 economies in Asia.

Pillar III. Singapore's Long-term Economic Growth Strategies and Public Policies Analysis

The third and imminent research pillar focuses on Singapore's long-term economic growth strategies in the context of changing circumstances, future trends, and emerging opportunities for Singapore in the decades ahead. In particular, ACI will take on the task of critically examining Singapore's public policy strengths and areas of improvement by assessing policy successes of the past, identifying new issues to address and the current policy gaps, through a systematic and evidence-based research inquiry using quantitative methodology and empirical data, leveraging on our network of policy experts.

Founding Patron and International Advisory Panel

Founding Patron

Mr George Yeo
Visiting Scholar, Lee Kuan Yew School of Public Policy, National University of Singapore & Former Minister of Foreign Affairs, Singapore

International Advisory Panel

Co-Chairs:

Professor Michael Porter (2006-2010)
Bishop William Lawrence University Professor

Ms Marjorie Yang (2006-2012)
Chairman, Esquel Group

Members:

Professor Kishore Mahbubani
Dean, Lee Kuan Yew School of Public Policy, National University of Singapore

Dr Kuntoro Mangkusubroto
Head, President's Delivery Unit for Developing Monitoring and Oversight (UKP4), Indonesia

Mr Narayana Murthy
Chairman, Infosys Technologies Limited

Mr Philip Yeo
Chairman, SPRING Singapore

Mr Loh Khum Yean
Permanent Secretary, Ministry of Trade and Industry

Ms Yong Ying-I
Permanent Secretary, Public Service Division

Professor Chan Kam Leung Alan
Dean, College of Humanities, Arts and Social Sciences, Nanyang Technological University

Asia Competitiveness Institute

Co-Directors:

Associate Professor Tan Khee Giap (2011 till now)
Professor Tan Kong Yam (2011 till now)

Asia Competitiveness Institute - World Scientific Series

(ISSN: 2424-9912)

Series Editor: Tan Khee Giap (*Lee Kuan Yew School of Public Policy, NUS, Singapore*)

In the tradition of the Asia Competitiveness Institute (ACI) at the Lee Kuan Yew School of Public Policy, National University of Singapore (NUS), our research publications make a distinctive contribution to the understanding of economic development in Asia. These books, first published in 2013, in the Asia Competitiveness Institute - World Scientific Series evaluate and track competitiveness for the sub-national economies of China, India, Indonesia and ASEAN annually through combining leading-edge methodologies with an extensive dataset. The study covers four environments of competitiveness: (1) Macroeconomic Stability, (2) Government and Institutional Setting, (3) Financial, Businesses and Manpower Conditions, and (4) Quality of Life and Infrastructure Development. It also conducts "what-if" policy simulations to propose policy suggestions.

2016

2016 Annual Competitiveness Analysis and Growth Slowdown Analysis for ASEAN-10
by Tan Khee Giap, Nguyen Le Phuong Anh & Luu Nguyen Trieu Duong (Lee Kuan Yew School of Public Policy, NUS, Singapore)

2016 Growth Slowdown Analysis by Income Thresholds and Annual Update of Competitiveness Analysis for 34 Greater China Economies
by Tan Khee Giap, Wang Peng & Xie Teleixi (Lee Kuan Yew School of Public Policy, NUS, Singapore)

Inaugural 2016 Ease of Doing Business Index on Attractiveness to Investors, Business Friendliness and Competitive Policies (EDB Index ABC) for 21 Sub-National Economies of India
by Tan Khee Giap, Sasidaran Gopalan, Jigyasa Sharma & Tan Kong Yam (Lee Kuan Yew School of Public Policy, NUS, Singapore)

2016 Annual Competitiveness and Growth Slowdown Analysis for Sub-National Economies of India
by Tan Khee Giap, Sasidaran Gopalan, Anuja Tandon & Tan Kong Yam (Lee Kuan Yew School of Public Policy, NUS, Singapore)

2016 Growth Slowdown Analysis, Ease of Doing Business Index, and Annual Competitiveness Studies of Indonesia's Sub-National Economies
by Tan Khee Giap, Mulya Amri, Nursyahida Ahmad & Tan Kong Yam (Lee Kuan Yew School of Public Policy, NUS, Singapore)

2016 Annual Competitiveness Analysis and Development Strategies for Indonesian Provinces
by Tan Khee Giap, Mulya Amri & Nursyahida Ahmad (Lee Kuan Yew School of Public Policy, NUS, Singapore)

2015

2015 Annual Competitiveness Analysis, Agricultural Productivity and Development Vision for ASEAN-10
by Tan Khee Giap, Nguyen Le Phuong Anh, Sasidaran Gopalan & Luu Nguyen Trieu Duong (Lee Kuan Yew School of Public Policy, NUS, Singapore)

*More information on this series can also be found at http://www.worldscientific.com/series/aciwss

(Continued at end of book)

Asia Competitiveness Institute - World Scientific Series

2016 Annual Competitiveness Analysis and Growth Slowdown Analysis for ASEAN-10

Tan Khee Giap
Co-Director, Asia Competitiveness Institute
Lee Kuan Yew School of Public Policy, National University of Singapore

Nguyen Le Phuong Anh
Research Fellow, Asia Competitiveness Institute
Lee Kuan Yew School of Public Policy, National University of Singapore

Luu Nguyen Trieu Duong
Research Associate, Asia Competitiveness Institute
Lee Kuan Yew School of Public Policy, National University of Singapore

Special Remarks

Heng Swee Keat
Minister for Finance, Singapore

George Yeo
Visiting Scholar, Lee Kuan Yew School of Public Policy, National University of Singapore
Former Minister for Foreign Affairs, Singapore

Reviewers

Tan Sri Rastam Mohd Isa
Chairman and Chief Executive, Institute of Strategic and International Studies (ISIS), Malaysia

Kirida Bhaopichitr
Research Director, Thailand Development Research Institute (TDRI), Thailand

Gilberto M. Llanto
President, Philippine Institute for Development Studies (PIDS), Philippines

Darwin Marcelo
Infrastructure Economist, The World Bank Group

Nguyen Dinh Cung
President, Central Institute for Economic Management (CIEM), Vietnam

Lee Kuan Yew School of Public Policy
Asia Competitiveness Institute
NUS National University of Singapore
World Scientific

Published by

World Scientific Publishing Co. Pte. Ltd.
5 Toh Tuck Link, Singapore 596224
USA office: 27 Warren Street, Suite 401-402, Hackensack, NJ 07601
UK office: 57 Shelton Street, Covent Garden, London WC2H 9HE

British Library Cataloguing-in-Publication Data
A catalogue record for this book is available from the British Library.

Asia Competitiveness Institute – World Scientific Series
2016 ANNUAL COMPETITIVENESS ANALYSIS AND GROWTH SLOWDOWN ANALYSIS FOR ASEAN-10

ISBN 978-981-3226-75-3

Desk Editor: Jiang Yulin

Typeset by Stallion Press
Email: enquiries@stallionpress.com

Printed in Singapore

Contents

*Based on the speech on "Building Deep Capabilities for the Future Economy" by Mr Heng Swee Keat, Minister for Finance of Singapore at the Economic Society of Singapore (ESS) Annual Dinner on Wednesday, 2 August 2017

Foreword

The year 2017 marks more than three decades of the launch of Vietnam's economic reform *Doi Moi* (Renovation). Over the past 30 years, Vietnam has witnessed an evident leap from low-income to middle-income economy with an average of 5 percent growth per annum in real GDP per capita between 1986 and 2015. Nonetheless, further development is not guaranteed. It is imperative to head for a new direction and invigorate the reforms in Vietnam. The Vietnamese business community, in particular, still have a long way to go to mark their presence in both the domestic and global markets.

Against this backdrop, the Vietnam Chamber of Commerce and Industry (VCCI) seeks to represent and steer the Vietnamese business community to forge ahead. The annual competitiveness analysis and simulation study for ASEAN-10 conducted by the Asia Competitiveness Institute (ACI) at the Lee Kuan Yew School of Public Policy (LKYSPP), National University of Singapore (NUS) serves as an instructive roadmap for this purpose. The ACI's competitiveness framework does not only provides an overview of competitiveness in each ASEAN member state through the ranking of each economy, but has gone beyond that to identify strengths and weaknesses in various aspects such as macroeconomic stability and governance. The rigorous and systematic studies also shed light on concrete policy recommendations for policy-makers in the respective economy.

Meanwhile, as Vietnam is deepening its integration into the global economy, the growth slowdown analysis undertaken by ACI in this edition sends a timely alert for the economy, especially the business actors, to adapt to rising socio-economic uncertainties which may stall global growth. In addition, the chapter dedicated to the transitional economies is particularly useful for Vietnam as the country has come to a monumental juncture which requires deep reflections on the current development trajectory and careful planning for the way forward. By having the priorities of improving economic competitiveness, enhancing institutional capacity and facilitating balanced development in mind, this publication can act as a catalyst for future reforms.

2017 is also a critical year for Vietnam to demonstrate its leadership as it hosts the APEC. In this context, the extensive evidence-based research conducted by ACI will also serve as a basis for APEC's future development agenda in the post-Bogor era. I believe that VCCI can leverage on the excellent work by ACI which provides important and constructive insights for the Vietnamese economy and the business community to make headway amidst rising global uncertainties. I extend whole hearted support for ACI's research projects and look forward to collaborating with ACI in the forthcoming studies on Vietnamese Small and Medium Enterprises (SMEs).

Dr Vu Tien Loc
Chairman and President
Vietnam Chamber of Commerce and Industry (VCCI)

Preface

This year's celebration of Association of Southeast Asian Nations' (ASEAN's) 50th anniversary is a toast to the diversity of the regional cooperation which has brought us together rather than driven us apart. The Asia Competitiveness Institute (ACI) at the Lee Kuan Yew School of Public Policy (LKYSPP), National University of Singapore (NUS) aspires to spearhead the public discourse on regional and sub-national competitiveness. Among ACI's flagship projects is the annual empirical competitiveness analysis of ASEAN. The Annual Competitiveness Analysis for ASEAN-10 is now in its fourth edition. It sheds light on the pertinent challenges faced by the respective ASEAN economies and provides inputs for policy formulation.

Notwithstanding the impressive growth of the ASEAN economies from riding on the globalisation wave, trade has also brought about adverse effects on income distribution between and within countries. Moreover, the path ahead is full of uncertainties against the backdrop of rising protectionism and increasing geopolitical tensions. In this context, this publication is timely as it includes extensive growth slowdown analysis of the ASEAN economies. The methodological approach categorises the economies into income groups and enables customised solutions to the growth and development issues that each ASEAN member faces. The framework goes beyond ranking the economies to incorporate *what-if* policy simulations on how each economy can improve its competitiveness. A customised approach is vital for a region as diverse as ASEAN.

This edition also presents in-depth studies on four transitional economies in ASEAN, namely Cambodia, Laos, Myanmar and Vietnam. The research has included the reform progress and prevailing challenges which have impeded development of the economies. This offers insights to the stakeholders in fostering better reform policies and more importantly to call for concerted efforts in bridging the development gaps among ASEAN countries for inclusive development in Southeast Asia.

ACI has been on the forefront of Asian competitiveness studies with this publication on ASEAN, as well as companion competitiveness series on Greater China, India and Indonesia. We hope this study augments the ongoing policy dialogue in ASEAN and contributes to the ambitious blueprint for the establishment of the ASEAN Community.

Professor Kishore Mahbubani
Dean
Lee Kuan Yew School of Public Policy
National University of Singapore

Acknowledgements

We from the Asia Competitiveness Institute (ACI) at the Lee Kuan Yew School of Public Policy (LKYSPP), National University of Singapore (NUS), have combined leading-edge research methodologies with extensive data collection efforts to evaluate and track economic competitiveness since 2000 at both national and sub-national levels for over 100 Asian economies including Greater China, India, Indonesia and ASEAN-10.

In this book on *2016 Annual Competitiveness Analysis and Growth Slowdown Analysis for ASEAN-10*, we benefit from the insights of Mr George Yeo, Former Minister for Foreign Affairs of Singapore, who provided a thoughtful reflection on identities and their continued relevance for policy-making. The annual competitiveness analysis for ASEAN-10 is also updated. Holistically, ACI offers evidence-based assessment of both economic, institutional and social indicators at the macro level and sectoral indicators at the micro level for competitiveness evaluation. Given prevailing worries about ASEAN economies falling into the "middle-income trap", we also conduct the growth slowdown analysis for the ASEAN economies. Through income-group specific econometric models, we identify determinants of growth slowdown and compute the predictive probability of slowdown for each ASEAN economy. Concerning the transitional economies, we evaluate the progress of economic reforms in Cambodia, Laos, Myanmar and Vietnam, from which we draw policy implications for these countries' future development. Finally, recognising the possible disruptive changes in the future economy, the insightful speech by Mr Heng Swee Keat, Minister for Finance of Singapore has shed light on the path ahead for Singapore.

We would like to place on record our heartfelt gratitude for Mr George Yeo for his contribution to Chapter 1 of this book. In the current context of rising socio-economic uncertainties around the globe, his deliberation on identities is a timely reminder of the powerful political and sociological forces shaping our world today. We are also very grateful to Mr Heng Swee Keat for his inputs in Chapter 5 of this book. Mr Heng's policy discussion on building capabilities among the firms and people serves as a clear roadmap to prepare Singapore for the future economy.

The publication of this book would also not have been possible without the tremendous support from various country experts who attended the ACI-World Bank ASEAN Economic Forum jointly organised by ACI and the World Bank at LKYSPP, NUS on 9th September 2016. We wish to thank the following reviewers who gave their constructive comments and offered instructive insights on the respective chapters as incorporated in this book:

Tan Sri Rastam Mohd Isa
Chairman and Chief Executive, Institute of Strategic and International Studies (ISIS), Malaysia

Dr Gilberto M. Llanto
President, Philippine Institute for Development Studies (PIDS), Philippines

Dr Nguyen Dinh Cung
President, Central Institute for Economic Management (CIEM), Vietnam

Dr Darwin Marcelo
Infrastructure Economist, The World Bank Group

Dr Kirida Bhaopichitr
Research Director, Thailand Development Research Institute (TDRI), Thailand

We would also like to place on record our appreciation for the support and encouragement from Dean Kishore Mahbubani; Associate Professor Eduardo Araral, Vice Dean (Research); Mr Donald Low, Associate Dean (Research and Executive Education); Mr Thomas Chan Hean Boon (Associate Director, Research Support Unit) and other colleagues at LKYSPP. Finally, this book would not have been possible without the dedicated effort of all research and administrative staff at ACI. Thus we note with tremendous appreciation the high team spirit of all ACI staff including Nguyen Duy, Chuah Hui Yin, Yap Xin Yi, Tracy Cai Jiao and Nurliyana Binte Yusoff.

Tan Khee Giap
Nguyen Le Phuong Anh
Luu Nguyen Trieu Duong

Asia Competitiveness Institute
Lee Kuan Yew School of Public Policy
National University of Singapore

About the Authors

Tan Khee Giap is a Co-Director of the Asia Competitiveness Institute (ACI) and Associate Professor at the Lee Kuan Yew School of Public Policy, National University of Singapore. He is also the Chairman of the Singapore National Committee for Pacific Economic Cooperation. Upon graduating with a PhD from University of East Anglia, England, in 1987 under the Overseas Research Scheme awarded by the Committee of Vice-Chancellors and Principals of the Universities of the United Kingdom, he joined the banking sector as a treasury manager and served as secretary to the Assets and Liabilities Committee for three years, thereafter he taught at the Department of Economics and Statistics, National University of Singapore, 1990–1993. Dr Tan joined Nanyang Technological University in 1993 and was Associate Dean, Graduate Studies Office, 2007–2009. He is now with Lee Kuan Yew School of Public Policy, National University of Singapore.

Dr Tan has consulted extensively with the various government ministries, statutory boards and government-linked companies of Singapore government including Ministry of Finance, Ministry of Trade & Industry, Ministry of Manpower, Housing & Development Board, Civil Aviation Authority of Singapore, Singapore Tourism Board, Trade Development Board, Maritime Port Authority, Ministry of Information, Culture & Arts, Economic Development Board, Ministry of National Development, Media Development Authority, Ministry of Environment and Water Resources, Singapore Design Council, Ministry of Community Development, Youth & Sports, Singapore Press Holdings, Mendaki, StarHub, CapitaLand and Great Eastern Life on policies concerning financial, fiscal, trade, tourism, public housing, labour, telecommunication, tourism, liveable cities, creative industry, media, community development, airport and seaport activities. He has also served as a consultant to international agencies such as the Asian Development Bank, Asian Development Bank Institute, United Nations Industrial Development Group, World Gold Council, ASEAN Secretariat, Central Policy Unit of Hong Kong, Kerzner International, Las Vegas Sands and Marina Bay Sands.

Dr Tan is the lead author for 27 books, serving as journals editor and published widely in international refereed journals. His current research interests include econometric forecasting, Cost of Living Index, Global Liveable Cities Index and competitiveness analysis on 31 provinces in China, 35 states in India and ASEAN-10 economies.

Dr Tan was Deputy President of the Singapore Economic Society, 2004. He served in the 2002 Economic Review Committee (ERC). He has also served as Chairman of the Task Force on Portable Medical Benefits (PMB), as the Deputy Chairman of the IPS Forum for Economic Restructuring (IFER) in 2003 and as a member of the Resource Panel of the Government Parliamentary Committee for Transport and Government Parliamentary Committee for Finance and Trade & Industry and Government Parliamentary Committee for Defence and Foreign Affairs since 2007.

Dr Tan has extensively advised and guided multinational corporations leading to public listings especially those companies from Mainland China and Taiwan. He is also currently an

Independent Director of the publicly listed BreadTalk Group, Boustead Projects, TEE Land and Chengdu Rural Commercial Bank.

Nguyen Le Phuong Anh is a Research Fellow at the Asia Competitiveness Institute (ACI) at the Lee Kuan Yew School of Public Policy (LKYSPP), National University of Singapore (NUS). Phuong Anh received her Bachelor (Honours) degree in Economics from Nanyang Technological University (NTU), Singapore, and a Master of Science degree in Development Studies from London School of Economics and Political Science (LSE), United Kingdom. Prior to joining ACI, she gained extensive experience working in the financial sector with OCBC, DBS and Bloomberg L.P. in Singapore, and additionally held a research internship position at the Mekong Institute in Khon Kaen, Thailand. At ACI, she co-authored two books titled *2014 Annual Indices for Expatriates and Ordinary Residents on Cost of Living, Wages and Purchasing Power for World's Major Cities* and *2014 Annual Competitiveness Ranking and Simulation Study for ASEAN-10 and Development Strategies to Enhance Asia Economic Connectivity*, and an editorial opinion on Vietnam for *The Straits Times*. She is currently coordinating the annual competitiveness study of the ASEAN-10 economies. Phuong Anh's research interests include economic development policy, international political economy, ASEAN economies and applied econometrics.

Luu Nguyen Trieu Duong is a Research Associate at the Asia Competitiveness Institute (ACI), Lee Kuan Yew School of Public Policy (LKYSPP), National University of Singapore (NUS). Luu graduated from NUS in 2015 with a Second Upper Class Honours Bachelor of Social Sciences in Economics. Luu was a recipient of the ASEAN Undergraduate Scholarship and was placed on the Dean's List and Dean's Scholar List on separate occasions during his course of study. At ACI, he is the lead coordinator of the ACI's flagship project "Cost of Living, Wages and Purchasing Power Indices for Expatriates and Ordinary Residents in World's Major Cities", the lead coordinator of the project "Econometric Modelling of Domestic and External Engines of Growth for ASEAN Economies" and the co-coordinator of the ASEAN research cluster overseeing all projects related to ASEAN-10. He also participated extensively in the research on growth slowdown analysis by income thresholds and the study on the effects of exchange rate on foreign direct investments. Luu has co-authored journal articles, books and editorial-opinions on cost of living in world's major cities as well as economic development in ASEAN economies. Luu's research interests include growth and development, ASEAN economies, applied econometrics, international trade and public economics.

List of Abbreviations

ACI	Asia Competitiveness Institute
ADB	Asian Development Bank
AEC	ASEAN Economic Community
AFC	Asian Financial Crisis
AI	Artificial Intelligence
AIIB	Asian Infrastructure Investment Bank
ASEAN	Association of Southeast Asian Nations
ASW	ASEAN Single Window
BKPM	Indonesia Investment Coordinating Board
BMA	Bayesian Model Averaging
BMT	Basic Military Training
BRIC	Brazil, Russia, India and China
CEO	Chief Executive Officer
CFE	Committee on the Future Economy
CIEM	Central Institute for Economic Management, Vietnam
CLMV	Cambodia, Laos, Myanmar and Vietnam
CMIE	Centre for Monitoring Indian Economy Pvt. Ltd
COC	Code of Conduct
COT	Competitiveness-Over-Time
CSO	Civil Society Organisation
CUI	Catch-Up Index
EAS	East Asia Summit
ECM	Error Correction Model
EFI	Enterprise Future Initiative
EIU	Economist Intelligence Unit
ESS	Economic Society of Singapore
EU	European Union
FBMC	Financial, Businesses and Manpower Conditions
FDI	Foreign Direct Investment
FTA	Free Trade Agreement
GAM	Gerakan Aceh Merdeka
GCR	Global Competitiveness Report
GDP	Gross Domestic Product
GFC	Global Financial Crisis
GIA	Global Innovation Alliance
GIS	Government and Institutional Setting
GLCI	Global Liveable City Index

GMID	Global Market Information Database
GNI	Gross National Income
GRDP	Gross Regional Domestic Product
HDI	Human Development Index
HPAEs	High-Performing Asian Economies
IAI	Initiative for ASEAN Integration
ICT	Information and Communications Technology
ILO	International Labour Organisation
IMD	Institute for Management Development
IMF	International Monetary Fund
IP	Intellectual Property
IS	Islamic State
ISIS	Institute of Strategic and International Studies, Malaysia
ITE	Institute of Technical Education
ITMs	Industry Transformation Maps
IWSP	Integrated Work-Study Programme
LDCs	Least Developed Countries
LPI	Logistic Performance Index
LKYSPP	Lee Kuan Yew School of Public Policy
MDG	Millennium Development Goal
MFA	Ministry of Foreign Affairs Singapore
MNC	Multinational Corporation
MOE	Ministry of Education
MOSPI	Ministry of Statistics and Programme Implementation
MS	Macroeconomic Stability
MSMEs	Micro, Small and Medium Enterprises
MSR	Maritime Silk Road
MTI	Ministry of Trade and Industry
NEM	New Economic Mechanism
NGO	Non-governmental Organisation
NIEs	Newly Industrialising Economies
NS	National Service
NSW	National Single Window
NTU	Nanyang Technological University
NUS	National University of Singapore
OBOR	One Belt, One Road Initiative
ODA	Official Development Assistance
OECD	Organisation for Economic Cooperation and Development
ORD	Operationally Ready Date
PET	Pre-employment Training
PIAAC	Programme for the International Assessment of Adult Competencies
PIDS	Philippine Institute for Development Studies, Philippines

PIP	Posterior Inclusion Probability
PLC	Promising Local Enterprise
PPP	Purchasing Power Parity
PRC	People's Republic of China
PRK	People's Republic of Kampuchea
PSTD	Posterior Standard Deviation
QLID	Quality of Life and Infrastructure Development
RCA	Revealed Comparative Advantage
RCEP	Regional Comprehensive Economic Partnership
RSVI	Ranked Standardised Value of Indicator
SAF	Singapore Armed Forces
SCCCI	Singapore Chinese Chamber of Commerce and Industry
SCS	Singapore Computer Society
SD	Standard Deviation
SFI	Skills Future Initiative
SIT	Singapore Institute of Technology
SITF	Singapore Infocomm Technology Federation
SMEs	Small and Medium Enterprises
SOE	State-owned Enterprise
STEM	Science, Technology, Engineering and Mathematics
SVI	Standardised Value of Indicator
TACs	Trade Associations and Chambers
TCP/IP	Transmission Control Protocol/Internet Protocol
TDRI	Thailand Development Research Institute
TeSA	TechSkills Accelerator
TFP	Total Factor Productivity
TOT	Terms of Trade
TPP	Trans-Pacific Partnership
UIS	UNESCO Institute for Statistics
UK	United Kingdom
UN	United Nations
UNCTAD	United Nations Conference on Trade and Development
UNDP	United Nations Development Programme
UNICEF	United Nations International Children's Emergency Fund
US	United States
VCP	Vietnamese Communist Party
VUCA	Volatility, Uncertainty, Complexity and Ambiguity
WCY	World Competitiveness Yearbook
WEF	World Economic Forum
WTO	World Trade Organisation

List of Figures and Tables

Figures

Chapter 2

Chapter 5

Chapter 6

Tables

Chapter 1

Chapter 2

Discussant Notes 2.2

Chapter 3

Chapter 4

Chapter 6

Chapter 1

A Sense of Self in an Age of Globalisation and ASEAN's Respect for Diversity

1.1 Introduction

Established in 1967 initially as a security grouping, the Association of Southeast Asian Nations (ASEAN), currently with 10 members, has evolved to become one of the most enduring regional associations in the developing world today. Having braved through multiple domestic, regional and global economic crises, particularly the Asian Financial Crisis of 1997–1998 and the Global Financial Crisis of 2008–2009, ASEAN as a whole has proven its increasing resilience in the face of an increasingly uncertain global economic landscape and become the seventh largest economy in the world with a combined Gross Domestic Product (GDP) of 2.4 trillion US dollars by 2014.[1] It has also been tipped to become the fourth-largest economy after the United States (US), the European Union (EU) and China by as early as 2030.[2]

Nevertheless, challenges remain. There are still substantial socio-economic gaps between the ASEAN-6, which includes Brunei, Indonesia, Malaysia, Philippines, Thailand and Singapore, and the less developed Cambodia, Laos, Myanmar and Vietnam (CLMV). In fact, disparities exist even among the ASEAN-6 countries, with Singapore leading the pack by some distance in many important measures such as GDP per capita and Human Development Index as seen in Table 1.1 below. Moreover, the optimistic economic projections for ASEAN can only be realised if the member states can sustain the positive growth momentums by carrying out suitable reforms to address longstanding structural weaknesses.

In the tradition of the Asia Competitiveness Institute (ACI) at the Lee Kuan Yew School of Public Policy (LKYSPP), National University of Singapore (NUS), our research publications make a distinctive contribution to the literature by focusing on pertinent regional and national economic issues of ASEAN as one of our flagship projects.[3] The subsequent chapters of this book will cover the prevailing major economic trends, the potential opportunities and challenges as well as the corresponding policy implications for the ASEAN economies. However, first, it is important to recognise that development is not just a function of economic variables. It is also driven by sociological and political factors which shape the domestic, regional and global institutional structures on which economic growth depends.

In Southeast Asia, managing the incredible diversity within the region remains the primary challenge for policy-makers. Dubbed "the Balkans of Asia", the ASEAN member states include

[1] See McKinsey Global Institute (2014).

[2] This assessment was made by J.P. Morgan, see https://www.jpmorgan.com/country/US/EN/cib/investment-banking/trade-asean-future (accessed on 28 March 2017).

[3] See Tan *et al.* (2013), Tan *et al.* (2015) and Tan *et al.* (2017a) for previous publications on ASEAN. See Tan *et al.* (2017b); Tan *et al.* (2017c); Tan *et al.* (2017d) and Tan *et al.* (2017e) for other flagship projects on Greater China, India and Indonesia.

Table 1.1: ASEAN-10 in a Snapshot, 2014

Country	Population (Millions)	GDP (Million Constant 2010 US Dollars)	GDP per Capita (Constant 2010 US Dollars)	Human Development Index
Brunei	0.4	13,715.4	32,859.7	0.864
Cambodia	15.3	14,858.2	969.3	0.558
Indonesia	254.5	942,339.2	3,703.4	0.686
Laos	6.7	9,702.2	1,450.4	0.582
Malaysia	29.9	314,333.9	10,512.1	0.787
Myanmar	53.4	65,742.5	1,230.3	0.552
Philippines	99.1	251,010.9	2,531.9	0.679
Singapore	5.5	281,367.1	51,440.8	0.924
Thailand	67.7	381,679.4	5,635.6	0.738
Vietnam	90.7	144,834.7	1,596.3	0.678

Source: World Bank and the United Nations Development Programme (UNDP).

240 million Muslims, 130 million Christians, 140 million Buddhists, 7 million Hindus and 50 million followers of folk religions.[4] They also vary greatly in terms of political systems, languages and cultures. Over the past 50 years, ASEAN has played a crucial role in maintaining cohesion between its members through a respect for such diversity. Nevertheless, the bloc is under risk of losing its solidarity, especially because of territorial disputes between the ASEAN countries and China in the South China Sea.

At this juncture, as ASEAN approaches the 50th anniversary of its founding, it is appropriate that we reflect on the economic, sociological and political forces which underline the development trajectory of the region. In Section 1.2 below, we provide a lecture delivered by Mr George Yeo, former Minister for Foreign Affairs of Singapore, on "A Sense of Self in an Age of Globalisation". Drawing on a vast well of historical and modern examples, Mr Yeo emphasised the continued relevance of human beings' identities for policy-making. With respect to ASEAN, he provided a very timely reminder: "*Here in Southeast Asia, we have to be mindful of not riding roughshod over deep identities. We ignore these identities at our peril*". Section 1.3 will then outline the overall roadmap for the rest of the book.

1.2 A Sense of Self in an Age of Globalisation[5]

Having left the Ministry of Foreign Affairs (MFA) over five years ago, this feels like a homecoming. After spending more than a decade in the Foreign Ministry, foreign affairs and diplomacy have become a part of me. I am honoured to be invited back as one of your own.

---

[4] See Mahbubani (2015).

[5] This section is a reprint with permission of the speech by Mr George Yeo, Former Minister for Foreign Affairs of Singapore at the 9th S. Rajaratnam Lecture on Friday, 11 November 2016 at 1430hrs at The Ritz–Carlton Millenia

Sometimes, when I get animated about matters concerning Singapore's foreign policy, my wife reminds me that I am no longer in office and can I please be more detached in expressing my views to friends and colleagues in Singapore and Hong Kong.

1.2.1 Human Identity

Human identity is a strange thing. Next month, I will address the International Teochew Doctors Association Conference. I was intrigued to receive the invitation some months ago. The doctors refer to PhD holders. What has it got to do with being Teochew? If it is Teochew food or Teochew opera, I could understand but "Teochew doctors" seemed a bit strange. I did not reply immediately. A few weeks later, I was officially admitted into the Hong Kong Teochew Association. I must confess that I applied to join principally because it has a good Teochew restaurant which members are entitled to dine in. When I arrived for the induction, one of the Association leaders immediately asked me if I would be attending the "Teochew Doctors" Association Conference in Singapore. Oh, this is bigger than I thought. On the wall of the main dining room, I saw pictures of patrons and donors from prominent Teochew families going back decades including the picture of a young Li Ka-shing. Some were from my own ancestral village of Anbu. That night, I replied that I would be taking part in the December conference after being assured that I won't have to speak in the Teochew dialect.

Each of us has multiple identities. They run deep and are important to us. These identities could be religious, national, ethnic, tribal or personal but they are not to be trifled with. Among close friends, it is alright to make fun of a person's identity but, even so, one has to be careful.

Depending on the situation, some identities become more important than others. When young Singaporean men enter National Service (NS), they have their hair cut very short. Parents visiting their sons in Basic Military Training (BMT) have difficulty recognising them because they all look alike. There is a reason for this, which is to acculturate them to a highly disciplined organisation. When we want individuals to have a strong group identity, we make them wear uniform and suppress their other identities.

This imposed discipline is not natural. Once the discipline is taken away, or in a context where the higher identity is unimportant, the deeper identities assert themselves. We see this immediately in NS soldiers who reach Operationally Ready Date (ORD). But, after two years, the Singapore Armed Forces (SAF) leaves its imprint on their identity. When they are mobilised, they quickly fall into line again. This NS programming in Singapore men is obvious when they are overseas, especially in an emergency.

1.2.2 Cycles of History

Human society goes through cycles. In response to challenges, human society can become highly organised, sometimes into empires. Elaborate hierarchies are established. Those who conform are affirmed and rewarded. Those who don't are put down or punished. When Qin Shi Huang unified China more than 2000 years ago, scholars who advocated divergent ideas were

---

Singapore. The full text of the speech is also available at https://www.mfa.gov.sg/content/mfa/media_centre/press_room/pr/2016/201611/mfa-press-release--speech-by-mr-george-yeo--former-minister-for-.html (accessed 1 March, 2017).

buried alive and books were burnt so that there was a single orthodoxy. The unification of China enabled the economy to become much more productive. With a national system of roads and canals, and the standardisation of weights and measures, Qin China made possible an elaborate division of labour on a continental scale. Since then, every time China was reunified, it quickly became the world's biggest economy.

However, the harsh rule of Qin Shi Huang did not last long after him. His son was toppled and Han replaced Qin. An empire maintained by draconian law and the frequent use of force was replaced by a softer system based on Confucianist values. The unbending legalist principle of *fa* as replaced by the Confucianist ideal of proper behaviour, *li*. Thus if a prince behaves in a noble way, the people will accept his rule, naturally. If a father is a good father, the sons will be good sons, naturally. Of course, this was often not the case. Carrots and sticks had still to be used for effective governance but what was constantly held up as the ideal was proper behaviour.

Chinese history goes through long periods of unity followed by long periods of disunity. When it is united, its productivity is awesome. But when it is divided, the chaos is equally awesome. During the periods of disunity and dispersal, local Chinese communities continue to be held together by Confucianist values of *li*. Today, new Chinese diaspora communities sprouting in Europe, Africa and South America show similar characteristics. This gives Chinese people a deep identity which, contains within it, a belief that the ideal world is one where the entire world is one big happy family.

The Arabs have a similar longing for unity, strange though this may seem when one thinks of the Middle East today. There is a famous Arab Bedouin saying: I against my brother; my brother and I against my cousins; my cousins, brothers and I against the world. Islam arose out of Arab culture and gave it a higher unity in the *umma*. The hope for Arab unity is never extinguished; the Islamic ideal of a universal caliphate is not a hope, it is a millenarian quest.

Some years ago, I accompanied members of the Singapore Arab Association to the Yemen. I combined it with an official visit to what was then a peaceful, united country. The Foreign Minister Dr Al Kirby, a medical doctor, was my host in Sana'a, a wonderful human being. We first spent two days in the Wadi Hadramaut where many of the Arabs in Southeast Asia hail from originally. Most of the Arab Syeds in Southeast Asia are descendants of a common ancestor Syed Ahmed bin Isa al-Muhajir, himself a tenth descendent of the Prophet, who travelled from Basra and settled in the Hadhramaut, a thousand years ago. In our delegation was Dr Ho Eng Seng, a scholar from Penang, who wrote an interesting book on the Syeds of the Hadhramaut called *"The Graves of Tarim"*. Eng Seng is now the Director of our Middle East Institute. An essential ritual for a visit by Hadhrami Arabs to the Hadhramaut is the recitation of certain prayers by a Syed at the tomb of Syed Ahmed, the Muhajir. The only Syed in our delegation was Alwi Aidid, a Hadhrami from Penang, son of a Chinese mother. So it fell upon him to say the prayers. Normally a good-humoured friend, he was all coiled up that day. It seemed as if the entire burden of his ancestors was on his shoulders. After the obligatory prayers were said, he was his old relaxed self again. I bought many copies of Eng Seng's book and gave it to my Arab friends including Ali Alatas, Alwi Shihab and Hamid Albar.

In Southeast Asia, the prestige of the Syeds go up and down depending on political circumstances. Malay Sultans were eager to have them as sons-in-law so that their grandchildren would become descendants of the Prophet. This history of Hadhrami Syeds marrying into Malay royal families is well-recorded in *"The Graves of Tarim"*. In Indonesia, the Syeds had to play down their ancestry because of republicanism. But they know who they are and maintain certain rituals and traditions in the family. There was an Indonesian politician of Arab descendant whom I suspected to be a Syed. I decided to ask him point blank one day. When he replied that he was, I passed him a copy of Eng Seng's book. His immediate reaction was to turn to the index page of his family's name.

These deeper identities of human beings will become more important in the new age of globalisation.

1.2.3 Fragmentation and Neural Networks

Technological change is undermining hierarchies everywhere and an important reason for the anger against institutions based on hierarchies. This is a big subject now commonly subsumed under the phrase "The Fourth Industrial Revolution". In the past, institutions were maintained by ritual, by fear, by mystification, by hypocrisy, sometimes by outright lies. With cameras and microphones now ubiquitous, this is no longer possible. Those who pretend to be what they are not get quickly exposed and laughed at in the social media.

The support for Brexit expressed popular frustration with the loss of control to Brussels, to institutions so complicated that they no longer enjoy the affection of ordinary people. Thus, the larger issue of Brexit is not the United Kingdom but the nature of the European construction itself. In their hearts, the Europeans remain a collection of tribal peoples who are proud of their distinct identities. The sense of Roman citizenship, which was an overlay, disappeared a long time ago. Although the Western Roman Empire was reincarnated in the Roman Church, Christianity as a higher identity uniting Europeans lost its force during the religious wars which culminated in the Treaty of Westphalia in 1648. The anti-clericalism of the French Revolution in 1789 spread into many parts of Europe.

In the United States (US), the election of Donald Trump reflected a widespread loss of trust in the institutions which have made the US the most stable country in the world. Great institutions are never easily changed or dismantled. There must first be a period of creative destruction which means years of political upheaval and unhappiness. It will not be easy to break up encrusted vested interests.

We are seeing fragmentation everywhere. The nation-state itself is weakening as talent, capital and knowledge become more mobile. Patriotism based on the multinational state is weakening. The digital revolution is dramatically redistributing power in human society. Today, good teachers learn from their students; good parents learn from their children. Political or corporate leaders can no longer act as if they have a monopoly of knowledge, wisdom and moral authority.

Fragmentation, however, does not dissolve into chaos. The fragments are still held together by deeper identities which link them up across political borders, and across economic and cultural domains into complex neural networks. The apps on our smart phones are a manifestation of such network formation. For good or for ill, people are linking up to others with similar identities or interests. Being physically together no longer ensures interaction. Through the smart phone, the passengers in a train are each in his own world. We have become comfortable ignoring people around us. Sometimes, one gets the same feeling even around a family dining table.

The growth of networks creates new challenges. The Internet makes it easier to extend networks around the world. Birds of the same feather seek out each other. The Internet can broaden our minds but it can also narrow them. Those who have a deep interest in particular subjects are fed more material on the same subjects and encouraged to network with others who share them. That's how self-radicalisation happens.

1.2.4 New Challenges Ahead

The governance of networks is difficult because they straddle national jurisdictions. The dominant form of governance in the world today is through national governments. No government has full control over the Internet. International cooperation is difficult and slow. During the Cold War, it was the US which led the non-Communist world. Today, the world has become increasingly multipolar, calling into question US leadership. Superpower leadership is costly, having to be backed by expensive military power. Both at the national and international levels, governance has become more complicated and less effective.

The Soviet Empire was the first major casualty of the Fourth Industrial Revolution. Once the central governance structure cracked, the countries of Central and Eastern Europe became independent, and within the Soviet Union itself, each republic became an independent state. Those new countries which are held together by a deeper sense of identity are stable, including the core of Russia itself. Others like Yugoslavia broke up into smaller pieces. Even a smaller piece like Bosnia–Herzegovina would not hold together without strong outside intervention.

For a time, the US seeing itself as the sole superpower, the New Rome as some neo-conservatives call it, intervened to re-create the Middle East on the basis of democracy. September 11 became a reason to remove Saddam Hussein in Iraq and the Arab Spring a reason to remove Muammar Gaddhafi in Libya and Bashar al-Assad in Syria. It has been an absolute disaster. Without strong, brutal leaders holding tight the reins of power, these countries broke up into warring factions. Even as we meet today, horrible battles are taking place in Aleppo and Mosul, sister cities with long histories.

In Libya, the deep identity is tribal and the conflict there is therefore mostly tribal in nature. In such a situation without a dictator, it is Salafi Islam which is most able to unite tribes against common enemies. Ironically, the beneficiaries of the removal of Gaddafi are groups like Al Qaeda and ISIS acting against the West.

It was the underestimation by the Americans of the depth of the Sunni-Shiite divide in the Middle East that led to civil war and external interference in Iraq and Syria. An Arab ruler in the Gulf once told me that the most stable border in the entire region is that between Turkey and Iran. It is the same border which separated the Ottomans from the Safavids. The Safavids made Iran a Shiite country five hundred years ago. Children were taught to curse the first three caliphs — Abu Bakr, Umar and Uthman. Ali was the rightful successor of the Prophet. Safavid Iran became a Shiite kingdom. The Ottomans were Sunni. The agreement between them was that no Shiite in the Ottoman realm would bear arms. In this way, the Shiites in the Ottoman realm could not easily become a fifth column for Iran. This kept the peace. When the American coalition invaded Iraq, a major objective was the transfer of power to the Shiite majority. An old understanding had been unwounded with cataclysmic repercussions across the entire Fertile Crescent. Iran benefited while alarm bells rang in the Saudi Kingdom. The predominantly Sunni cities of Aleppo and Mosul are right now being recaptured by soldiers who are predominantly Shiite or Shiite-led, one with the help of Russia, the other with the help of the US.

It may be that Humpty Dumpty would have fallen anyway, eventually. But, if we had known how fragile the shell is, we might have found a better, gentler way to bring Humpty Dumpty down from the wall. But all this is in hindsight. It is easy to be wise after the event.

Here in Southeast Asia, we have to be mindful of not riding roughshod over deep identities. We ignore these identities at our peril. Indonesia's relatively smooth transition to a modern democracy could not have been foreseen during the Asian financial crisis when the vast country was in danger of breaking up. If there had been civil war, Singapore would not be left in peace. After East Timor became independent, successive Indonesian Presidents had the wisdom to accommodate the Acehnese. I remember talking to President Abdurrahman Wahid when he visited Singapore. As the Minister-in-Attendance, I was in the car with him. His touching wish was for an agreement which enables the Acehnese to feel that the land they live on is their own. After the Boxing Day tsunami, President Yudhoyono held the Indonesian Army back so that Vice President Jusuf Kalla could negotiate a peace agreement with the Gerakan Aceh Merdeka (GAM). Pak Jusuf, who monitored proceedings from Jakarta through two mobile phones, asked Minister Hamid Awaludin to invite GAM leaders in Helsinki for an informal meeting to break the ice first and build up trust before the start of negotiations. There can be no stable peace without the respect and accommodation of differences.

The challenge of the ethnic groups in Myanmar is an ongoing struggle. Many Western and Islamic countries are pressuring Daw Aung San Suu Kyi to solve the Rohingya problem in Rakhine State. There is an urgent need to ameliorate the suffering of the Rohingyas but this is a difficult political issue. Daw Suu cannot settle the Rohingya issue without first achieving a peace agreement with the other minority ethnic groups who collectively make up one third of the population. When her father Aung San signed the Panglong Agreement with the seven most important minority groups in 1947 on the eve of independence, which included the Rakhines, Bengalis were recognised as an ethnic minority but not Rohingyas. The ethnic issue is further complicated by the fact that many ethnic groups straddle the borders with Bangladesh, India, China and Thailand.

Myanmar's peaceful transition from a military government to a democratically elected government is a miracle which could not have been achieved without the patient support and understanding of ASEAN and other countries. What is needed now is economic development without which there can be no solution to the ethnic problem. During Daw Suu's recent visit to China, China agreed to play a helpful role. Earlier attempts to have a peace agreement without involving China could not succeed. For every Kachin living in Myanmar, there are two living in China. For every Wa living in Myanmar, there is another living in China.

1.2.5 ASEAN's Respect for Diversity

ASEAN is culturally the most diverse region in the world because of its complex geography. As a result of the Australian plate crashing into Asian tectonic plates, the entire region between the Himalayas and Australia is corrugated into high mountain ridges, deep valleys, indented coasts and the world's biggest archipelago, with strangely shaped islands like Mindanao, Sulawesi and Halmahera. Over the centuries, tribes have migrated southwards from the Chinese mainland, down the peninsulas and into the islands. Some were forced up the mountains. As empires waxed and waned on opposite sides, they brought to our shores aspects of their civilisation and bits of their DNA.

There can only be peace in Southeast Asia if we recognise and respect this diversity and build institutions based upon acceptance of diversity. While we should influence each other positively, we should never impose our views or our wills on one another.

The Malays describe the region as the lands below the winds (*tanah di bawa angin*). The winds blow one way six months of the year and the other way the other six months. The region is in between China and India not only geographically but also culturally. The instinct in coastal Southeast Asia is therefore to be open and neutral, welcoming all who come peacefully to our shores. Every time the China trade flowed strongly, it brought opportunity and prosperity to the kingdoms and principalities in the region. The China trade which flowed in the 19th century, which was the one which created modern Singapore, was however different. Trade was opened up by gunboats and had to conform to western rules. During that period, Southeast Asia was carved up into colonial domains except for Thailand which astutely adjusted to whichever was the prevailing power.

The new China trade of the 21st century will revert back to earlier China trades which allowed for greater diversity. President Xi Jinping's One Belt, One Road, is based on a voluntary principle. There is no requirement to change one's internal operating system in order to become part of it. Like the Internet, one can participate in the network by accepting certain protocols, similar to the Transmission Control Protocol/Internet Protocol (TCP/IP). This is now unfolding on an epic scale, transforming the face of Eurasia. Powers which see China as a rival are reacting uneasily to this development. The US and Japan are refusing to join the Asian Infrastructure Investment Bank (AIIB). India is not enthusiastic, worried that the Kashgar–Gwadar corridor will affect it adversely. These countries fear that China will pull too many of the strings.

China will fail if it tries to dominate its neighbours by force or intimidation. Deng Xiaoping once said that if China ever tries to be a new hegemon, other countries should unite with the Chinese people to defeat it. What China is doing instead is to make use of its economic strength to win friends and influence people. Those who are friendly to China are rewarded while those who are not so friendly find themselves economically disadvantaged. However, the Chinese know that they cannot expect an exclusive position for themselves in Southeast Asia which was precisely the point made by Premier Zhu Rongji in Phnom Penh in 2002 when he signed the Framework Agreement for the ASEAN-China Free Trade Agreement (FTA) with ASEAN leaders. No one in ASEAN wants China as an enemy. The more China is a friend, the more the US, Japan, India and Europe will also be welcomed as friends because that gives us diversification. The more, the merrier.

Territorial disputes in the South China Sea must, however, be well managed. The US is understandably concerned. However, trying to play off the US against China, or vice versa, is a dangerous game for ASEAN countries. All of us in ASEAN are small powers in comparison to these two. We end up being minor pieces on their global chessboard to be sacrificed when expedient. The high tension earlier this year seems to have ameliorated as all four countries with competing claims and China are talking in a constructive way. Because of long contact with Southeast over many centuries, China has a fine sense of ASEAN's diversity and calibrates its foreign policy to this reality.

ASEAN itself is slowly but steadily inculcating in its people a sense of ASEAN citizenry. The ASEAN flag now flies alongside national flags of member states in all overseas missions. Next year, ASEAN celebrates its 50th Anniversary. I hope we will be able to field an ASEAN soccer team for the World Cup one day, cheered on by all the people of ASEAN.

1.2.6 Singapore's Identity and Destiny

Singapore's identity is rooted in our geography and history. At the southernmost tip of the Eurasia landmass, we are where ships turn as the winds change direction. Singapore is a child of the maritime silk route. In the coming decades, this China trade will flow with greater strength than ever before. Behind China, there is a rising India. As Prof Wang Gungwu put it beautifully, we are where the *mandalas* of China and India intersect. The growth of One Belt, One Road is therefore a historic opportunity for Singapore which, provided we seize it with both hands, will take us far.

Singapore's destiny is in Southeast Asia. We are at the heart of ASEAN and the most *ASEAN-ised* of all the ASEAN countries. Every member country in ASEAN has a strong presence in Singapore. The rich diversity of ASEAN has its reflection in the Singapore crystal. We are densely connected economically and culturally with all the other nine countries. It is for this reason that Singapore has always been a strong advocate of ASEAN unity and integration. ASEAN's role as a neutral platform friendly to all major powers is irreplaceable. Provided we do not take sides, all the major powers will wish us well and support our deeper unity and integration. ASEAN must always be reluctant to *ASEAN-ise* bilateral problems which individual ASEAN countries may have with major powers. Unless there are overriding reasons for ASEAN as a whole to be involved in such bilateral disputes, it should refrain from doing so. On the South China Sea, for example, ASEAN does have a strong interest in freedom of navigation but ASEAN should take no position on territorial disputes between the four claimant states and China. ASEAN should also studiously avoid taking sides in the unavoidable rivalry between the US and China.

There is a strong alignment between Singapore's foreign policy and ASEAN's foreign policy. Despite having left the Government for some years, in my present capacity in the private sector, I am constantly reminded by ASEAN friends of the important role Singapore plays in fostering ASEAN unity.

Singapore's Chineseness is an inseparable part of our existence in Southeast Asia. It was our Chineseness that impelled so many Singaporeans to support China's war against Japan, that led the Japanese militarists to kill many young men after the British were defeated, that made the British keep Singapore out of the Malayan Federation, that enabled Lee Kuan Yew to persuade the Tunku to take Singapore into Malaysia, and that caused Singapore to separate not long afterwards in 1965. That same Chineseness continues to link us in a myriad ways to the unfolding drama of China's great transformation in the 21st century and to the situation of the ethnic Chinese in Southeast Asia. Singapore's Chineseness is a huge advantage in this period of history but it also complicates our foreign policy. One senior Chinese diplomat once noted to me that "there is considerable mutual affection between the people of China and the people of Singapore". The other side of this emotional coin is the occasional overreaction to disagreements between us. I remember Indonesian Foreign Minister Pak Ali Alatas once expressing to me his deep concern about Singapore's deteriorating relations with China many years ago over an incident which I've long forgotten. His concern came as a pleasant surprise to me.

Singapore's links with Malaysia and Indonesia, with India and with the Muslim world are similarly fraught with emotional complications. The POA issue with Malaysia took over twenty years to resolve largely because the emotional trauma of separation for both sides took time to heal. After 51 years, we are still very much one people separated in two countries. In a group, it is difficult to distinguish Singaporeans from Malaysians. Among Indonesian leaders, there is sometimes a sense that Chinese Singapore is somehow exploiting Indonesia, benefiting disproportionately from the relationship. At Pak Mochtar Riady's book launch in Singapore recently, which I was honoured to speak at, an accompanying video displayed both the Indonesian and the People's Republic of China (PRC) flags. Being Chinese and being Indonesian are equally important identities to him. The ethnic Chinese connection with Singapore is woven into the fabric of economic life in Southeast Asia and complicates our relationship with Indonesia. Notwithstanding all this, Singapore and Indonesia remain the closest of partners. With One Belt, One Road, our two countries will grow even closer together in the coming decades.

Singapore's links to India are also profound and will be a growing advantage not only to us, but to the entire region. By 2050, India will either be the second or the third biggest economy in the world. Some of my Indian friends consider Singapore to be virtually a part of India. *Singapore* is of course an Indian name, Sanskrit in origin.

Singapore's links to the Muslim world are inseparable from our other links to Southeast Asia, China and India. The recent picture of President Tony Tan meeting Singapore religious students in Egypt's Al-Azhar University shows how intimately connected we are to the Middle East and the Muslim world. Every coin has two sides. While we celebrate the connections, we are also ineluctably affected by the turmoil in the Middle East including the challenge of Jihadi terrorism.

What all this means is that the Singapore identity is complex and dynamic. This complexity is part of our everyday life. We will never stop worrying about it. We will never stop arguing over policies affected by our multiple identities in education and housing, language and culture, national security and foreign policy. The latest debate is the Elected Presidency.

In having to grapple with these tensions, which are never fully resolved, we develop a Singapore culture, a higher Singapore identity, which is accommodating and inclusive, while being always sensitive to issues touching on race, language and religion. Each and every

Singaporean has multiple identities. Being Singaporean means understanding and accepting this reality, even celebrating it. The Singaporean has to be big-hearted and broadminded in order to embrace others not like himself. This is the Singapore idea which is worth living and fighting for. Indeed it is an idea the world desperately needs. Singapore is only Singapore if it has this universal appeal.

1.3 Chapter Organisation of the Book

The rest of the book is structured as follows. Chapter 2 provides an update on ACI's competitiveness analysis of ASEAN-10. Through a comprehensive and rigorous methodological framework, we not only produce annual rankings of economic competitiveness for the 10 ASEAN countries from 2000 to 2013 but also provide a policy roadmap for member states to identify their respective strengths and weaknesses. Through such analysis, ACI's research seeks to contribute to the realisation of the vision of sustainable and inclusive economic development in the region.

Chapter 3 celebrates the economic achievements of ASEAN over the past 50 years which has lifted millions out of poverty. Nevertheless, it highlights that further development is not guaranteed and pundits have raised concerns that certain ASEAN economies may be caught in the so-called "middle-income trap". While not taking a stance on whether such a trap exists, which is still a highly contentious issue in the literature, we recognise the importance of identifying potential threats, weaknesses and impediments to economic growth. Using econometric techniques including logistic regression and Bayesian Model Averaging, we investigate the determinants of growth slowdown specific to different levels of development. We then make plausible predictions about the possibilities of certain economies experiencing growth slowdown assuming they continue on their current growth paths.

In Chapter 4, the persistence of the development gap between ASEAN-6 and CLMV is again emphasised. We undertake a comprehensive review of the modern economic history of CLMV, focusing particularly on the economic reforms implemented over the past three decades through which these countries transition from centrally planned economies to more market-oriented systems. The achievements of reforms are acknowledged but more importantly, outstanding bottlenecks are identified. Drawing on theoretical frameworks such as the Flying Geese Model and actual development experiences of the High-Performing Asian Economies between the 1960s and late-1980s, we also discuss the policy options for CLMV in the next phase of their development.

Chapter 5 centres on the comprehensive discussion by Mr Heng Swee Keat, Minister for Finance of Singapore, on the challenges faced by Singapore as it moves forward into the future economy. Good policy-making entails adeptly navigating the immediate risks while not losing sight of the other upcoming trends in long-term planning. Among the key unfolding challenges are ageing population and rapid technological advancements, both of which will have profound social, political and economic implications for all economies, especially one as open as Singapore. The Chapter shall present Mr Heng's thoughts on the necessary policy initiatives, targeting at both the micro and macro levels, to prepare Singapore for the future. Though cast in the Singapore context, the insights derived from this Chapter are also applicable to other ASEAN economies, as they will also face similar challenges in the next phase of their development.

Chapter 6 summarises the research findings presented in this book. It also outlines policy implications for mitigating the risk of growth slowdown and narrowing the development divide. It also highlights new challenges in terms of managing the urban transition as urbanisation has progressed rapidly across Southeast Asia over the past two to three decades. In addition, the chapter will also bring home the message that success in preserving ASEAN's unity and navigating geopolitical headwinds are paramount for continued peace and prosperity. Finally, we discuss possible ideas for future research.

References

Mahbubani, Kishore. 2015. "ASEAN as a Living, Breathing Modern Miracle". *CIRSD Horizons* (2): 136–148.

McKinsey Global Institute. 2014. *Southeast Asia at the crossroads: Three paths to prosperity,* available at http://www.mckinsey.com/global-themes/asia-pacific/three-paths-to-sustained-economic-growth-in-southeast-asia (accessed on 29 March 2017).

Tan, Khee Giap, Linda Low, Tan Kong Yam, and Lim Lijuan Amanda. 2013. *Annual Analysis of Competitiveness, Development Strategies and Public Policies on ASEAN-10: 2000–2010.* Singapore: Pearson Education.

Tan, Khee Giap, Sangiita Wei Cher Yoong, Sasidaran Gopalan, and Le Phuong Anh Nguyen. 2015. *2014 Annual Competitiveness Ranking and Simulation Study for ASEAN-10 and Development Strategies to Enhance Asia Economic Connectivity*. Singapore: World Scientific.

Tan, Khee Giap, Nguyen Le Phuong Anh, Sasidaran Gopalan, and Luu Nguyen Trieu Duong. 2017a. *2015 Annual Competitiveness Analysis, Agricultural Productivity and Development Vision for ASEAN-10.* Singapore: World Scientific.

Tan, Khee Giap, Randong Yuan, and Teleixi Xie. 2017b. *2015 Estimation of Agricultural Productivity and Annual Update of Competitiveness Analysis for Greater China*. Singapore: World Scientific.

Tan, Khee Giap, Sasidaran Gopalan, and Anuja Tandon. 2017c. *2015 Agricultural Total Factor Productivity and Competitiveness Analysis for Sub-national Economies of India*. Singapore: World Scientific.

Tan, Khee Giap, Nurina Merdikawati, Mulya Amri, and Kong Yam Tan. 2017d. *2015 Agricultural Productivity, Decentralisation, and Competitiveness Analysis for Provinces and Regions of Indonesia.* Singapore: World Scientific.

Tan, Khee Giap, Nurina Merdikawati, Mulya Amri, and Nursyahida Binte Ahmad. 2017e. *2015 Annual Competitiveness Analysis and Development Strategies for Indonesian Provinces.* Singapore: World Scientific.

Yeo, George. 2016. Speech at the ninth S. Rajaratnam Lecture on "A Sense of Self in an Age of Globalisation". Singapore, 11 November.

Chapter 2

2016 Update on Annual Competitiveness Analysis for ASEAN-10

2.1 Introduction

ASEAN is a vibrant region with remarkable potential for upgraded development. By 2015, total population in ASEAN was over 630 million people. It is geographically advantageous, located between the Asia-Pacific and the Indian sub-continent. Nevertheless, despite rapid, growth across ASEAN over the past two to three decades, the development divide between the 10 ASEAN members remains stark. As of 2014, Singapore's real Gross Domestic Product (GDP) per capita, the highest in the region, was more than 53 times the level of Cambodia. In terms of the Human Development Index (HDI), Singapore's HDI value was 1.7 times that of Myanmar.[1]

2015 marks another momentous milestone in the history of the regional grouping as the ASEAN Community was officially established on 31 December, taking regional integration to a greater height. Nonetheless, as analysed in great detail in Chapter 1 of the *2015 Annual Competitiveness Analysis, Agricultural Productivity and Development Vision for ASEAN-10*,[2] the third instalment of our publication series on ASEAN, while economic integration initiatives such as the ASEAN Economic Community (AEC), which is one of the three pillars of the ASEAN Community, may provide a platform for the ASEAN member states to enhance competitiveness, narrow the development divide and achieve prosperity, individual members have to be earnest in implementing far-reaching domestic reforms. Without decisive and wide-ranging domestic reforms, the benefits of economic integration would be at best elusive.

In this regard, ACI has crafted a comprehensive and rigorous methodological framework not only to produce annual rankings of competitiveness for ASEAN but also to provide an ingenious policy roadmap for individual member states to identify gaps that need to be addressed to achieve greater competitiveness on their respective pathways to sustainable and inclusive economic development. Unlike other existing global competitiveness rankings, ACI's framework centres upon ASEAN with its own distinct characteristics, opportunities and challenges. Our methodology thus represents a customised approach to evaluating and improving national competitiveness, rather than a one-size-fits-all solution, for a region as diverse as ASEAN.

With this latest competitiveness ranking and simulation study covering data from 2000 to 2013, ACI also seeks to contribute to realising the AEC. While it was officially launched on 31 December 2015, the consensus is that the process of community building in ASEAN remains a work-in-progress beyond the 2015 milestone. ACI's annual competitiveness analysis of the 10 ASEAN economies can thus offer a complement to the AEC blueprint as it is conducted with the same objective of turning ASEAN into a competitive and sustainable region.

[1] Based on data from the World Bank and the United Nations Development Programme (UNDP).

[2] See Tan *et al*. (2017).

Following this Introduction, Section 2.2 details the methodology and data used to derive the rankings as well as the simulation analysis showing how the ASEAN economies can improve their competitiveness in various dimensions. This makes ACI's contribution more instructive than other competitiveness indices which merely report the rankings. Section 2.3 discusses the results of the competitiveness analysis and the top 20 percent strengths and weaknesses of individual ASEAN member states. This is followed by *what-if* policy simulation that demonstrates changes in the standardised scores as well as the rankings for individual economies following an improvement of their top 20 percent weaknesses. Section 2.4 concludes with policy implications.

2.2 ACI Competitiveness Framework and Methodology

2.2.1 Literature Review on Competitiveness

The notion of regional or *in-situ* competitiveness has been explored in various ways. Initially, in the 1980's, "competitiveness" was considered as part of the private sector domain, especially in relation to a firm's performance.[3] Over time, the discourse expanded onto the domain of macroeconomics, as shown by the establishment of "Council on Competitiveness" or similar institutions in various advanced industrialised countries. Some scholars acknowledge that it is primarily firms that compete, not nations, regions, or places.[4] However, the performance of those firms depends on various factors that are embedded in the firm's location. These include quality of labour and infrastructure, governance, costs of doing business, as well as the performance of competing and complementary firms around the area.[5]

Two of the most highly cited cross-country competitiveness studies at the moment are the World Competitiveness Yearbook (WCY) by the Institute for Management Development (IMD) World Competitiveness Centre and the World Economic Forum's (WEF) Global Competitiveness Report (GCR). The WCY defines competitiveness as composed of four factors: (i) economic performance, (ii) government efficiency, (iii) business efficiency, and (iv) infrastructure. Each factor is further made up of five criteria, so that there are 20 criteria in total. The WCY uses equal weights such that each criterion contributes 5 percent weight, and each factor contributes 25 percent weight to the overall competitiveness index.[6] Most of the data used are statistical indicators sourced from international, regional and national organisations. However, substantial perception data sourced from executive surveys supplement the statistical data.

The GCR breaks down its Global Competitiveness Index into three sub-indices: (i) basic requirements, (ii) efficiency enhancers, and (iii) innovation and sophistication factors.[7] Each of the three sub-indices has a different number of pillars. The basic requirements sub-index has four pillars: institutions, infrastructure, macroeconomic environment, and health and primary

[3] See Porter (1980).

[4] See Krugman (1994).

[5] See Camagni (2002), Kitson, Martin, and Tyler (2004) and Bristow (2010).

[6] See IMD World Competitiveness Center (2014).

[7] See World Economic Forum (2014).

education. The efficiency enhancers sub-index is composed of six pillars: higher education and training, goods market efficiency, labour market efficiency, financial market development, technological readiness and market size. Lastly, the innovation and sophistication factors sub-index consists of two pillars: business sophistication and innovation. Most of the data that make up these pillars and sub-indices come from executive opinion surveys.

2.2.2 ACI Competitiveness Framework

While the notion of competitiveness has been defined in various ways, ACI's approach to competitiveness is eclectic and comprehensive as it takes into account different factors that collectively shape the ability of a nation or region to achieve substantial and inclusive economic development over a sustained period of time.

In line with this overarching thrust, ACI defines competitiveness through four environments: (i) Macroeconomic Stability (MS), (ii) Government and Institutional Setting, (iii) Financial, Businesses and Manpower Conditions, and (iv) Quality of Life and Infrastructure Development. These four environments carry equal weightage (25 percent) in the computation of the Overall Competitiveness score. Following a nested approach, each environment comprises three sub-environments of the same weightage (33.3 percent) (see Figure 2.1). While giving different weights to different environments and sub-environments based on their importance seems more

Figure 2.1: ACI Competitiveness Framework

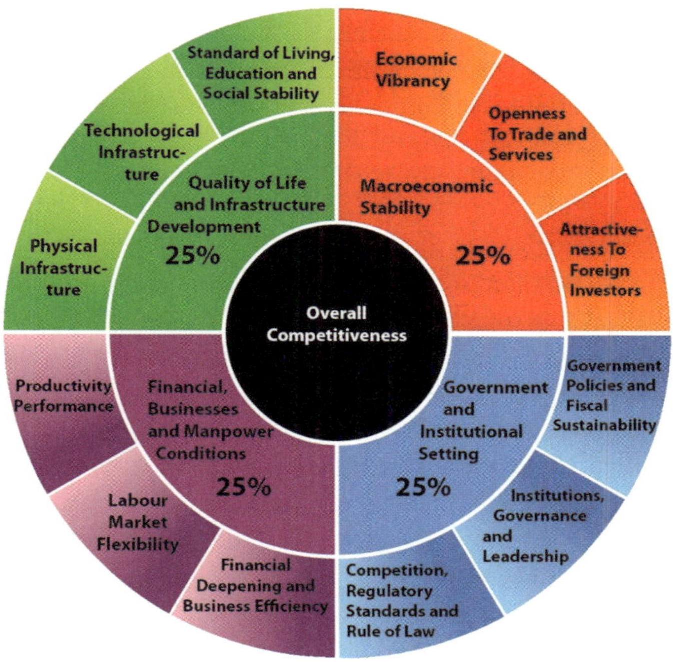

Source: Asia Competitiveness Institute

appropriate, the method is nonetheless arbitrary and contentious. Thus, equal distribution of weight reflects a balanced view towards the different factors that make up an overall notion of competitiveness.

ACI's framework provides a holistic, integrated and systematic way of examining national competitiveness. Two environments are specifically related to economic performance, namely Macroeconomic Stability (MS) and Financial, Businesses and Manpower Conditions (FBMC). MS encompasses aggregated macroeconomic conditions which include: (i) Economic Vibrancy, (ii) Openness to Trade and Services, and (iii) Attractiveness to Foreign Investors. FBMC, on the other hand, represents the microeconomy, particularly firms and factors that impact their performances. FBMC thus comprises: (i) Financial Deepening and Business Efficiency, (ii) Labour Market Flexibility, and (iii) Productivity Performance). The remaining two environments are institutional and social in character. Government and Institutional Setting (GIS) covers efficacy of government institutions and rule of law. This environment consists of: (i) Government Policies and Fiscal Sustainability, (ii) Institutions, Governance and Leadership, and (iii) Competition, Regulatory Standards and Rule of Law. Lastly, Quality of Life and Infrastructure Development (QLID) combines infrastructure, health and education services, environmental standards and social security. The three sub-environments are: (i) Physical Infrastructure, (ii) Technological Infrastructure, and (iii) Standard of Living, Education and Social Stability.

There are a total of 121 indicators used in ACI's competitiveness rankings and simulations for ASEAN-10 economies in the period 2000–2013 (see Appendix 4). The extensive number of indicators ensures robust interpretation of each environment and sub-environment in the Overall Competitiveness score. Depending on data availability, some environments and sub-environments may have more indicators than others. Nonetheless, this is not an issue as they simply average out. This also allows a certain amount of flexibility in adding or removing indicators when updating the rankings in the future, so long as the overall structure of the four environments and 12 sub-environments remains unchanged.

2.2.3 Data Sources

The data for the 121 indicators used in this study were collected from various sources, of which the bulk came from official data sources such as the World Bank, World Development Indicators, Asian Development Bank (ADB) and World Economic Forum Global Competitiveness Index. Other sources include Economist Intelligence Unit (EIU), Global Market Information Database (GMID), UNESCO Institute for Statistics, International Monetary Fund (IMF) World Economic Outlook Database, United Nations Conference on Trade and Development (UNCTAD), IMD World Competitiveness Yearbook, International Telecommunication Union ICT Indicators Database, United Nations Development Programme (UNDP), Reporters Without Border and the Ciingranelli–Richards Human Rights Dataset.

2.2.4 Computation of Standardised Scores

The next important question in terms of methodology is how to aggregate the different types of data into one coherent way of analysis. Given 121 different indicators in this research, all in different values or quantity terms, such as GDP in millions of US dollars, or population in numbers, how do we resolve these different units of measurement?

The ACI uses a statistical methodology of 'standardised score'. The standardised score is a relative comparison to see how well is the performance of a certain economy in comparison to the average economy. Therefore, the unit of measurement is no longer relevant. The standardised score has no unit of measurement because it simply measures relative performance among economies, whatever the indicator is.

In statistical terms, it measures how many standard deviations away is each economy from the average economy (see Appendix 5 for technical explanation). If an economy has a standardised score of zero, it is basically an average performer in terms of that particular indicator. Having a negative score means the economy performs below average. Having a positive score, on the other hand, means above-average performance.

The further away the score is from zero, the further away is the performance of said economy from the ASEAN-10 average. If an economy has a high positive score, it means it is much above the average score. The standardised scores for each indicator are then aggregated at the sub-environment level, and then reaggregated at the environment level, and finally aggregated again at the overall level. This allows comparison of performance of the 10 ASEAN economies at different levels, from the Overall Competitiveness to specific indicators in four environments.

2.2.5 *What-if* Competitiveness Simulation Analysis

A competitiveness ranking in itself is like a beauty contest; it merely identifies who are doing well and who are facing challenges, but stops short of giving more constructive advice on improving the rankings. The ACI index goes one step further by tackling the 'so what?' question. What is the policy implication of a competitiveness ranking result for a particular economy? The data used in the ACI index allows us to do an in-depth analysis of the performance of each economy according to the different indicators, sub-environments, and environments. By analysing the said data, we are able to identify not just the Overall Competitiveness ranking, but also specific indicators for which the economy is doing well or struggling. This allows us to come up with policy recommendations for each economy.

The ACI has *what-if* competitiveness simulation that is based on an improvement of each economy's top 20 percent weakest indicators,[8] and a recalculation of the standardised score based on such improvements. To do this, we first look at each economy and sorted the different indicators for each economy from the highest to the lowest score. This allows us to identify the 24 weakest indicators that each economy has. Why 24? Because we are looking from the bottom 20 percent of the 121 indicators used in the ASEAN study.

Next, we raise the scores of these 24 weakest indicators moderately to match the average score. This means their average score is raised to zero if it has been negative previously. For other economies which were already competitive, we leave their scores alone. Their scores are not discounted if they are already competitive. Once these scores are raised, we recalculate the

[8] Counting from the bottom given a list of 121 as the weakest, while the top 20 percent strongest will count from the top of the 121 listing of indicators.

ranking, assuming that other economies stay constant. Each economy would then have a new, improved standardised score. This allows us to answer the question: if a particular economy improves on its set of weakest indicators, and assuming other economies remain constant, how will that economy's competitiveness ranking improve?

2.3 Competitiveness Analysis for ASEAN-10 Economies, 2000–2013

In this section, we present the Overall Competitiveness rankings as well as the rankings for the four environments as derived from the standardised scores for each economy over the period 2000–2013. The scores for individual sub-environments are visualised in the median and maximum web analysis. Findings on the *what-if* competitiveness simulation are also discussed.

2.3.1 Overall Competitiveness

Table 2.1 shows the Overall Competitiveness Rankings along with the Standardised scores of individual ASEAN member states over the period of 2000–2013. In the year 2013, Singapore demonstrated a marked improvement in its score to 2.0793 from 2.0279 in 2012 although it has

Table 2.1: Overall Competitiveness Rankings and Standardised Scores, 2000–2013

OVERALL										
	1		2		3		4		5	
Rank	Economy	Score	Economy	Score	Economy	Score	Economy	Score	Economy	Score
2000	Singapore	2.1141	Malaysia	0.9680	Thailand	0.5623	Brunei	0.3798	Philippines	–0.1224
2001	Singapore	2.0723	Malaysia	0.9289	Thailand	0.6469	Brunei	0.4071	Philippines	–0.1039
2002	Singapore	1.9301	Malaysia	1.0545	Thailand	0.8011	Brunei	0.3711	Philippines	–0.1766
2003	Singapore	1.9638	Malaysia	1.0595	Thailand	0.7471	Brunei	0.3819	Indonesia	–0.1258
2004	Singapore	1.9299	Malaysia	1.0859	Thailand	0.7300	Brunei	0.4120	Indonesia	–0.0896
2005	Singapore	1.9799	Malaysia	1.0708	Thailand	0.7229	Brunei	0.3642	Indonesia	–0.1969
2006	Singapore	1.9484	Malaysia	1.0945	Thailand	0.6819	Brunei	0.3722	Indonesia	–0.0605
2007	Singapore	2.0127	Malaysia	1.0779	Thailand	0.5711	Brunei	0.3179	Indonesia	0.0082
2008	Singapore	2.0879	Malaysia	0.9690	Thailand	0.5432	Brunei	0.3462	Indonesia	0.0555
2009	Singapore	2.1505	Malaysia	0.8700	Thailand	0.5297	Brunei	0.3391	Indonesia	0.0844
2010	Singapore	2.0535	Malaysia	0.9653	Thailand	0.5435	Brunei	0.3973	Indonesia	0.1152
2011	Singapore	2.0633	Malaysia	1.0700	Thailand	0.5208	Brunei	0.3764	Indonesia	0.0456
2012	Singapore	2.0279	Malaysia	1.0799	Thailand	0.5306	Brunei	0.3746	Indonesia	–0.0142
2013	Singapore	2.0793	Malaysia	1.0099	Thailand	0.5286	Brunei	0.3770	Indonesia	–0.0138

(Continued)

Table 2.1: ***(Continued)***

OVERALL										
	6		7		8		9		10	
Rank	Economy	Score	Economy	Score	Economy	Score	Economy	Score	Economy	Score
2000	Indonesia	−0.1264	Vietnam	−0.3583	Cambodia	−0.9156	Laos	−1.1951	Myanmar	−1.3065
2001	Indonesia	−0.1592	Vietnam	−0.3390	Cambodia	−0.9186	Laos	−1.1063	Myanmar	−1.4282
2002	Indonesia	−0.1931	Vietnam	−0.2820	Cambodia	−0.9333	Laos	−1.1159	Myanmar	−1.4557
2003	Vietnam	−0.2479	Philippines	−0.2799	Cambodia	−0.9741	Laos	−1.1493	Myanmar	−1.3753
2004	Philippines	−0.2546	Vietnam	−0.3296	Cambodia	−0.9395	Laos	−1.0568	Myanmar	−1.4876
2005	Philippines	−0.2085	Vietnam	−0.3074	Cambodia	−0.9324	Laos	−0.9954	Myanmar	−1.4972
2006	Philippines	−0.2370	Vietnam	−0.3292	Cambodia	−0.9278	Laos	−1.0055	Myanmar	−1.5370
2007	Philippines	−0.2369	Vietnam	−0.2838	Cambodia	−0.9357	Laos	−0.9975	Myanmar	−1.5339
2008	Philippines	−0.2850	Vietnam	−0.2901	Cambodia	−0.9364	Laos	−0.9796	Myanmar	−1.5106
2009	Vietnam	−0.1939	Philippines	−0.4302	Laos	−0.8705	Cambodia	−0.9547	Myanmar	−1.5243
2010	Vietnam	−0.2024	Philippines	−0.4313	Cambodia	−0.9551	Laos	−0.9636	Myanmar	−1.5223
2011	Philippines	−0.3797	Vietnam	−0.4106	Cambodia	−0.8641	Laos	−0.9015	Myanmar	−1.5201
2012	Philippines	−0.2979	Vietnam	−0.4176	Cambodia	−0.7054	Laos	−0.9603	Myanmar	−1.6175
2013	Philippines	−0.3258	Vietnam	−0.3835	Cambodia	−0.7739	Laos	−0.8861	Myanmar	−1.6116

Source: Asia Competitiveness Institute

not returned to its peak performance in 2009 with a score of 2.1505. Nonetheless, Singapore has not only remained at the top for 14 consecutive years but also widened its competitiveness gap with Malaysia which ranked second in 2013 with a score of 1.0099.

Thailand and Brunei maintained their third and fourth place, respectively, throughout the study period. However, Thailand has experienced large fluctuations in its scores; for instance, from 0.8011 in 2002 to 0.5286 in 2013, which signifies the need for constant monitoring and improvement of national competitiveness. Meanwhile, Indonesia has overtaken Philippines at fifth since 2003. While the largest country in ASEAN registered a slight increase in its score in 2013 (−0.0138) as compared to 2012 (−0.0142), it still has not managed to decidedly graduate into the rank of economies with positive, or above-average, scores in the region. Philippines' competitiveness has deteriorated significantly as its standardised score plunged even more negatively in 2013 relative to 2012 and 2000.

The newer, less developed group of ASEAN members remained at the bottom of the ranking in 2013. Vietnam, while maintaining its seventh place, seems to have narrowed its competitiveness divide *vis-à-vis* Philippines as its score rose to −0.3835 while that of Philippines slipped to −0.3258 in 2013. Cambodia appears to have firmly overtaken Laos and Myanmar at the eighth position. Laos, at the ninth place, has seen a notable increase in its score from −1.1951 in 2000 to −0.8861 in 2013, while Myanmar fared worse in 2013 with a score of −1.6116 relative to 2000.

Figure 2.2: Overall Competitiveness — 2000, 2012 and 2013

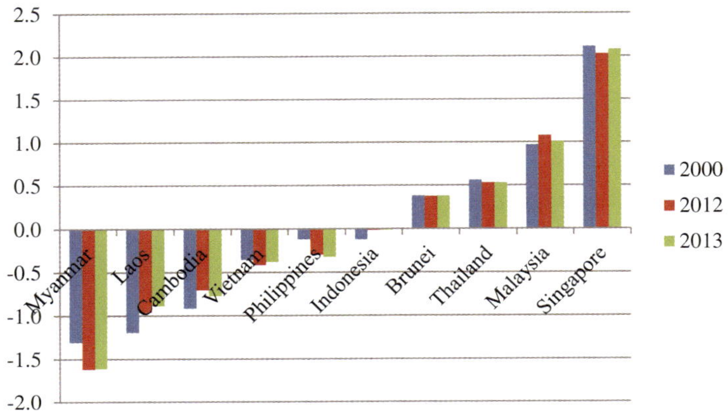

Source: Asia Competitiveness Institute

As seen in Figure 2.2, which depicts the 10 ASEAN economies' performances in 2000, 2012 and 2013, competitiveness upgrading within ASEAN has been uneven with countries such as Indonesia, Laos and Cambodia converging towards the regional average while Myanmar, Philippines, and to a lesser extent, Thailand deteriorating in 2013 relative to 2000. Malaysia and Vietnam appear to stagnate as they fared worse in 2013 as compared to 2012, while Brunei's performance has remained virtually unchanged over the study period.

2.3.2 Macroeconomic Stability

Table 2.2 presents the rankings and standardised scores for the first environment, Macroeconomic Stability, over the period of 2000–2013. While Singapore has once again remained at the top throughout the study period, Thailand overtook Malaysia at the second place in 2013 as Malaysia's score slipped from 0.7278 to 0.6385 and that of Thailand markedly rose from 0.6330 to 0.7336 between 2012 and 2013. Indonesia shows enormous potential for competitiveness catching-up as it ranked above Brunei at fourth. Vietnam seems to have decidedly overtaken Philippines at the sixth place as Philippines' score plunged more negatively in 2013 relative to 2012. Although Laos' score improved markedly from –1.3645 in 2000 to –0.8807 in 2013, it remained at ninth in 2013 while Cambodia and Myanmar took the eighth and tenth place, respectively.

The relative performances of the 10 ASEAN member states as well as the evolution of competitiveness in Macroeconomic Stability are illustrated in Figure 2.3. Laos appears to make the most remarkable leap in its score in 2013 relative to 2000. Singapore, Thailand, Indonesia, Brunei and Vietnam registered moderate improvement in 2013 as compared to 2000 while Myanmar, Cambodia, Philippines and Malaysia fared worse over the same period.

Among the three sub-environments constituting Macroeconomic Stability, Indonesia slipped from the top in 2012 to second in 2013 in terms of Economic Vibrancy (Figure 2.4) while Thailand overtook Malaysia at the second place for Openness to Trade and Services (Figure 2.5).

Table 2.2: Macroeconomic Stability Rankings and Standardised Scores, 2000–2013

MACROECONOMIC STABILITY										
	1		2		3		4		5	
Rank	Economy	Score	Economy	Score	Economy	Score	Economy	Score	Economy	Score
2000	Singapore	2.1392	Malaysia	0.8781	Thailand	0.6753	Indonesia	0.3183	Brunei	−0.1827
2001	Singapore	2.0382	Malaysia	0.8462	Thailand	0.7007	Indonesia	0.2620	Brunei	0.0469
2002	Singapore	1.9540	Malaysia	0.8797	Thailand	0.7457	Indonesia	0.3596	Brunei	0.0108
2003	Singapore	2.1089	Malaysia	0.8397	Thailand	0.6821	Indonesia	0.4915	Brunei	−0.1102
2004	Singapore	2.1186	Malaysia	0.8369	Thailand	0.7764	Indonesia	0.3865	Brunei	−0.1547
2005	Singapore	2.1180	Malaysia	0.8674	Thailand	0.7507	Indonesia	0.3222	Brunei	−0.1041
2006	Singapore	2.0724	Malaysia	0.8401	Thailand	0.7496	Indonesia	0.4479	Brunei	−0.1019
2007	Singapore	2.0662	Malaysia	0.8925	Thailand	0.7401	Indonesia	0.4877	Philippines	−0.2098
2008	Singapore	2.0721	Malaysia	0.7847	Thailand	0.7444	Indonesia	0.6583	Brunei	−0.1767
2009	Singapore	2.1795	Thailand	0.7072	Indonesia	0.6619	Malaysia	0.6423	Brunei	−0.1404
2010	Singapore	2.1882	Malaysia	0.6956	Indonesia	0.5945	Thailand	0.5899	Brunei	0.0303
2011	Singapore	2.2247	Malaysia	0.7504	Indonesia	0.6225	Thailand	0.4619	Brunei	0.0307
2012	Singapore	2.1370	Malaysia	0.7278	Thailand	0.6330	Indonesia	0.5317	Brunei	0.0133
2013	Singapore	2.2126	Thailand	0.7336	Malaysia	0.6385	Indonesia	0.3844	Brunei	0.0033
	6		7		8		9		10	
Rank	Economy	Score	Economy	Score	Economy	Score	Economy	Score	Economy	Score
2000	Philippines	−0.2475	Vietnam	−0.3660	Cambodia	−0.5421	Myanmar	−1.3081	Laos	−1.3645
2001	Vietnam	−0.2294	Philippines	−0.3218	Cambodia	−0.5403	Laos	−1.0914	Myanmar	−1.7113
2002	Philippines	−0.2328	Vietnam	−0.2552	Cambodia	−0.6423	Laos	−1.0812	Myanmar	−1.7382
2003	Vietnam	−0.3347	Philippines	−0.3672	Cambodia	−0.7220	Laos	−1.2190	Myanmar	−1.3691
2004	Philippines	−0.3340	Vietnam	−0.4869	Cambodia	−0.6050	Laos	−1.0448	Myanmar	−1.4929
2005	Philippines	−0.3965	Vietnam	−0.4519	Cambodia	−0.6138	Laos	−0.8994	Myanmar	−1.5927
2006	Philippines	−0.3111	Vietnam	−0.4971	Cambodia	−0.7165	Laos	−0.8641	Myanmar	−1.6194
2007	Brunei	−0.2782	Vietnam	−0.4819	Cambodia	−0.8028	Laos	−0.8626	Myanmar	−1.5512
2008	Philippines	−0.3764	Vietnam	−0.4994	Cambodia	−0.8080	Laos	−0.9253	Myanmar	−1.4737
2009	Vietnam	−0.3987	Philippines	−0.6122	Laos	−0.7676	Cambodia	−0.8402	Myanmar	−1.4318
2010	Vietnam	−0.4229	Philippines	−0.4696	Cambodia	−0.8001	Laos	−0.9886	Myanmar	−1.4173
2011	Philippines	−0.4257	Vietnam	−0.6003	Cambodia	−0.7583	Laos	−0.9179	Myanmar	−1.3880
2012	Philippines	−0.3218	Vietnam	−0.5409	Cambodia	−0.7029	Laos	−0.8773	Myanmar	−1.6000
2013	Vietnam	−0.3074	Philippines	−0.5552	Cambodia	−0.6976	Laos	−0.8807	Myanmar	−1.5315

Source: Asia Competitiveness Institute

Figure 2.3: Macroeconomic Stability — 2000, 2012 and 2013

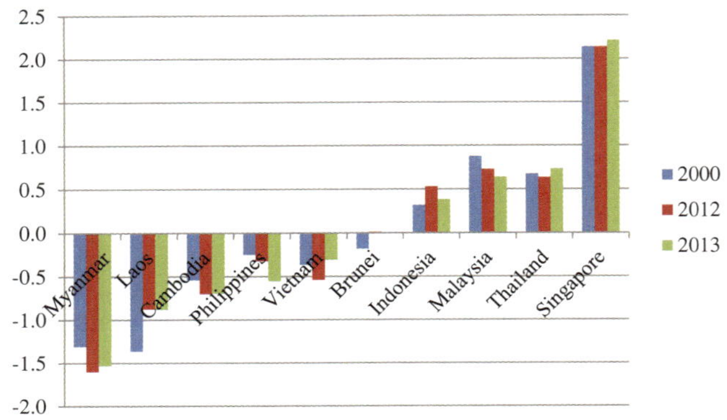

Source: Asia Competitiveness Institute

Figure 2.4: Macroeconomic Stability (Economic Vibrancy) — 2000, 2012 and 2013

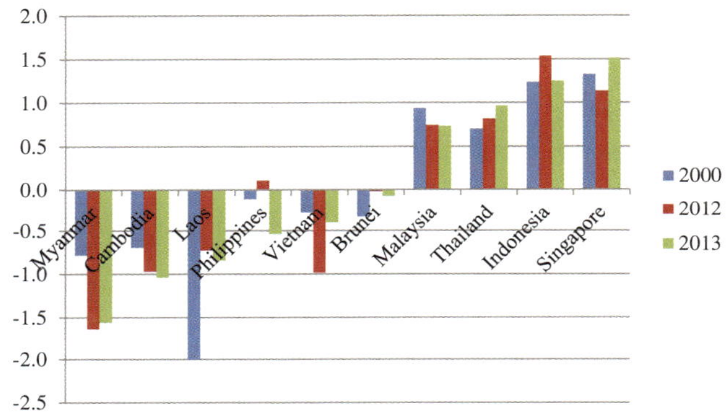

Source: Asia Competitiveness Institute

Figure 2.5: Macroeconomic Stability (Openness to Trade and Services) — 2000, 2012 and 2013

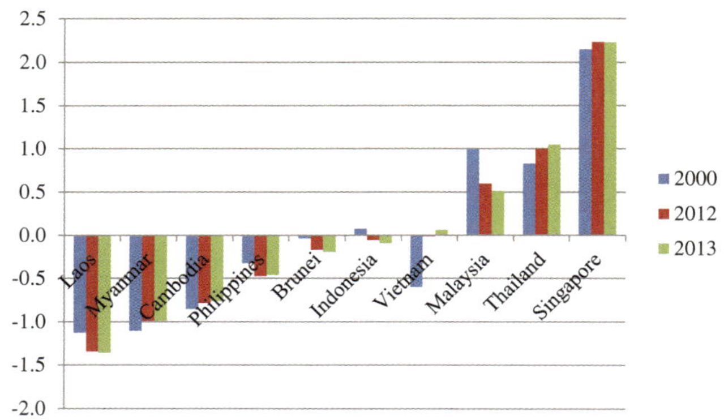

Source: Asia Competitiveness Institute

Figure 2.6: Macroeconomic Stability (Attractiveness to Foreign Investors) — 2000, 2012 and 2013

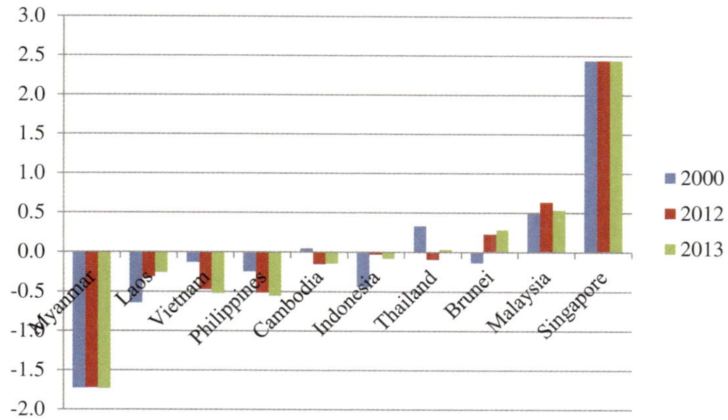

Source: Asia Competitiveness Institute

It is heartening that Vietnam's score turned positive for Openness to Trade and Services in 2013. Likewise, Thailand's score in terms of Attractiveness to Foreign Investors improved and became positive in 2013 (Figure 2.6).

On the flip side, Philippines' score for Economic Vibrancy plunged from positive in 2012 to negative in 2013. Its performance in the remaining two sub-environments under Macroeconomic Stability also deteriorated in 2013 relative to 2000. Consequently, Philippines fell into the bottom four in all three sub-environments. Indonesia and Cambodia's competitiveness seems to have eroded in 2013 as compared to 2000 in terms of Openness to Trade and Services and Attractiveness to Foreign Investors, respectively.

2.3.3 Government and Institutional Setting

The same duo, Singapore and Malaysia, dominated the first and second place in the rankings for Government and Institutional Setting throughout the study period (Table 2.3). Singapore is ahead of its neighbours as a developmental state with an able government that is not captured by private interests. While Brunei seems to have decidedly overtaken Thailand at the third place since 2010, Thailand's performance in this environment improved markedly in 2013 as compared to 2012 as indicated by its scores. Likewise, Philippines' score, while remaining negative or below regional average, increased between 2012 and 2013, enabling it to firmly surpass Indonesia at the fifth position. In the bottom four, the gaps in the scores remained relatively large between Cambodia, Laos and Myanmar at the eighth, ninth and tenth place, respectively, and Vietnam at seventh.

As seen in Figure 2.7, Laos, Indonesia, Malaysia and, to a lesser extent, Brunei have made steadfast improvement in Government and Institutional Setting in 2013 relative to 2000 while the remaining six ASEAN member states fared worse over time. Thailand, while improving in 2013 as compared to 2012, has not returned to its original competitiveness level in this environment in 2000.

Nevertheless, Thailand's score for Government Policies and Fiscal Sustainability rose steadily between 2000 and 2013 (Figure 2.8). As a result, Thailand not only surpassed Malaysia at the

Table 2.3: Government and Institutional Setting Rankings and Standardised Scores, 2000–2013

GOVERNMENT AND INSTITUTIONAL SETTING										
	1		2		3		4		5	
Rank	Economy	Score	Economy	Score	Economy	Score	Economy	Score	Economy	Score
2000	Singapore	2.2679	Malaysia	0.7806	Thailand	0.5763	Brunei	0.4504	Philippines	−0.0755
2001	Singapore	2.2594	Malaysia	0.7816	Thailand	0.5879	Brunei	0.3864	Philippines	−0.0424
2002	Singapore	2.1383	Malaysia	0.9486	Thailand	0.7376	Brunei	0.2594	Philippines	−0.1423
2003	Singapore	2.1132	Malaysia	0.9141	Thailand	0.8732	Brunei	0.2459	Vietnam	−0.1648
2004	Singapore	2.0510	Malaysia	1.0261	Thailand	0.7439	Brunei	0.4190	Philippines	−0.2626
2005	Singapore	2.0372	Malaysia	1.0836	Thailand	0.7287	Brunei	0.4025	Philippines	−0.1927
2006	Singapore	2.1110	Malaysia	0.9706	Thailand	0.6668	Brunei	0.4264	Philippines	−0.2507
2007	Singapore	2.1883	Malaysia	0.9676	Thailand	0.5605	Brunei	0.4297	Philippines	−0.2289
2008	Singapore	2.3522	Malaysia	0.7753	Thailand	0.4806	Brunei	0.4449	Vietnam	−0.2897
2009	Singapore	2.4590	Malaysia	0.5640	Thailand	0.4661	Brunei	0.3983	Indonesia	−0.2145
2010	Singapore	2.3072	Malaysia	0.7557	Brunei	0.5219	Thailand	0.4327	Indonesia	−0.1416
2011	Singapore	2.2321	Malaysia	0.9598	Brunei	0.5532	Thailand	0.4124	Indonesia	−0.3237
2012	Singapore	2.2724	Malaysia	0.9448	Brunei	0.4848	Thailand	0.2765	Philippines	−0.1949
2013	Singapore	2.2585	Malaysia	0.9212	Brunei	0.5123	Thailand	0.3455	Philippines	−0.1649
	6		7		8		9		10	
Rank	Economy	Score	Economy	Score	Economy	Score	Economy	Score	Economy	Score
2000	Vietnam	−0.3383	Indonesia	−0.5650	Cambodia	−0.8076	Myanmar	−1.1236	Laos	−1.1653
2001	Vietnam	−0.2841	Indonesia	−0.5145	Cambodia	−0.8571	Laos	−1.0518	Myanmar	−1.2654
2002	Vietnam	−0.2113	Indonesia	−0.4756	Cambodia	−0.8817	Laos	−1.0591	Myanmar	−1.3138
2003	Philippines	−0.3161	Indonesia	−0.3775	Cambodia	−1.0703	Myanmar	−1.0798	Laos	−1.1378
2004	Vietnam	−0.2703	Indonesia	−0.4397	Laos	−0.9140	Cambodia	−0.9872	Myanmar	−1.3661
2005	Vietnam	−0.2918	Indonesia	−0.5425	Cambodia	−0.9415	Laos	−0.9513	Myanmar	−1.3321
2006	Indonesia	−0.2609	Vietnam	−0.3942	Laos	−0.9336	Cambodia	−0.9555	Myanmar	−1.3799
2007	Indonesia	−0.3596	Vietnam	−0.3897	Cambodia	−0.9232	Laos	−0.9340	Myanmar	−1.3108
2008	Philippines	−0.3257	Indonesia	−0.4272	Laos	−0.8608	Cambodia	−0.9922	Myanmar	−1.1573
2009	Vietnam	−0.2762	Philippines	−0.4842	Laos	−0.7991	Cambodia	−0.9332	Myanmar	−1.1803
2010	Vietnam	−0.3172	Philippines	−0.4060	Laos	−0.9527	Cambodia	−0.9723	Myanmar	−1.2278
2011	Philippines	−0.3411	Vietnam	−0.4738	Cambodia	−0.8091	Laos	−0.9063	Myanmar	−1.3034
2012	Vietnam	−0.3732	Indonesia	−0.4146	Cambodia	−0.7233	Laos	−0.8383	Myanmar	−1.4342
2013	Indonesia	−0.3956	Vietnam	−0.4256	Cambodia	−0.8120	Laos	−0.8579	Myanmar	−1.3816

Source: Asia Competitiveness Institute

Figure 2.7: Government and Institutional Setting — 2000, 2012 and 2013

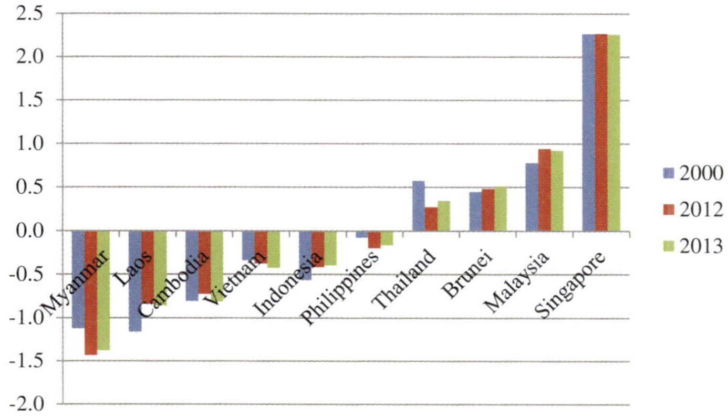

Source: Asia Competitiveness Institute

Figure 2.8: Government and Institutional Setting (Government Policies and Fiscal Sustainability) — 2000, 2012 and 2013

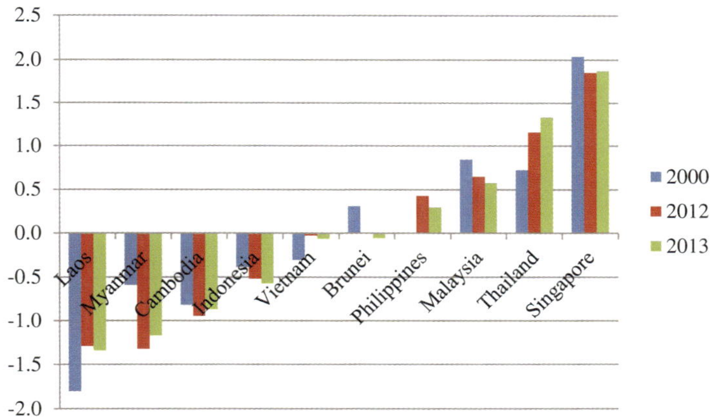

Source: Asia Competitiveness Institute

second place but also narrowed its gap with the top performer Singapore in this environment. Laos was the only ASEAN country which improved in all three sub-environments over the study period (Figures 2.8–2.10). The majority of ASEAN fared better in one or two sub-environments while deteriorating in others, which signifies the enormous challenges in establishing good governance in the region.

Figure 2.9: Government and Institutional Setting (Institutions, Governance and Leadership) — 2000, 2012 and 2013

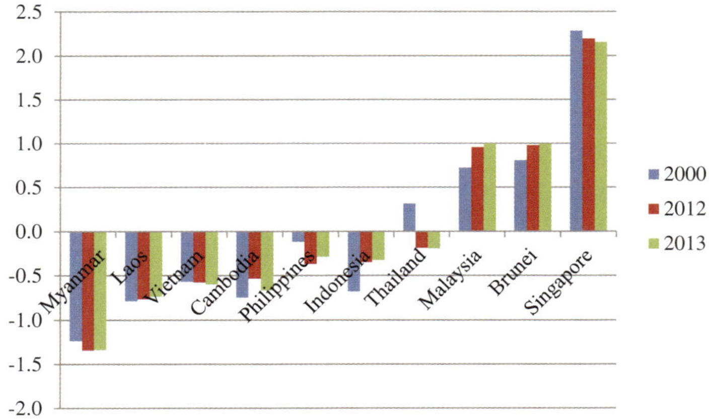

Source: Asia Competitiveness Institute

Figure 2.10: Government and Institutional Setting (Competition, Regulatory Standards and Rule of Law) — 2000, 2012 and 2013

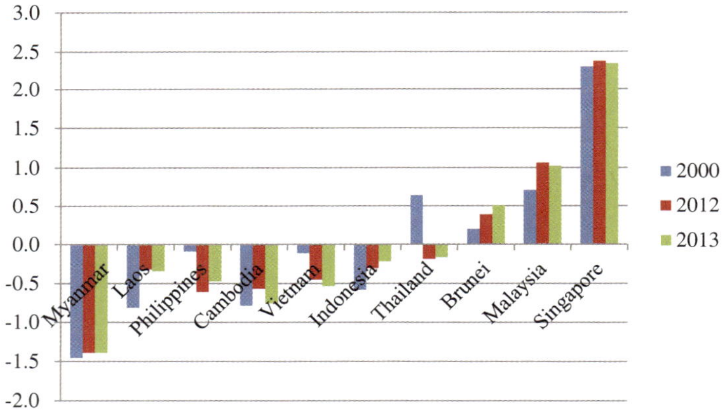

Source: Asia Competitiveness Institute

2.3.4 Financial, Businesses and Manpower Conditions

Table 2.4 and Figure 2.11 show the rankings and standardised scores for Financial, Businesses and Manpower Conditions in the selected years from 2000 to 2013. While Singapore has maintained its top position throughout the study period, Malaysia at second has substantially narrowed its gap with Singapore as its score rose from 1.2182 in 2000 to 1.5363 in 2013 while Singapore's score dropped from 1.8940 to 1.6265 over the same period. Indonesia improved significantly in 2013 relative to 2012 and has consequently overtaken Vietnam at fifth, after Thailand and Brunei at the third and fourth place, respectively. Vietnam and Philippines ranked

Table 2.4: Financial, Businesses and Manpower Conditions Rankings and Standardised Scores, 2000–2013

FINANCIAL, BUSINESSES AND MANPOWER CONDITIONS										
	1		2		3		4		5	
Rank	Economy	Score	Economy	Score	Economy	Score	Economy	Score	Economy	Score
2000	Singapore	1.8940	Malaysia	1.2182	Thailand	0.5349	Brunei	0.3022	Indonesia	–0.0297
2001	Singapore	1.9166	Malaysia	1.0831	Thailand	0.7188	Brunei	0.3058	Philippines	–0.0339
2002	Singapore	1.5835	Malaysia	1.3368	Thailand	0.9782	Brunei	0.3350	Vietnam	–0.1303
2003	Singapore	1.5506	Malaysia	1.3929	Thailand	0.8509	Brunei	0.4750	Vietnam	–0.0200
2004	Singapore	1.5106	Malaysia	1.4126	Thailand	0.8312	Brunei	0.4396	Vietnam	–0.0605
2005	Singapore	1.7237	Malaysia	1.2274	Thailand	0.8517	Brunei	0.2694	Vietnam	–0.0059
2006	Singapore	1.6381	Malaysia	1.4197	Thailand	0.7785	Brunei	0.3309	Vietnam	–0.1008
2007	Singapore	1.6370	Malaysia	1.4852	Thailand	0.5277	Brunei	0.3267	Indonesia	0.0340
2008	Singapore	1.7360	Malaysia	1.3597	Thailand	0.5436	Brunei	0.2074	Indonesia	0.1133
2009	Singapore	1.7290	Malaysia	1.3510	Thailand	0.5689	Brunei	0.1913	Vietnam	0.0921
2010	Singapore	1.5959	Malaysia	1.4455	Thailand	0.7146	Brunei	0.2137	Indonesia	0.0676
2011	Singapore	1.5884	Malaysia	1.5581	Thailand	0.7958	Indonesia	0.0700	Brunei	0.0557
2012	Singapore	1.5710	Malaysia	1.5690	Thailand	0.7850	Brunei	0.1827	Indonesia	0.0070
2013	Singapore	1.6265	Malaysia	1.5363	Thailand	0.6283	Brunei	0.1943	Indonesia	0.1252
	6		7		8		9		10	
Rank	Economy	Score	Economy	Score	Economy	Score	Economy	Score	Economy	Score
2000	Vietnam	–0.0921	Philippines	–0.1549	Laos	–1.1079	Cambodia	–1.2534	Myanmar	–1.3113
2001	Indonesia	–0.1461	Vietnam	–0.1778	Laos	–1.1477	Cambodia	–1.2569	Myanmar	–1.2619
2002	Philippines	–0.1639	Indonesia	–0.2542	Cambodia	–1.2139	Laos	–1.2166	Myanmar	–1.2546
2003	Indonesia	–0.2919	Philippines	–0.2919	Cambodia	–1.1128	Laos	–1.1382	Myanmar	–1.4146
2004	Indonesia	–0.0770	Philippines	–0.3062	Cambodia	–1.1198	Laos	–1.2118	Myanmar	–1.4187
2005	Philippines	–0.0594	Indonesia	–0.3061	Laos	–1.1183	Cambodia	–1.1469	Myanmar	–1.4356
2006	Philippines	–0.2237	Indonesia	–0.2258	Cambodia	–0.9699	Laos	–1.1992	Myanmar	–1.4477
2007	Vietnam	–0.0196	Philippines	–0.3370	Cambodia	–0.9554	Laos	–1.1761	Myanmar	–1.5226
2008	Vietnam	–0.0551	Philippines	–0.2518	Cambodia	–0.9151	Laos	–1.1100	Myanmar	–1.6280
2009	Indonesia	0.0574	Philippines	–0.3722	Laos	–0.9518	Cambodia	–1.0041	Myanmar	–1.6616
2010	Vietnam	0.0633	Philippines	–0.5804	Laos	–0.9243	Cambodia	–0.9525	Myanmar	–1.6433
2011	Vietnam	–0.2559	Philippines	–0.3513	Cambodia	–0.9301	Laos	–0.9900	Myanmar	–1.5407
2012	Philippines	–0.4050	Vietnam	–0.4187	Cambodia	–0.6164	Laos	–1.0878	Myanmar	–1.5868
2013	Philippines	–0.2870	Vietnam	–0.4229	Cambodia	–0.7067	Laos	–1.0670	Myanmar	–1.6269

Source: Asia Competitiveness Institute

Figure 2.11: Financial, Businesses and Manpower Conditions — 2000, 2012 and 2013

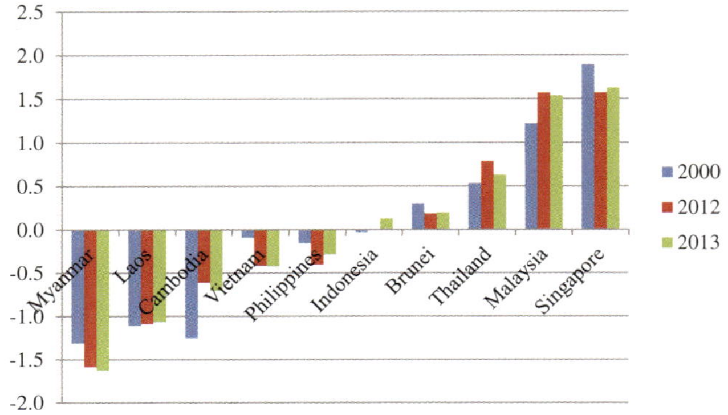

Source: Asia Competitiveness Institute

Figure 2.12: Financial, Businesses and Manpower Conditions (Financial Deepening and Business Efficiency) — 2000, 2012 and 2013

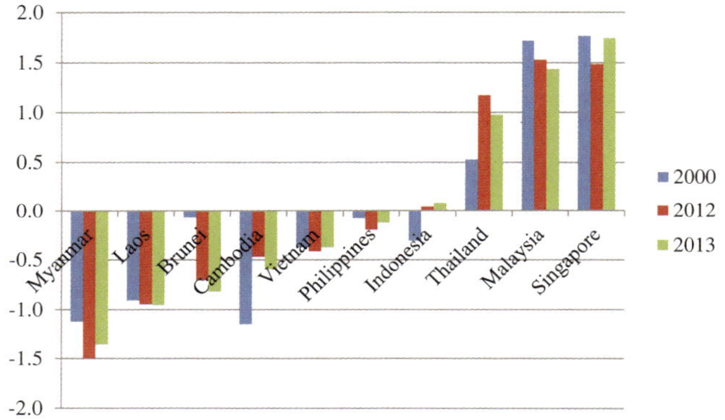

Source: Asia Competitiveness Institute

Figure 2.13: Financial, Businesses and Manpower Conditions (Labour Market Flexibility) — 2000, 2012 and 2013

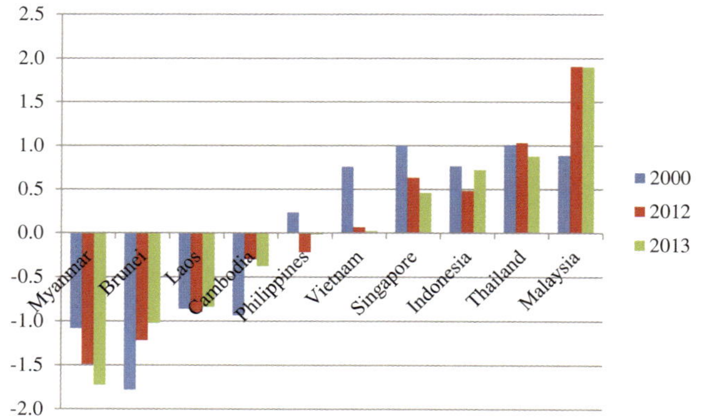

Source: Asia Competitiveness Institute

Figure 2.14: Financial, Businesses and Manpower Conditions (Productivity Performance) — 2000, 2012 and 2013

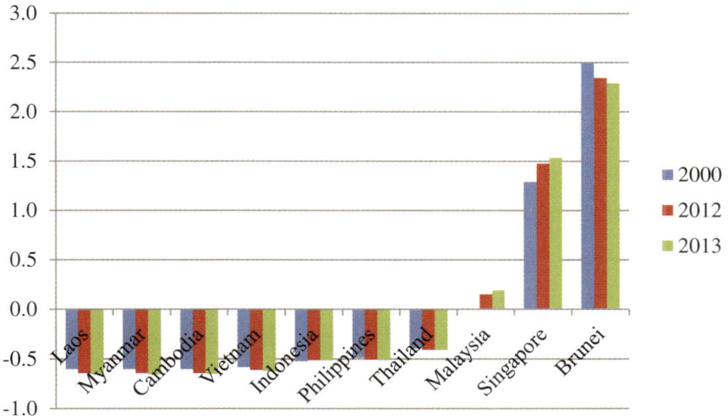

Source: Asia Competitiveness Institute

at sixth and seventh, respectively, as their scores plunged more negatively between 2000 and 2013. In the bottom three, Cambodia and Laos improved markedly while Myanmar fared worse.

The standardised scores of individual ASEAN member states for the three sub-environments are illustrated in Figures 2.12–2.14. Interestingly, while Singapore has remained at the top for Financial Deepening and Business Efficiency, Malaysia and Brunei took the top spot for Labour Market Flexibility and Productivity Performance, respectively, by a large margin. Nonetheless, in terms of Productivity Performance, Brunei's competitiveness appears to be eroding as indicated by its declining scores while Singapore at second and Malaysia at third have made some notable progress over time. The remaining seven ASEAN economies have remained below average in this environment although Indonesia shows signs of slight improvement in 2012 and 2013 relative to 2000.

2.3.5 Quality of Life and Infrastructure Development

In the ranking for Quality of Life and Infrastructure Development (Table 2.5), Malaysia has overtaken Brunei at the second place, after Singapore, since 2010, followed by Thailand as the only four economies with positive scores throughout the study period. Indonesia has surpassed both Philippines and Vietnam at the fifth position. In the bottom three, Laos at the eighth place shows remarkable improvement as its score rose from –1.0355 in 2000 to –0.6600 in 2013. Cambodia and Myanmar at the ninth and tenth place, respectively, fared worse in 2013 relative to 2012.

As seen in Figure 2.15, only Laos and Indonesia demonstrated steady improvement in scores in 2000, 2012 and 2013 while for Vietnam and Cambodia, progress in terms of Quality of Life and Infrastructure Development seems to be unstable as their scores plunged more negatively in 2013 relative to 2012. However, more alarming are Myanmar and Philippines which fared worse in 2012 and 2013 as compared to 2000. Among the top four economies with positive scores, only

Table 2.5: Quality of Life and Infrastructure Development Rankings and Standardised Scores, 2000–2013

QUALITY OF LIFE AND INFRASTRUCTURE DEVELOPMENT										
	1		2		3		4		5	
Rank	Economy	Score	Economy	Score	Economy	Score	Economy	Score	Economy	Score
2000	Singapore	1.9655	Brunei	0.9152	Malaysia	0.9083	Thailand	0.4121	Philippines	−0.0007
2001	Singapore	1.9282	Malaysia	0.9388	Brunei	0.8606	Thailand	0.5343	Philippines	−0.0103
2002	Singapore	1.8934	Malaysia	0.9703	Brunei	0.8499	Thailand	0.6800	Philippines	−0.1536
2003	Singapore	1.8969	Malaysia	0.9912	Brunei	0.8809	Thailand	0.5113	Philippines	−0.1179
2004	Singapore	1.8663	Malaysia	0.9705	Brunei	0.9071	Thailand	0.5031	Philippines	−0.0927
2005	Singapore	1.8899	Malaysia	1.0234	Brunei	0.8611	Thailand	0.5054	Philippines	−0.1694
2006	Singapore	1.8342	Malaysia	1.0704	Brunei	0.8069	Thailand	0.4845	Philippines	−0.1458
2007	Singapore	1.9862	Malaysia	0.8735	Brunei	0.7662	Thailand	0.4068	Indonesia	−0.1302
2008	Singapore	1.9744	Brunei	0.8732	Malaysia	0.8556	Thailand	0.3478	Indonesia	−0.1282
2009	Singapore	1.9971	Brunei	0.8696	Malaysia	0.8267	Thailand	0.3180	Vietnam	−0.1715
2010	Singapore	1.9411	Malaysia	0.8791	Brunei	0.7880	Thailand	0.3889	Indonesia	−0.0698
2011	Singapore	2.0002	Malaysia	0.9040	Brunei	0.8280	Thailand	0.3605	Indonesia	−0.1911
2012	Singapore	1.9468	Malaysia	0.9798	Brunei	0.7834	Thailand	0.3797	Indonesia	−0.1797
2013	Singapore	2.0345	Malaysia	0.8537	Brunei	0.7644	Thailand	0.3597	Indonesia	−0.1680
	6		7		8		9		10	
Rank	Economy	Score	Economy	Score	Economy	Score	Economy	Score	Economy	Score
2000	Indonesia	−0.2177	Vietnam	−0.6047	Cambodia	−0.9771	Laos	−1.0355	Myanmar	−1.3654
2001	Indonesia	−0.2270	Vietnam	−0.6405	Cambodia	−0.9552	Laos	−1.0558	Myanmar	−1.3732
2002	Indonesia	−0.3870	Vietnam	−0.5092	Cambodia	−0.9222	Laos	−1.0194	Myanmar	−1.4023
2003	Indonesia	−0.3135	Vietnam	−0.4485	Cambodia	−0.8993	Laos	−0.9936	Myanmar	−1.5076
2004	Indonesia	−0.2201	Vietnam	−0.4713	Cambodia	−0.9616	Laos	−0.9617	Myanmar	−1.5396
2005	Indonesia	−0.2461	Vietnam	−0.4566	Laos	−0.9368	Cambodia	−0.9563	Myanmar	−1.5147
2006	Indonesia	−0.1990	Vietnam	−0.3015	Laos	−0.9540	Cambodia	−1.0035	Myanmar	−1.5922
2007	Philippines	−0.1514	Vietnam	−0.2194	Laos	−0.9315	Cambodia	−0.9810	Myanmar	−1.6192
2008	Philippines	−0.1565	Vietnam	−0.2861	Laos	−0.9207	Cambodia	−0.9330	Myanmar	−1.6264
2009	Indonesia	−0.1765	Philippines	−0.2047	Laos	−0.8676	Cambodia	−0.9360	Myanmar	−1.6552
2010	Vietnam	−0.1149	Philippines	−0.2310	Laos	−0.9039	Cambodia	−1.0112	Myanmar	−1.6662
2011	Vietnam	−0.2712	Philippines	−0.3626	Laos	−0.7009	Cambodia	−0.8717	Myanmar	−1.6952
2012	Philippines	−0.2430	Vietnam	−0.2997	Cambodia	−0.7150	Laos	−0.9505	Myanmar	−1.7018
2013	Philippines	−0.2671	Vietnam	−0.3440	Laos	−0.6600	Cambodia	−0.8103	Myanmar	−1.7629

Source: Asia Competitiveness Institute

Figure 2.15: Quality of Life and Infrastructure Development — 2000, 2012 and 2013

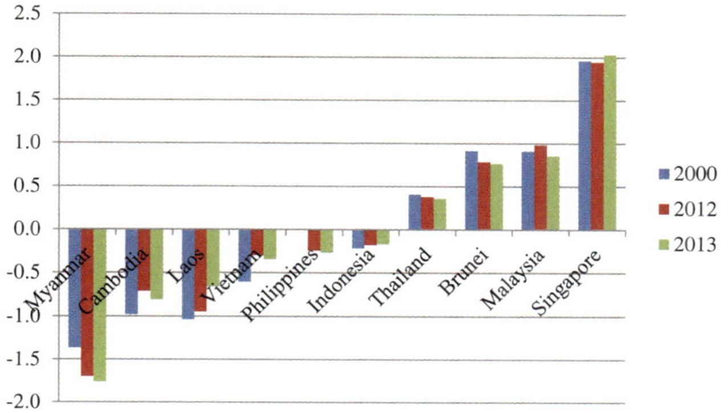

Source: Asia Competitiveness Institute

Figure 2.16: Quality of Life and Infrastructure Development (Physical Infrastructure) — 2000, 2012 and 2013

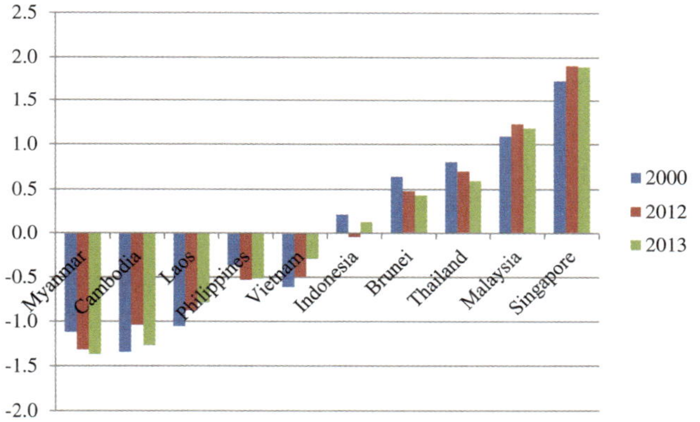

Source: Asia Competitiveness Institute

Figure 2.17: Quality of Life and Infrastructure Development (Technological Infrastructure) — 2000, 2012 and 2013

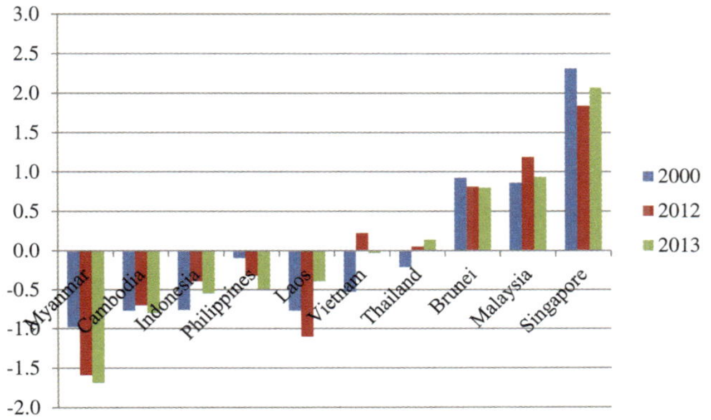

Source: Asia Competitiveness Institute

Figure 2.18: Quality of Life and Infrastructure Development (Standard of Living, Education and Social Stability) — 2000, 2012 and 2013

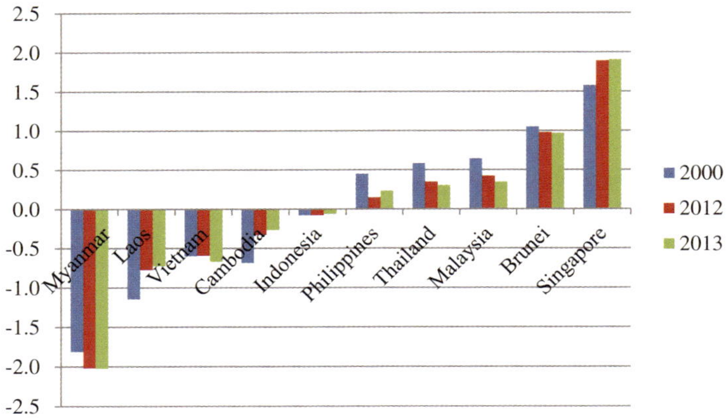

Source: Asia Competitiveness Institute

Singapore exceeded its own performance in 2013 as compared to 2000, while Malaysia, Brunei and Thailand seem to be losing in competitiveness in this environment.

Among the three sub-environments under Quality of Life and Infrastructure Development, Singapore and Malaysia held the top two spots for Physical Infrastructure (Figure 2.16) and Technological Infrastructure (Figure 2.17). However, Brunei has remained ahead of Malaysia in terms of Standard of Living, Education and Social Stability (Figure 2.18). Indonesia appears to have rebounded in terms of Physical Infrastructure as its score turned from negative in 2012 to positive in 2013 although it has not returned to its 2000 level. More impressive is Thailand which seems to have decidedly joined the rank of ASEAN economies with positive scores for Technological Infrastructure. On the flip side, Vietnam's score for Technological Infrastructure plunged from positive in 2012 to negative in 2013.

2.3.6 Competitiveness-Over-Time Analysis

For a better comparison of the competitive performances over time, we split the study period into two sub-periods, 2000–2006 (Period A) and 2007–2013 (Period B). Our Competitiveness Over-Time (COT) analysis is conducted for Overall Competitiveness as well as each of the 12 sub-environments, which is instructive for policy-making as it reveals where individual economies are losing competitiveness. For all COT Figures 2.19–2.31, countries above the 45-degree line improved their competitiveness in Period B relative to Period A; below the line means they performed better in the Period A; and on the line means no change over both sub-periods.

As shown in Figure 2.19 for Overall Competitiveness, Singapore at the top of the 45-degree line is consistent with its top-notch performance detailed in Section 2.3.1. Malaysia, Brunei and Vietnam are on or very close to the 45-degree line, indicating a lack of improvement in their competitiveness over time. Thailand, Philippines and Myanmar fall below the line, which implies that their competitiveness has deteriorated in Period B relative

Figure 2.19: Competitiveness Over Time Analysis for Overall Competitiveness, Period B (2007–2013) Against Period A (2000–2006)

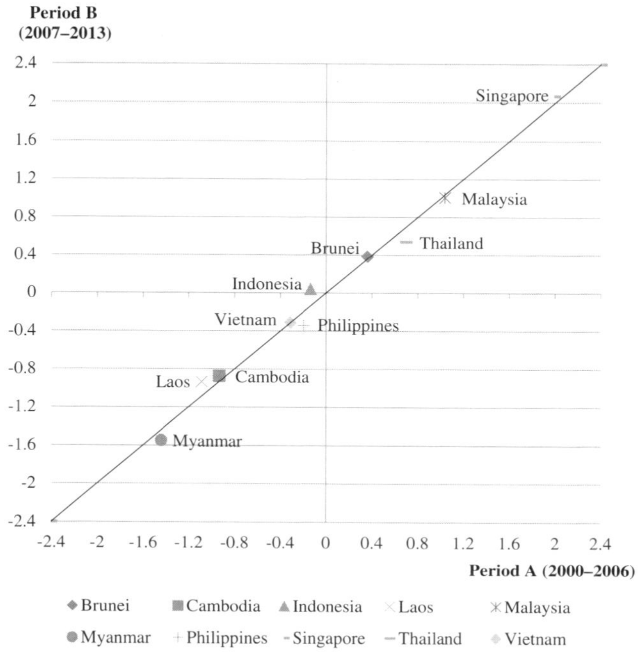

Source: Asia Competitiveness Institute

Figure 2.20: Competitiveness Over Time Analysis for Economic Vibrancy, Period B (2007–2013) Against Period A (2000–2006)

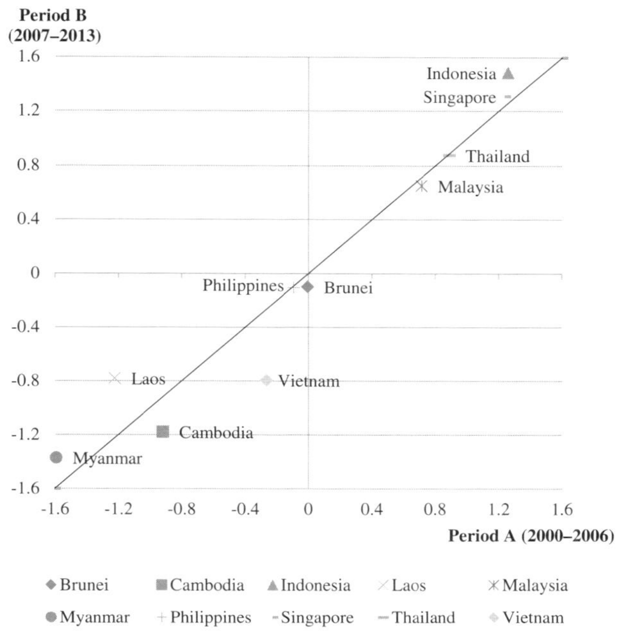

Source: Asia Competitiveness Institute

Figure 2.21: Competitiveness Over Time Analysis for Openness to Trade and Services, Period B (2007–2013) Against Period A (2000–2006)

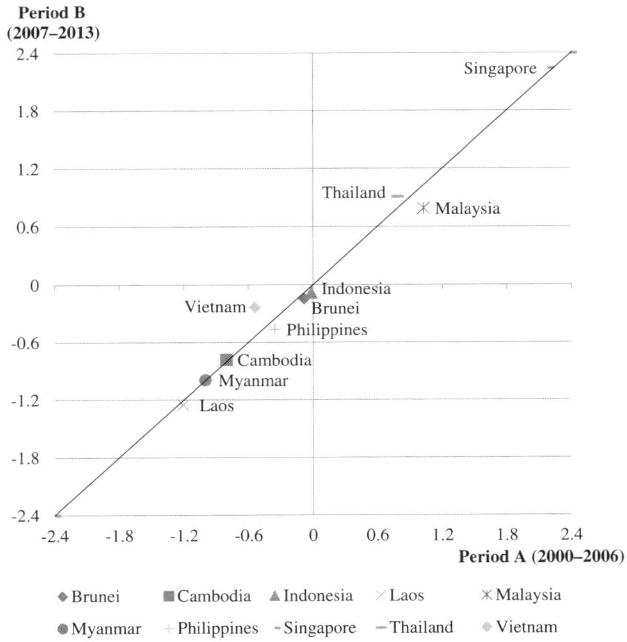

Source: Asia Competitiveness Institute

to Period A. In contrast, Indonesia, Laos and to a lesser extent, Cambodia performed better in Period B than in Period A.

In Figure 2.20 for Economic Vibrancy, a sub-environment under Macroeconomic Stability, Indonesia rose to the top as well as fared better in Period B than in Period A. Among the bottom four economies, Laos and Myanmar show marked improvement over time, while Vietnam and Cambodia are losing in competitiveness in this sub-environment. Singapore as second to Indonesia improved in Period B relative to Period A, while Malaysia and Brunei fared worse over time and Thailand and Philippines stagnated.

In the remaining two sub-environments under Macroeconomic Stability, most ASEAN economies clustered along the 45-degree line, which indicates little to no improvement in competitiveness, with the exception of Vietnam and Thailand lying above the line for Openness to Trade and Services (see Figure 2.21), and Indonesia and Brunei which fared better over time in terms of Attractiveness to Foreign Investors (see Figure 2.22).

As seen in Figures 2.23–2.25, Singapore remains at the top for all three sub-environments under Government and Institutional Setting and even shows notable improvement over time for Government Policies and Fiscal Sustainability and Competition, Regulatory Standards and Rule of Law. It is heartening that Thailand and Philippines fared better in terms of Government Policies and Fiscal Sustainability, while Indonesia significantly improved in Competition, Regulatory Standards and Rule of Law in Period B as compared to Period A. Nonetheless, except for Singapore and Laos which performed better in all sub-environments in Period B

Figure 2.22: Competitiveness Over Time Analysis for Attractiveness to Foreign Investors, Period B (2007–2013) Against Period A (2000–2006)

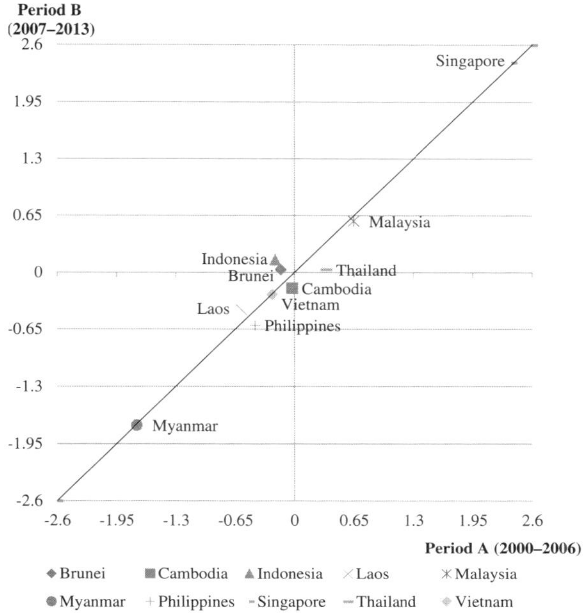

Source: Asia Competitiveness Institute

Figure 2.23: Competitiveness Over Time Analysis for Government Policies and Fiscal Sustainability, Period B (2007–2013) Against Period A (2000–2006)

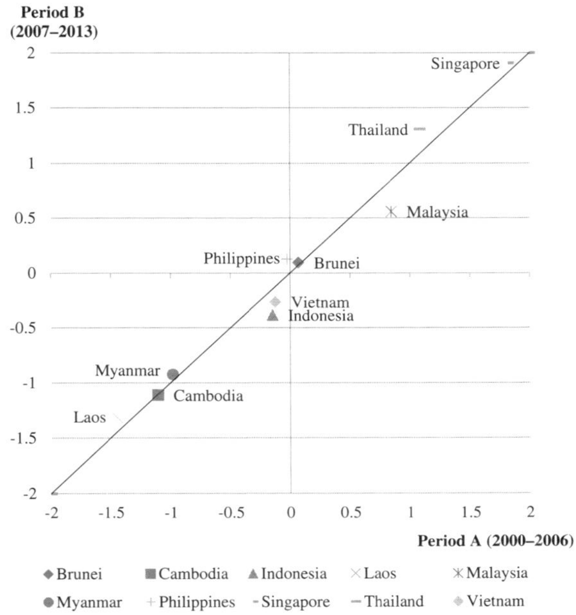

Source: Asia Competitiveness Institute

Figure 2.24: Competitiveness Over Time Analysis for Institutions, Governance and Leadership, Period B (2007–2013) Against Period A (2000–2006)

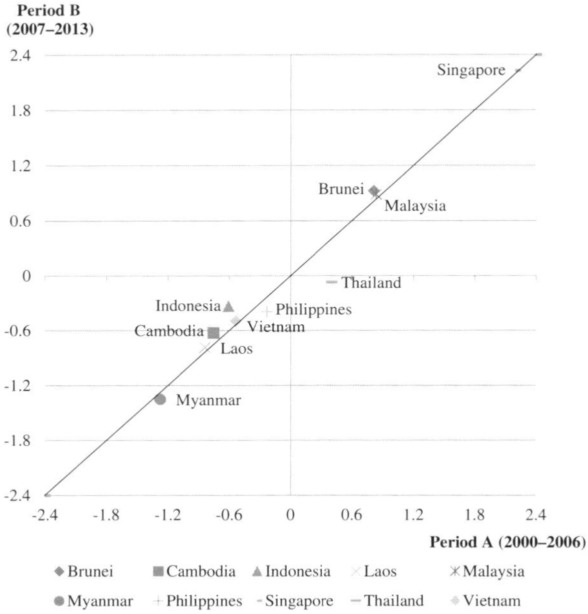

Source: Asia Competitiveness Institute

Figure 2.25: Competitiveness Over Time Analysis for Competition, Regulatory Standards and Rule of Law, Period B (2007–2013) Against Period A (2000–2006)

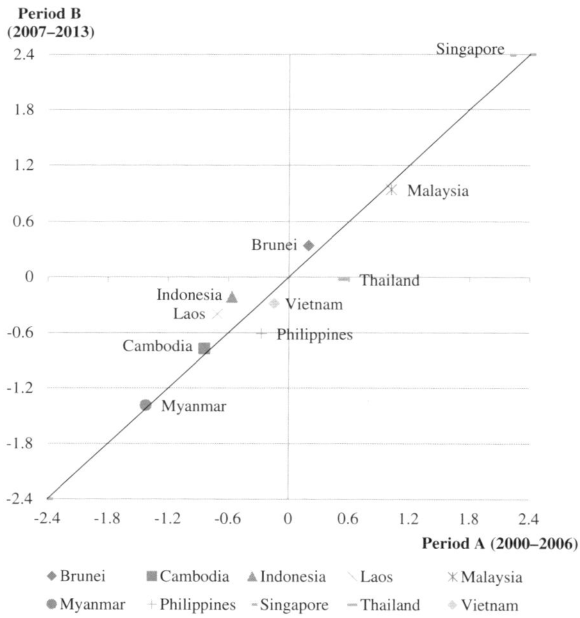

Source: Asia Competitiveness Institute

Figure 2.26: Competitiveness Over Time Analysis for Financial Deepening and Business Efficiency, Period B (2007–2013) Against Period A (2000–2006)

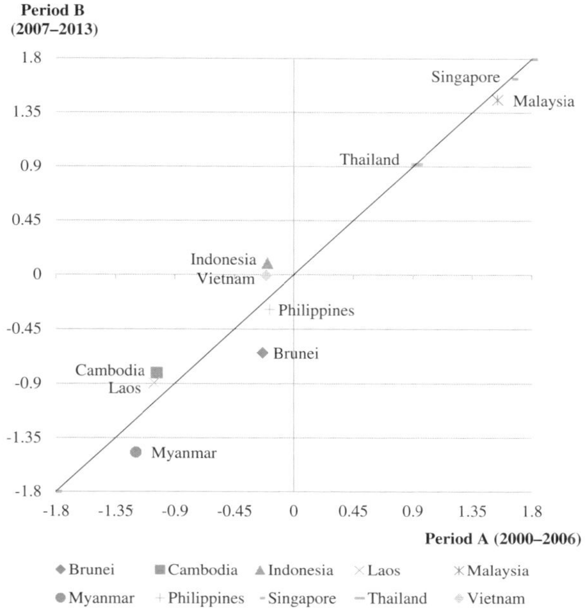

Source: Asia Competitiveness Institute

relative to Period A, the remaining eight ASEAN economies improved in certain sub-environments while deteriorating in others, which signifies the enormous challenges in maintaining sound governance in the region.

Among the three sub-environments under Financial, Businesses and Manpower Conditions, Singapore has maintained its top spot for Financial Deepening and Business Efficiency (Figure 2.26) while Malaysia and Brunei have been the most competitive in terms of Labour Market Flexibility (Figure 2.27) and Productivity Performance (Figure 2.28), respectively. However, while Malaysia has become remarkably more competitive over time in Labour Market Flexibility, Brunei's competitiveness in productivity appears to be eroding as it fared worse in Period B relative to Period A. With the exception of Singapore and Malaysia which slightly improved in productivity over time, the rest of ASEAN clustered on the 45-degree line.

In Figures 2.29–2.31 for the three sub-environments under Quality of Life and Infrastructure Development, Vietnam shows significant improvement in terms of Technological Infrastructure (Figure 2.30), while Indonesia and Laos have made great strides in Standard of Living, Education and Social Stability. Nonetheless, improving physical infrastructure appears to be a regional challenge as, except for Singapore, Vietnam, Laos and Cambodia, the remaining six ASEAN countries either fall below or lie on the 45-degree line, which indicates that they fared worse or stagnated in Period B relative to Period A. It is also alarming for Malaysia, Thailand and Philippines as the older, more mature economies in ASEAN that their competitiveness in terms of Standard of Living, Education and Social Stability appears to be eroding over time.

Figure 2.27: Competitiveness Over Time Analysis for Labour Market Flexibility, Period B (2007–2013) Against Period A (2000–2006)

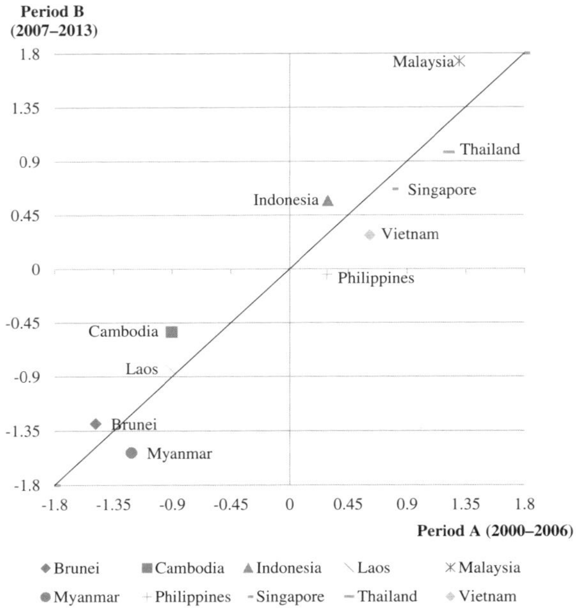

Source: Asia Competitiveness Institute

Figure 2.28: Competitiveness Over Time Analysis for Productivity Performance, Period B (2007–2013) Against Period A (2000–2006)

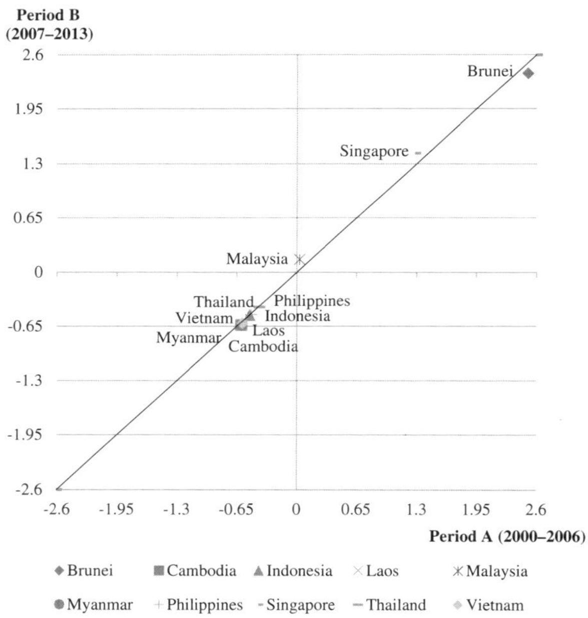

Source: Asia Competitiveness Institute

Figure 2.29: Competitiveness Over Time Analysis for Physical Infrastructure, Period B (2007–2013) Against Period A (2000–2006)

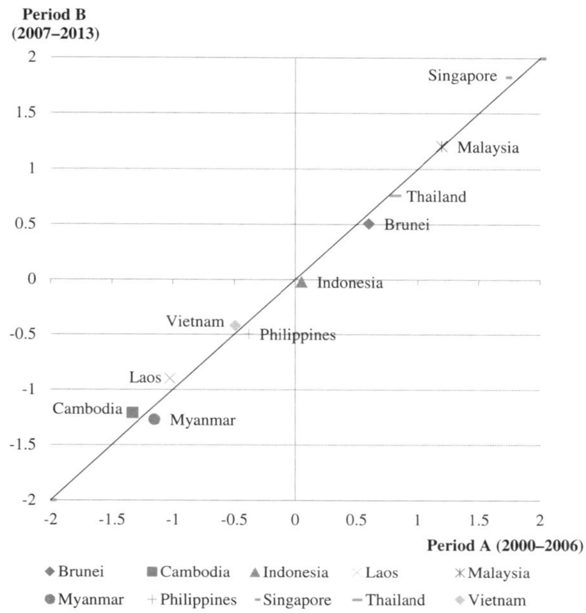

Source: Asia Competitiveness Institute

Figure 2.30: Competitiveness Over Time Analysis for Technological Infrastructure, Period B (2007–2013) Against Period A (2000–2006)

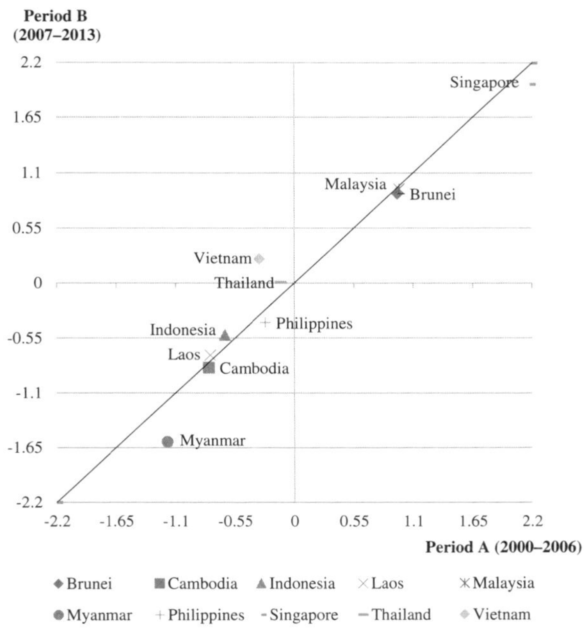

Source: Asia Competitiveness Institute

Figure 2.31: Competitiveness Over Time Analysis for Standard of Living, Education and Social Stability, Period B (2007–2013) Against Period A (2000–2006)

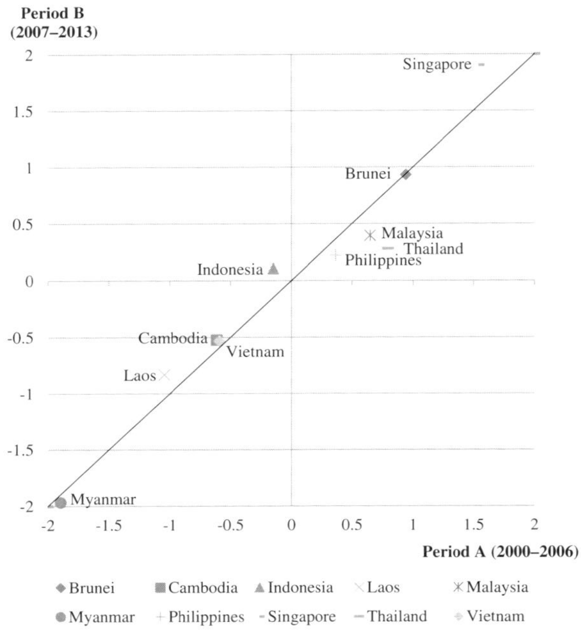

Source: Asia Competitiveness Institute

Our COT analysis shows that the majority of ASEAN-10 have improved in competitiveness over time, albeit to various degrees and in different sub-environments. Indonesia stands out as a clear outlier, showing impressive progress in the majority of sub-environments, while Singapore remains the top-performing economy by a large margin. However, for the remaining older, more mature economies in ASEAN, particularly Thailand and Philippines, maintaining competitiveness has been problematic as global as well as regional competition intensifies with the emergence of numerous low-cost, labour-abundant investment destinations. For the transitional economies in ASEAN, while Cambodia, Laos and Vietnam have made significant strides in attracting foreign direct investment (FDI) and multinational corporations (MNCs) as part and parcel of the initial take-off stage, with Myanmar rising as the new frontier, keeping them remains a challenge as institutional capacity, infrastructure and productivity fail to come up to par. Self-competition is thus paramount regardless of where one stands in the rankings.

2.3.7 Maximising Strengths and Minimising Weaknesses

In this section, the top 20 percent strongest indicators and top 20 percent weakest indicators for individual ASEAN economies will be first discussed. This is followed by the analysis of spider web charts depicting each economy's competitiveness in each sub-environments *vis-à-vis* the ASEAN median and maximum (set by the regional top performer).

2.3.7.1 *Top 20 Percent Strongest and Weakest Indicators*

Brunei's top 20 percent strongest and top 20 percent weakest indicators are listed in Tables 2.6 and 2.7, respectively. As oil prices have tumbled, the diminutive oil-rich state needs to step up its efforts in diversifying its economy. Labour productivity (#1 and #2 in Table 2.6) and fiscal balance (#3 and #4) are the two most notable strengths which can serve as important catalysts for the country's economic restructuring.

On the other hand, Brunei's high labour costs can be prohibitive to potential foreign and local investors (#118 and #120 in Table 2.7). Among its top weaknesses is the private sector (#108, #111) which is constrained by the lack of ease of starting business (#117), a relatively underdeveloped financial sector (#115, #119) and tax burden (#121).

Table 2.6: Top 20 Percent Strongest Indicators List for Brunei, 2013

Rank	20 Percent Strongest Indicator	Score	Environment
1	Agriculture, Value Added Per Worker	2.8861	FBMC
2	Industry, Value Added Per Worker	2.2822	FBMC
3	Budget Balance	2.1657	GIS
4	Current Account Balance	1.9977	MS
5	Government Environmental Protection Policies	1.9913	GIS
6	Access to Print Media	1.9363	QLID
7	Personal Computers	1.9172	QLID
8	Gross Domestic Savings	1.9136	MS
9	Government Consumption Expenditure	1.8549	GIS
10	Air Quality	1.7234	QLID
11	Inflation	1.6101	MS
12	Sovereign Debt Risk	1.5635	FBMC
13	Religious Unrest	1.5412	QLID
14	Corporate Income Tax	1.4630	MS
15	Secondary Schooling	1.4501	QLID
16	Political Change	1.4369	GIS
17	Government Stability	1.4276	GIS
18	Government Responsiveness	1.3861	GIS
19	Human Development Index	1.3844	QLID
20	Public Security and Safety	1.3809	QLID
21	Information and Communication Technology (ICT) Expenditure	1.3779	QLID
22	High Quality Management Staff	1.3760	FBMC
23	Quality of Judiciary	1.2678	GIS
24	Access to Sanitation	1.1599	QLID

Source: Asia Competitiveness Institute

Table 2.7: Top 20 Percent Weakest Indicators List for Brunei, 2013

Rank	20 Percent Weakest Indicator	Score	Environment
98	Population	−0.8582	QLID
99	Output Industry (Value Added)	−0.8627	MS
100	Output Agriculture (Value Added)	−0.8756	MS
101	International Reserves	−0.8838	GIS
102	Health Expenditure	−0.8867	QLID
103	Urban Population Growth	−0.8939	QLID
104	Labour Force	−0.9055	FBMC
105	Government Revenue (Including Grants)	−0.9089	GIS
106	Imports of Goods and Services	−0.9267	MS
107	Tax Revenue	−0.9517	GIS
108	Market Capitalisation	−1.0035	FBMC
109	Gross Domestic Product	−1.0067	MS
110	Real GDP Growth	−1.0097	MS
111	Listed Domestic Companies	−1.0108	FBMC
112	Output Services (Value Added)	−1.0120	MS
113	Regional Competitiveness	−1.0462	GIS
114	Deposit Interest Rate	−1.0744	GIS
115	Domestic Credit Provided by the Financial Sector	−1.0780	FBMC
116	Gross Fixed Capital Formation	−1.2308	MS
117	Ease of Starting Business	−1.5132	GIS
118	Cost of Management Staff	−1.8299	FBMC
119	Claims on Private Sector	−1.9212	FBMC
120	Cost of Production Labour	−1.9659	FBMC
121	Tax Burden	−2.1336	GIS

Source: Asia Competitiveness Institute

Table 2.8: Top 20 Percent Strongest Indicators List for Cambodia, 2013

Rank	20 Percent Strongest Indicator	Score	Environment
1	Freedom of Religion	2.2361	QLID
2	Health Expenditure	2.0419	QLID
3	Claims on Private Sector	1.8536	FBMC
4	Freedom of Speech	1.5275	QLID
5	Unemployment Rate	1.3255	FBMC
6	Government Environmental Protection Policies	1.2982	GIS
7	Daily Organic Water Pollutant Emissions	1.1413	QLID
8	Corporate Income Tax	0.9728	MS
9	Real GDP Growth	0.9678	MS
10	Primary Schooling	0.9021	QLID
11	International Monetary Fund Credit	0.7737	GIS
12	Cost of Management Staff	0.7648	FBMC
13	External Debt	0.7647	GIS
14	Cost of Production Labour	0.6264	FBMC
15	Freedom of Press	0.6095	QLID
16	Traffic Congestion	0.5915	QLID
17	Tax Burden	0.5677	GIS
18	Exchange Rate Appreciation	0.5182	GIS
19	Cellular Mobile Telephone Subscribers	0.4932	QLID
20	Inflation	0.4000	MS
21	Religious Unrest	0.2757	QLID
22	Business Impact of Rules on FDI	0.2276	MS
23	Urban Population Growth	0.0818	QLID
24	Telecommunications System	0.0684	QLID

Source: Asia Competitiveness Institute

Table 2.9: Top 20 Percent Weakest Indicators List for Cambodia, 2013

Rank	20 Percent Weakest Indicator	Score	Environment
98	Net Foreign Assets	−0.9254	GIS
99	Policy Towards Private Enterprise Rating	−0.9312	GIS
100	Quality of Police	−0.9554	GIS
101	Government Effectiveness	−0.9745	GIS
102	University and Post-Graduate Education	−0.9796	QLID
103	Market Capitalisation	−1.0035	FBMC
104	Output Services (Value Added)	−1.0038	MS
105	Ease of Starting Business	−1.0049	GIS
106	Sovereign Debt Risk	−1.0085	FBMC
107	Gross Domestic Product	−1.0101	MS
108	Listed Domestic Companies	−1.0108	FBMC
109	Government Revenue (Including Grants)	−1.0188	GIS
110	Tax Revenue	−1.0264	GIS
111	Interest Rate Spread	−1.0773	GIS
112	Information and Communication Technology (ICT) Expenditure	−1.1009	QLID
113	Internet Subscribers	−1.1013	QLID
114	Quality of Judiciary	−1.2403	GIS
115	Electric Power	−1.3107	QLID
116	Urban Population	−1.3466	QLID
117	Gross Domestic Savings	−1.4711	MS
118	Access to Water	−1.7563	QLID
119	Access to Sanitation	−2.0885	QLID
120	Literacy Rate	−2.1106	QLID
121	Air Quality	−2.1667	QLID

Source: Asia Competitiveness Institute

Cambodia is clearly accelerating its catching-up as it has decidedly overtaken Laos at the eighth place in the Overall Competitiveness ranking (Table 2.1). Employment creation and a conducive environment for private sector development are among its top five strengths (#3 and #5 in Table 2.8). Low labour cost (#12 and #14) may provide the extra boost to strengthen the private sector but more heed needs to be paid to the education system (#102, #120 in Table 2.9) as well as public services (#115, #118, #119) to upgrade human resources. Improving enterprise policy (#99) and ease of starting business (#105) are also imperative for entrepreneurship to thrive.

Indonesia's top 20 Percent strongest indicators list (Table 2.10) has population, agricultural value added and labour force as the top three, suggesting that labour-intensive agriculture in a dualistic economic structure is viable. It is also heartening that industry and services value added

Table 2.10: Top 20 Percent Strongest Indicators List for Indonesia, 2013

Rank	20 Percent Strongest Indicator	Score	Environment
1	Population	2.6427	QLID
2	Output Agriculture (Value Added)	2.6043	MS
3	Labour Force	2.5609	FBMC
4	Output Industry (Value Added)	2.4306	MS
5	Output Services (Value Added)	2.0712	MS
6	Freedom of Speech	1.5275	QLID
7	Gross Fixed Capital Formation	1.4546	MS
8	Gross Domestic Product	1.4042	MS
9	Deposit Interest Rate	1.1144	GIS
10	Market Capitalisation	1.0371	FBMC
11	Political System Risk	0.8923	GIS
12	Government Revenue (Including Grants)	0.8577	GIS
13	Tax Revenue	0.8572	GIS
14	Freedom of Press	0.8016	QLID
15	Tax Burden	0.7946	GIS
16	Claims on Private Sector	0.7871	FBMC
17	Cost of Management Staff	0.7648	FBMC
18	Availability of Scientists and Engineers	0.7473	FBMC
19	Regional Competitiveness	0.6851	GIS
20	Listed Domestic Companies	0.5710	FBMC
21	Secondary Schooling	0.5510	QLID
22	Cost of Production Labour	0.5243	FBMC
23	Imports of Goods and Services	0.5192	MS
24	Extent of Staff Training	0.4558	FBMC

Source: Asia Competitiveness Institute

Table 2.11: Top 20 Percent Weakest Indicators List for Indonesia, 2013

Rank	20 Percent Weakest Indicator	Score	Environment
98	Personal Computers	−0.6594	QLID
99	Institutional Sophistication	−0.7156	GIS
100	Freedom of Religion	−0.7454	QLID
101	Quality of Political Leadership	−0.7588	GIS
102	Domestic Credit to Private Sector	−0.7603	FBMC
103	Internet Subscribers	−0.7923	QLID
104	Labour Activism	−0.7952	QLID
105	Openness to Trade	−0.8475	MS
106	Government Stability	−0.8566	GIS
107	High Quality Management Staff	−0.8761	FBMC
108	Lack of Discrimination Against Investors	−0.8866	MS
109	Quality of Central Bank/Monetary Authority	−0.8879	GIS
110	Labour Market Rating	−0.9082	FBMC
111	Lack of Market Distortion due to State-Ownership	−0.9145	GIS
112	Policy Towards Private Enterprise Rating	−0.9312	GIS
113	Access to Sanitation	−0.9833	QLID
114	Money Supply (M2)	−1.0908	GIS
115	Information and Communication Technology (ICT) Expenditure	−1.1009	QLID
116	Inflation	−1.2410	MS
117	Unemployment Rate	−1.5149	FBMC
118	Real GDP Growth	−1.7000	MS
119	Exchange Rate Appreciation	−1.8415	GIS
120	External Debt	−2.0281	GIS
121	International Monetary Fund Credit	−2.1696	GIS

Source: Asia Competitiveness Institute

are among the country's top five strengths, which means Indonesia can leverage on its large workforce to develop resource-based industries and services, for instance, agro-processing, and simultaneously tackle its unemployment problem (#117 in Table 2.11).

Nonetheless for Indonesia, a stable and enabling macroeconomic environment remains one of its top weaknesses (#109, #114, #116, #119). Equally important is prudent fiscal management as high external debt (#120) exposes the country to insolvency and liquidity risks. While entrepreneurial growth is among Indonesia's top strengths (#10 and #20), improvement is required in terms of enterprise policy (#112) to minimise market distortion and level the playing field (#108, #111).

Laos seems to be quietly rising to join the more developed ASEAN members, as evident in its top strengths that include technological infrastructure and investment (#1 and #5 in Table 2.12). Socio-political stability (#9, #16, #23), low labour cost (#14) and a relatively conducive business environment (#15, #19, #20) are among Laos' top 20 percent strengths that the country needs to leverage on in its development trajectory.

On the flip side, human capital remains a key challenge for Laos to keep up with the demands of industrialisation (#102, #112, #115, #118 in Table 2.13). More heed should also be paid to fiscal management (#105, #107, #119) to minimise sovereign debt risk (#100).

While Malaysia as the second most competitive economy in ASEAN has not successfully narrowed its gap with the top-performing Singapore, it can leverage on its top strengths including a

Table 2.12: Top 20 Percent Strongest Indicators List for Laos, 2013

Rank	20 Percent Strongest Indicator	Score	Environment
1	Telecommunications System	2.7301	QLID
2	Urban Population Growth	2.4141	QLID
3	Real GDP Growth	1.5315	MS
4	Daily Organic Water Pollutant Emissions	1.1413	QLID
5	Gross Fixed Capital Formation	0.9831	MS
6	Exchange Rate Appreciation	0.9192	GIS
7	International Monetary Fund Credit	0.8253	GIS
8	Unemployment Rate	0.8048	FBMC
9	Labour Unrest	0.8026	QLID
10	Cost of Management Staff	0.7648	FBMC
11	External Debt	0.7405	GIS
12	Government Consumption Expenditure	0.6578	GIS
13	Traffic Congestion	0.6445	QLID
14	Cost of Production Labour	0.6264	FBMC
15	Monopolies and Cartel	0.5635	GIS
16	Religious Unrest	0.5328	QLID
17	Electric Power	0.5051	QLID
18	Primary Schooling	0.5021	QLID
19	Levelness of Playing Field	0.5010	MS
20	Corporate Income Tax	0.4732	MS
21	Government Environmental Protection Policies	0.4555	GIS
22	Effectiveness of Legal System	0.3122	GIS
23	Political Change	0.2441	GIS
24	Business Impact of Rules on FDI	0.2120	MS

Source: Asia Competitiveness Institute

Table 2.13: Top 20 Percent Weakest Indicators List for Laos, 2013

Rank	20 Percent Weakest Indicator	Score	Environment
98	Net Foreign Assets	−0.9810	GIS
99	Market Capitalisation	−1.0035	FBMC
100	Sovereign Debt Risk	−1.0085	FBMC
101	Listed Domestic Companies	−1.0108	FBMC
102	University and Post-Graduate Education	−1.0239	QLID
103	Output Services (Value Added)	−1.0411	MS
104	Human Development Index	−1.0445	QLID
105	Government Revenue (Including Grants)	−1.0502	GIS
106	Gross Domestic Product	−1.0545	MS
107	Tax Revenue	−1.0579	GIS
108	Information and Communication Technology (ICT) Expenditure	−1.1009	QLID
109	Cellular Mobile Telephone Subscribers	−1.1045	QLID
110	Health Expenditure	−1.2070	QLID
111	Inflation	−1.2181	MS
112	Secondary Schooling	−1.2784	QLID
113	Port Facilities	−1.2896	QLID
114	Freedom of Press	−1.4514	QLID
115	Availability of Scientists and Engineers	−1.4583	FBMC
116	Access to Water	−1.5187	QLID
117	Regional Competitiveness	−1.7019	GIS
118	Literacy Rate	−1.8190	QLID
119	Current Account Balance	−1.9789	MS
120	Lending Rate	−2.2353	GIS
121	Interest Rate Spread	−2.5754	GIS

Source: Asia Competitiveness Institute

thriving private sector (#1 and #3 in Table 2.14) and a strong legislature and financial system (#2 and #4) to expedite catching-up. Malaysia's high-quality manpower (#9, #10, #17) and strong institutional capacity (#8, #18, #23) pose a credible challenge to Singapore's overall top spots in Financial, Businesses and Manpower Conditions and Government and Institutional Setting, respectively. Also highly competitive is its physical infrastructure including rail (#5), roads (#19) and ports (#22).

Nonetheless, attracting FDI inflows has been challenging for Malaysia (#104 in Table 2.15) amidst rising labour cost (#103) and declining labour pool (#112, #113). Fiscal vulnerability has to be addressed (#114, #120, #121) if the country is to effectively maintain a stable macroeconomic environment crucial to growth.

Table 2.14: Top 20 Percent Strongest Indicators List for Malaysia, 2013

Rank	20 Percent Strongest Indicator	Score	Environment
1	Listed Domestic Companies	2.1632	FBMC
2	Legislature/Parliament (Functioning of Government System)	1.5510	GIS
3	Ease of Starting Business	1.5068	GIS
4	Money Supply (M2)	1.4814	GIS
5	Rail Facilities	1.4715	QLID
6	Government Stability	1.4276	GIS
7	Market Capitalisation	1.4126	FBMC
8	Government Responsiveness	1.3861	GIS
9	Availability of Scientists and Engineers	1.3761	FBMC
10	High Quality Management Staff	1.3760	FBMC
11	Domestic Credit to Private Sector	1.3448	FBMC
12	Quality of Banking and Financial System	1.3174	FBMC
13	Domestic Credit Provided by the Financial Sector	1.3110	FBMC
14	Corporate Governance	1.2633	GIS
15	Internet Subscribers	1.1825	QLID
16	Monopolies and Cartel	1.1314	GIS
17	Extent of Staff Training	1.1114	FBMC
18	Bureaucracy/Red Tape	1.1064	GIS
19	Local Road System	1.1044	QLID
20	Lending Rate	1.0832	GIS
21	Quality of Stock Market Regulatory Authority	1.0620	FBMC
22	Port Facilities	1.0489	QLID
23	Government Effectiveness	1.0366	GIS
24	Transparency of Processes for Investors	1.0258	MS

Source: Asia Competitiveness Institute

Table 2.15: Top 20 Percent Weakest Indicators List for Malaysia, 2013

Rank	20 Percent Weakest Indicator	Score	Environment
98	Secondary Schooling	0.1069	QLID
99	Air Quality	0.0992	QLID
100	Exchange Rate Appreciation	0.0785	GIS
101	Urban Population Growth	0.0340	QLID
102	Health Expenditure	−0.0055	QLID
103	Cost of Production Labour	−0.0081	FBMC
104	Foreign Direct Investment Inflows	−0.0265	MS
105	Unemployment Rate	−0.0473	FBMC
106	Real GDP Growth	−0.0550	MS
107	Deposit Interest Rate	−0.0912	GIS
108	GDP Per Capita	−0.1259	MS
109	Industry, Value Added Per Worker	−0.1714	FBMC
110	Tax Burden	−0.1945	GIS
111	Traffic Congestion	−0.3376	QLID
112	Population	−0.4470	QLID
113	Labour Force	−0.5348	FBMC
114	Budget Balance	−0.5943	GIS
115	Freedom of Speech	−0.6547	QLID
116	Claims on Private Sector	−0.6834	FBMC
117	Corporate Income Tax	−0.7145	MS
118	Freedom of Religion	−0.7454	QLID
119	Daily Organic Water Pollutant Emissions	−1.0902	QLID
120	International Monetary Fund Credit	−1.1852	GIS
121	External Debt	−1.5202	GIS

Source: Asia Competitiveness Institute

Myanmar as a latecomer to competitiveness is not without its strengths among which are taxes (#1 in Table 2.16), macroeconomic stability (#6, #18) and labour cost (#5, #7). Myanmar's immense potential as a food basket is evident in its agricultural output and productivity (#19, #21), high water and air quality (#3, #22) and labour force (#13, #15). With Ease of Starting Business as one of its top 20 percent strengths (#23), Myanmar seems poised to become the next investment hotspot in ASEAN and Asia.

That said, socio-political instability may derail Myanmar's growth trajectory (#111, #118 in Table 2.17). In light of the strong mandate given to the National League for Democracy in the watershed 2015 general election, strengthening public governance (#98, #100, #101, #105) would be imperative as a prerequisite to economic growth.

Table 2.16: Top 20 Percent Strongest Indicators List for Myanmar, 2013

Rank	20 Percent Strongest Indicator	Score	Environment
1	Tax Burden	1.7959	GIS
2	Deposit Interest Rate	1.7498	GIS
3	Daily Organic Water Pollutant Emissions	1.3622	QLID
4	Claims on Private Sector	0.9955	FBMC
5	Cost of Management Staff	0.7648	FBMC
6	External Debt	0.7543	GIS
7	Cost of Production Labour	0.6264	FBMC
8	Traffic Congestion	0.5587	QLID
9	International Monetary Fund Credit	0.5311	GIS
10	Interest Rate Spread	0.2933	GIS
11	Literacy Rate	0.2083	QLID
12	Access to Sanitation	0.0672	QLID
13	Labour Force	−0.0039	FBMC
14	Gross Domestic Savings	−0.0968	MS
15	Population	−0.1166	QLID
16	Urban Population Growth	−0.1179	QLID
17	Unemployment Rate	−0.1420	FBMC
18	Money Supply Growth (M2)	−0.2094	MS
19	Output Agriculture (Value Added)	−0.3751	MS
20	Current Account Balance	−0.4433	MS
21	Agriculture, Value Added Per Worker	−0.4690	FBMC
22	Air Quality	−0.5200	QLID
23	Ease of Starting Business	−0.5485	GIS
24	GDP Per Capita	−0.5740	MS

Source: Asia Competitiveness Institute

Table 2.17: Top 20 Percent Weakest Indicators List for Myanmar, 2013

Rank	20 Percent Weakest Indicator	Score	Environment
98	Government Effectiveness	−1.5583	GIS
99	Government Consumption Expenditure	−1.6027	GIS
100	Quality of Regulatory Environment	−1.6121	GIS
101	Effectiveness of Legal System	−1.6150	GIS
102	Corporate Income Tax	−1.6572	MS
103	Local Road System	−1.6710	QLID
104	Public Security and Safety	−1.7364	QLID
105	Legislature/Parliament (Functioning of Government System)	−1.8042	GIS
106	Levelness of Playing Field	−1.8116	MS
107	Primary Schooling	−1.8157	QLID
108	Gross Fixed Capital Formation	−1.8896	MS
109	Foreign Owned Companies	−1.9332	MS
110	Airport Facilities	−1.9534	QLID
111	Labour Unrest	−1.9677	QLID
112	Quality of Stock Market Regulatory Authority	−1.9771	FBMC
113	Strength of Auditing and Reporting Standards	−2.0103	GIS
114	Exchange Rate Appreciation	−2.0634	GIS
115	Quality of Banking and Financial System	−2.0897	FBMC
116	Monopolies and Cartel	−2.1406	GIS
117	Business Impact of Rules on FDI	−2.1729	MS
118	Religious Unrest	−2.3514	QLID
119	Extent of Staff Training	−2.3530	FBMC
120	Tax Revenue/Government Revenue	−2.3993	GIS
121	Cellular Mobile Telephone Subscribers	−2.4483	QLID

Source: Asia Competitiveness Institute

For Philippines, its talent pool is an enormous strength to tap (#3 in Table 2.18) if the lack of productive employment can be resolved at home (#120 in Table 2.19), which will translate into a transfusion of skills and capital, particularly from the professionally skilled diaspora around the world. Much is dependent on improving the domestic business environment that is plagued with bureaucratic inertia (#106, #107, #109). Democracy may enable voices to be heard (#2, #17) but will hinder growth without political stability (#116) and good governance (#103, #106). Infrastructure, both physical and technological, is another major impediment in Philippines' growth path (#100, #102, #108, #112).

Table 2.18: Top 20 Percent Strongest Indicators List for Philippines, 2013

Rank	20 Percent Strongest Indicator	Score	Environment
1	Labour Activism	1.6899	QLID
2	Freedom of Speech	1.5275	QLID
3	High Quality Management Staff	1.4228	FBMC
4	Tax Revenue/Government Revenue	1.1500	GIS
5	Daily Organic Water Pollutant Emissions	0.9532	QLID
6	Lack of Market Distortion due to State-Ownership	0.8555	GIS
7	Lending Rate	0.8237	GIS
8	Real GDP Growth	0.7729	MS
9	Freedom of Religion	0.7454	QLID
10	Strength of Auditing and Reporting Standards	0.6731	GIS
11	Literacy Rate	0.6526	QLID
12	Quality of Stock Market Regulatory Authority	0.6114	FBMC
13	Cost of Production Labour	0.5334	FBMC
14	Population	0.5168	QLID
15	Traffic Congestion	0.4974	QLID
16	Interest Rate Spread	0.4835	GIS
17	Freedom of Press	0.4242	QLID
18	Extent of Staff Training	0.3937	FBMC
19	Exchange Rate Appreciation	0.3865	GIS
20	Inflation	0.3740	MS
21	Market Capitalisation	0.3518	FBMC
22	Tax Burden	0.3506	GIS
23	Social Unrest	0.3159	QLID
24	Labour Force	0.3083	FBMC

Source: Asia Competitiveness Institute

Table 2.19: Top 20 Percent Weakest Indicators List for Philippines, 2013

Rank	20 Percent Weakest Indicator	Score	Environment
98	Money Supply (M2)	–0.6352	GIS
99	Business Impact of Rules on FDI	–0.6397	MS
100	Port Facilities	–0.6647	QLID
101	Domestic Credit to Private Sector	–0.6823	FBMC
102	Personal Computers	–0.6872	QLID
103	Institutional Sophistication	–0.7156	GIS
104	Openness to Trade	–0.7180	MS
105	Access to Print Media	–0.7192	QLID
106	Government Responsiveness	–0.7338	GIS
107	Bureaucracy/Red Tape	–0.7450	GIS
108	Rail Facilities	–0.7511	QLID
109	Quality of Judiciary	–0.8001	GIS
110	Telephone Main Lines	–0.8293	QLID
111	Monopolies and Cartel	–0.8393	GIS
112	Airport Facilities	–0.8485	QLID
113	Government Environmental Protection Policies	–0.9284	GIS
114	Levelness of Playing Field	–0.9300	MS
115	Corporate Income Tax	–1.0539	MS
116	Political Change	–1.0734	GIS
117	Gross Domestic Savings	–1.1461	MS
118	Urban Population Growth	–1.3642	QLID
119	Primary Schooling	–1.8157	QLID
120	Unemployment Rate	–1.8936	FBMC
121	Money Supply Growth (M2)	–2.5525	MS

Source: Asia Competitiveness Institute

Singapore is *sui generis* as one of the four Asian Tigers, evolving from a port city in the *entrepôt* trade to an economic powerhouse within less than half a century. Its globalised way is reflected in its strengths in attracting FDI (#1 in Table 2.20) and high productivity (#2), both reinforced by quality of political leadership (#11, #12, #17, #23) and a transparent, enabling business environment (#13, #16, #19).

Despite dominating the top spot in the rankings of Overall Competitiveness as well as the majority of sub-environments over the study period from 2000 to 2013, Singapore is not without its weaknesses. Rising manpower costs (#119, #120 in Table 2.21), exacerbated by a small labour pool (#113, #114), threaten to erode its competitiveness in attracting MNCs as newcomers with large, young and increasingly educated workforce emerge.

Table 2.20: Top 20 Percent Strongest Indicators List for Singapore, 2013

Rank	20 Percent Strongest Indicator	Score	Environment
1	Foreign Direct Investment Inflows	2.8284	MS
2	GDP Per Capita	2.6917	MS
3	Services, Value Added Per Worker	2.6876	FBMC
4	Telephone Main Lines	2.6394	QLID
5	Openness to Trade	2.5921	MS
6	Barriers to Trade	2.5902	GIS
7	Social Unrest	2.5724	QLID
8	Quality of Central Bank/Monetary Authority	2.5650	GIS
9	Total Value of Stocks Traded	2.5285	FBMC
10	Networked Readiness Index	2.5226	QLID
11	Quality of Political Leadership	2.4933	GIS
12	Lack of Corruption	2.4140	GIS
13	Lack of Discrimination Against Investors	2.4124	MS
14	Integrity of Legal System	2.4121	GIS
15	Exports of Goods and Services	2.4067	MS
16	Transparency of Processes for Investors	2.3591	MS
17	Transparency of Government	2.3591	GIS
18	Institutional Sophistication	2.3585	GIS
19	Policy Towards Private Enterprise Rating	2.3425	GIS
20	Imports of Goods and Services	2.3073	MS
21	Intellectual Property Rights Protection	2.3039	GIS
22	International Reserves	2.2630	GIS
23	Quality of Government Policies	2.1914	GIS
24	Lack of Cronyism	2.1804	GIS

Source: Asia Competitiveness Institute

Table 2.21: Top 20 Percent Weakest Indicators List for Singapore, 2013

Rank	20 Percent Weakest Indicator	Score	Environment
98	Exchange Rate Appreciation	0.4657	GIS
99	Freedom of Press	0.3833	QLID
100	Health Expenditure	0.3036	QLID
101	Real GDP Growth	0.2858	MS
102	Interest Rate Spread	0.2423	GIS
103	Tax Burden	0.2407	GIS
104	Claims on Private Sector	0.2107	FBMC
105	Output Industry (Value Added)	0.1872	MS
106	Unemployment Rate	0.1420	FBMC
107	Government Consumption Expenditure	−0.2572	GIS
108	Agriculture, Value Added Per Worker	−0.3177	FBMC
109	Tax Revenue/Government Revenue	−0.4423	GIS
110	Freedom of Speech	−0.6547	QLID
111	Telecommunications System	−0.6624	QLID
112	Daily Organic Water Pollutant Emissions	−0.7783	QLID
113	Population	−0.7883	QLID
114	Labour Force	−0.8226	FBMC
115	Output Agriculture (Value Added)	−0.8766	MS
116	Urban Population Growth	−1.0610	QLID
117	Government Environmental Protection Policies	−1.1266	GIS
118	Deposit Interest Rate	−1.1271	GIS
119	Cost of Management Staff	−1.8299	FBMC
120	Cost of Production Labour	−1.9659	FBMC
121	Traffic Congestion	−2.8550	QLID

Source: Asia Competitiveness Institute

Notwithstanding its political tumult since the 2006 *coup d'etat*, Thailand continues to be one of the top tourism destinations (#1 in Table 2.22). Amidst political uncertainty, Thailand has been relatively successful in maintaining an enabling business environment (#13, #16), strengthened by an effective financial system (#2, #5), which contribute to its stable Overall Competitiveness scores as shown in Table 2.1. Fiscal balance is also not compromised (#5, #10).

However, prolonged political instability (#116, #118, #119, #121 in Table 2.23), coupled with cronyism (#117) and ineffective governance (#107, #108, #110), will eventually undermine the confidence of both domestic and foreign investors. More heed should also be paid to productivity performance (#100, #101) for the country to restore its attractiveness as an investment destination.

Table 2.22: Top 20 Percent Strongest Indicators List for Thailand, 2013

Rank	20 Percent Strongest Indicator	Score	Environment
1	International Tourism Receipts	2.5620	MS
2	Domestic Credit Provided by the Financial Sector	1.9120	FBMC
3	Tax Revenue	1.6819	GIS
4	University and Post-Graduate Education	1.6246	QLID
5	Domestic Credit to Private Sector	1.2795	FBMC
6	Government Revenue (Including Grants)	1.2579	GIS
7	Money Supply (M2)	1.2203	GIS
8	Net Foreign Assets	1.2201	GIS
9	Gross Domestic Product	1.2096	MS
10	Government Consumption Expenditure	1.1616	GIS
11	Unemployment Rate	1.1362	FBMC
12	Tax Revenue/Government Revenue	1.0969	GIS
13	Ease of Starting Business	1.0414	GIS
14	Regional Competitiveness	1.0164	GIS
15	International Reserves	0.9942	GIS
16	Market Capitalisation	0.9648	FBMC
17	Total Value of Stocks Traded	0.8647	FBMC
18	Secondary Schooling	0.8353	QLID
19	Imports of Goods and Services	0.8310	MS
20	Freedom of Press	0.8159	QLID
21	Airport Facilities	0.8064	QLID
22	Access to Sanitation	0.7938	QLID
23	Output Industry (Value Added)	0.7925	MS
24	Access to Water	0.7869	QLID

Source: Asia Competitiveness Institute

Table 2.23: Top 20 Percent Weakest Indicators List for Thailand, 2013

Rank	20 Percent Weakest Indicator	Score	Environment
98	Rail Facilities	–0.3455	QLID
99	Monopolies and Cartel	–0.3606	GIS
100	Agriculture, Value Added Per Worker	–0.3828	FBMC
101	Industry, Value Added Per Worker	–0.3972	FBMC
102	Corporate Governance	–0.4310	GIS
103	Public Security and Safety	–0.4387	QLID
104	Levelness of Playing Field	–0.4618	MS
105	Religious Unrest	–0.5173	QLID
106	Tax Burden	–0.5342	GIS
107	Bureaucracy/Red Tape	–0.5557	GIS
108	Government Responsiveness	–0.5684	GIS
109	International Monetary Fund Credit	–0.6019	GIS
110	Integrity of Legal System	–0.6030	GIS
111	Freedom of Speech	–0.6547	QLID
112	External Debt	–0.6608	GIS
113	Quality of Police	–0.7020	GIS
114	Intellectual Property Rights Protection	–0.7253	GIS
115	Claims on Private Sector	–0.7307	FBMC
116	Government Stability	–0.7614	GIS
117	Lack of Cronyism	–0.8115	GIS
118	Social Unrest	–0.8123	QLID
119	Political System Risk	–0.8923	GIS
120	Daily Organic Water Pollutant Emissions	–1.2920	QLID
121	Political Change	–1.3812	GIS

Source: Asia Competitiveness Institute

Vietnam as the frontrunner among the newer, less developed group of economies of ASEAN, which also comprises Cambodia, Laos and Myanmar, has broad-based strengths that include public services such as health care (#2 in Table 2.24) and education (#6), a low-cost workforce (#7, #13) and socio-political stability (#22, #24), which reinforce the country's attractiveness to FDI inflows.

Nonetheless, notwithstanding the 30-year *Doi Moi* (renovation) reform towards a market economy, remnants of the central planning era such as market distortion as a result of state ownership (#109) and weak corporate governance (#113, #120) continue to prevail at the expense of the private sector. Perhaps, another more far-reaching and comprehensive round of *Doi Moi* is what it takes for Vietnam to propel itself into the rank of the more developed economies in ASEAN. Policy-makers should also keep a watchful eye on the country's macroeconomic stability, fiscal

Table 2.24: Top 20 Percent Strongest Indicators List for Vietnam, 2013

Rank	20 Percent Strongest Indicator	Score	Environment
1	Deposit Interest Rate	1.4350	GIS
2	Health Expenditure	1.1234	QLID
3	Tax Revenue/Government Revenue	0.9454	GIS
4	Money Supply (M2)	0.9258	GIS
5	Money Supply Growth (M2)	0.8420	MS
6	Primary Schooling	0.8007	QLID
7	Cost of Management Staff	0.7648	FBMC
8	Domestic Credit to Private Sector	0.7214	FBMC
9	Regional Competitiveness	0.6766	GIS
10	Interest Rate Spread	0.6686	GIS
11	Labour Force	0.6400	FBMC
12	Domestic Credit Provided by the Financial Sector	0.6376	FBMC
13	Cost of Production Labour	0.6264	FBMC
14	Cellular Mobile Telephone Subscribers	0.5914	QLID
15	Traffic Congestion	0.5903	QLID
16	Access to Water	0.5596	QLID
17	Unemployment Rate	0.5207	FBMC
18	Openness to Trade	0.4520	MS
19	Urban Population Growth	0.4507	QLID
20	Political Change	0.4309	GIS
21	International Monetary Fund Credit	0.4154	GIS
22	Religious Unrest	0.4111	QLID
23	Population	0.3949	QLID
24	Government Stability	0.3807	GIS

Source: Asia Competitiveness Institute

Table 2.25: Top 20 Percent Weakest Indicators List for Vietnam, 2013

Rank	20 Percent Weakest Indicator	Score	Environment
98	Freedom of Religion	−0.7454	QLID
99	Labour Activism	−0.7952	QLID
100	Effectiveness of Legal System	−0.8098	GIS
101	Extent of Staff Training	−0.8145	FBMC
102	Quality of Stock Market Regulatory Authority	−0.8191	FBMC
103	Market Capitalisation	−0.8290	FBMC
104	Urban Population	−0.8317	QLID
105	Tax Burden	−0.8746	GIS
106	High Quality Management Staff	−0.8761	FBMC
107	Air Quality	−0.8879	QLID
108	Corporate Income Tax	−0.8936	MS
109	Lack of Market Distortion due to State-Ownership	−0.9145	GIS
110	Bureaucracy/Red Tape	−0.9268	GIS
111	Barriers to Trade	−0.9630	GIS
112	Government Environmental Protection Policies	−0.9689	GIS
113	Strength of Auditing and Reporting Standards	−0.9869	GIS
114	Intellectual Property Rights Protection	−0.9976	GIS
115	Sovereign Debt Risk	−1.0085	FBMC
116	Local Road System	−1.0372	QLID
117	Government Consumption Expenditure	−1.0870	GIS
118	Secondary Schooling	−1.2784	QLID
119	Inflation	−1.3256	MS
120	Corporate Governance	−1.4965	GIS
121	Freedom of Press	−1.5291	QLID

Source: Asia Competitiveness Institute

sustainability and fiscal stability as sovereign debt (#115) may become a cause for concern should economic growth slows down. Vietnam should implement fiscal consolidation measures, improve efficiency in public spending and undertake reforms in its baking and financial sector.

2.3.7.2 *Median Competitiveness Web Analysis*

As another roadmap for policy-makers, the spider web charts are employed to show how competitive individual ASEAN economies are in each of the 12 sub-environments relative to ASEAN-10 median and to ASEAN-10 maximum.

Starting with Brunei in Figure 2.32, its Productivity Performance, Institutions, Governance and Leadership and Standard of Living, Education and Social Stability exceed the ASEAN-10 median by a large margin, signifying the paramount importance of institutional capability in spurring growth and raising living standards. However, despite its stellar performance in Institutions, Governance and Leadership, Brunei's Labour Flexibility and Financial Deepening and Business Efficiency lie oddly below the regional median. For Economic Vibrancy and Openness to Trade and Services, the oil-rich state is either at, or close to, the median level, suggesting more can be done in these areas, leveraging on its strengths in Institutions, Governance and Leadership and Competition, Regulatory Standards and Rule of Law.

For Cambodia (Figure 2.33), its Attractiveness to Foreign Investors coincides with the ASEAN-10 median, while its Physical Infrastructure is way off, which highlights the need for bolstering infrastructure to retain foreign investors as well as stimulate local investment. Improvement on Government Policies and Fiscal Sustainability and Openness to Trade and

Figure 2.32: Median Competitiveness Web Analysis for Brunei, 2013

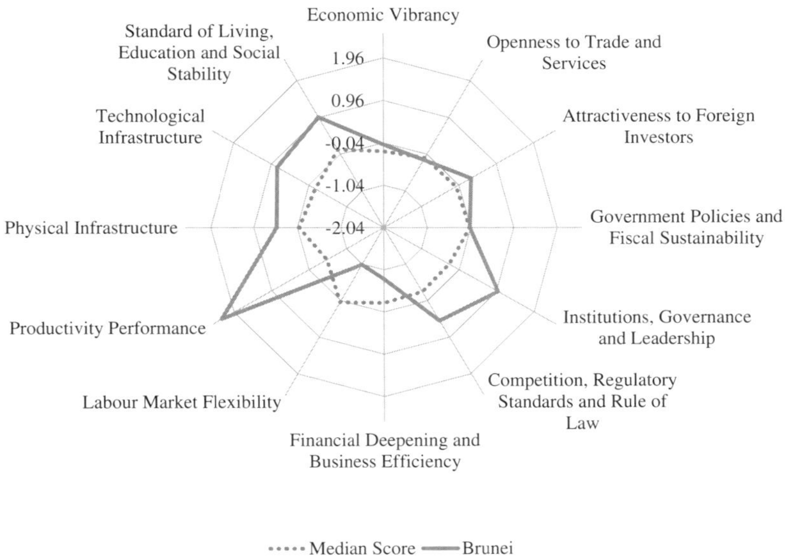

Source: Asia Competitiveness Institute

Services is imperative for Cambodia to catch up with ASEAN-10 median in terms of Economic Vibrancy and Financial Deepening and Business Efficiency.

Figure 2.33: Median Competitiveness Web Analysis for Cambodia, 2013

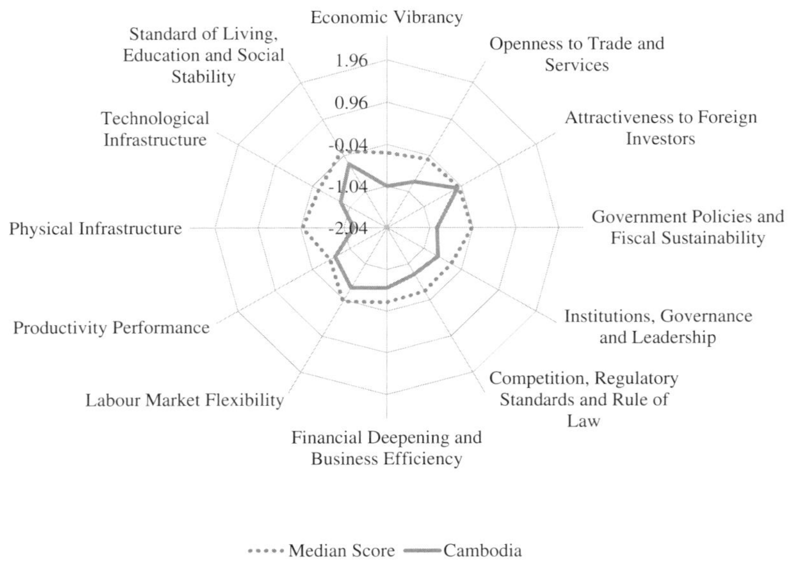

Source: Asia Competitiveness Institute

In Figure 2.34, Indonesia has performed exceptionally well above the ASEAN-10 median for Economic Vibrancy. The largest country in ASEAN also exceeds the regional median for

Figure 2.34: Median Competitiveness Web Analysis for Indonesia, 2013

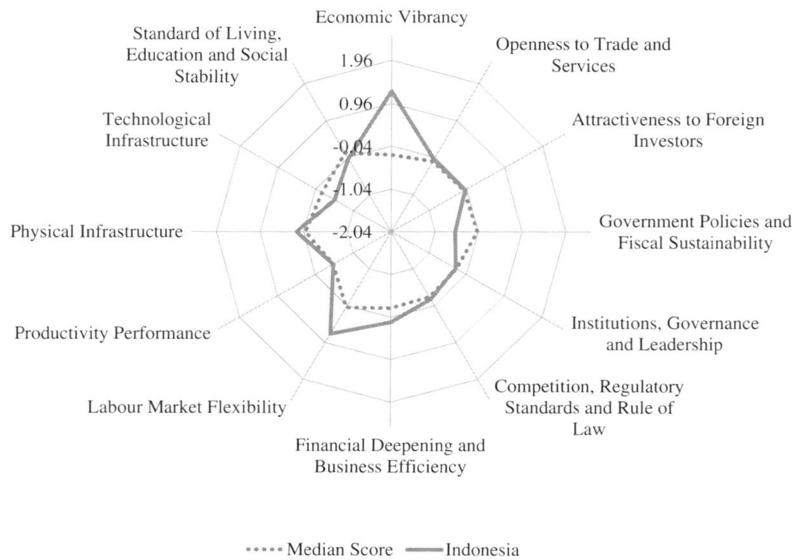

Source: Asia Competitiveness Institute

Labour Flexibility and Physical Infrastructure, albeit to a lesser extent. However, Indonesia either lies at or close to the median level for the majority of the sub-environments, namely, Openness to Trade and Services, Attractiveness to Foreign Investors, Institutions, Governance and Leadership, Competition, Regulatory Standards and Rule of Law and Productivity Performance. Concerted efforts need to be made in terms of Government Policies and Fiscal Sustainability, which is well below the ASEAN-10 median, for Indonesia to make significant strides in the lagging areas and accelerate its catching-up with the top-performing economies in the region.

Laos as depicted in Figure 2.35 remains far below the ASEAN-10 median in most sub-environments but not without potential. It is heartening that Laos's Competition, Regulatory Standards and Rule of Law coincides with the regional median, while its Attractiveness to Foreign Investors, Technological Infrastructure and Productivity Performance are close to the median level. Meanwhile, Laos's Openness to Trade and Services and Financial Deepening and Business Efficiency remain far below the ASEAN-10 median. Improvement on Government Policies and Fiscal Sustainability would be paramount for Laos to bring these sub-environments up to par.

It is no surprise that Malaysia, the second most competitive economy in ASEAN over the study period of 2000–2013, is well above the regional median in all sub-environments (Figure 2.36). In line with its top spot in the 2013 ranking of Labour Market Flexibility, Malaysia exceeds the median margin by the largest margin. With existing strengths in Financial Deepening and Business Efficiency and Physical Infrastructure, more can be done to bring Productivity Performance and Standard of Living, Education and Social Stability up to similar levels.

Figure 2.35: Median Competitiveness Web Analysis for Laos, 2013

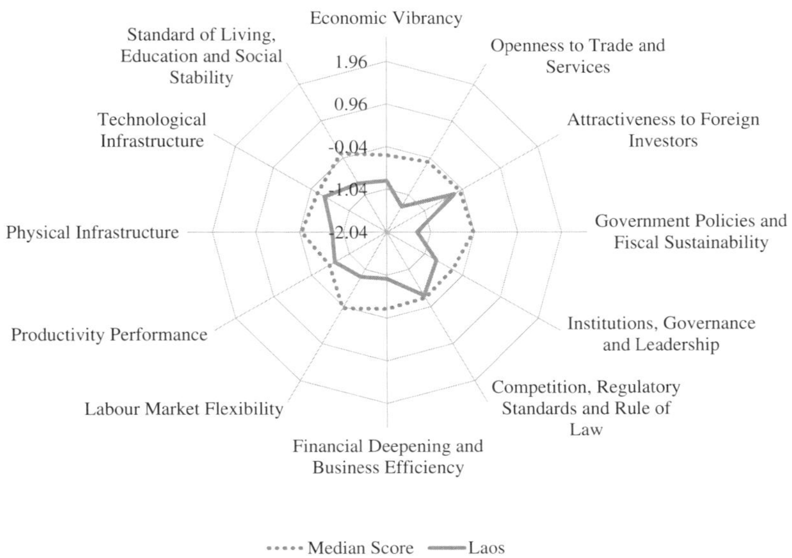

Source: Asia Competitiveness Institute

Figure 2.36: Median Competitiveness Web Analysis for Malaysia, 2013

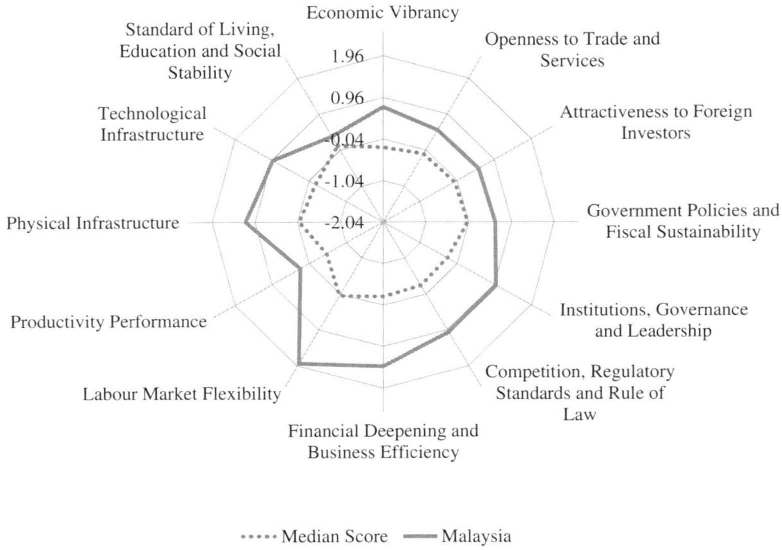

Source: Asia Competitiveness Institute

Myanmar, as the bottom-performing economy in the majority of the sub-environments, is unsurprisingly below the regional median in all sub-environments (Figure 2.37), with Standard of Living, Education and Social Stability being the lowest. However, its Productivity Performance lies very close to the ASEAN-10 median, which provide ample grounds for hope. Earnest efforts need to be made in terms of Institutions, Governance and Leadership and Government Policies and Fiscal Sustainability to bring the lagging sub-environments closer to the median level.

Figure 2.37: Median Competitiveness Web Analysis for Myanmar, 2013

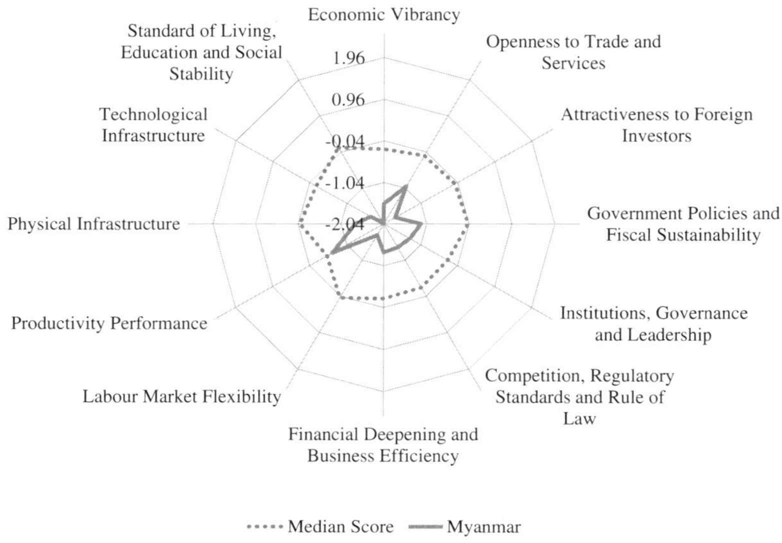

Source: Asia Competitiveness Institute

Figure 2.38: Median Competitiveness Web Analysis for Philippines, 2013

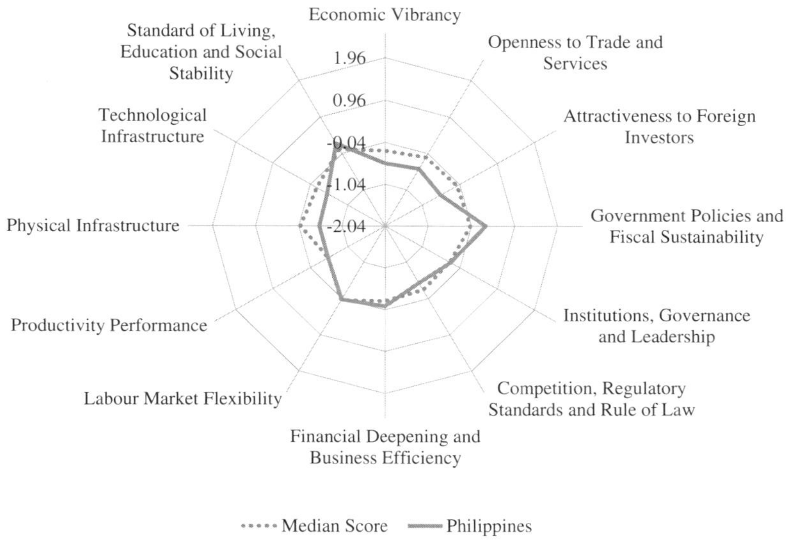

Source: Asia Competitiveness Institute

Philippines's strengths lie in Government Policies and Fiscal Sustainability, Standard of Living, Education and Social Stability, and Financial Deepening and Business Efficiency, which exceed the ASEAN-10 median levels (Figure 2.38). Nonetheless, it is well below the regional median in Physical Infrastructure, Attractiveness to Foreign Investors and Openness to Trade and Services. More heed should be paid to these lagging sub-environments, together with Technological Infrastructure, to strengthen Economic Vibrancy as well as Philippines's overall competitiveness.

Consistently ranked at the top in Overall Competitiveness, Singapore in Figure 2.39 far exceeds the regional median in all sub-environments. Nonetheless, it has to closely watch Labour Market Flexibility, which is its weakest area. Maintaining competitiveness on the back of productivity and value add should also be the way forward for the city-state.

As the third most competitive ASEAN member state between 2000 and 2013, Thailand, as shown in Figure 2.40, lies well above the regional median in most aspects of competitiveness, notably Government Policies and Fiscal Sustainability, Openness to Trade and Services, Financial Deepening and Business Efficiency and Economic Vibrancy. Despite its various strengths, Thailand's Attractiveness to Foreign Investors and Standard of Living, Education and Social Stability are not up to standard as they remain very close to the median levels. Improving Institutions, Governance and Leadership, Competition, Regulatory Standards and Rule of Law as well as Productivity Performance should be Thailand's top priority if it is to credibly challenge Malaysia for the second spot.

Vietnam (Figure 2.41) exceeds the regional median in Technological Infrastructure and Openness to Trade and Services, and coincides with the median for Government Policies and Fiscal Sustainability and Labour Market Flexibility. Nonetheless, it is lagging well below the ASEAN-10 median for Attractiveness to Foreign Investors and Standard of Living, Education and Social Stability, suggesting that its reform momentum is running out of steam. Much needs to be done in terms of Institutions, Governance and Leadership and Competition, Regulatory

Standards and Rule of Law as the primary drivers of reform, or it risks being surpassed by Cambodia and Laos. With Financial Deepening and Business Efficiency and Productivity Performance being close to the regional median, private sector dynamism could be unleashed for the country to successfully upgrade its national competitiveness.

Figure 2.39: Median Competitiveness Web Analysis for Singapore, 2013

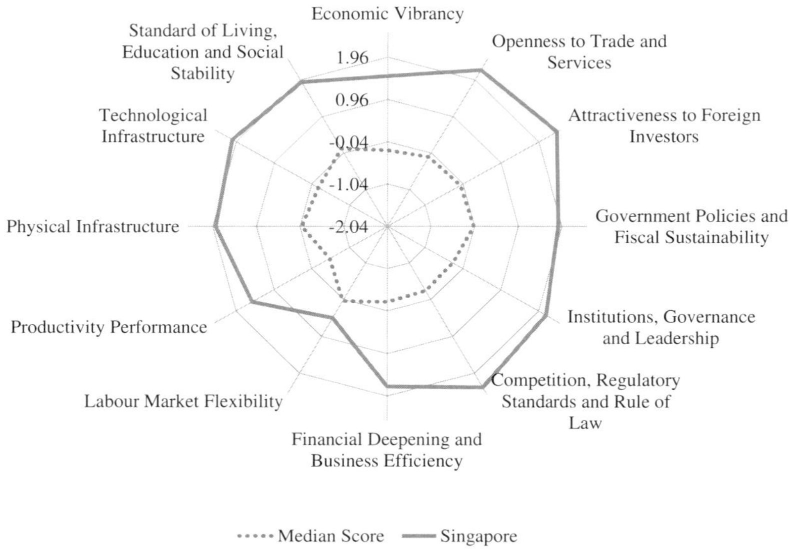

Source: Asia Competitiveness Institute

Figure 2.40: Median Competitiveness Web Analysis for Thailand, 2013

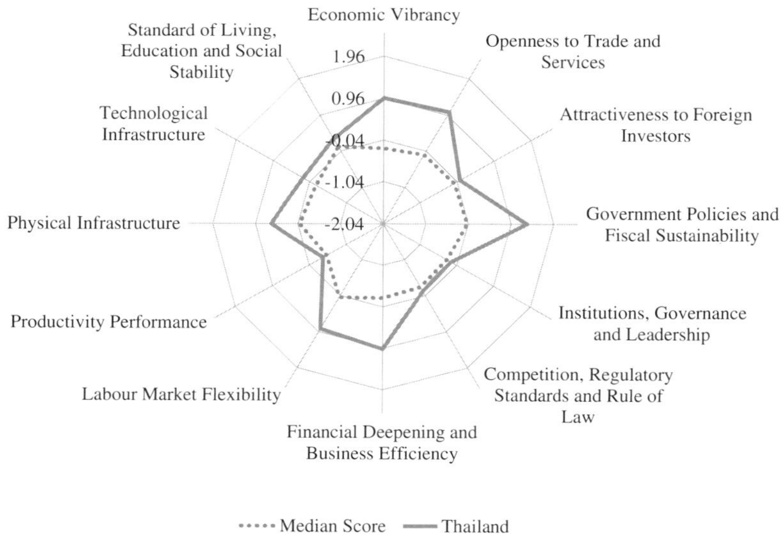

Source: Asia Competitiveness Institute

Figure 2.41: Median Competitiveness Web Analysis for Vietnam, 2013

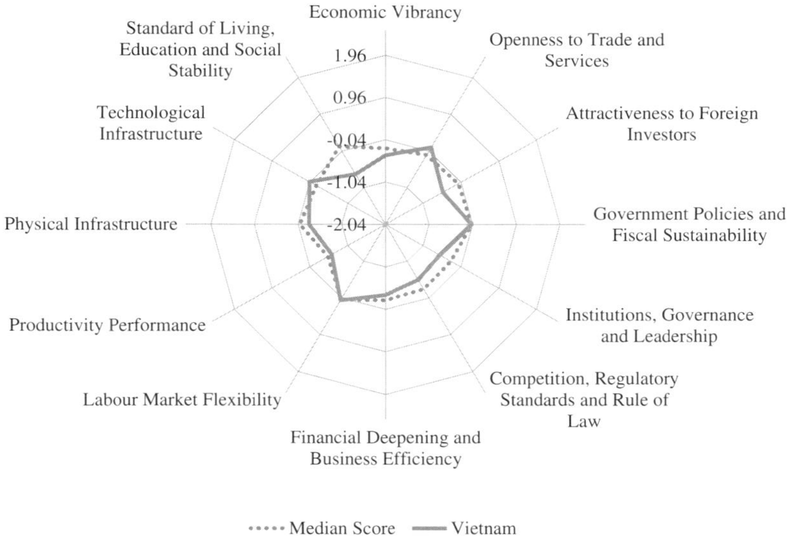

Source: Asia Competitiveness Institute

2.3.7.3 *Maximum Competitiveness Web Analysis*

Maximum competitiveness web analysis presented in this sector reveals how far individual ASEAN economies are from the highest scores for each of the 12 sub-environments.

Brunei, as shown in Figure 2.42, sets the regional maximum for Productivity Performance but is well below the regional maximum for Labour Market Flexibility. Other aspects of competitiveness including Economic Vibrancy, Openness to Trade and Services and Government Policies and Fiscal Sustainability also leave much to be desired although Brunei is in the high-income band with Singapore. Reforms in terms of Institutions, Governance and Leadership should be the starting point for the oil-rich state to diversify its economy towards a sustainable future.

Cambodia (Figure 2.43) is well below the ASEAN maximum in all sub-environments. In view of its gaps relative to the top performer, Attractiveness to Foreign Investors could be prioritised for employment creation to improve Standard of Living, Education and Social Stability. With sound Institutions, Governance and Leadership, foreign investment can be harnessed to facilitate development in other aspects of competitiveness.

As seen in Figure 2.44, Indonesia's Economic Vibrancy is only a tad below the regional maximum, signifying the country's competitiveness potential. Labour Market Flexibility and Physical Infrastructure, which register positive scores, could be Indonesia's starting point to narrow its gap with the top four economies in the Overall Competitiveness ranking (Singapore, Malaysia, Thailand and Brunei).

Figure 2.42: Maximum Competitiveness Web Analysis for Brunei, 2013

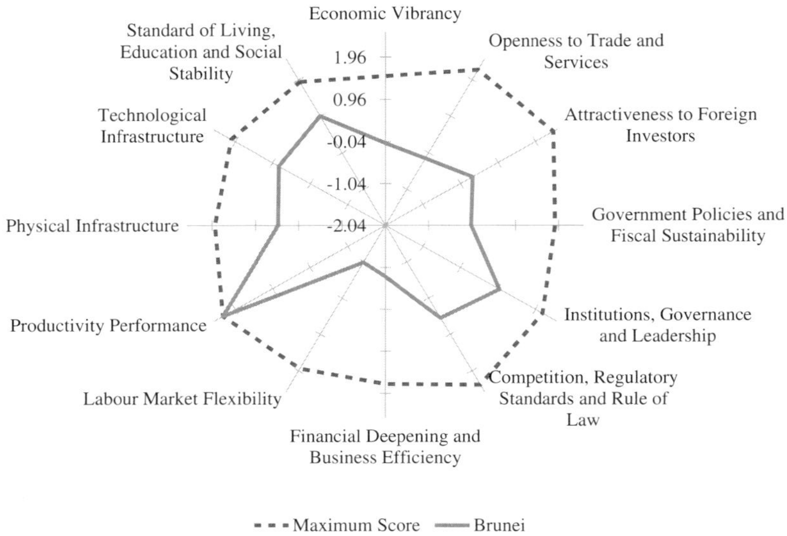

Source: Asia Competitiveness Institute

Figure 2.43: Maximum Competitiveness Web Analysis for Cambodia, 2013

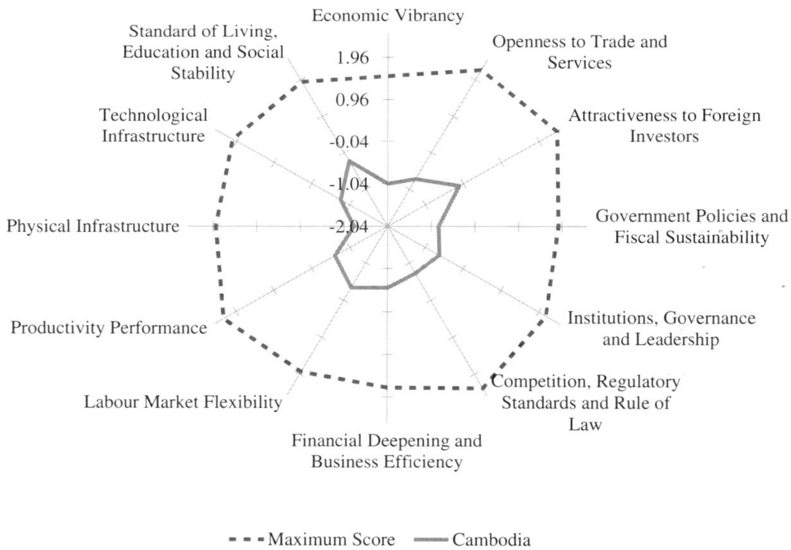

Source: Asia Competitiveness Institute

Figure 2.44: Maximum Competitiveness Web Analysis for Indonesia, 2013

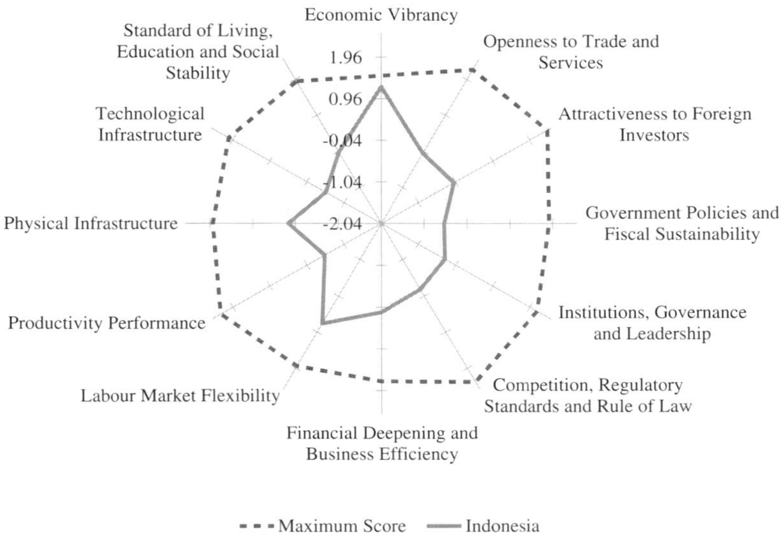

Source: Asia Competitiveness Institute

Laos (Figure 2.45) remains far distant from the ASEAN maximum in all sub-environments. With Attractiveness to Foreign Investors and Competition, Regulatory Standards and Rule of Law being the closest to the regional maximum, attracting and retaining foreign investment on the back of a transparent and impartial regulatory framework could help the country to expedite the catching-up process.

Malaysia (Figure 2.46) as the second most competitive economy in ASEAN sets the regional maximum for Labour Market Flexibility. Nevertheless, it remains distant from the ASEAN maximum for the majority of the remaining sub-environments, with Productivity Performance being the furthest from the maximum level. Equally important is bringing Standard of Living, Education and Social Stability up to par with the other components of competitiveness.

Myanmar (Figure 2.47) is far below the ASEAN maximum for all sub-environments. Expectations are high for the new administration under the National League for Democracy party to deliver substantial improvements in terms of Institutions, Governance and Leadership as well as Government Policies and Fiscal Sustainability to move the country forward. Expediting its opening-up under the newly established AEC for increased trade and investment flows should be the country's top priority to narrow its development gap with, first, Laos, Cambodia and Vietnam and subsequently, the rest of ASEAN-10.

Figure 2.45: Maximum Competitiveness Web Analysis for Laos, 2013

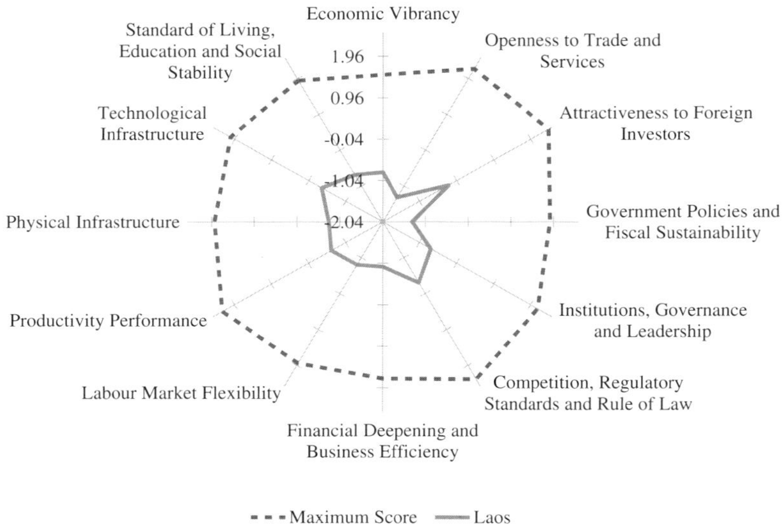

Source: Asia Competitiveness Institute

Figure 2.46: Maximum Competitiveness Web Analysis for Malaysia, 2013

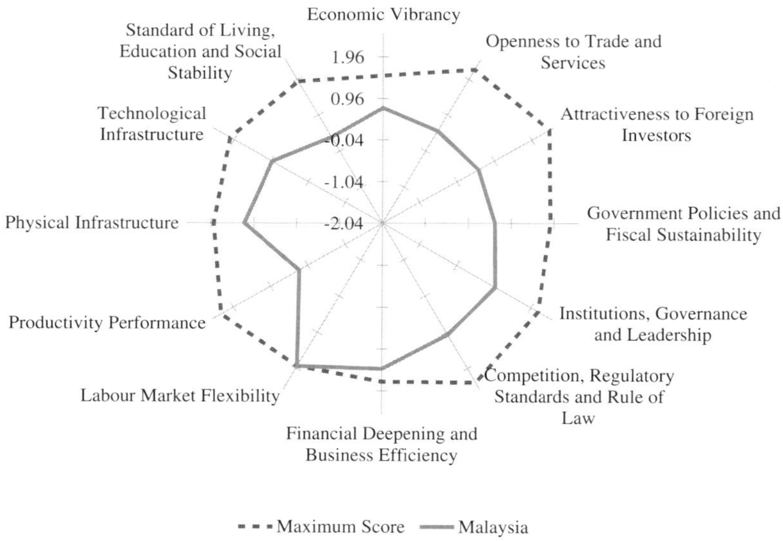

Source: Asia Competitiveness Institute

Figure 2.47: Maximum Competitiveness Web Analysis for Myanmar, 2013

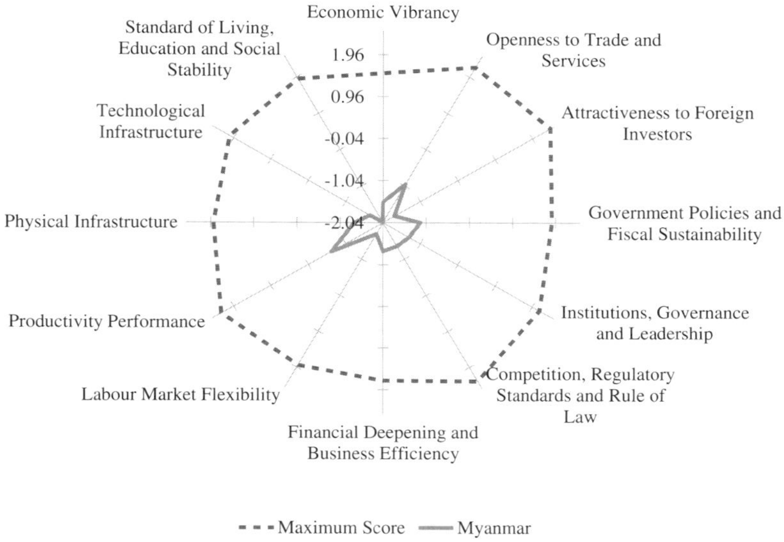

Source: Asia Competitiveness Institute

Despite being one of the more mature economies in ASEAN, Philippines (Figure 2.48) is remarkably distant from the regional maximum for Attractiveness to Foreign Investors, Economic Vibrancy and Physical as well as Technological Infrastructure. As noted earlier, the creation of productive employment at home is critical for the country to regain its deteriorating

Figure 2.48: Maximum Competitiveness Web Analysis for Philippines, 2013

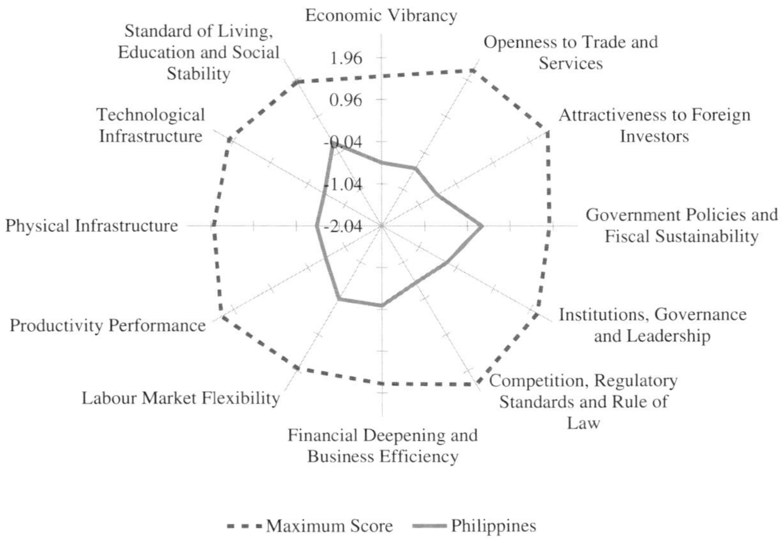

Source: Asia Competitiveness Institute

competitiveness standing. Reform could begin with strengthening Competition, Regulatory Standards and Rule of Law, which would pave the way for foreign as well as local private sector investment as dual engines of growth.

As the top-performing economy in ASEAN, Singapore (Figure 2.49) sets the regional maximum for the majority of sub-environments. However, it is disappointingly lagging in Productivity Performance. Raising labour productivity, particularly in the small- and medium-sized enterprise sector, would be the crucial first step in Singapore's trajectory towards a knowledge-based economy it is aspiring to become.

Thailand (Figure 2.50) is close to the ASEAN-10 maximum for Economic Vibrancy, Government Policies and Fiscal Sustainability and Financial Deepening and Business Efficiency. Nonetheless, it is oddly well below the regional maximum for Standard of Living, Education and Social Stability given its strong performances in the aforementioned aspects. More heed should be paid to Institutions, Governance and Leadership and Competition, Regulatory Standards and Rule of Law to restore the country's Attractiveness to Foreign Investors as well as improving other aspects of competitiveness.

As seen in Figure 2.51, Vietnam is well below ASEAN maximum in all sub-environments although it has narrowed the distance for Openness to Trade and Services, Technological Infrastructure and Labour Market Flexibility. With growing competition from Cambodia, Laos and Myanmar, Vietnam cannot be complacent in regaining its reform momentum which seems to be fizzling, particularly for Economic Vibrancy and Attractiveness to Foreign Investors.

Figure 2.49: Maximum Competitiveness Web Analysis for Singapore, 2013

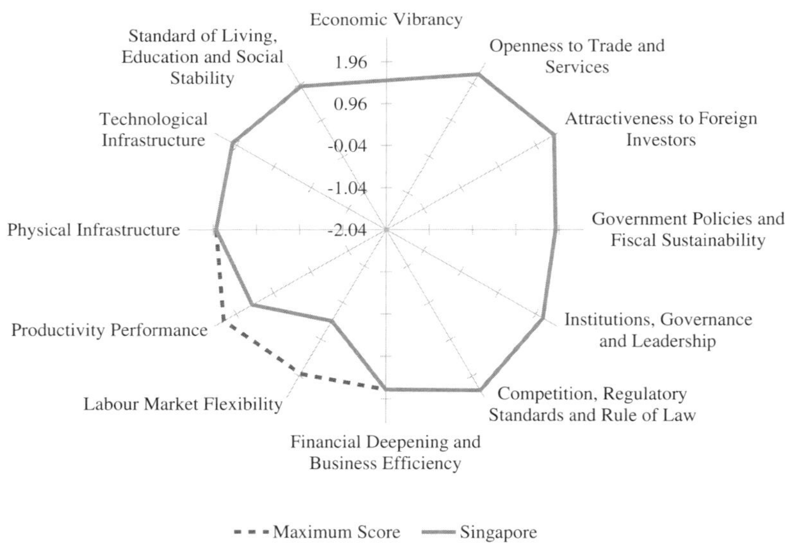

Source: Asia Competitiveness Institute

Figure 2.50: Maximum Competitiveness Web Analysis for Thailand, 2013

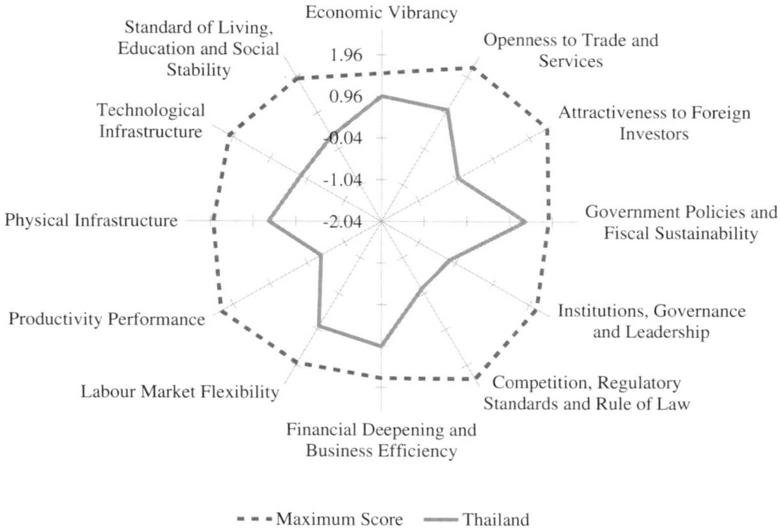

Source: Asia Competitiveness Institute

Figure 2.51: Maximum Competitiveness Web Analysis for Vietnam, 2013

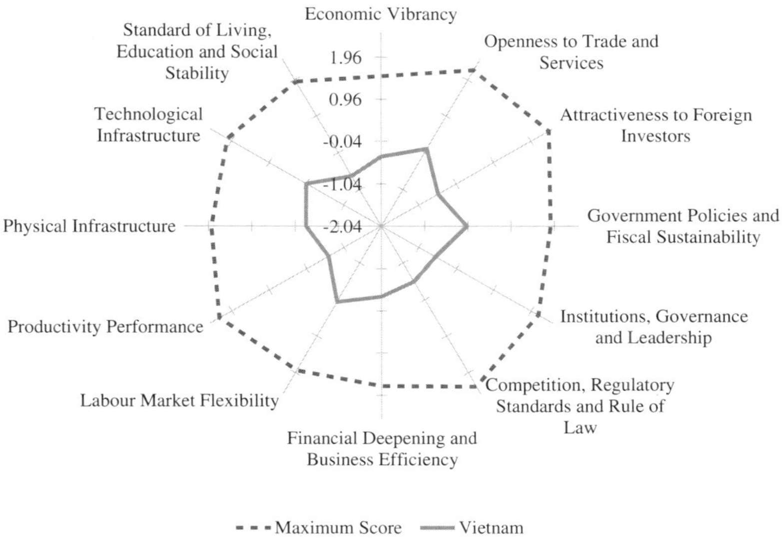

Source: Asia Competitiveness Institute

2.3.8 Upgrading Competitiveness through *What-if* Simulation Analysis

This section discusses the *what-if* simulation analysis by the methodology detailed in Section 2.2.5. The simulation is conducted for the Overall Competitiveness as well as each of the four environments. Tables 2.26–2.30 show the standardised scores and rankings of individual ASEAN-10 economies before and after simulation.

Table 2.26: *What-if* Competitiveness Simulation Analysis on Overall Competitiveness, 2013

	Rank		Score	
Economy	**Before**	**After**	**Before**	**After**
Brunei	4	3	0.3770	0.8467
Cambodia	8	7	–0.7739	–0.4324
Indonesia	5	5	–0.0138	0.3549
Laos	9	7	–0.8861	–0.4436
Malaysia	2	2	1.0099	1.1177
Myanmar	10	10	–1.6116	–1.0834
Philippines	6	5	–0.3258	–0.0033
Singapore	1	1	2.0793	2.2474
Thailand	3	3	0.5286	0.6762
Vietnam	7	6	–0.3835	–0.0971

Source: Asia Competitiveness Institute

Table 2.27: *What-if* Competitiveness Simulation Analysis on Macroeconomic Stability, 2013

	Rank		Score	
Economy	**Before**	**After**	**Before**	**After**
Brunei	5	4	0.0033	0.4214
Cambodia	8	7	–0.6976	–0.4856
Indonesia	4	3	0.3844	0.6308
Laos	9	7	–0.8807	–0.5342
Malaysia	3	3	0.6385	0.6854
Myanmar	10	10	–1.5315	–1.0688
Philippines	7	6	–0.5552	–0.1475
Singapore	1	1	2.2126	2.2399
Thailand	2	2	0.7336	0.7565
Vietnam	6	6	–0.3074	–0.1793

Source: Asia Competitiveness Institute

Table 2.28: *What-if* Competitiveness Simulation Analysis on Government and Institutional Setting, 2013

	Rank		Score	
Economy	**Before**	**After**	**Before**	**After**
Brunei	3	3	0.5123	0.8528
Cambodia	8	8	–0.8120	–0.4779
Indonesia	6	5	–0.3956	0.0867
Laos	9	6	–0.8579	–0.4287
Malaysia	2	2	0.9212	1.0780
Myanmar	10	8	–1.3816	–0.8540
Philippines	5	5	–0.1649	0.0148
Singapore	1	1	2.2585	2.3109
Thailand	4	3	0.3455	0.6112
Vietnam	7	5	–0.4256	–0.1212

Source: Asia Competitiveness Institute

Table 2.29: *What-if* Competitiveness Simulation Analysis on Financial, Businesses and Manpower Conditions, 2013

	Rank		Score	
Economy	**Before**	**After**	**Before**	**After**
Brunei	4	3	0.1943	1.1668
Cambodia	8	8	–0.7067	–0.5297
Indonesia	5	3	0.1252	0.5820
Laos	9	8	–1.0670	–0.6634
Malaysia	2	1	1.5363	1.6375
Myanmar	10	9	–1.6269	–1.0527
Philippines	6	5	–0.2870	0.0449
Singapore	1	1	1.6265	2.1096
Thailand	3	3	0.6283	0.7762
Vietnam	7	6	–0.4229	–0.0043

Source: Asia Competitiveness Institute

In Table 2.26 for Overall Competitiveness, most impressive is Laos, jumping two spots from ninth to seventh after the simulation. The first (Singapore), second (Malaysia), third (Thailand) and fifth (Indonesia) rankings remain unchanged but with improved scores. For instance, while Indonesia stays at fifth, it attains a positive score of 0.3549 as compared to the negative –0.0138 before the simulation. The remaining economies climb one place after having the scores of the top 20 percent weakest indicators raised to zero (the average score).

Table 2.30: *What-if* Competitiveness Simulation Analysis on Quality of Life and Infrastructure Development, 2013

	Rank		Score	
Economy	**Before**	**After**	**Before**	**After**
Brunei	3	2	0.7644	0.8629
Cambodia	9	5	−0.8103	−0.1948
Indonesia	5	5	−0.1680	0.0923
Laos	8	5	−0.6600	−0.1055
Malaysia	2	2	0.8537	0.9678
Myanmar	10	10	−1.7629	−1.2397
Philippines	6	5	−0.2671	0.0748
Singapore	1	1	2.0345	2.1861
Thailand	4	4	0.3597	0.5045
Vietnam	7	5	−0.3440	−0.0753

Source: Asia Competitiveness Institute

Likewise for Macroeconomic Stability (Table 2.27), Laos sees the most significant improvement in its ranking from ninth to seventh after the simulation. The first (Singapore), second (Thailand), third (Malaysia) and sixth (Vietnam) rankings stay the same but with higher scores. The rest of ASEAN-10 all move up one place after the policy simulation.

In Table 2.28 for Government and Institutional Setting, Laos climbs three places from ninth to sixth, while Myanmar and Vietnam jumps two spots from tenth to eighth and seventh to fifth, respectively, after the simulation. Indonesia and Thailand both move up one place to join Philippines and Brunei at fifth and third, respectively.

As shown in Table 2.29, Indonesia shows the most impressive jump in ranking after the simulation for Financial, Businesses and Manpower Conditions from fifth to third. With the exception of Singapore at first, Thailand at third and Cambodia at eighth remaining unchanged, the rest of ASEAN move up one place after having their top 20 percent weakest indicators raised to the average score (zero).

As seen in Table 2.30 for Quality of Life and Infrastructure Development, Cambodia remarkably leaps four spots while Laos and Vietnam jump three and two places, respectively, to tie at the fifth place after the simulation. Such notable improvements in the rankings of Cambodia, Laos and Vietnam following the simulation makes complacency not an option for the more mature ASEAN economies.

2.4 Concluding Notes

In general, the rankings of the Overall Competitiveness do not see considerable changes over the period 2000–2013. The development divide in the ASEAN-10 is evident in our annual rankings where Singapore, Malaysia, Thailand and Brunei remain in the top four for 14 consecutive years.

Indonesia has decidedly surpassed the Philippines and Vietnam at fifth. The bottom four are Vietnam, Cambodia, Laos and Myanmar. With the exception of the top four, the standardised scores of the remaining six economies were negative in 2013, indicating their below-average performances. The four environments and 12 sub-environments, however, are more diverse in rankings with Thailand overtaking Malaysia at second for Macroeconomic Stability and Brunei leading the region in Productivity Performance.

Overall, our competitiveness analysis of ASEAN-10 indicates wide variations not only in levels of economic development but also in paces of catching-up within the bloc. Indonesia, for instance, has been surging ahead, particularly in sub-environments such as Economic Vibrancy and Labour Market Flexibility, as shown in our results of its top 20 percent strongest indicators and median web chart. For Vietnam, the catching-up momentum seems to be running out of steam as signified in its below-median Attractiveness to Foreign Investors, Institutions, Governance and Leadership as well as Competition, Regulatory Standards and Rule of Law. Cambodia and Laos seems quietly rising with marked improvement in many aspects of competitiveness. The Philippines risks being outstripped by the newer members as its standardised scores plunged more negatively over time. Thailand, too, cannot be complacent on the socio-political front if it is to restore trust and confidence in both domestic and foreign investors.

As noted in Section 2.2.5, a competitiveness ranking in itself is like a beauty contest that stops short of offering insights on how to improve the rankings. The top 20 percent strongest and weakest indicators are thus revealed for the ASEAN member states to harness their strengths and resolve their weaknesses for fostering a more competitive and prosperous economy. Furthermore, our policy simulation analysis shows how much individual countries improve in terms of standardised scores and rankings if their scores of the top 20 percent weaknesses are raised to the average. The post-simulation results for the CLMV grouping are particularly impressive, proving that improved competitiveness is totally feasible with the right solutions.

While economic convergence is certainly desirable, diversity in development stages as well as competitiveness can be a powerful source of synergy, complementing and supplementing one another for increased overall regional competitiveness. A dualistic economic structure with agriculture and agro-based industrialisation-cum-servicisation is totally viable, leveraging on the strengths of individual member states. Thailand, for instance, has been a successful dualistic economy. Malaysia and Indonesia are endowed with abundant fertile soil conducive for a wide variety of agricultural products from rubber to palm oil. CLMV are currently net exporters of rice. The more developed ASEAN-6 and the newer, transitional CLMV form a pair like two hands clapping in terms of agricultural resource endowments and potential dualism.

Part and parcel in such dualistic economic structure, as well as for more seamless flows of trade and investment amongst the 10 ASEAN economies, is enhanced regional economic integration which is the primary thrust of the ASEAN Economic Community launched on 31st December 2015. Nonetheless, while the AEC aspires to become "a single market and production base" by the 2015 milestone, only about 80 percent of the stipulated measures under the blueprint were completed by then. Thorny issues where implementation has been most problematic include: (i) non-tariff barriers to trade, (ii) trade facilitation through the establishment of the

ASEAN Single Window, (iii) trade in services, (iv) free movement of skilled labour, and (v) the launch of the ASEAN Single Aviation Market, or the Open Skies policy.[9] Given the multiple flexibilities allowed both in the design of the AEC blueprint and in its implementation, the realisation of a "single market and production base" will not end even as 100 percent of the requirements have been fulfilled. In fact, as recognised by the ASEAN Secretariat, policy-makers and scholars in the region, community building in ASEAN is an ongoing and dynamic journey in which 2015 is a significant milestone.[10]

It is useful to highlight that several of the key obstacles that have stood in the way of realising the full potential of AEC pertain to the reluctance of member countries in ASEAN to embrace free trade in both goods and services. Trade liberalisation in general has been acknowledged for decades for having been a positive force for global economic development thus enabling several developing economies including those in ASEAN to reap aggregate welfare gains. However, it has also generated adverse distributive effects along the way, affecting workers in industries lacking comparative advantage especially when the transition to other sectors has not been easy. This is particularly evident in the case of China where phenomenal economic growth through export-oriented manufacturing that led to broad-based expansion in employment appears to be confronting bottlenecks in light of rising labour costs and a maturing manufacturing sector.

With China gradually losing its cost competitiveness to emerging rivals in the ASEAN region, and several manufacturing facilities relocating away from China to countries like Indonesia and Vietnam, it is important for other developing economies in the ASEAN region that are poised to become the next manufacturing hubs to be prepared to deal with similar challenges. In fact, their window for manufacturing-led growth may be considerably smaller than what China has enjoyed and disruptive technological changes, particularly in automation, coupled with diminishing demographic dividends due to rapid growth of their aging population will further erode their advantage in manufacturing in due course.

Hence, there is a need for policy-makers in the ASEAN region to prepare for policy reforms to ensure that the economy is resilient to structural challenges and future disruptions. One such priority is to develop the service sector in tandem with the manufacturing sector. The economic literature suggests that services gain in importance as an engine of growth and a source of employment creation as the economy develops. Nonetheless, the development of the service sector is not a natural progression achieved solely through market forces. Governments have an important role to facilitate an appropriate regulatory framework which fosters competitive and efficient service markets.

Investment in infrastructure is essential for service industries to grow, specifically in the case of logistics, information and tourism. Taking the case of tourism for instance, in light of the growing middle class in ASEAN, a policy strategy encouraging coordinated tourism can potentially be a new source of growth for the ASEAN-10. In fact, tourism remains one of the fastest growing economic sectors in the region, especially in some countries such as Malaysia,[11]

[9] See Tan *et al.* (2016, forthcoming, Chapter 1).

[10] See, for instance, ASEAN Secretariat (2015), Lim (2015), Ong (2014).

[11] See, for instance, the discussion in Tan, Gopalan, and Ye (2016) on the potential of the tourism industry in Malaysia using a Geweke causality analysis; research contribution by Blake Harley Berger in this paper is acknowledged.

Thailand and Singapore.[12] Tourism and travel have been promoted as an integral part of the national development strategies for decades in these countries and there are significant benefits to be reaped from a coordinated tourism policy in ASEAN-10. Beyond economics, tourism policy that is designed to market the distinctiveness of local traditions and culture can pave the way for better cultural exchanges between countries which can foster bilateral relations between countries in the region. Since tourism by its very nature involves and requires inter-country cooperation on many fronts, tourism policy assumes significance in order to shape a country's engagement with the rest of the world.[13]

In conclusion, beyond the 2015 milestone achieved by the AEC, enormous work awaits the 10 ASEAN member states to realise the common dream of inclusive and sustainable prosperity. Narrowing the development divide remains a work-in-progress, which requires not only capacity building and technical assistance from the more mature economies in the bloc but also, and even more importantly, far-reaching domestic reforms, particularly in the less developed CLMV grouping. In this regard, ACI's competitiveness ranking and simulation study provide an instructive roadmap for policy-makers in individual ASEAN member states to identify gaps that need to be addressed in their respective trajectories to national prosperity. Building institutional capacity remains the first and foremost prerequisite to foster greater competitiveness and sustainable growth as evident in the experience of Singapore. In all, competition in parallel with cooperation is the cornerstone of the vision for a highly competitive and resilient ASEAN.

References

ASEAN Secretariat. 2015. *A Blueprint for Growth — ASEAN Economic Community 2015: Progress and Key Achievements*. Jakarta: ASEAN Secretariat.

Bristow, Gillian. 2010. *Critical Reflections on Regional Competitiveness: Theory, Policy, Practice* (*Routledge Studies in Human Geography*). Oxon: Routledge.

Camagni, Roberto. 2002. "On the Concept of Territorial Competitiveness: Sound or Misleading?" *Urban Studies* 39(13): 2395–2411.

IMD World Competitiveness Center. 2014. *IMD World Competitiveness Yearbook*. Lausanne: International Institute for Management Development.

Kitson, Michael, Ronald Martin, and Peter Tyler. 2004. "Regional Competitiveness: An Elusive yet Key Concept?" *Regional Studies* 38(9): 991–99.

Krugman, Paul. 1994. "Competitiveness: A Dangerous Obsession." *Foreign Affairs* 73(2): 28–44.

Lim, Hng Kiang. 2015. Speech at the ASEAN Conference 2015 on "Progress of the ASEAN Economic Community 2015: Opportunities, Challenges and the Road Ahead." Singapore, May 20.

Ong, Keng Yong. 2014. Speech at the 28th Asia-Pacific Roundtable Plenary Session 6 on "ASEAN's Post-2015 Agenda: Strengthening and Deepening Community Building." Kuala Lumpur, June 2–4.

[12] See, Tan, Tan, and Kwan (2016) for an empirical analysis of drivers of growth in travel and tourism industry in Thailand and Singapore.

[13] Prideaux (2005).

Porter, Michael E. 1980. *Competitive Strategy: Techniques for Analyzing Industries and Competitors*. New York: Free Press.

Prideaux, B. 2005. "Factors Affecting Bilateral Tourism Flows," *Annals of Tourism Research*, 32, 780–801.

Tan, Khee Giap, Sasidaran Gopalan, and Ye Ye. 2016. "Drivers of growth in the travel and tourism industry in Malaysia: A Geweke causality analysis." *Economies*, 4(3), 1–15.

Tan, Khee Giap, Evan Tan Beng Kai, and Vincent Kwan Wen Seng. 2016. "Drivers of growth in the travel and tourism industry in Thailand and Singapore: A Geweke causality analysis." *Public Enterprise*, 22(1), 56–78.

Tan, Khee Giap, Nguyen Le Phuong Anh, Sasidaran Gopalan, and Luu Nguyen Trieu Duong. 2017. *2015 Annual Competitiveness Analysis, Agricultural Productivity and Development Vision for ASEAN-10*. Singapore: World Scientific.

World Economic Forum. 2014. *Global Competitiveness Report 2013–2014*. Geneva: World Economic Forum.

Discussant Notes 2.1

Tan Sri Rastam Mohd Isa

Chairman and Chief Executive,

Institute of Strategic and International Studies (ISIS), Malaysia

Introduction

This short paper servers to provide some comments and observations on the '2016 Annual Update on ACI's Competitiveness Ranking and Simulations of ASEAN-10.'

Motivation for the Study

The motivation for the study is very much on a sound basis. ASEAN is a successful regional organisation that is transforming itself into a community. It is not only the ASEAN member states that are concerned about ASEAN's future. The rest of the world is also tracking its progress.

Nowadays ASEAN tends to hit the news headlines not just because of its economic integration and other regional cooperation initiatives, but also because of geopolitical and strategic issues that concern the region, for example the South China Sea and major power competition. Regardless, ASEAN is an important region which is the envy of many, a region where people are interested to invest and do business in as well as trade with. If others are excited about the prospects in ASEAN, why shouldn't we?

The coming into being of the ASEAN Community, especially the AEC, provides for greater opportunities for growth and development for the ASEAN countries. Therefore it is important that these know how competitive they are because individual countries remain the ultimate beneficiary if they are highly competitive or loser if they are not. In this regard, ASEAN would be the vehicle for promoting their interests. This 2016 update is, therefore, most appropriate and timely.

Objectives of the Study

I would agree with the view that the study could afford policy-makers the opportunity and ability to identify national strengths and weaknesses as well as the region's collective strengths and weaknesses. This is especially more relevant now with ASEAN pledging closer regional economic integration through the implementation of common action plans and programmes under the AEC.

Tracking competitiveness over time to show resilience and flexibility of strategic policy responses to external shocks is a very good approach. The objective of offering regional solutions to regional challenges is also very good. However, ASEAN and the member states also have to contend with not just regional challenges and problems. There are global challenges and issues which also impact on ASEAN such as the oil price shock, China's economic slowdown and political and economic developments in the United States and Europe.

One thing to remember also is that business, trade, investment and tourism in ASEAN cannot flourish without external sources, demand and supply. Trade and investment flows among the ASEAN-10 are still quite low although these are now on the increase. Therefore the role of external players remain crucial to fuel further growth and development in the ASEAN countries, either other governments in terms of providing funding and support for various projects or the private sector in terms of investments, trade, tourism and other economic activities.

It is important that the study be recommended to the ASEAN member governments, relevant ASEAN ministerial bodies and the ASEAN Secretariat. Let us ensure that ASEAN leaders, ministers and officials quote more the ACI competitiveness report than those put out by others, in particular the World Economic Forum (WEF), although those tend to be less comprehensive and rather selective in approach and objective.

Methodology, Ranking and Simulations

The methodology employed is very comprehensive. The division into four environments, 12 sub-environments and 121 indicators provides for a rigorous approach to the subject. The ACI study also focusses specifically on the ASEAN countries. This contrasts with the method used by others, even in respect of the two "highly cited cross-country competitiveness studies", the WCY by the IMD World Competitiveness Centre and the WEF's GCR. Their study components are more limited although the approach tends to be more from a global perspective. The GCR 2015–2016 covers 140 countries and nine ASEAN countries are included. Brunei is not on the list. The latest WCY compares 61 economies around the world using several indicators, including government policy, real GDP growth per capita, exchange rate stability and political risk. Only five ASEAN countries — Indonesia, Malaysia, Philippines, Singapore and Thailand are included. According to the WCY, Asia's competitiveness has declined.

The WCY and GCR tend to be cited more often perhaps because of the global approach that they take and overall rankings assigned to the countries studied. It is quite attractive for a leader or minister to quote the GCR for example, especially if his/her country is ranked favourably overall against the 140 countries surveyed, even if there are many shortcomings in specific areas. Without diminishing the policy relevance of such rankings, I would say that in some instances the GCR would be good for public relations and political purposes, whether to convince potential investors or to fend off criticisms from political adversaries and validate government policies and programmes.

As mentioned in the ACI report, scholars say that it is "firms that compete and not nations, regions or places." But it can be argued that nations, regions and places also need to compete for resources, financing support and investment. Some countries, regions and provinces spend vast sums of money on investment and trade promotion efforts. Therefore, competitiveness reports are important to governments just as the private sector would no doubt value them. Therefore, the more comprehensive the study, the more valuable it would be.

In the context of the ASEAN Community, this ACI study is most relevant to both government and the private sector. It should be able to assist governments assess their strengths and weaknesses and make the necessary policy adjustments whether domestically or in the larger ASEAN framework. For the private sector, the study will help them in making important business and investment decisions in the ASEAN region.

Observation

It is no surprise that Singapore continues to top the overall ranking. After all Singapore is also always at the top in the competitiveness studies done by others. Singapore meets or even surpasses most of the criteria set in these studies. There are many lessons that others can learn from Singapore. For sure, the field of education is one area of interest. What is encouraging is that the COT analysis in the ACI study shows that the majority of the ASEAN-10 has improved in competitiveness over time, albeit to varying degrees and indifferent sub-environments.

While ACI has taken a very comprehensive approach, there are perhaps a few issues that require further attention that may have relevance to the study in future. For a start, while the environments and sub-environments could remain as they are, the indicators could be adjusted to align to the blueprints of all the three pillars of the ASEAN Community. This may mean either adjusting the 121 indicators that are currently used or adding more indicators in particular under the 'financial, businesses and manpower conditions' and 'quality of life and infrastructure development ' environments.

Let us look at the issue of migrants, women and youth. To illustrate, the ASEAN Socio-Cultural Community Blueprint 2025 states that "intra-ASEAN migration is on the rise, from 1.5 million in 1990 to 6.5 million in 2013. Almost 50 percent of international migrants are women, who are increasingly migrating to seek employment opportunities." Additionally, "one in eight migrant workers is a young person between the age of 15 and 24".

The above points to the potential problems within ASEAN related to employment and employability. As it stands, Malaysia depends a lot on foreign workers to help develop the country and grow the economy. The migration issue needs to be addressed policy-wise by ASEAN collectively and the member states individually. The experience of Europe should be instructive to us.

ASEAN is now paying quite a lot of attention to the issue of women and youth under the socio-cultural pillar. According to the WEF, ASEAN countries generally do not fare well in handling gender equality issues. In the WEF 2014 report on the World Gender Gap, only the Philippines merits a ranking above 50th at 9th. The rest ranked below 50th, starting with Singapore at 59th. Malaysia stood at 107th out of 142 countries. Women could play a more prominent role in the labour force in ASEAN countries in the future. In Malaysia, there are more women enrolled in universities and colleges than men.

One of the distinct characteristics of the ASEAN economic and business environment is the overwhelming presence of micro, small and medium enterprises (MSMEs). They make up 97 percent of businesses in ASEAN. Under the AEC, ASEAN is giving a lot of priority towards MSME development and empowerment. This should be factored into the competitiveness study.

While looking at the labour-related indicators, the issue of education and skills need to be considered as well. It is fine to look at percentages of literacy rates and schooling and university enrolments. But issues such as vocational qualification, language and soft skills and technical competencies need to be given weightage as well. A recent report in the Jakarta Post cites problems relating to the skills of Indonesian graduates as revealed by the results of the Programme for the International Assessment of Adult Competencies (PIAAC) conducted by the OECD. The report calls for a total overhaul of the Indonesian workforce because the PIAAC results for Indonesians had exposed weaknesses in the Indonesian education system and by implication presenting problems for Indonesian competitiveness. Indonesia is the only ASEAN country that participated in the PIAAC. The same programme, if applied to other ASEAN countries, might reveal similar results. As it is, many employers in Malaysia, for instance, complain about the poor skills of graduates.

Another matter that would be relevant to competitiveness is research and innovation. A recent study by Thomson Reuters entitled "ASEAN – The emerging Research and Innovation Hub" suggests that research and innovation activities have been on the increase in the ASEAN countries. ASEAN has nearly doubled its share of the world's scientific literature between 2006 and 2015 and that patent activity in ASEAN has increased more than 40 percent in the last three years. A business- friendly and innovation-supportive environment is cited as one of the key achievements of the AEC. Thus it would be fitting for the ACI competitiveness study to give due treatment to research and innovation.

Looking at the detailed COT analysis, it would appear that despite the objectivity and good intention obviously forming the basis of enquiry, some findings appear unreasonable and rather subjective. For example, among Malaysia's weakest indicators are air quality and traffic congestion. The former is measured in micrograms per cubic meter and the latter by the number of vehicles per kilometre of roads. The reader would be puzzled as to how Malaysia could be considered as having poor air quality when haze coming from elsewhere envelopes parts of the country only a few weeks in a year. Similarly, whilst there is traffic congestion in Kuala Lumpur, the situation is no worse than other major ASEAN capital cities. It may be helpful if some of the methods of gathering and analysing data could be improved in the future.

On the whole, this has been an excellent study and update. It would have been nice if it had been released before the ASEAN Summit and made available to the leaders, ministers, officials and business people gathered in Vientiane.

Discussant Notes 2.2

Dr Gilberto M. Llanto

President, Philippine Institute for Development Studies (PIDS), Philippines

First, please allow me to congratulate the research team headed by Professor Tan Khee Giap for producing a document that will be very useful to ASEAN leaders and policymakers. Other institutions also publish global competitiveness ranking but the ACI-LKY team went beyond the reporting of competitiveness rankings. They innovated by delving deeper into the competitiveness issues faced by each ASEAN member state through specific indicators of economic performance and, by providing a "what-if" competitiveness simulation that will show the economic effects of addressing particular weak areas of an economy. This is a very important contribution and the ACI-LKY team has to be congratulated for providing each ASEAN member state a practical and practicable set of critical recommendations to improve competitiveness. It may be helpful to determine which of those indicators, if improved, would have the most significant impact to the economy and competitiveness.

Different ASEAN member states face different sets of challenges and there is not one uniform pathway to growth and development. In this sense, the approach taken by the research team enlightens the discovery of a relevant pathway. Each economy's journey to growth and development is unique and ASEAN leaders and policymakers will surely benefit from evidence-based results of the exercise undertaken by the ACI research team. Thus, the exercise is informative, practical and very useful to policy makers.

The second point I like to underscore is the Methodology used by the research team. It is a clever approach to use "standardised scores" in arriving at the performance of an economy from the vantage point of competitiveness. The Methodology enabled the research team to use a diverse data set without having to worry about different units of measurements of the different variables used in the exercise. In contrast, other attempts to measure competitiveness have relied heavily on executive opinion surveys where bias could not be completely ruled out or where representativeness of the answers cannot be assured. In my opinion, the Methodology used by the research team could provide more robust results.

The third point I have is a question: how is it that economies that are lower in competitiveness ranking managed to outperform those economies which rank higher? Please see Table 1. I think the next Update will even be more useful if the research team can demonstrate empirically how improved competitiveness drives growth performance. The competitiveness ranking will be more appreciated by decision makers if it can be linked to economic growth performance.

Table 1: Growth Rates, ASEAN and ASEAN Plus-Three Economies, 2010–2014 (Percent)

	2010	2011	2012	2013	2014	2010–2014
ASEAN						
Indonesia	6.2	6.2	6.0	5.6	5.0	5.8
Cambodia	6.0	7.1	7.3	7.5	7.1	7.0
Lao PDR	8.5	8.0	8.0	8.5	7.5	8.1
Myanmar				8.2	8.5	8.4
Malaysia	7.4	5.3	5.5	4.7	6.0	5.8
Philippines	7.6	3.7	6.7	7.1	6.1	6.2
Singapore	15.2	6.2	3.4	4.4	2.9	6.4
Thailand	7.5	0.8	7.3	2.8	0.9	3.9
Viet Nam	6.4	6.2	5.2	5.4	6.0	5.9
Plus-Three Countries						
Japan	4.7	–0.5	1.8	1.6	–0.1	1.5
South Korea	6.5	3.7	2.3	2.9	3.3	3.7
China	10.6	9.5	7.8	7.7	7.3	8.6

Source: World Bank (2016). *World Development Indicators*. Washington, D.C.

The final point I would like to make is the need for even greater collaboration, cooperation and solidarity among ASEAN member states. The strength of a chain really depends on its weakest link. There is a need for greater intra-ASEAN collaboration in addressing the different factors affecting the competitiveness and productivity of member states. This is motivated by the fact that last year the ASEAN Community was officially established as a single market and production base. I assume that each member state believes in the wisdom of looking after each other for the common good of the community.

Discussant Notes 2.3

Dr Nguyen Dinh Cung

President, Central Institute for Economic Management (CIEM), Vietnam

Firstly, let me thank ACI, especially Associate Professor, ACI's Co-Director Tan Khee Giap very much for inviting me as a discussant in the ACI ASEAN Economic Forum. I also thank Ms Phuong Anh and Mr Trieu Duong for very interesting and informative research and presentations.

Annually, we see many competitiveness reports such as the World Economic Forums Global Competitiveness Report, the Index of Economic Freedom, the World Bank's Ease of Doing Business Index, and the World Bank's Global Governance Index. ACI's ranking of ASEAN states drew similar results. Singapore was the number one, Malaysia number two, and Thailand number three, followed by Brunei, Indonesia, Philippines, and others. These similarities endorse the strength of the ACI's methodology. Furthermore, I find ACI's update to be attractive, and useful for policy makers in the following aspects.

Firstly, ACI's competitiveness framework is comprehensive. It addressed almost all the factors affecting competitiveness, included in four environments, 12 sub-environments and 121 indicators. The update tracked competitiveness of each member country from 2000 to 2013, allowing member states to identify means to make improvements in general, or, with respect to specific indicators. They also showed us the gaps between specific states and the regional average, or their peers in ASEAN. Lastly, it identified each member state's strengths and weaknesses. I concur with the five concluding remarks, and it seems to me that domestic reforms in less developed countries are not strong and comprehensive enough. As a result, they have not caught up to the pace of the ASEAN-5 in terms of competitiveness ranking. The gap has not narrowed.

Moving on, I observe that unlike the World Economic Forum, ACI's update did not differentiate countries according to their level of development. However, in my opinion, it is apparent that areas of priority, requiring reform differ greatly over nations at varying stages of development. Furthermore, while ACI's update identified strengths and weaknesses, it did not identify their cause, nor did it provide methodology, nor information for addressing them. As such I think that deeper country specific diagnostics should be carried out.

In summary, I highly appreciate ACI's report and its presentation of the competitiveness rankings and simulations of the ASEAN-10, and think that it may inspire far reaching reforms in Vietnam. Furthermore, I look forward to our cooperation in organising a workshop in Hanoi, to share ACI's 2016 Annual Competitiveness updates with our policy-makers and the public. Thank you very much.

Chapter 3
Growth Slowdown Analysis by Income Thresholds for ASEAN Economies

3.1 Introduction

3.1.1 Background

Over the past 50 years, the members of ASEAN have become increasingly connected by business and trade relations as well as people-to-people exchanges. Robust economic growth across the regions has lifted millions out of poverty and created a growing middle class. Over the period 2000–2014, the average compound annual growth rate of real Gross Domestic Product (GDP) of the 10 ASEAN economies was 5.7 percent.[1] The region has also attracted a lot of foreign direct investment (FDI) in recent years.

Despite the impressive performances of the ASEAN economies over the past two decades, further development is not guaranteed. Many pundits have expressed concern that growth may be derailed in the future. For example, according to a 2014 World Bank report, Indonesia, the largest economy in ASEAN, will face very real risk of a growth slowdown if structural reforms are not carried out.[2] Meanwhile, the Asian Development Bank (ADB) has suggested that it is possible for Indonesia to fall into the "middle-income trap".[3] This risk is not unique to Indonesia. Many observers have also warned of the possibility that other economies in the region, such as Malaysia, Philippines, Thailand and Vietnam, will be stuck at the middle-income level.[4]

There are many potential challenges to ASEAN's future growth. The ongoing slowdown of the Chinese economy is expected to have significant negative impacts on the economic performances of the ASEAN economies due to extensive economic links between ASEAN and China.[5] It is already observed that weakening import demand in China has slowed ASEAN exports.[6] In addition, the effort to establish the ASEAN Economic Community (AEC) and transform the region into a competitive "single market and production base" remains very much a work in progress. Though the AEC was officially established on 31 December 2015,[7] major challenges remain in the areas of non-tariff barriers, barriers to services trade and the ratification of the ASEAN Open Skies agreements. The bloc's economic

---

[1] Asia Competitiveness Institute based on data from the International Monetary Fund, World Economic Outlook database.

[2] See World Bank (2014).

[3] See Rhee (2012).

[4] See, for example, Ohno (2009); Yusuf and Nabeshima (2009); Flaaen, Ghani, and Mishra (2013) and Tran (2013).

[5] See Wei (2015).

[6] See Kyozuka (2016).

[7] The ASEAN Economic Community is one of the three pillars of the ASEAN Community. On 22 November 2015, the Heads of State/Government of the ASEAN members signed the 2015 Kuala Lumpur Declaration on the Establishment of the ASEAN Community declaring the formal establishment of the ASEAN Community on 31

agenda also risks being disrupted by a potential loss of ASEAN's cohesiveness. In particular, in territorial disputes between some ASEAN members and China, the main disputants including Vietnam, the Philippines and Malaysia differ in their approaches to deal with latter. ASEAN as a grouping also does not feature in these disputes. Furthermore, geopolitical tussles between major foreign powers, particularly the United States, and China, present a risk to ASEAN's unity as member states may be tempted or forced to choose side. Finally, if constructed, the Isthmus of Kra Canal, which allows ships to bypass the Strait of Malacca, may enable some ASEAN members to benefit at the expense of others[8] and thus may create friction within ASEAN.

In addition, each ASEAN economy faces various domestic challenges. Brunei has to contend with high labour costs and a relatively underdeveloped financial sector. Cambodia has weak enterprise policy and has to improve its citizenry's access to public services, particularly water, sanitation and primary education. Indonesia is still overly reliant on concentration of economic activities in Java. While more special economic zones have been planned outside Java, their operationalisation remains a challenge in terms of efficient logistics and transportation costs as well as capable human resources. Laos needs to accelerate its industrialisation process and concurrently improve physical infrastructure in rural areas for narrowing the urban–rural income gap. The economy also faces challenges in terms of its human capital. As for Malaysia, rising labour cost is a threat to the country's attractiveness to foreign investors. In Myanmar, the long-running civil war is detrimental for growth. In addition, Myanmar's Information and Communications Technology (ICT) infrastructure is particularly lacking. For the Philippines, lack of productive employment at home is hindering the transfusion of skills and capital, particularly from the professionally skilled diaspora around the world. In Singapore, small population and rising manpower costs are threatening to erode its attractiveness to multinational corporations (MNCs) as new competitors with large, young and increasingly highly-educated workforce emerge. Meanwhile, Thailand's economic prospect has been dampened by prolonged political tumult. Finally, for Vietnam, a lagging private sector, saddled by inefficient and unproductive state-owned enterprises, is a bane to Vietnam's efforts to move up the value chain as supporting industries remain underdeveloped. Also, low human capital quality and technological capability undermine not only the economy's attractiveness to MNCs but also the development of its private sector.

Nevertheless, there is also potential for future growth in the region. Home to more than 600 million people, ASEAN is one of the largest markets in the world. Meanwhile, while ASEAN is likely to be buffeted by economic slowdown in China, it also stands to benefit from China's ailments. With China's rising wages and thus diminishing competitiveness in labour-intensive manufacturing, ASEAN has, in recent years, become one of the top investment destinations for export-oriented MNCs. Consequently, ASEAN's presence in the global value chains is poised to become more prominent. At the same time, the ASEAN economies will also benefit

---

December 2015. See http://www.asean.org/storage/2015/12/KL-Declaration-on-Establishment-of-ASEAN-Community-2015.pdf (accessed on 26 February 2015).

[8] See Shimada (2015).

from the China-led One Belt, One Road initiative, especially from the Maritime Silk Road (MSR). In particular, the China–Singapore Economic Corridor, an initiative to facilitate the realisation of the MSR, can be expected to draw in the entire development of western China, creating tangible opportunities for Singapore as a business-economic hub as well as other ASEAN economies along the route. Indonesia also stands to gain from the MSR as it is complimentary to President Widodo's vision for Indonesia to become a maritime power. Finally, deeper regional economic integration holds much promise as the AEC can be expected to generate substantial economic benefits for ASEAN members, provided that the members are earnest in adopting the AEC integration programme.

This chapter provides a comprehensive analysis of growth slowdown for the ASEAN economies against the backdrop of other developing Asian economies including the economies of Greater China,[9] the states and union territories of India and the provinces of Indonesia (henceforth referred to as the Indian and Indonesian "sub-national economies").[10] In other words, we investigate episodes where growth had hitherto been fast but has then slowed substantially. Our analysis covers economies at all levels of development, including low-, lower-middle-, upper-middle- and high-income economies. We construct income group-specific logistic model in order to identify the relevant determinants of growth slowdown. In doing so, we aim to answer two research questions. First, are determinants of economic slowdown likely to differ across income groups? Second, what are the probabilities that economies in ASEAN will experience a growth slowdown in the near future?

3.1.2 Understanding Growth Slowdown and "Income Traps"

Economists have expended great efforts to understand the challenges to continued economic growth at different levels of development. Many have conceptualised the problems to growth through the idea of income traps. "Poverty trap" and, more recently, "middle-income trap" are common parlances in the development policy community. This section provides a brief review on existing researches on poverty-trap and middle-income-trap and seeks to distinguish our study on growth slowdown from these literature.

Much have been written about poverty-trap. The literature on poverty trap is motivated by the observation that the very rich and very poor countries do not seem to converge in GDP per capita over time. Several studies in this literature have pointed out that the cross-country income distribution has become increasingly bimodal, with probability mass concentrated at the two extremes.[11] In other words, while a handful of countries have grown to achieve high GDP per capita, many others have continued to be stuck in poverty. "Poverty trap" is one of the arguments proposed to explain this phenomenon. According to the poverty-trap theory, economies clustering around the lower end of the income distribution are beset with self-reinforcing mechanisms

[9] Greater China economies refer to the mainland China provinces, Hong Kong, Macau and Taiwan.

[10] Due to data constraints, some economies are not included in the sample, such that our study covers 107 economies in total. See Section 3.5 for more details.

[11] See, for example, Azariadis and Stachurski (2005) and Quah (1993).

which cause the persistence of poverty. These self-reinforcing mechanisms are the so-called traps.[12]

Both the theoretical and empirical literatures about poverty trap are well developed. The theoretical models for poverty trap suggest the existence of multiple equilibria and elaborate the ways in which "bad" equilibria of low growth and low income may be selected. According to Azariadis and Stachurski (2005), there are in general two "canonical" classes of models. The first model is called *historical* self-reinforcement, a process whereby initial conditions of the endogenous variables, such as the stocks of physical and human capital or technological progress, can shape long-run outcomes. The second is the *inertial* self-reinforcement hypothesis which emphasises the role of beliefs and expectations in selecting "bad" equilibria and the role of societal conventions, norms and institutions in perpetuating poverty by preserving expectations and beliefs. In terms of the empirics, there have been efforts to test for the existence of poverty trap.[13] There have also been many studies which empirically examine specific trap mechanisms[14] or traps which occur at the individual or group level.[15]

In contrast to poverty trap, the term middle-income trap has only gained currency in academic and policy discourses in recent years. Over the past few years, a debate has arisen around the observation that there are countries which have attained middle-income status for an extended period of time but have not yet been able to catch up to the high-income economies. Some authors, such as Gill and Kharas (2007); Felipe (2012a) and Aiyar *et al.* (2013) claimed that these economies have fallen into a "middle-income trap" while others, such as Im and Rosenblatt (2013) and Bulman, Eden, and Nguyen (2014), disputed the existence of such trap. More recently, Ye and Robertson (2016) concluded that if middle-income traps do exist, they are not very common. In fact, much remains to be clarified about the concept. As Gill and Kharas (2015) have noted, different authors define "middle-income traps" in various ways. Despite the lack of consensus about the definition and existence of middle-income traps in the academic literature, policy-makers tend to be concerned about them nonetheless. This has motivated a rich body of researches into factors which are key in helping an economy avoid being trapped at the middle-income level.[16]

Our research has important differences with both the poverty-trap and middle-income-trap literature. We focus on growth slowdown at different levels of development.[17] In other words, unlike the poverty-trap literature, we do not investigate mechanisms and factors which hamper the ability of low-income economies to generate growth. Instead, we are interested in episodes of reversals in growth rate *after the economy has enjoyed extended periods of fast growth.*

---

[12] Definition is adopted from Azariadis and Stachurski (2005).

[13] See Bloom, Canning, and Sevilla (2003).

[14] See Azariadis and Stachurski (2005, 339–340) for a comprehensive review.

[15] For instance, Jalan and Ravallion (2002) investigates geographical poverty traps arising from factor endowments among rural households from post-reform rural China.

[16] See, for example, Yusuf and Nabeshima (2009), Felipe (2012b), Bulman, Eden, and Nguyen (2014), D. Zhang (2014), Agenor (2015), Gill and Kharas (2015) and Kasenda (2015).

[17] Our study classifies economies into low-, lower-middle-, upper-middle- and high-income economies. See Section 3.3 for details.

The focus on growth slowdown is more relevant for low-income economies of our interest in ASEAN, Greater China, India and Indonesia as the main challenge for these economies is not so much how to generate but how to sustain growth. Meanwhile, in contrast to most of the middle-income trap literature, we do not wade into the debate on the trap existence. Instead, our research sharply focuses on factors which may make growth slowdown more likely at the middle-income level. Regardless of whether the "middle-income trap" exists, policy-makers in middle-income economies should be concerned with potential weaknesses which may cause their economies to slow down.

In essence, our study is in line with the budding literature focusing on growth dynamics which has emerged in the wake of Pritchett (2000). Pritchett (2000) observed that instability was a fundamental property of the growth series of developing countries as there were many upturns and downturns over time. Because of this instability, arguing Pritchett, studies which focus on the long-term growth rates are unlikely to be able to offer any useful insights. Instead, it is far more important to examine the "hills, plateaus, mountains and plains" — the various growth patterns — in the data series. In recent years, an increasing number of empirical researches have emerged to chart this territory.[18] Works which are most similar to ours include Eichengreen, Park, and Shin (2012), Eichengreen, Park, and Shin (2013), Aiyar *et al.* (2013) and L. Zhang and Puy (2015). The first three examined episodes of growth slowdown in middle-income economies while the fourth analysed growth slowdown in low-income economies. As compared to these studies, ours is more comprehensive as we analyse economies at all levels of development, including low-, lower-middle-, upper-middle- and high-income economies.

3.1.3 Motivation and Expected Contributions

Our study makes several significant contributions. We are among the first, if not the first, to provide a systematic quantitative analysis on the issue of growth slowdown at the high-income level on top of investigating growth slowdown for economies in other income groups. The subject of high-income slowdown has only begun to garner attention in public and policy discourses in recent years.[19] Nevertheless, it is highly relevant. As Japan's anaemic economic performance over the past 20 years demonstrates, further development after an economy attains high-income status is hardly assured and the failure to address the impediments to growth can be costly. As such, high-income economies, as well as those that are about to progress into this income group also need to be mindful of the risk of growth slowdown.

Our research is of particular interest for ASEAN policy-makers and researchers who focus on ASEAN economies. We are more comprehensive than the existing literature and study all

[18] Examples of these researches include Hausmann, Pritchett, and Rodrik (2005) which studied factors that trigger growth accelerations, Hausmann, Rodríguez, and Wagner (2006) which studied growth collapses, Jerzmanowski (2006) which highlighted the importance of institutions in determining the probability of economies switching between different regimes of growth, Reddy and Minoiu (2008) which investigated real income stagnations, Aiyar *et al.* (2013), L Zhang and Puy (2015), Eichengreen, Park, and Shin (2012) and Eichengreen, Park, and Shin (2013) which examined growth slowdown.

[19] For example, see Neumann (2015) and Dehn (2014).

ASEAN economies for which data are available. Our sample includes, among others, Myanmar. According to our classification, Myanmar had been a low-income economy until 2005 when it attained lower-middle-income status.[20] To date, we have yet come across any empirical study on growth slowdown or middle-income trap which account for Myanmar's growth experience.

In addition, our research benchmarks the ASEAN economies against fellow Asian developing economies, including the Greater China economies and sub-national economies in Indonesia and India.[21] We track the development progress of these economies and assess the risk that they will experience growth slowdown. In doing so, we have created a dataset of internationally comparable data on real Gross Regional Domestic Product (GRDP) per capita for the Greater China economies and the sub-national economies of India and Indonesia where GRDP refers to the GDP of each of these economies. To the best of our knowledge, we are the pioneers in this respect as such data are not available elsewhere in the literature. Our dataset presents GRDP per capita in 1990 constant prices Purchasing Power Parity (PPP) dollar data for 33 Greater China economies, 32 Indian states and union territories and 33 Indonesian provinces from the early 1990s to the present. The dataset is reported in Section 3.2 while the method to obtain it is detailed in Section 3.4.1. The method can easily be applied to calculate the GRDP per capita in 1990 PPP dollars for sub-national economies in any other country, leaving great potential to expand our unique dataset.

Finally, our research has important policy implications. The empirical findings from our model specifications enable us to perform statistical predictions for each economy in our study on the probability of it experiencing growth slowdown in the near future. This probability can be interpreted as preliminary caution for national and local governments so that they can take targeted actions in order to minimise the chances of economic slowdown. Meanwhile, variables identified as determinants of growth slowdown by our models indicate areas where policy actions and supportive reforms are needed.

The rest of the chapter is organised as follows. Section 3.2 provides some stylised facts about the economic growth landscape of the ASEAN economies. Section 3.3 summarises existing literatures on income thresholds classification, identification of growth slowdown, as well as drivers of growth and determinants of growth slowdown. Section 3.4 details the methodology adopted by our study while Section 3.5 discusses data description, statistical computation and sources. Section 3.6 reveals our empirical findings, followed by Section 3.7 which compares strengths and weaknesses of ASEAN economies. Lastly, Section 3.8 draws relevant policy implications for each ASEAN economy based on our results and concludes the chapter.

3.2 Stylised Facts on the Economic Growth Landscape of ASEAN

First, a quick clarification about the term "GRDP". In mainland China, GRDP denotes the provincial counterpart of national GDP. In India and Indonesia, "Gross State Domestic Product" and

---

[20] See Section 3.2 for more details.

[21] For a more comprehensive discussion of the datasets for Greater China economies, Indian and Indonesian sub-national economies, see Tan, Lian, and Xie (2016), Tan, Luu and Yoong (2016) and Tan, Ahmad, and Gopalan (2016).

"Gross Regional Product" are used instead. For consistency and ease of reference, we standardise the terminology to GRDP in this chapter. This means that the GDP of the ASEAN countries as well as that of the Greater China economies besides mainland China will also be referred to as such henceforth.

We classify the ASEAN economies into four income groups based on the level of GRDP per capita measured in 1990 PPP dollars[22] of each economy. We adopt the classification thresholds proposed by Felipe (2012a) which were derived from the World Bank's Gross National Income (GNI) per capita thresholds.[23] Accordingly, an economy is categorised as low-income if its GRDP per capita in 1990 PPP dollars is less than 2,000, lower-middle-income if its GRDP per capita is at least 2,000 but less than 7,250, upper-middle-income if its GRDP per capita is at least 7,250 but less than 11,750, and high-income if its GRDP per capita is 11,750 or higher. These thresholds are held constant over time.[24]

Tables 3.1–3.5 display the GRDP per capita in 1990 PPP dollars of the ASEAN economies between 1960 and 2014. The distribution of the economies by income group over time is shown in Figures 3.1, 3.3. We use red to denote the low-income group, yellow for the lower-middle-income group, green for the upper-middle-income group and blue for the high-income group. Brunei's GRDP per capita in 1990 PPP dollars data are not available throughout the period while Laos' data are only available until 2008.

According to the classification criteria we employ, as many as eight ASEAN economies were categorised as low-income in 1960 (see Figure 3.2). Singapore was the only economy in the region which had by then attained lower-middle-income status. However, the number of low-income economies has decreased over the years, as reflected in the shrinkage of the red area in Figure 3.1. In particular, Malaysia graduated from the low-income group in the late 1960s. Philippines and Thailand graduated in the early and mid-1970s while Indonesia made the transition in the mid-1980s. The early and mid-2000s saw the most instances of transitions from the low-income to the lower-middle-income group as Cambodia, Myanmar and Vietnam graduated during this period. By 2006, Laos was the only economy which had not escaped the low-income group.[25]

Some economies went on to make further transitions. Malaysia grew to become an upper-middle-income economy in 1996 while Thailand attained the same status in 2003. Meanwhile, Singapore moved from the lower-middle- to the upper-middle-income group in 1978 and a

[22] GRDP per capita in 1990 PPP dollars of the ASEAN economies are calculated based on data obtained from the Total Economy Database, May 2015, Maddison (2010) and the World Bank Word Development Indicators 2015. See Section 3.5 for detailed data descriptions.

[23] The World Bank's GNI thresholds take into account both income and non-income measures of well-being. Since they are based on the World Bank's classification, the thresholds proposed by Felipe also retain the same underlying information. See Felipe (2012a, 6).

[24] As noted in Felipe (2012a), World Bank's GNI thresholds are adjusted for inflation annually and therefore remain constant in real terms. Thus, using constant thresholds of GRDP per capita measured in real terms (1990 PPP dollars) is in principle equivalent to the World Bank's income classification method. See Felipe (2012a, 7).

[25] In 2008, the last year for which data for Laos were available, the economy was still a low-income economy. Its GRDP per capita in 1990 PPP dollars stood at 1,816 dollars.

Table 3.1: GRDP Per Capita in 1990 PPP Dollars for ASEAN Economies, 1960–1969

Economy	1960	1961	1962	1963	1964	1965	1966	1967	1968	1969
Brunei	NA	NA	NA	NA	NA	NA	NA	NA	NA	NA
Cambodia	675	652	687	720	685	702	720	745	767	767
Indonesia	1,095	1,139	1,110	1,041	1,053	1,037	1,011	963	1,030	1,128
Laos	740	745	751	756	762	767	773	778	783	788
Malaysia	1,581	1,636	1,674	1,697	1,748	1,819	1,857	1,838	1,948	2,010
Myanmar	599	600	638	642	639	640	599	601	625	634
Philippines	1,603	1,638	1,660	1,720	1,723	1,758	1,780	1,820	1,856	1,887
Singapore	2,310	2,422	2,520	2,701	2,541	2,667	2,891	3,163	3,540	3,965
Thailand	1,084	1,107	1,158	1,214	1,258	1,318	1,423	1,497	1,572	1,647
Vietnam	728	750	828	837	860	852	842	721	693	735

- Low-Income ($y_t < 2,000$)
- Upper-Middle-Income ($7,250 \le y_t < 11,750$)
- Not Available
- Lower-Middle-Income ($2,000 \le y_t < 7,250$)
- High-Income ($11,750 \le y_t$)

Note: y_t denotes GRDP per capita in 1990 PPP dollars of an economy in year t.

Source: Asia Competitiveness Institute based on data from Total Economy Database, May 2015; Maddison (2010) and the World Bank, World Development Indicators

Table 3.2: GRDP Per Capita in 1990 PPP Dollars for ASEAN Economies, 1970–1979

Economy	1970	1971	1972	1973	1974	1975	1976	1977	1978	1979
Brunei	NA	NA	NA	NA	NA	NA	NA	NA	NA	NA
Cambodia	681	634	586	783	662	575	626	695	787	825
Indonesia	1,215	1,250	1,357	1,519	1,558	1,520	1,614	1,699	1,735	1,786
Laos	792	795	797	800	805	813	826	841	858	874
Malaysia	2,079	2,178	2,286	2,553	2,679	2,639	2,900	3,065	3,257	3,441
Myanmar	647	652	641	628	646	657	680	704	732	749
Philippines	1,902	1,948	1,996	2,113	2,127	2,183	2,310	2,373	2,428	2,496
Singapore	4,439	4,904	5,460	5,977	6,276	6,430	6,797	7,224	7,752	8,362
Thailand	1,704	1,736	1,758	1,880	1,912	1,956	2,084	2,236	2,403	2,475
Vietnam	732	752	800	834	783	711	811	822	809	796

■ Low-Income ($y_t < 2{,}000$) ■ Lower-Middle-Income ($2{,}000 \le y_t < 7{,}250$)
■ Upper-Middle-Income ($7{,}250 \le y_t < 11{,}750$) ■ High-Income ($11{,}750 \le y_t$)
■ Not Available

Note: y_t denotes GRDP per capita in 1990 PPP dollars of an economy in year *t*.

Source: Asia Competitiveness Institute based on data from Total Economy Database, May 2015; Maddison (2010) and the World Bank World Development Indicators

Table 3.3: GRDP Per Capita in 1990 PPP Dollars for ASEAN Economies, 1980–1989

Economy	1980	1981	1982	1983	1984	1985	1986	1987	1988	1989
Brunei	NA	NA	NA	NA	NA	NA	NA	NA	NA	NA
Cambodia	852	854	896	924	948	971	996	948	944	939
Indonesia	1,896	1,980	1,864	1,897	1,984	1,991	2,066	2,126	2,205	2,360
Laos	887	897	904	908	911	913	916	917	919	921
Malaysia	3,638	3,801	3,926	4,059	4,258	4,099	4,034	4,125	4,359	4,631
Myanmar	794	820	844	862	885	891	865	815	710	724
Philippines	2,553	2,569	2,589	2,568	2,316	2,089	2,103	2,136	2,220	2,298
Singapore	9,058	9,460	9,674	10,330	10,982	10,764	10,966	11,827	12,821	13,599
Thailand	2,536	2,633	2,721	2,821	2,929	3,010	3,118	3,352	3,731	4,120
Vietnam	757	769	818	848	907	942	947	958	991	1,013

■ Low-Income ($y_t < 2{,}000$) □ Lower-Middle-Income ($2{,}000 \le y_t < 7{,}250$)
■ Upper-Middle-Income ($7{,}250 \le y_t < 11{,}750$) ■ High-Income ($11{,}750 \le y_t$)
■ Not Available

Note: y_t denotes GRDP per capita in 1990 PPP dollars of an economy in year *t*.

Source: Asia Competitiveness Institute based on data from Total Economy Database, May 2015; Maddison (2010) and the World Bank, World Development Indicators

Table 3.4: GRDP Per Capita in 1990 PPP Dollars for ASEAN Economies, 1990–1999

Economy	1990	1991	1992	1993	1994	1995	1996	1997	1998	1999
Brunei	NA	NA	NA	NA	NA	NA	NA	NA	NA	NA
Cambodia	909	945	975	979	1,033	1,066	1,091	1,121	1,148	1,262
Indonesia	2,524	2,702	2,848	3,004	3,179	3,386	3,596	3,709	3,176	3,155
Laos	922	922	944	1,010	1,045	1,074	1,074	1,106	1,116	1,181
Malaysia	4,932	5,259	5,579	5,976	6,364	6,814	7,307	7,646	6,909	7,160
Myanmar	732	716	774	809	857	903	948	987	1,030	1,128
Philippines	2,309	2,240	2,195	2,190	2,235	2,287	2,367	2,435	2,369	2,390
Singapore	14,220	14,745	15,323	16,664	17,914	18,599	19,203	20,109	19,005	20,003
Thailand	4,520	4,849	5,253	5,670	6,080	6,520	6,837	6,577	6,006	6,207
Vietnam	1,045	1,087	1,160	1,232	1,318	1,421	1,529	1,628	1,695	1,750

■ Low-Income ($y_t < 2{,}000$) ■ Lower-Middle-Income ($2{,}000 \leq y_t < 7{,}250$)
■ Upper-Middle-Income ($7{,}250 \leq y_t < 11{,}750$) ■ High-Income ($11{,}750 \leq y_t$)
■ Not Available

Note: y_t denotes GRDP per capita in 1990 PPP dollars of an economy in year *t*.

Source: Asia Competitiveness Institute based on data from Total Economy Database, May 2015; Maddison (2010) and the World Bank, World Development Indicators

Table 3.5: GRDP Per Capita in 1990 PPP Dollars for ASEAN Economies, 2000–2014

Economy	2000	2001	2002	2003	2004	2005	2006	2007	2008	2009	2010	2011	2012	2013	2014
Brunei	NA	NA	NA	NA	NA	NA	NA	NA	NA	NA	NA	NA	NA	NA	NA
Cambodia	1,339	1,413	1,484	1,582	1,717	1,915	2,090	2,271	2,389	2,357	2,459	2,589	2,730	2,882	3,028
Indonesia	3,263	3,333	3,433	3,546	3,672	3,826	3,979	4,172	4,361	4,500	4,717	4,959	5,202	5,438	5,645
Laos	1,228	1,278	1,335	1,393	1,462	1,541	1,640	1,729	1,816	NA	NA	NA	NA	NA	NA
Malaysia	7,620	7,498	7,744	8,035	8,420	8,705	9,022	9,416	9,694	9,380	9,903	10,236	10,636	10,956	11,434
Myanmar	1,270	1,401	1,558	1,762	1,989	2,245	2,523	2,807	3,074	3,374	3,689	3,858	4,117	4,387	4,684
Philippines	2,443	2,461	2,499	2,570	2,690	2,766	2,859	2,997	3,070	3,054	3,232	3,294	3,457	3,642	3,799
Singapore	21,408	20,640	21,314	22,590	24,439	25,659	27,072	28,334	27,345	26,373	29,859	31,058	31,340	32,206	32,719
Thailand	6,409	6,553	6,877	7,292	7,679	7,942	8,291	8,717	8,847	8,759	9,391	9,424	10,057	10,313	10,354
Vietnam	1,844	1,946	2,060	2,186	2,328	2,495	2,640	2,797	2,925	3,050	3,212	3,377	3,517	3,661	3,825

■ Low-Income ($y_t < 2{,}000$)
■ Lower-Middle-Income ($2{,}000 \le y_t < 7{,}250$)
■ Upper-Middle-Income ($7{,}250 \le y_t < 11{,}750$)
■ High-Income ($11{,}750 \le y_t$)
■ Not Available

Note: y_t denotes GRDP per capita in 1990 PPP dollars of an economy in year t.

Source: Asia Competitiveness Institute based on data from Total Economy Database, May 2015; Maddison (2010) and the World Bank, World Development Indicators

Figure 3.1: Area Chart for Distribution of ASEAN Economies by Income Categories, 1960–2014

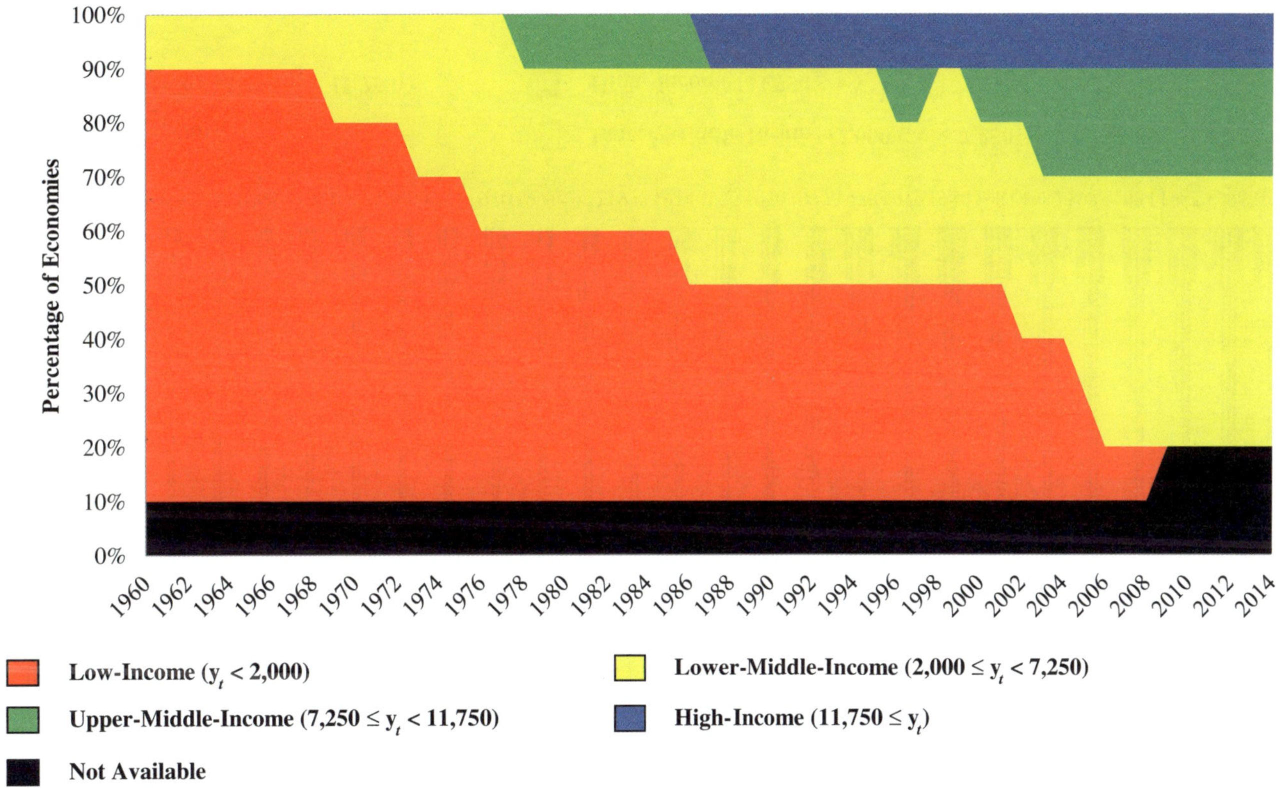

Note: y_t denotes GRDP per capita in 1990 PPP dollars of an economy in year *t*.
Source: Asia Competitiveness Institute based on data from Total Economy Database, May 2015; Maddison (2010) and the World Bank, World Development Indicators

Figure 3.2: Bar Chart for Distribution of ASEAN Economies by Income Categories, 1960–1989

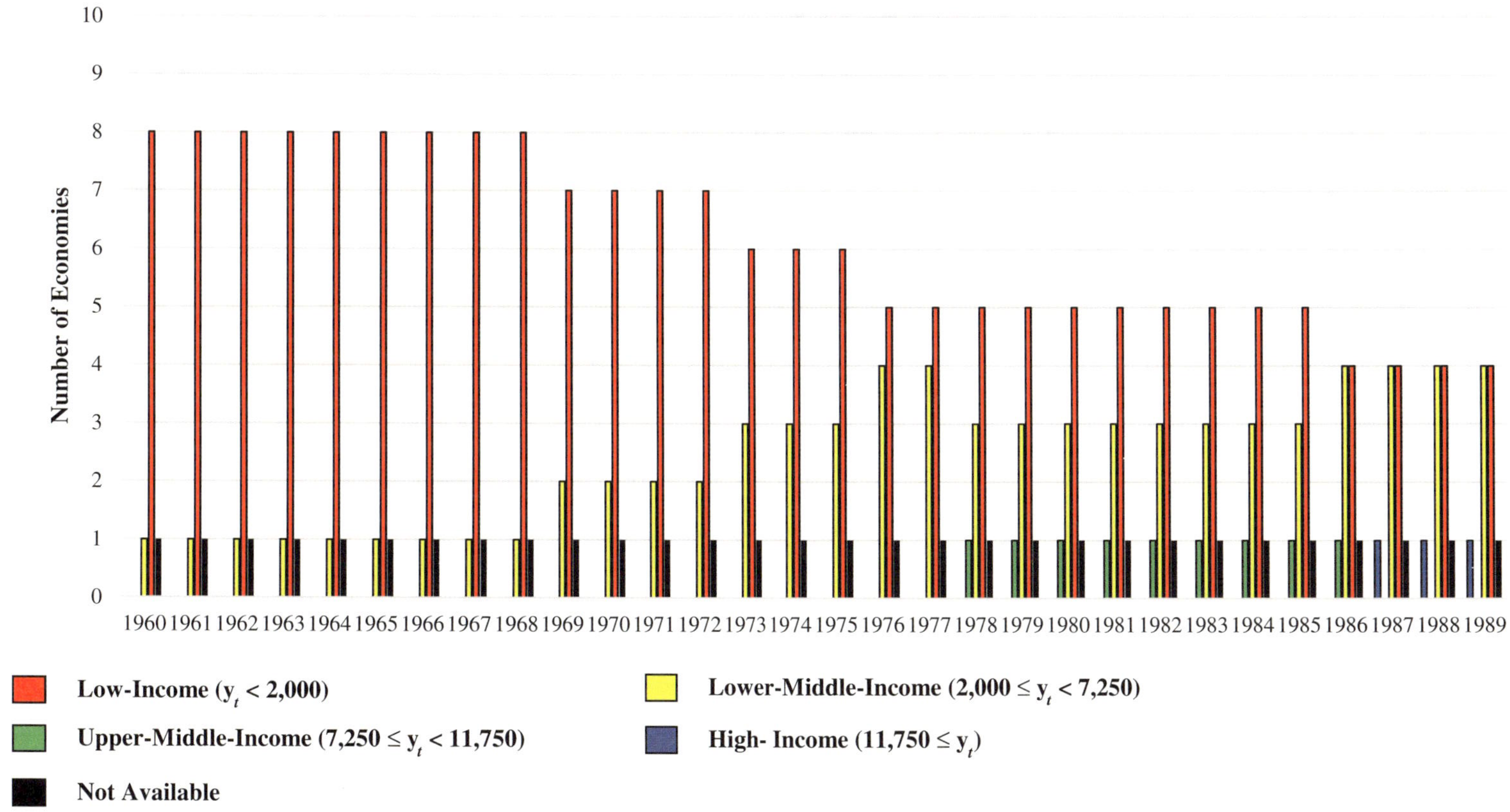

Note: y_t denotes GRDP per capita in 1990 PPP dollars of an economy in year *t*.
Source: Asia Competitiveness Institute based on data from Total Economy Database, May 2015; Maddison (2010) and the World Bank, World Development Indicators

Figure 3.3: Bar Chart for Distribution of ASEAN Economies by Income Categories, 1990–2014

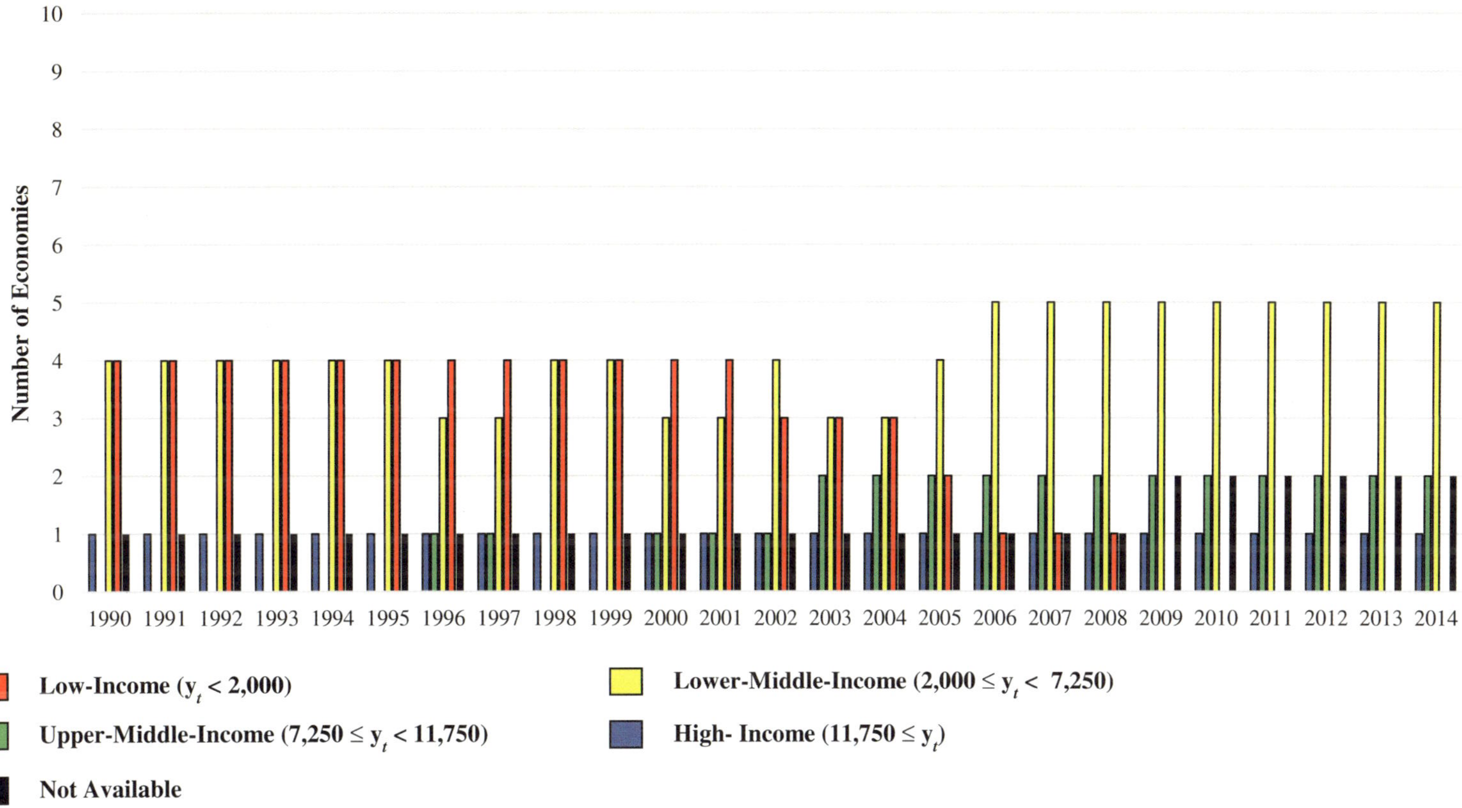

Note: y_t denotes GRDP per capita in 1990 PPP dollars of an economy in year *t*.
Source: Asia Competitiveness Institute based on data from Total Economy Database, May 2015; Maddison (2010) and the World Bank, World Development Indicators

decade later, became a high-income economy (see Tables 3.2–3.5). Singapore was the only high-income economy in ASEAN as of 2014.

The 1997 Asian Financial Crisis adversely affected economic growth momentums in the region. The ASEAN-5 countries were hit particularly hard as they experienced negative real income growth during the crisis. As can be seen in Table 3.4, Malaysia's GRDP per capita declined and the economy regressed from upper-middle-income status to lower-middle-income status in 1998. Meanwhile, the GRDP per capita of Thailand, where the crisis originated, started to decrease in 1997 and declined further in 1998. Negative growth hit Philippines, Singapore and Indonesia in 1998 and persisted in Indonesia until after 1999. In contrast, Cambodia, Laos, Myanmar and Vietnam were less adversely affected. During the Asian Financial Crisis, these economies still posted positive, albeit slower, real income growth.

Recent trends in the economic growth landscape of the ASEAN economies offer grounds for both optimism and concern. The first encouraging sign is the region's remarkable resilience during the Global Financial Crisis. GRDP per capita of Cambodia, Malaysia, Philippines and Thailand all declined in 2009 but growth quickly resumed and by 2010, these economies' GRDP per capita have surpassed their 2008 levels. Singapore, which was hit the hardest by the crisis as it endured 2 years of negative real income growth in 2008 and 2009, also recovered quickly to see its GRDP per capita in 2010 exceeding the level in 2007 (see Table 3.5).

Secondly, the less developed economies in ASEAN have exhibited robust growth. Table 3.6 shows the compound annual growth rates of GRDP per capita in 1990 PPP dollars in eight

Table 3.6: Compound Annual Growth Rates of GRDP Per Capita in 1990 PPP Dollars for ASEAN Economies, 2000–2014

Economy	Compound Annual Growth Rate of GRDP Per Capita in 1990 PPP Dollars for ASEAN Economies, 2000–2014 (Percent)
Cambodia	6.0
Indonesia	4.0
Malaysia	2.9
Myanmar	9.8
Philippines	3.2
Singapore	3.1
Thailand	3.5
Vietnam	5.4
Average of Cambodia, Myanmar and Vietnam	7.0
Average of Indonesia, Malaysia, Philippines, Thailand and Singapore	3.3

Notes: (i) Brunei's GRDP per capita data are not available while Laos' GRDP per capita data are only available until 2008. (ii) Averages reported are simple averages.

Source: Asia Competitiveness Institute based on data from Total Economy Database, May 2015; Maddison (2010) and the World Bank, World Development Indicators

ASEAN economies for which we have data over the 2000–2014 period. On average, GRDP per capita in 1990 PPP dollars of Cambodia, Myanmar and Vietnam grew at 7.0 percent annually. This was more than twice as much as the average compound annual growth rate of ASEAN-5, which stood at 3.3 percent. If Cambodia, Myanmar and Vietnam are able to maintain their impressive growth trajectories, it is likely that they will be able to narrow the development gap and eventually catch up with their more developed counterparts in ASEAN. In fact, Vietnam's GRDP per capita already exceeded Philippines' GRDP per capita in 2013.[26]

Nevertheless, the late developers cannot afford to be complacent as the experience of the earlier graduates into the lower-middle-income and upper-middle-income groups suggests that positive growth momentums may fizzle out. As of 2014, Malaysia and Thailand have still not been able to transform into high-income economies even though they became upper-middle-income economies in 1996 and 2003, respectively. More startlingly, despite attaining lower-middle-income status in the 1970s and 1980s, Philippines and Indonesia have not graduated into the upper-middle-income group. This means that by 2014, these two economies had spent 42 and 29 years respectively in the lower-middle-income group.

3.3 Literature Review

In this section, we review existing literature on works related to growth slowdown, including various ways of classifying economies into income groups and defining a growth slowdown episode. We will also discuss drivers of growth and determinants of growth slowdown used in other similar studies.

3.3.1 Income Thresholds Classification

In current literature, there are two main approaches to income classification. The first is based on absolute levels of income. The World Bank's categorisation of economies into low-, lower-middle-, upper-middle- and high-income economies based on the economies' nominal GNI per capita exemplifies this approach. The World Bank adopts GNI per capita as a classification criterion because it is a useful and readily available indicator which is also correlated with other, non-income measures of welfare such as life expectancy at birth, mortality rates of children and enrolment rates in school. As of 2016, the World Bank defined low-income economies as those with GNI per capita of 1,045 US dollars or less in 2014, lower-middle-income economies as those whose GNI per capita lies between 1,045 US dollars and 4,125 US dollars, upper-middle-income economies as those with GNI per capita between 4,125 US dollars and 12,736 US dollars and high-income economies as those with GNI per capita of 12,736 US dollars or more.[27] The GNI thresholds are adjusted for inflation and thus remain constant in real terms over time.

[26] In 2013, Vietnam's GRDP per capita in 1990 PPP dollars was 3,661 dollars while that of Philippines was 3,642 dollars. See Table 3.5.

[27] See http://data.worldbank.org/about/country-and-lending-groups (accessed on 22 February 2016).

Felipe (2012a) also followed the absolute income level approach. However, the author proposed thresholds of GDP per capita in constant 1990 PPP dollars. He first defined different sets of GDP per capita in 1990 PPP dollars thresholds, where each set was made up of three different thresholds $t_0 < t_1 < t_2$. The t_0 distinguished low-income and lower-middle-income economies, t_1 separated lower-middle-income economies from upper-middle-income economies, while t_2 differentiated the upper-middle-income group from the high-income group. The three thresholds t_0, t_1 and t_2 could take different values at 250-dollar intervals, where $1{,}500 \leq t_0 \leq 4{,}750$, $5{,}000 \leq t_1 \leq 8{,}750$, and $9{,}000 \leq t_2 \leq 20{,}000$. Thus, for example, a set of thresholds might contain $t_0 = 1{,}500$, $t_1 = 5{,}000$, and $t_2 = 9{,}000$ and another set may contain $t_0 = 1{,}750$, $t_1 = 5{,}000$, $t_2 = 9{,}000$. In total, 10,080 sets were produced. Felipe used these sets of thresholds to classify all economies which the World Bank also classified over the period 1987–2010. He then calculated the pairwise correlation between the World Bank's classification and the 10,080 classifications using polychoric correlation. The set which yielded the highest correlation was selected as each income group classified according to these criteria was likely to retain the same underlying information (both income and non-income measures of well-being) encapsulated in the corresponding World Bank income category. The author eventually selected the set with $t_0 = 2{,}000$, $t_1 = 7{,}250$ and $t_2 = 11{,}750$.

Employing similar methodology as Felipe (2012), Aiyar *et al.* (2013) also used the World Bank's GNI per capita thresholds as benchmarks to create income thresholds measured in GDP per capita in 2005 PPP dollars. However, unlike Felipe (2012a), each potential set of thresholds in Aiyar *et al.* (2013) consisted of only two thresholds t_1 and t_2 ($t_1 < t_2$) where t_1 separated low-income from middle-income while t_2 distinguished middle-income from high-income. Both t_1 and t_2 could take a set of values at 1,000-dollar intervals, where $1{,}000 \leq t_1 \leq 3{,}000$ and $12{,}000 \leq t_2 \leq 16{,}000$, creating in total 15 combinations. The authors eventually selected the set with $t_1 = 2{,}000$ and $t_2 = 15{,}000$ as the classification that resulted from this set overlapped the most with the World Bank's classification. Clearly, as compared to Aiyar *et al.* (2013), the set of classification criteria in Felipe (2012a) provided a finer differentiation of the economies as it distinguished the lower-middle-income group from the upper-middle-income group. Furthermore, Felipe (2012a)'s thresholds were more precisely defined as the gap between each threshold was much smaller.

The second approach to income classification is based on relative levels of income. The Catch-Up Index (CUI) proposed by Woo (2012) exemplifies this approach. The CUI of an economy expressed the percentage of the economy's income level relative to that of the United States in the same year. Countries were classified as high-income if their CUIs were more than 55 percent, middle-income if their CUIs were between 55 percent and 20 percent, and low-income if their CUIs were less than 20 percent (Woo, 2012). Fundamentally, classification based on relative level of income is problematic as it is subjected to economic fluctuations in the benchmark economy. For example, the CUI values of the ASEAN economies during the 2008 Global Financial Crisis and its aftermaths could have been artificially inflated. This is because, on the one hand, the United States experienced severe contractions in output and could only manage a slow recovery while on the other hand, ASEAN economies were much less affected and also recovered faster. As such, using CUI values to classify the ASEAN economies during this period risks mischaracterising (with an upward bias) their levels of development.

3.3.2 Growth Slowdown Identification

There are several definitions for growth slowdown in the existing literature. Aiyar *et al.* (2013) and Zhang and Puy (2015) characterised growth slowdown as "large, sudden and sustained deviations from the predicted growth path". These authors identified a country i as experiencing a growth slowdown in period t if the following two conditions were fulfilled simultaneously: (i) $res_t^i - res_{t-1}^i < p(0.20)$ and (ii) $res_{t+1}^i - res_{t-1}^i < p(0.20)$, where res_t^i is the residual of the country i in period t and $p(0.20)$ denotes the 20th percentile of the empirical distribution of differences in residuals from one time period to another. Both authors defined $t = 5$. The residual res_t^i was defined as the gap between the actual growth rate and the predicted growth rate of economy i which was estimated based on a regression of per capita GDP growth against lagged income level and measures of human and physical capital. Condition (i) thus requires the difference of residual between period t and period $t - 1$ to be smaller than the 20th percentile of the empirical distribution, indicating that the actual performance of the economy falls substantially below expectation. Condition (ii) requires the difference of residual between period $t + 1$ and period $t - 1$ to be smaller than the 20th percentile of the empirical distribution, thereby ensuring that the slowdown is sustained over a prolonged duration. This definition of growth slowdown requires estimation of predicted growth rates, which are difficult to be implemented in our context due to data constraints.

On the other hand, Eichengreen, Park, and Shin (2012) defined growth slowdown as an episode where growth has hitherto been fast but has now slowed non-negligibly. The methodology, which was also adopted in Eichengreen, Park, and Shin (2013), was based on the analysis of growth accelerations by Hausmann, Pritchett, and Rodrik (2005). Formally, the authors identified a slowdown when three conditions were satisfied: (i) $g_{t,t-n} \geq 0.035$, (ii) $g_{t,t-n} - g_{t,t+n} \geq 0.02$, and (iii) $y_t > 10{,}000$, where y_t is the GDP per capita in constant 2005 PPP dollars in year t, while $g_{t,t-n}$ and $g_{t,t+n}$ are the average growth rate of the GDP per capita from year $t - n$ to t and the average growth rate of the GDP per capita from year t to $t + n$, respectively. In both Eichengreen, Park, and Shin (2012) and Eichengreen, Park, and Shin (2013), $n = 7$. Intuitively, the three conditions can be interpreted as follows. First, condition (i) requires that the average growth rate of GDP per capita of an economy to be at least 3.5 percent or greater before the slowdown. Next, condition (ii) identifies slowdown episodes when the average growth rate of GDP per capita declines by at least 2 percentage points, implying that the slowdown is non-negligible. Lastly, condition (iii) restricts identification of slowdown to those economies with GDP per capita in 2005 PPP dollars that is larger than 10,000 dollars as the authors wanted to rule out crises in not yet successful developing economies.

3.3.3 Drivers of Growth and Determinants of Growth Slowdown

Table 3.7 lists potential drivers of growth and determinants of growth slowdown based on various existing literatures. The papers referred to in this table have empirically investigated the causes of growth slowdown and key growth drivers of economies which might be income group-specific.

Table 3.7: List of Potential Drivers of Growth and Determinants of Growth Slowdown

No.	Variable	Definition and Explanation of the Variable	Authors Who Use the Variable
1	Size of Government Index	This index measures the involvement of government in the economy. The index is made up of component indicators such as government investment and consumption spending, subsidies and transfers as a percentage of GDP, top marginal income tax rate and government ownership of enterprises.	Aiyar *et al.* (2013)
2	Rule of Law Index	The index is made up of indicators for judicial independence, military interference in the rule of law, contract enforcement, the protection of property rights and regulatory restrictions on the sale of real property.	Aiyar *et al.* (2013)
3	Freedom to Trade Internationally Index	The index is constructed from measures of trade taxes, non-tariff barriers, black market exchange rates and international capital market controls.	Aiyar *et al.* (2013)
4	Regulation Index	The index measures the extent of credit market regulations, labour regulations and business regulations.	Aiyar *et al.* (2013)
5	Chinn-Ito Index for Financial Openness	The index is based on binary dummy variables codifying the tabulation of restrictions on cross-border financial transactions.	Aiyar *et al.* (2013); Eichengreen, Park, and Shin (2012)
6	Total Dependency Ratio	Ratio of the number of old people (ages 65 and above) and young people (ages 15 and below) to the number of people of working age (ages between 15 and 64).	Aiyar *et al.* (2013); Eichengreen, Park, and Shin (2012)
7	Old Dependency Ratio	Ratio of the number of old people (ages 65 and above) to the number of people of working age (ages between 15 and 64).	Eichengreen, Park, and Shin (2012); Eichengreen, Park, and Shin (2013)
8	Young Dependency Ratio	Ratio of the number of young people (ages 15 and below) to the number of people of working age (ages between 15 and 64).	Eichengreen, Park, and Shin (2012); Eichengreen, Park, and Shin (2013)
9	Fertility Rate	Average number of births per woman.	Aiyar *et al.* (2013); Eichengreen, Park, and Shin (2012)
10	Sex Ratio	Ratio of total number of males in the population to the total number of females.	Aiyar *et al.* (2013)
11	Telephone Lines Per 100 People	Self-explanatory.	Aiyar *et al.* (2013)
12	Gigawatts of Power Generating Capacity Per 100 People	Self-explanatory.	Aiyar *et al.* (2013)

13	Length of Road Network Per 100 People	Self-explanatory.	Aiyar *et al.* (2013)
14	GDP Per Capita	Self-explanatory.	Eichengreen, Park, and Shin (2012); Eichengreen, Park, and Shin (2013)
15	Pre-slowdown Growth Rate of GDP Per Capita	Growth rate of GDP per capita in the years preceding the slowdown.	Eichengreen, Park, and Shin (2012); Eichengreen, Park, and Shin (2013)
16	Openness to Trade	Ratio of the sum of imports and exports to GDP.	Aiyar *et al.* (2013); Eichengreen, Park, and Shin (2012); Eichengreen, Park, and Shin (2013)
17	Terms of Trade (TOT) Shocks	TOT is defined as the ratio of export price index to import price index. The specification of "shock" is based on the difference between the current value of the TOT and past values.	Aiyar *et al.* (2013); Eichengreen, Park, and Shin (2012); Eichengreen, Park, and Shin (2013)
18	Commodity Price Shocks	Shocks in world oil price and food price.	Aiyar *et al.* (2013)
19	Ratio of Gross Capital Inflows to Gross Domestic Product	Self-explanatory.	Aiyar *et al.* (2013)
20	Ratio of Public Debt to Gross Domestic Product	Self-explanatory.	Aiyar *et al.* (2013)
21	Banking Crisis Dummy	A binary variable which identifies if the economy has experienced at least one banking crisis (=1 if yes, = 0 if no) in recent times.	Aiyar *et al.* (2013)
22	Financial Crises Dummy	A binary variable which identifies if the economy has experienced at least one financial crisis, of any kind (banking crisis, currency crisis, etc.) in recent times; variable =1 if yes, = 0 if no.	Eichengreen, Park, and Shin (2012); Eichengreen, Park, and Shin (2013)
23	Inflation Rate	Self-explanatory.	Aiyar *et al.* (2013); Eichengreen, Park, and Shin (2012); Eichengreen, Park, and Shin (2013)
24	Nominal Exchange Rate	Standard deviation of past nominal exchange rate over a certain past period (e.g. seven periods preceding the current one).	Eichengreen, Park, and Shin (2012); Eichengreen, Park, and Shin (2013)

(Continued)

Table 3.7: (*Continued*)

No.	Variable	Definition and Explanation of the Variable	Authors Who Use the Variable
25	Real Exchange Rate	Self-explanatory.	Aiyar *et al.* (2013); Eichengreen, Park, and Shin (2012); Eichengreen, Park, and Shin (2013)
26	Share of Employment in Manufacturing in Total Employment	Self-explanatory.	Eichengreen, Park, and Shin (2012)
27	Share of Total Value-added from Agriculture Sector in Gross Domestic Product	Self-explanatory.	Aiyar *et al.* (2013)
28	Share of Total Value-added from Services Sector in Gross Domestic Product	Self-explanatory.	Aiyar *et al.* (2013)
29	Government Share in Gross Domestic Product Per Capita	Self-explanatory.	Eichengreen, Park, and Shin (2012); Eichengreen, Park, and Shin (2013)
30	Investment Share in Gross Domestic Product Per Capita	Self-explanatory.	Eichengreen, Park, and Shin (2012); Eichengreen, Park, and Shin (2013)
31	Consumption Share in Gross Domestic Product Per Capita	Self-explanatory.	Eichengreen, Park, and Shin (2012); Eichengreen, Park, and Shin (2013)
32	Variables Measuring the Extent of Diversification of the Export Basket	The extent of diversification is measured either by an index or the number of exports with revealed comparative advantage ratio (RCA)[28] ≥ 1.	Aiyar *et al.* (2013); Felipe (2012b)

[28] Formally, the RCA ratio is given by

$$RCA = \left(\frac{xval_{ci}}{\sum_i xval_{ci}} \right) \Big/ \left(\frac{\sum_c xval_{ci}}{\sum_i \sum_c xval_{ci}} \right)$$

where $xval_{ci}$ is the value of country c's export of product i.

33	Variables Related to the Sophistication of Goods Exports:			
	33.1	Share of High-Tech Exports in Total Manufactured Exports	Definition of "high-tech exports" follows the World Bank. "High-tech exports" are products with high research and development intensity, such as aerospace, computers, pharmaceuticals, scientific instruments and electrical machinery.	Eichengreen, Park, and Shin (2013)
	33.2	Index of Sophistication of Goods Exports[29]	The index is proposed by Hausmann, Hwang, and Rodrik (2005). The index is a weighted average of the sophistication level of each good in the export basket. The sophistication level of the good, in turn, is determined based on the assumption that goods exported by rich country are sophisticated.	Flaaen, Ghani, and Mishra (2013); Felipe (2012b)
34	Variables Related to the Sophistication of Service Exports			
	34.1	Share of Modern Service Exports in Total Service Exports	"Modern services" are supposedly impersonal, hence less labour-intensive and therefore more productive. The authors pick out five among eleven service categories reported in the International Monetary Fund's Balance of Payments data to be modern services: communications, insurance, financial, computer and information and other business services.	Flaaen, Ghani, and Mishra (2013)
	34.2	Index of Sophistication of Service Exports	An imitation of the index of sophistication of goods exports.	Flaaen, Ghani, and Mishra (2013)

(Continued)

[29] Formally, the export sophistication index for country c is given by

$$Index_c = \sum_i \frac{xval_{ci}}{\sum_i xval_{ci}} * PRODY_i$$

where $xval_{ci}$ is the value of country c's export of product i, and

$$PRODY_i = \sum_c \left[\left(\frac{xval_{ci}}{\sum_i xval_{ci}} \right) \Big/ \sum_c \left(\frac{xval_{ci}}{\sum_i xval_{ci}} \right) \right] * GDPPC_c$$

with $GDPPC_c$ — gross domestic product per capita of country c.

Table 3.7: (*Continued*)

No.	Variable	Definition and Explanation of the Variable	Authors Who Use the Variable
35	Variables Related to FDI:		
	35.1 Ratio of Total FDI Inflows to GDP	Self-explanatory.	Zhang (2014)
	35.2 Foreign Direct Investment Regulatory Restrictiveness Index	The index is constructed by the OECD, at the sectorial (e.g. manufacturing, tertiary) and sub-sectorial (e.g. business services, communication) levels for national economies. The higher the index value, the more restrictive to FDI the country is.	Flaaen, Ghani, and Mishra (2013)
36	Growth Rate of Real Gross Domestic Product of the World	Self-explanatory.	Eichengreen, Park, and Shin (2013)
37	Gross Domestic Product Weighted Distance to Other Countries	Weighted sum of distance from the country in question to the rest in the sample. The weight is the percentage of the destination country in global GDP.	Aiyar *et al.* (2013)
38	Total Amount of Intra-Regional Trade (Exports and Imports to Economies in the Same Region)	Self-explanatory.	Aiyar *et al.* (2013)
39	Variables Related to the Political Conditions:		
	39.1 "Positive Changes" — from Authoritarian to More Democratic	A binary variable which identifies if the country became more democratic in the preceding periods (= 1 if yes, = 0 if no). This is done by observing the change in value of the Polity Index, an index constructed by the Centre for Systemic Peace to measure the degree of authority of a political regime.	Eichengreen, Park, and Shin (2012); Eichengreen, Park, and Shin (2013)
	39.2 "Negative Changes" — from Democratic to More Authoritarian	A binary variable which identifies if the country became more authoritarian in the preceding periods (= 1 if yes, = 0 if no). This is the counterpart to the "positive changes" variable.	Eichengreen, Park, and Shin (2012); Eichengreen, Park, and Shin (2013)
40	Wars and Civil Conflicts Dummy	A binary variable which identifies if the country has experienced wars or civil conflicts in recent times (=1 if yes, = 0 if no).	Aiyar *et al.* (2013)
41	Natural Disaster Dummy	A binary variable which identifies if the country has experienced natural disaster in recent times (=1 if yes, = 0 if no).	Aiyar *et al.* (2013)
42	Fraction of Country's Land Area in the Tropic Zone	Self-explanatory.	Aiyar *et al.* (2013)

43	Ethno-Linguistic Fractionalisation Index	Index measuring the probability of two random people in a country speaking different languages.	Aiyar *et al.* (2013)
44	Fraction of Buddhist Population in Total Population	Self-explanatory.	Aiyar *et al.* (2013)
45	Spanish Colony Dummy	Variable = 1 if country was a Spanish colony in the past, = 0 if not.	Aiyar *et al.* (2013)
46	Variables Related to the Education Level of the Population:		
	46.1 Years of Schooling	Average number of years of schooling for population aged 15 and above.	Eichengreen, Park, and Shin (2013)
	46.2 Years of Schooling at Secondary and Higher Level	Average number of years of schooling at secondary and higher level for population aged 15 and above.	Eichengreen, Park, and Shin (2013)
47	Scientific Journal Articles Per 10,000 People	Self-explanatory.	Zhang (2014)
48	Latitude	Absolute value of latitude of approximate centre of country.	Bloom, Canning, and Sevilla (2003)
49	Landlocked	Dummy variable = 1 for landlocked countries and = 0 for all others.	Bloom, Canning, and Sevilla (2003)
50	Percentage Land Coastal	Percentage of land within 100 km of coast.	Bloom, Canning, and Sevilla (2003)
51	Maximum Temperature	Average maximum temperature of capital city in degrees centigrade.	Bloom, Canning, and Sevilla (2003)
52	Rainfall	Average annual rainfall in capital city in centimetres.	Bloom, Canning, and Sevilla (2003)
53	Homogeneity	Percentage of population in largest single group that shares the same ethnic, linguistic, and religious characteristics.	Bloom, Canning, and Sevilla (2003)
54	Proportion of Villages That Have a Mountainous Terrain	Self-explanatory.	Jalan and Ravallion (2002)
55	Cultivated Area Per 10,000 Persons Per km^2	Self-explanatory.	Jalan and Ravallion (2002)
56	Infant Mortality Rate	Infant mortality rate per 1,000 live births.	Jalan and Ravallion (2002)
57	Medical Personnel Per 10,000 Persons	Self-explanatory.	Jalan and Ravallion (2002)
58	Proportion of Population Living in the Urban Areas	Self-explanatory.	Jalan and Ravallion (2002)

Source: Asia Competitiveness Institute

3.4 Methodological Approach[30]

In this section, we discuss our methodology. Section 3.4.1 describes the method through which we obtain GRDP per capita in 1990 PPP dollars data for the economies in our sample. Next, Section 3.4.2 discusses the set of thresholds used to divide economies into income groups. Section 3.4.3 then describes what constitute an episode of growth slowdown. Section 3.4.4 discusses the income group-specific regression analysis that we use to identify factors associated with the occurrences of growth slowdown at each level of development. When studying economies in the upper-middle-income and high-income groups, we also employ the Bayesian Model Averaging (BMA) technique which is outlined in Section 3.4.5. Lastly, Section 3.4.6 presents the approach taken to obtain predictive probability for each economy on its likelihood of experiencing growth slowdown in the near future.

3.4.1 Obtaining GRDP Per Capita in 1990 PPP Dollars

GRDP per capita of all economies in our study are measured in 1990 PPP dollars. For the ASEAN economies, GRDP per capita in 1990 PPP dollars is calculated by dividing GRDP in 1990 PPP dollars data from the Total Economy Database, May 2015 version and Maddison (2010) to total population statistics reported by the World Bank. Meanwhile, GRDP per capita in 1990 PPP dollars data for Hong Kong and Taiwan is obtained directly from the Total Economy Database.

However, data for the sub-national economies of mainland China, India and Indonesia are only reported in their respective local currency units. There is no existing database which compiles GRDP per capita in 1990 PPP dollars for sub-national economies. Furthermore, there is no readily available conversion factor for 1990 PPP dollars. Therefore, we take the following steps to obtain GRDP per capita data measured in 1990 PPP dollars for the sub-national economies in mainland China, India and Indonesia.

First, GRDP data in current prices of local currency are collected and divided by the corresponding population data. All data sources are listed in Section 3.5. The resultant nominal GRDP per capita in local currency is then converted to constant 1990 PPP dollars by multiplying them with a year-specific conversion factor, which is calculated as follows:

$$\begin{aligned}&\textit{Conversion factor for Country C in year t}\\&=\frac{\textit{Country C's GDP per capita in 1990 PPP dollar in year t}}{\textit{Country C's GDP per capita in current prices of local currency unit in year t}}\end{aligned}$$

where country C can be either China, India or Indonesia, depending on the sub-national economy concerned and year t spans between 1993 and 2013 which is the study period.

[30] This section builds on Tan, Luu, and Lian (2017, forthcoming).

All sub-national economies of the same country therefore share a common conversion factor for each year. By doing so, we assume that the ratio of GRDP per capita expressed in 1990 PPP dollars to that of the current prices of local current unit for a sub-national economy is the same as that at country level. All data for national GDP per capita in 1990 PPP dollars are retrieved from the Total Economy Database, May 2015 version while national GDP per capita in current prices of local currency units are collected from the World Bank, World Development Indicator.

3.4.2 Classification of Income Thresholds

To classify the economies into different income groups, we adopt the classification criteria based on absolute level of GRDP per capita in 1990 PPP dollars as proposed by Felipe (2012a). The classification thresholds are outlined in Table 3.8 and are held constant over time.

Felipe (2012a)'s thresholds are ideal for our study for at least two reasons. Firstly, the income thresholds proposed are defined based on GDP per capita rather than the GNI per capita. Although the World Bank's income classification, measured in current GNI per capita, is the most widely used to divide economies into income groups, it cannot be applied directly to our work as most of the economies included in our study are sub-national economies for which GNI per capita data are not available. Secondly, income thresholds by Felipe are obtained through finding the closest threshold values defined in terms of GDP per capita in 1990 PPP dollars to those of the World Bank. This ensures that each income category still retains the same underlying information as their World Bank counterparts.

Due to data constraint whereby we have insufficient observations to run separate regression analyses for the upper-middle-income and high-income economies, we have merged economies from these two groups into a single category, namely the combined group of upper-middle-income and high-income economies, when investigating potential determinants that are associated with growth slowdown.

3.4.3 Identification of Growth Slowdown

Following Eichengreen, Park, and Shin (2012), which is based on the analysis of growth accelerations by Hausmann, Pritchett, and Rodrik (2005), we define an episode as a growth

Table 3.8: Income Thresholds Classification Adopted

Income Group	Classification Thresholds
Low-income	GRDP per capita < 2,000
Lower-middle-income	2,000 ≤ GRDP per capita < 7,250
Upper-middle-income	7,250 ≤ GRDP per capita < 11,750
High-income	GRDP per capita ≥ 11,750

Source: Asia Competitiveness Institute

slowdown if growth has hitherto been fast but has slowed non-negligibly. Episodes of slowdown are isolated according to income groups because we suspect that determinants of growth slowdown at various stages of development may be different from each other. Other empirical works, such as Aiyar *et al.* (2013) and Bulman, Eden, and Nguyen (2014), offer evidence supporting this hypothesis.

Formally, a slowdown is identified when conditions (1) and (2) below are fulfilled along with one of the conditions (3), depending on whether the economy at time t is in the low-income group (i.e. condition 3a), lower-middle-income group (i.e. condition 3b), or combined group of upper-middle-income and high-income economies (i.e. condition 3c). The three conditions are as follows:

$$g_{t,t-n} \geq 0.035 \quad (1)$$

$$g_{t,t-n} - g_{t,t+n} \geq 0.02 \quad (2)$$

$$y_t < 2{,}000 \quad (3a)$$

$$2{,}000 \leq y_t < 7{,}250 \quad (3b)$$

$$y_t \geq 7{,}250 \quad (3c)$$

where y_t is the GRDP per capita in 1990 PPP dollars in year t while $g_{t,t-n}$ and $g_{t,t+n}$ are the least square growth rate of the GRDP per capita from year $t - n$ to t and the least square growth rate of the GRDP per capita from year t to $t + n$, respectively. Mathematically, $g_{t,t-n}$ takes the following form:

$$ln\ (y_{t-n+i}) = a + ln\ (1 + g_{t,t-n}) * i, \quad \text{where } i = 0,1,\ldots,n \quad (4)$$

In this paper, we set $n = 5$. Due to the structures of conditions (1) and (2), this means that growth slowdown cannot be identified for the first and last 5 years of the study period. As our analysis covers the period 1993–2013, slowdown episodes between 1998 and 2008 are identified.

The intuitive interpretations of the conditions are as follows. Firstly, condition (1) requires that the least square growth rate of GRDP per capita of an economy to be at least 3.5 percent or greater before the slowdown. Economies satisfying this condition are those with high initial growth rates. Next, condition (2) identifies slowdown episodes when the least square growth rate of GRDP per capita declines by at least 2 percentage points, implying that the slowdown is non-negligible. Lastly, conditions (3a), (3b) and (3c) separate the occurrences of slowdown by their income groups. For instance, if GRDP per capita for an economy satisfies conditions (1), (2) and (3a), the economy is said to have experienced growth slowdown as a low-income economy. On the other hand, if another economy's GRDP per capita satisfies conditions (1),

Figure 3.4: Frequency of Growth Slowdown in Each Income Group for ASEAN, Greater China, India and Indonesia Economies

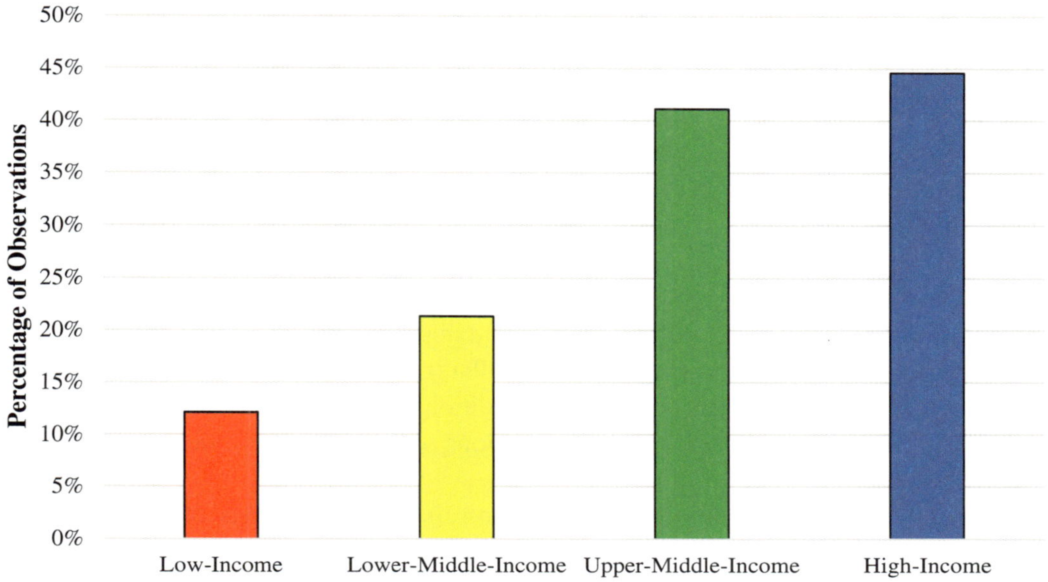

Note: Frequency of growth slowdown in each income group is calculated by dividing the number of slowdown occurrences by the total number of observations in that particular income group.
Source: Asia Competitiveness Institute

(2) and (3b) instead, that economy is deemed to undergo growth slowdown as a lower-middle-income economy.

In any particular year *t*, we assign the value 1 to economies for which a slowdown episode is identified. Economies which belong to the same income group but do not experience slowdown are coded as 0. In this way, we create income group-specific dummy variables representing the occurrence (or lack thereof) of growth slowdown. These dummies will serve as the dependent variables in the regression analysis.

Generally, economies in our sample do not stay within a single income group over the entire study period. As a result, the slowdown dummies generated for an economy over the years may be treated as observations for analyses of different income groups. For example, during the period 1993–2002, Thailand was a lower-middle-income economy. It subsequently graduated to the upper-middle-income group in 2003 and continued to stay in that group until the end of the study period. In this case, the slowdown dummies generated using data between 1993 and 2002 contribute to the analysis of growth slowdown in the lower-middle-income group while those generated using data from 2003 onwards are part of the analysis for the combined group of upper-middle-income and high-income economies.

Figure 3.4 shows the frequency of growth slowdown in each income group in the sample as identified by our approach. As the economies move across the income groups from low-income to lower-middle-income to upper-middle-income and lastly high-income group, the frequency of slowdown increases.

3.4.4 Regression Analysis on Determinants of Growth Slowdown

Having identified growth slowdown episodes, we now turn to studying their determinants. We specify income group-specific logistic regression models using the slowdown dummy created as the dependent variable to examine the impact of various determinants on the probability of an economy experiencing growth slowdown. We are guided by economic theories when picking potential independent variables. In other words, we specify three models of growth slowdown: one for the low-income economies, another for the lower-middle-income economies and a third for the combined group of upper-middle-income and high-income economies. Regressors in our model include GRDP per capita (in 1990 PPP dollars) as well as measures for demographic, infrastructure, human capital, macroeconomic conditions and exogenous factors. As for robustness check, we have also performed probit regressions on the same set of determinants as those by logistic models.

When conducting the regressions, we also pool all the observations of the same income group from economies in ASEAN, Greater China, India and Indonesia together. Although the regional traits are omitted as a result, this approach provides substantially more observations for each income group. Consequently, more precise estimates tend to be produced coupled with better probability predictive power of the regressions. Combining observations for economies from different geographical regions when running regressions to identify determinants of growth slowdown is a common approach in the literature. For instance, Aiyar *et al.* (2013) used annual data of 138 countries and segregates them according to income groups when performing separate regressions. Meanwhile, Eichengreen, Park, and Shin (2012) estimated a single regression using annual data of countries with GDP per capita that are greater than 10,000 in 2005 PPP dollars.

Since a relatively large number of potential regressors are examined in our study, model uncertainty is one major problem that we have to contend with. In an attempt to tackle this issue, we employ the BMA technique which is discussed in Section 3.4.5.

3.4.5 Bayesian Model Averaging as Robustness Check

The BMA technique is mainly employed to solve the "open-endedness of theories" problem. This is a fundamental challenge with growth regressions, in particular when determining which variables are to be included in the analysis (Brock and Durlauf, 2001). Open-endedness means that with the validation of one economic theory or model of growth, it does not simply imply that the others are false. BMA offers an alternative by considering all possible combinations of variables and assigns each combination a posterior model probability of being the "true" model based on Bayesian inference (Benkovskis *et al.*, 2015). BMA techniques will not generate the "best model". Instead, it generates a posterior inclusion probability (PIP) attached to each variable which can be interpreted as the probability of that variable belonging to the true empirical model. In other words, variables with high PIPs are considered robust determinants of growth slowdown (González-Aguado and Moral-Benito, 2013).

We mainly refer to the work by González-Aguado and Moral-Benito (2013) to develop the theoretical foundation for performing BMA techniques. In particular, the following equation shows a generic form of an empirical model:

$$\Psi = \theta X + \varepsilon$$

where Ψ is the dependent variable which in our case is the slowdown dummy, X represents a set of independent variables, θ is the vector of parameters, and ε is the error term. Suppose we have K possible independent variables to be selected. In this case, there will be 2^K different potential models which seek to explain the data, y, or 2^K different choices of X, indexed by $j = 1, 2, \ldots, 2^K$.

Next, we specify a prior mean model size $\bar{k}$ excluding the dependent variable. This is the prior belief of the right model size before seeing the data. In our case, we set $\bar{k} = 3$. Each variable then has a prior inclusion probability $\bar{k}/K$, and for a model, M_j, with m variables ($0 \le m \le K$), its prior model probability is calculated as follows:

$$P\left(M_j\right) = \left(\frac{\bar{k}}{K}\right)^m \left(1 - \frac{\bar{k}}{K}\right)^{K-m}$$

By Bayes' Rule, we can calculate the posterior model probability as follows:

$$P\left(M_j | y\right) = \frac{f(y \mid M_j) P\left(M_j\right)}{f(y)}$$

Here, $f(y \mid M_j)$ is usually called the marginal likelihood. It can be calculated using the following equation:

$$g\left(\theta^j | y, M_j\right) = \frac{f(y \mid \theta^j, M_j) g(\theta^j \mid M_j)}{f(y \mid M_j)}$$

where θ^j is the parameter set for the model M_j. If we integrate both sides of the above equation with respect to θ^j and use the fact that $\int g\left(\theta^j | y, M_j\right) d\theta^j = 1$ since g is a probability density function, we can obtain the following equation:

$$f\left(y | M_j\right) = \int f(y \mid \theta^j, M_j) g\left(\theta^j | M_j\right) d\theta^j$$

Moreover, considering θ a function of θ^j over $j = 1, \ldots, 2^K$, the posterior density of the parameters for all the models is as follows:

$$g(\theta|y) = \sum_{j=1}^{2^K} P(M_j|y)\, g(\theta \mid y, M_j)$$

By taking expectations on both sides, we obtain the estimation of the parameters,

$$E(\theta|y) = \sum_{j=1}^{2^K} P(M_j|y)\, E(\theta \mid y, M_j)$$

and the posterior variance is as follows:

$$Var(\theta|y) = \sum_{j=1}^{2^K} P(M_j|y)\, Var(\theta \mid y, M_j) + \sum_{j=1}^{2^K} P(M_j|y)\left(E(\theta \mid y, M_j) - E(\theta|y)\right)^2$$

Lastly, we can compute the posterior inclusion probability, or robustness, of each variable x by

$$posterior\ inclusion\ probability = P(\theta_x \neq 0|y) = \sum_{\theta_h \neq 0} P(M_j|y)$$

Following Benkovskis *et al.* (2015), we identify variables as robust if two criteria are met. Firstly, the posterior inclusion probability (PIP) should exceed the prior inclusion probability. For example, if the total number of variable considered is $K = 17$ and the prior mean model size is $\bar{k} = 3$, the prior inclusion probability $= \bar{k}/K = 3/17$. So, in order for a variable to be deemed as a robust determinant of growth slowdown, its posterior inclusion probability should be at least 3/17 in addition to fulfilling the second criterion. Secondly, the ratio of conditional posterior mean to conditional posterior standard deviation is larger than 1.65 in absolute value, which corresponds to a 90 percent coverage interval under Gaussian posterior parameter distribution. The mathematical representation is as follows:

$$\left| \frac{E(\theta|y)}{\sqrt{Var(\theta|y)}} \right| > 1.65$$

The two criteria need to be simultaneously satisfied for a variable to be considered robust.

In our study, we apply BMA techniques to the combined group of the upper-middle-income and high-income economies after logistic and probit estimations are conducted. The issue of model uncertainty is most acute in this case as growth slowdown in high-income economies is relatively unexplored in the literature. The BMA results are presented in Section 3.6.2.[31]

3.4.6 Obtaining Predictive Probability of an Economy Falling into a Slowdown

Based on the income group-specific models which link the probability of growth slowdown with the various determinants, we can compute the predictive probability of a particular economy experiencing growth slowdown in the near future by applying the relevant estimated logistic regression coefficients to the latest available data for that economy. This exercise enables us to identify high-risk economies which may require urgent policy interventions to help avert the prospect of slowing down. Since we set $n = 5$, the predictive probability of growth slowdown generated covers the next 5-year period starting from the year that the data represents.

Formally, suppose the logistic regression model for a particular income group includes the variables X_1, X_2, X_3 and X_4 with their respective coefficient estimates being $\widehat{\beta_1}, \widehat{\beta_2}, \widehat{\beta_3}$ and $\widehat{\beta_4}$ and the constant is estimated to be $\widehat{\beta_0}$. If the values of the four variables for an economy in that income group in year t are x_1, x_2, x_3 and x_4, the probability p of this economy experiencing growth slowdown during the period from year t to year $t + 5$ is given by

$$p = \frac{\delta}{1+\delta}$$

where

$$\delta = \exp\left(\widehat{\beta_0} + \widehat{\beta_1}x_1 + \widehat{\beta_2}x_2 + \widehat{\beta_3}x_3 + \widehat{\beta_4}\,x_4\right)$$

Since δ is positive, p is strictly between 0 and 1. As the latest year with available data for all determinants in the logistic models is 2012, we are able to generate predictive probabilities reflecting the likelihood of growth slowdown during the 2012–2017 period. Economies with higher probabilities face greater risks of growth slowdown over these years.

The interpretation of a low probability number is less straightforward. Low predictive probability does not necessarily imply a bright prospect for the economy. For a slowdown to be defined in our methodological framework, we first require the least square growth rate of GRDP per capita in 1990 PPP dollars to be at least 3.5 percent in the 5 years preceding the slowdown period (condition (1) presented in Section 3.4.3). Thus, low predictive probability may reflect either of the two following scenarios: the economy is indeed a fast growing economy which is likely to sustain its growth momentums or that the economy's growth rate is low to begin with

[31] The Asia Competitiveness Institute would like to express our heartfelt gratitude to Dr Carlos González-Aguado and Dr Enrique Moral-Benito for sharing their BMA programme.

and is therefore not identified as experiencing slowdown by definition. In other words, it is possible that economies with low predictive probability suffers from stagnation, which is beyond the scope of this paper.

3.5 Data Description, Statistical Computation and Sources

Our dataset covers 107 economies, containing nine ASEAN countries, 33 Greater China economies, 32 sub-national economies of India and 33 sub-national economies of Indonesia,[32] and spans the 1993–2013 period.[33] Following the methods outlined in Sections 3.4.1–3.4.3, we generate the growth slowdown dummy using data on GRDP and population. Various potential determinants of growth slowdown such as demographic, infrastructure, human capital, macroeconomic conditions and exogenous factors are also collected for each economy as independent variables. Regression analysis is then conducted based on the independent and dependent variables collected in order to identify potential determinants of growth slowdown for economies in each income group. Annual data are used in this study.

As mentioned in the previous sections, our analysis is conducted based on GRDP per capita data denoted in 1990 PPP dollars. For the ASEAN economies, including Cambodia, Indonesia, Laos, Malaysia, Myanmar, Philippines, Singapore, Thailand and Vietnam, we are able to collect the data on GRDP in 1990 PPP dollars directly from the Total Economy Database, May 2015 version.[34] GRDP per capita in 1990 PPP dollars is therefore obtained by dividing the GRDP in 1990 PPP dollars for each economy in each year with the corresponding total population number for the year. We use the population statistics published in the World Bank, World Development Indicator.

For Hong Kong and Taiwan, we collect GRDP per capita in 1990 PPP dollars directly from the Total Economy Database, May 2015 version. As for the 31 mainland China economies, we first collect nominal GRDP in yuan and then divide the GRDP data by the total population in order to obtain each economy's nominal GRDP per capita in yuan. The nominal GRDP data (in yuan) is collected from various provincial statistical yearbooks and from the website of the National Bureau of Statistics of China, while the population data are from the China Population & Employment Statistics Yearbook 2013, the China Statistical Yearbook 2014 and from the website of the National Bureau of Statistics of China. GRDP per capita in 1990 PPP dollars are then calculated using the method described in Section 3.4.1.

---

[32] The nine ASEAN economies included in our study are Cambodia, Indonesia, Laos, Malaysia, Myanmar, Philippines, Singapore, Thailand and Vietnam. As mentioned in Section 3.2, Brunei data are unavailable. The 33 Greater China economies covered in our study are the 31 mainland China provinces, Hong Kong and Taiwan, while Macau data are unavailable. The 32 sub-national economies of India included in our study are all the states and union territories of India excluding Dadra & Nagar Haveli, Daman & Diu and Lakshadweep. Andhra Pradesh and Telangana are treated as a single economy using the name Andhra Pradesh. The 33 subnational economies of Indonesia refer to all the provinces of Indonesia. Kalimantan Utara and Kalimantan Timur are treated as a single economy using the name 'Kalimantan Timur'.

[33] Unlike the rest of the economies, data for Laos are available from 1993 to 2008 only.

[34] All GRDP data for the economies listed above are obtained from the Total Economy Database, May 2015 version (The Conference Board 2015) except for Laos, which are unavailable in the database and are therefore retrieved from Maddison (2010).

Likewise, for the sub-national economies of India, we first collect nominal GRDP in current rupees and then divide the data by the total population to obtain each economy's nominal GRDP per capita (in rupees). The nominal GRDP data (in rupees) for the economies in India are retrieved from the website of the Ministry of Statistics and Programme Implementation (MOSPI), Central Statistics Office while the population data in census years (1991, 2001 and 2011) are collected from the Census of India. Population data for all other years during the 1993–2013 period are estimated based on census data. The conversion of nominal GRDP per capita data in rupees to that in 1990 PPP dollars follows the procedure outlined in Section 3.4.1.

For sub-national economies of Indonesia, the GRDP per capita in 1990 PPP dollars data are prepared in a similar way as that of the 31 mainland China economies and the sub-national economies of India. The nominal GRDP data (in rupiahs) are collected from the World Bank Indo-Dapoer and PDRB Menurut Penggunaan, while the population data are from the World Bank Indo-Dapoer. For the seven new Indonesian provinces created after 1993, namely, Maluku Utara, Papua Barat, Banten, Kepulauan Bangka Belitung, Gorontalo, Kepulauan Riau and Sulawesi Barat, we have backtracked their GRDP and population data until 1990.[35] We first calculate the ratios of the data between the newly created province and the province which it was formed from and then fit an exponential trend on the ratios. The GRDP and population data between 1993 and the year of bifurcation are then estimated based on the fitted exponential trend.

Our study examines different potential determinants of growth slowdown for economies in the context of different income groups, ranging from dependency ratios, openness to trade, exchange rates, world's GDP growth rate, employment structure, literacy rate, economic structure, productivity, infrastructure and government consumption expenditure. Ideally, many other explanatory variables should be considered as reviewed in Section 3.3.3. However, working on the countries of ASEAN over the span of two decades demands consistency in definition of indicators, which implies inevitable data gaps. We have also included some other potential determinants of growth slowdown which are important but not used in existing works, including productivity measures of the primary, secondary and tertiary industries. Table 3.9 summarises the list of potential independent variables we consider with details on the units and sources of data for economies in the various regions.

[35] Maluku Utara was created out of Maluku on 4 October 1999 (see http://www.bpkp.go.id/uu/filedownload/2/44/415.bpkp for official document), Papua Barat was created out of Papua on 4 October 1999 (see http://www.bpkp.go.id/uu/filedownload/2/44/414.bpkp for official document), Banten was created out of Jawa Barat on 17 October 2000 (see https://www.google.com/url?sa=t&rct=j&q=&esrc=s&source=web&cd=5&cad=rja&uact=8&ved=0CEUQFjAE&url=http%3A%2F%2Fwww.hukumonline.com%2Fpusatdata%2Fdownloadfile%2Ffl20334%2Fparent%2F17497&ei=yPa9U7WqMJWhugSjioLQCg&usg=AFQjCNHaW1Bh53l7ciaqHe7VVpg7p3yLjw&sig2=L7QDCmn0Oum-fJuVzr10yQ&bvm=bv.70138588,d.c2E for official document), Kepulauan Bangka Belitung was created out of Sumatera Selatan on 4 December 2000 (see http://www.hukumonline.com/pusatdata/downloadfile/fl20331/parent/17500 for official document), Gorontalo was created out of Sulawesi Utara on 22 December 2000 (see http://produk-hukum.kemenag.go.id/downloads/5ebedbf25a58f828cf9dc247eee8b1a8.pdf for official document), Kepulauan Riau was created out of Riau on 25 October 2002 (see http://produk-hukum.kemenag.go.id/downloads/f8ae5d8b4c760280ab00e0d3b68af661.pdf for official document), and Sulawesi Barat was created out of Sulawesi Selatan on 5 October 2004 (see http://produk-hukum.kemenag.go.id/downloads/fde4287a7b92c47ba9a82f49dbce0879.pdf for official document).

Table 3.9: Unit and Data Sources for Independent Variables

			Data Sources			
No.	**Independent Variables**	**Unit**	**ASEAN**	**Greater China**	**India**	**Indonesia**
1	Total Dependency Ratio	Percentage	• Abbas *et al.* (2010) • Barro and Lee (2013) • Bluedorn *et al.* (2013) • Centre for Research on the Epidemiology of Disaster, The International Disaster Database • Euromonitor International, Global Market Information Database • Fraser Institute, Economic Freedom of the World database • International Labour Organisation, Key Indicators of the Labour Market, 8th Edition	• Almanac of China's Population • China Compendium of Statistics 1949–2008 • China Energy Statistical Yearbook • China Population & Employment Statistical Yearbook • China Statistical Yearbook • China Statistical Yearbook on Science and Technology • Global Market Information Database (GMID)	• CEIC Database • Census of India: 1991, 2001 and 2011 • Centre for Monitoring Indian Economy Pvt. Ltd (CMIE): States of India database • Indiastat • Ministry of Statistics and Programme Implementation (MOSPI), Central Statistics Office • Ministry of Statistics and Programme Implementation (MOSPI), National Sample Survey Office	• CEIC Database • Indikator Kesejahteraan Rakyat • Investment Coordinating Board (BKPM) • Keuangan Pemerintah Provinsi • PDRB Menurut Penggunaan • PDRB Provinsi Menurut Lapangan Usaha • Proyeksi Penduduk Indonesia • Statistik Indonesia
2	Old Dependency Ratio	Percentage				
3	Young Dependency Ratio	Percentage				
4	Openness to Trade	Percentage of GRDP				
5	Percentage Change in Nominal Exchange Rate	Percentage				
6	World GDP Real Growth Rate	Percentage				
7	FDI Inflows as Percentage of GRDP	Percentage of GRDP				
8	Employment in Primary Industry as Percentage of Total Employment	Percentage of Total Employment				
9	Employment in Secondary Industry as Percentage of Total Employment	Percentage of Total Employment				
10	Employment in Tertiary Industry as Percentage of Total Employment	Percentage of Total Employment				
11	Literacy Rate	Percentage				
12	Overall Productivity	Constant 1990 PPP Dollars				

13	Primary Industry Value-added Per Worker	Constant 1990 PPP Dollars	• International Monetary Fund, World Economic Outlook Database, April 2015 • Maddison (2010) • The Conference Board, Total Economy Database, May 2015 version • United Nations Conference on Trade and Development • World Bank, World Development Indicators	• Hong Kong Annual Digest • Provincial Statistical Yearbook • Statistical Yearbook of the Chinese Investment in Fixed Assets • Taiwan Statistical Yearbook • Taiwan Statistical Data Book • The Conference Board, Total Economy Database, May 2015 version • World Bank, World Development Indicators	• The Conference Board, Total Economy Database, May 2015 version • World Bank, World Development Indicators	• Statistik Kesejahteraan Rakyat • Statistik Keuangan Pemerintah Provinsi • Statistik Perhubungan • Statistik Perhubungan • Statistik Transportasi • The Conference Board, Total Economy Database, May 2015 version • World Bank Indo-Dapoer • World Bank, World Development Indicators
14	Secondary Industry Value-added Per Worker	Constant 1990 PPP Dollars				
15	Tertiary Industry Value-added Per Worker	Constant 1990 PPP Dollars				
16	Length of Road	Kilometre				
17	Road Density	Kilometre Per Square Kilometre				
18	Length of Road Per Capita	Kilometre Per 10,000 People				
19	Primary Industry Value-added as Percentage of GRDP	Percentage of GRDP				
20	Secondary Industry Value-added as Percentage of GRDP	Percentage of GRDP				
21	Tertiary Industry Value-added as Percentage of GRDP	Percentage of GRDP				
22	Government Consumption Expenditure as Percentage of GRDP	Percentage of GRDP				

Source: Asia Competitiveness Institute

For certain independent variables which have a few years of missing data and display a clear linear trend, we employ linear interpolation or extrapolation to fill in the missing data. In the case whereby all the economies of the same region do not have data for the earlier years of the study period, we conduct estimation based on the exponential trend of available data.

In our dataset, there are a few sub-national economies which were created during the study period. For mainland China, Chongqing was separated from Sichuan on 14th March 1997. We obtain backdated Chongqing's data for the 1993–1997 period from the National Bureau of Statistics of China and the Chongqing Municipal Statistics Bureau. For the case of India, three bifurcations occurred during the study period: Chhattisgarh was separated from Madhya Pradesh on 1 November 2000, Uttarakhand (formerly known as Uttaranchal) was created from Uttar Pradesh on 9 November 2000, and Jharkhand was carved out of Bihar on 15 November 2000. Data for these three newly created economies are missing before 2000 for a few independent variables. For these missing data, we first calculate the ratios of the data between the newly created economy and the economy which it was formed from and then fit an exponential trend on the ratios. Data between 1993 and 2000 are then estimated based on the fitted exponential trend. For the case of Indonesia whereby seven economies were created during our study period, we employ the same technique to estimate missing data.

3.6 Empirical Findings

3.6.1 Determinants of Growth Slowdown by Income Thresholds

Table 3.10 summarises our research findings on determinants that are strongly associated with growth slowdown in the low-income group, lower-middle-income group and combined group of upper-middle-income and high-income economies. In all three income group-specific logistic regression models of growth slowdown, we employ GRDP per Capita (in 1990 PPP dollars) as a control variable to guard against omitted variable bias.

As illustrated in Table 3.10, growth slowdown in the low-income group is mainly associated with the level of GRDP per Capita, Literacy Rate, FDI Inflows as Percentage of GRDP, and Length of Road per Capita with the first two determinants being significant at the 5 percent level, while the last two at 10 percent level.

On the other hand, growth slowdown in the lower-middle-income group is associated with the level of GRDP per Capita, FDI Inflows as Percentage of GRDP, Old Dependency Ratio, Employment in Tertiary Industry as Percentage of Total Employment, and Literacy Rate, with the first three determinants being significant at 1 percent level, Employment in Tertiary Industry as Percentage of Total Employment at 5 percent level, and Literacy Rate at 10 percent level.

Meanwhile, growth slowdown in the combined group of upper-middle-income and high-income economies is associated with GRDP per Capita, Openness to Trade, Literacy Rate, Employment in Tertiary Industry as Percentage of Total Employment, and Secondary Industry Value added per Worker with the first two determinants being significant at 1 percent level while the last three determinants are significant at 5 percent level. The next few paragraphs discuss

Table 3.10: Determinants of Growth Slowdown for the Low-Income Group, Lower-Middle-Income Group and the Combined Group of Upper-Middle-Income and High-Income Economies, Logistic Model

	Growth Slowdown Models		
Income Groups	**Low-Income**	**Lower-Middle-Income**	**Combined Group of Upper-Middle-Income and High-Income Economies**
GRDP Per Capita	0.0013** (0.0005)	0.0005*** (0.0001)	0.0003*** (0.0001)
Literacy Rate	–0.0304** (0.0133)	–0.0197* (0.0114)	–0.1481** (0.0597)
FDI Inflows as Percentage of GRDP	–0.5082* (0.2629)	–0.1935*** (0.0523)	
Length of Road Per Capita	–0.0126* (0.0072)		
Employment in Tertiary Industry as Percentage of Total Employment		–0.0287** (0.0115)	–0.0426** (0.0172)
Old Dependency Ratio		0.0750*** (0.0287)	
Openness to Trade			–0.0091*** (0.0030)
Secondary Industry Value-added Per Worker			–0.00002** ($7.89e^{-6}$)
Constant	–1.0075 (1.0799)	–0.9246 (1.0452)	14.5001*** (5.5816)
No. of Observations	358	667	147
Pseudo R^2	0.0680	0.0876	0.1215

Note: Numbers in the parentheses are standard errors. *, ** and *** denote the coefficient is significant at 10 percent level, 5 percent level and 1 percent level, respectively.
Source: Asia Competitiveness Institute

each determinant in the three models, with the exception of the control variable GRDP per Capita, in further detail. It is worth noting that some determinants are associated with the occurrence of growth slowdown in more than one income group.

Literacy Rate appears as a significant variable in growth slowdown models for all three income groups, including the low-income group, lower-middle-income group, and the combined group of upper-middle-income and high-income economies. The signs of the coefficients are consistently negative, indicating that literacy is negatively associated with the probability of slowdown in all income groups. Basic literacy is the prerequisite for further educational attainment, and it facilitates and enables learning throughout a person's lifecycle after becoming literate. Thus, high literacy rate is necessary for an economy to achieve a high degree of human capital accumulation which is important for sustaining growth.

FDI Inflows as Percentage of GRDP is a significant variable in the slowdown model for the low-income and lower-middle-income economies. The signs of the coefficients in both models are negative, indicating an inverse relation between FDI inflows and the probability of slowdown for economies in the low- and lower-middle-income groups. This result is intuitive. The influx of capital through FDI increases capital accumulation in the host economy. More importantly, FDI promotes technological development through technological transfer and diffusion. It may also help augment managerial expertise in the host economy. Thus, FDI is an important driver of continued growth in low- and lower-middle-income economies as growth in these economies is usually hampered by capital inadequacies and technological backwardness.

Length of Road per Capita appears as a significant determinant of growth slowdown for the low-income group. The negative sign of the coefficient points to an inverse relation between road per capita and the probability of low-income economies experiencing growth slowdown. This result suggests that basic infrastructure development is important for low-income economies to sustain growth. Improving road networks and transport infrastructure in general grants producers in low-income economies access to new markets. At the same time, it also connects firms from more developed regions to labour in low-income economies, creating more opportunities for growth.

Employment in Tertiary Industry as Percentage of Total Employment is a significant variable in the slowdown models for lower-middle-income economies as well as the upper-middle- and high-income economies. The sign of the coefficients is consistently negative, indicating an inverse relation between employment in tertiary industry and the probability of slowdown for these economies. As an economy progresses, it becomes increasingly hard to sustain growth through exporting manufacturing products. This is because the economy slowly loses its cost advantage to less developed competitors. Thus, it is important for more advanced economies to diversify into the tertiary sector so that they can move up the value chain and create more opportunities for sustainable growth. Furthermore, certain high value-added industries such as research and development, financial services and consultancy services also help boost the potential, productivity and performance of other sectors and industries of the economy.

Old age Dependency Ratio is positively associated with the probability of growth slowdown for lower-middle-income economies. A high old dependency ratio means that the labour force has to support a higher number of elderlies. With fewer people of working age, the pool of productive labour shrinks. Furthermore, a smaller working-age population also means less domestic resources for productive investments as this group tends to save while the older population tends to dissave. Economies with high old dependency ratio are thus more prone to slowdown.

Openness to Trade is negatively associated with the probability of slowdown for the upper-middle-income and high-income economies. Having access to foreign markets provides the economy with more opportunities for growth. Trade with multiple international partners might also help diversify the demand risks from sole reliance on domestic market demand to a mix between domestic and external consumers. Furthermore, the exposure to global competition provides the impetus for domestic economic restructuring and other reform initiatives to address existing weaknesses and inefficiencies in the domestic economy which may otherwise hamper growth.

Finally, Secondary Industry Value added per Worker is negatively associated with the probability of slowdown for upper-middle-income and high-income economies. The result underscores the importance of improving productivity for continued growth in upper-middle-income and high-income economies. As an economy matures, it becomes increasingly difficult to grow by expanding industrial production as idle or underemployed factors of production become scarcer. Thus, productivity enhancement is necessary for sustaining growth and economies with lower productivity are more prone to slowdown.

As a robustness check, we have also performed probit regressions using the same set of determinants as shown in Table 3.10 for the three income groups. The results are reported in Appendix 6 and there is little difference between them and the results from logistic regressions.

3.6.2 Bayesian Model Averaging Results

In this section, we present three sets of BMA results for the combined group of upper-middle-income and high-income economies. This is because among the list of possible determinants for growth slowdown considered in our study (see Table 3.9), we have variables related to the employment structure of the primary, secondary and tertiary industries, the contribution of each sector to the economy's GRDP as well as value added per worker for each sector. Considering these three types of data in a single BMA estimation will pose multicollinearity problem as they are highly correlated.

We have therefore conducted three rounds of BMA estimations for the combined group of upper-middle-income and high-income economies. For the first round of BMA estimation, we include only variables related to employment structure and value added per worker while leaving out variables on economic structure. All the other potential determinants such as dependency ratios, openness to trade, exchange rates, etc. still remain in our BMA estimation. The second round of BMA estimation is similar to that of the first with the only difference being that variables related to economic structure are used in place of those on value added per worker. As for the third round of BMA estimation, economic structure-related variables and value added per worker variables are used while employment structure-related variables are omitted. The results for these three rounds of BMA estimations are thus labelled as Result (I), Result (II) and Result (III), respectively, in Tables 3.11–3.13.

Common to these three results, GRDP per capita, Overall Productivity, Employment in Tertiary Industry as Percentage of Total Employment, Road Density, Tertiary Industry Value added per Worker, and Government Consumption Expenditure as Percentage of GRDP are regarded as robust determinants of growth slowdown. Moreover, Secondary Industry Value added per Worker is considered a robust determinant in Result (I) (see Table 3.11). Note that three robust determinants identified through this BMA exercise are also in our logistic model for growth slowdown in the combined group of upper-middle-income and high-income economies, namely GRDP per capita, Employment in Tertiary Industry as Percentage of Total Employment, and Secondary Industry Value added per Worker.

Table 3.11: BMA Result (I) for the Combined Group of Upper-Middle-Income and High-Income Economies

Determinants	Posterior Inclusion Probability (PIP)	Posterior Mean	Posterior Standard Deviation (PSTD)	Posterior Mean / PSTD
GRDP Per Capita	0.99999	0.00064	0.00015	4.12338
Total Dependency Ratio	0.09732	−0.05030	0.02734	1.83994
Openness to Trade	0.06949	−0.00504	0.00337	1.49807
Percentage Change in Nominal Exchange Rate	0.04596	−0.02867	0.02289	1.25274
World Gross Domestic Product Real Growth Rate	0.04583	0.20967	0.15319	1.36868
FDI Inflows as Percentage of GRDP	0.02444	0.01589	0.03105	0.51174
Employment in Secondary Industry as Percentage of Total Employment	0.03662	0.02284	0.02063	1.10711
Employment in Tertiary Industry as Percentage of Total Employment	1.00000	−0.15190	0.03097	4.90544
Literacy Rate	0.03494	0.06195	0.06056	1.02297
Overall Productivity	0.21863	−0.00009	0.00004	2.35135
Primary Industry Value-added Per Worker	0.07917	−0.00004	0.00002	1.71429
Secondary Industry Value-added Per Worker	0.18367	−0.00002	0.00001	2.00000
Tertiary Industry Value-added Per Worker	0.99996	−0.00015	0.00003	4.38235
Road Density	1.00000	0.72957	0.13929	5.23795
Length of Road Per Capita	0.02424	−0.00521	0.01203	0.43301
Government Consumption Expenditure as Percentage of GRDP	0.99996	0.41966	0.08587	4.88716
Old Dependency Ratio	0.02482	0.04029	0.05927	0.67980

Notes: Those highlighted in yellow are considered robust determinants for growth slowdown in the combined group of upper-middle-income and high-income economies as they satisfy the two criteria simultaneously: (i) the posterior inclusion probability (PIP) exceeds the prior inclusion probability (i.e. $\frac{3}{17} = 0.17647$), and (ii) the ratio of conditional posterior mean to conditional posterior standard deviation is larger than 1.65 in absolute value, which corresponds to a 90 percent coverage interval under Gaussian posterior parameter distribution.
Source: Asia Competitiveness Institute

Table 3.12: BMA Result (II) for the Combined Group of Upper-Middle-Income and High-Income Economies

Determinants	Posterior Inclusion Probability (PIP)	Posterior Mean	Posterior Standard Deviation (PSTD)	Posterior Mean / PSTD
GRDP Per Capita	0.99998	0.00078	0.00014	5.63309
Total Dependency Ratio	0.05467	−0.04782	0.03672	1.30227
Openness to Trade	0.02569	−0.00181	0.00230	0.78472
Percentage Change in Nominal Exchange Rate	0.16702	−0.01240	0.00726	1.70756
World Gross Domestic Product Real Growth Rate	0.04764	0.19307	0.14079	1.37131
FDI Inflows as Percentage of GRDP	0.03552	−0.02699	0.02568	1.05081
Employment in Secondary Industry as Percentage of Total Employment	0.02115	−0.00380	0.02091	0.18150
Employment in Tertiary Industry as Percentage of Total Employment	0.20822	−0.05732	0.02624	2.18438
Literacy Rate	0.02056	−0.00564	0.06622	0.08515
Overall Productivity	0.99953	−0.00024	0.00005	5.22222
Road Density	1.00000	0.55152	0.10345	5.33114
Length of Road Per Capita	0.02133	−0.00254	0.01219	0.20866
Secondary Industry Value-added as Percentage of GRDP	0.06572	−0.02682	0.01872	1.43279
Tertiary Industry Value-added as Percentage of GRDP	0.99937	−0.10876	0.02273	4.78558
Government Consumption Expenditure as Percentage of GRDP	0.99939	0.37034	0.07734	4.78842
Old Dependency Ratio	0.02357	0.03587	0.05495	0.65280

Notes: Those highlighted in yellow are considered robust determinants for growth slowdown in the combined group of upper-middle-income and high-income economies as they satisfy the two criteria simultaneously: (i) The posterior inclusion probability (PIP) exceeds the prior inclusion probability (i.e. $\frac{3}{16} = 0.18750$), and (ii) the ratio of conditional posterior mean to conditional posterior standard deviation is larger than 1.65 in absolute value, which corresponds to a 90 percent coverage interval under Gaussian posterior parameter distribution.

Source: Asia Competitiveness Institute

Table 3.13: BMA Result (III) for the Combined Group of Upper-Middle-Income and High-Income Economies

Determinants	Posterior Inclusion Probability (PIP)	Posterior Mean	Posterior Standard Deviation (PSTD)	Posterior Mean / PSTD
GRDP Per Capita	0.99876	0.00071	0.00014	4.93056
Total Dependency Ratio	0.10938	−0.06037	0.03222	1.87374
Openness to Trade	0.02969	−0.00237	0.00241	0.98218
Percentage Change in Nominal Exchange Rate	0.09032	−0.01107	0.00782	1.41635
World Gross Domestic Product Real Growth Rate	0.03916	0.18080	0.14454	1.25085
FDI Inflows as Percentage of GRDP	0.05383	−0.03809	0.02627	1.44978
Literacy Rate	0.02926	0.05384	0.06011	0.89569
Overall Productivity	0.99686	−0.00022	0.00005	4.71739
Primary Industry Value-added Per Worker	0.01876	0.00000	0.00002	0.20000
Secondary Industry Value-added Per Worker	0.01938	0.00000	0.00001	0.16667
Tertiary Industry Value-added Per Worker	0.01988	0.00002	0.00004	0.41026
Road Density	1.00000	0.58675	0.11090	5.29069
Length of Road Per Capita	0.03187	−0.01070	0.01042	1.02707
Secondary Industry Value-added as Percentage of GRDP	0.02545	−0.01341	0.01715	0.78177
Tertiary Industry Value-added as Percentage of GRDP	0.99999	−0.12373	0.02311	5.35436
Government Consumption Expenditure as Percentage of GRDP	0.99990	0.41049	0.08471	4.84605
Old Dependency Ratio	0.01877	0.01127	0.05695	0.19795

Notes: Those highlighted in yellow are considered robust determinants for growth slowdown in the combined group of upper-middle-income and high-income economies as they satisfy the two criteria simultaneously: (i) the posterior inclusion probability (PIP) exceeds the prior inclusion probability (i.e. $\frac{3}{17} = 0.17647$), and (ii) the ratio of conditional posterior mean to conditional posterior standard deviation is larger than 1.65 in absolute value, which corresponds to a 90 percent coverage interval under Gaussian posterior parameter distribution.
Source: Asia Competitiveness Institute

3.6.3 Predictive Probability of Growth Slowdown for ASEAN Economies

Using our income group-specific logistic models, we compute predictive probabilities of near-future slowdown for the economies in ASEAN, Greater China, India and Indonesia. The predictive probability for an economy is computed using its 2012 data for the relevant determinants (see Section 3.4.6 for details). It is illustrative of the risk that the economy will experience growth slowdown in the 5 years following 2012, or the period 2012–2017: the higher the probability, the higher the likelihood of growth slowdown.

Figure 3.5 shows the scatterplot of the predictive probabilities for 107 economies in ASEAN, Greater China, India and Indonesia against the initial level of GRDP per capita in 1990 PPP dollars of each economy at the start of the prediction period in 2012. In general, upper-middle-income and high-income economies have higher probabilities of slowdown than lower-middle-income economies, which in turn are more likely to slow down than economies in the low-income group. In addition, within each income group, the likelihood of slowdown seems to increase with GRDP per capita level, as evident in the upward sloping trend line. Interestingly, the rate of increase is not uniform across income groups. The likelihood of slowdown seems to increase at decreasing rates as an economy graduates from one income group to another.

The next paragraph discusses in detail the predictive probabilities for ASEAN. For completeness, we have also calculated predictive probabilities using the probit specifications reported in Appendix 6. These probabilities are provided in Appendix 7.

By 2012, there are five lower-middle-income economies, two upper-middle-income economies and one high-income economy in ASEAN.[36] As seen in Figure 3.6, the regional average predictive probability of growth slowdown is 0.20890, indicating that on average, ASEAN economies have a 21 percent chance of experiencing growth slowdown in the 2012–2017 period. The average probability for the lower-middle-income economies is even lower at 0.14007 while the average probability for the combined group of upper-middle-income and high-income economies is higher at 0.32362. Singapore is the economy most likely to slow down in the region, yet its probability of slowdown is still less than 0.5.

The specific predictive probability for each ASEAN economy is displayed in Table 3.14. Among the lower-middle-income economies, Vietnam has the lowest probability of experiencing growth slowdown in the period 2012–2017 at 0.05736 while Indonesia has the highest probability at 0.26102. Meanwhile, among the upper-middle-income and high-income economies, Singapore has the highest probability at 0.44545 while Malaysia has the lowest probability at 0.22063.

ASEAN's low regional average probability of growth slowdown is impressive as compared to the prospects of economies in Greater China and India. The average predictive probability for the Greater China economies is 0.56872 while the average for the India subnational economies is 0.43071.[37] Thus, on average, ASEAN economies are less at risk of experiencing growth slowdown than the two giants. Building on strengths and improving on weaknesses of each ASEAN economy will help to further reduce the risk of growth slowdown.

[36] Brunei's GRDP per capita in 1990 PPP dollars are not available throughout the study period while Laos' GRDP per capita in 1990 PPP dollars are not available from 2009 onwards.

[37] See Tan, Wang, and Xie (2017, *forthcoming*) and Tan, Gopalan, Tandon, and Tan (2017, *forthcoming*).

Figure 3.5: Scatterplot Showing Predictive Probabilities of Growth Slowdown for Economies in ASEAN, Greater China, Indonesia and India for the Period 2012–2017 (Based on Income Group-Specific Logistic Models)

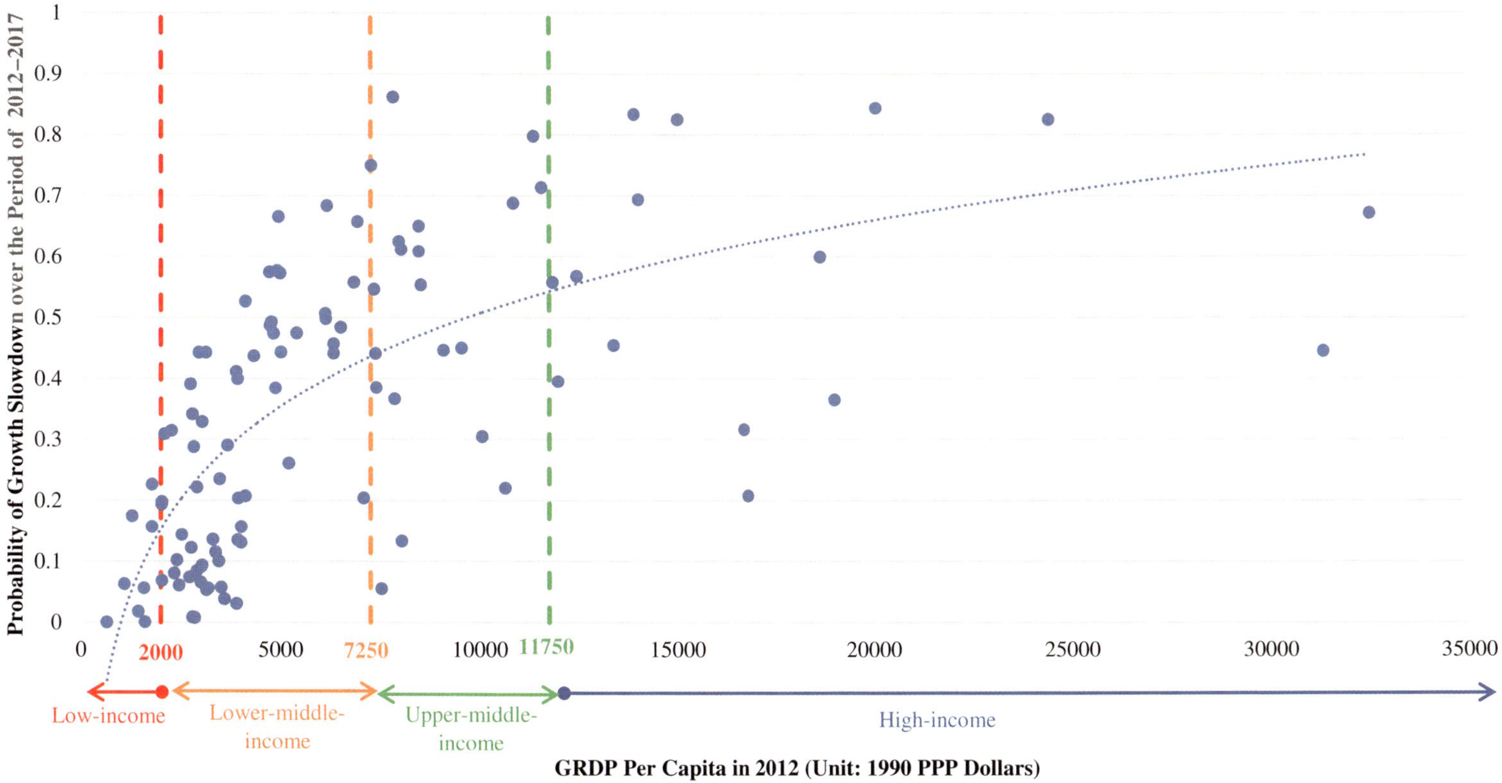

Source: Asia Competitiveness Institute

Figure 3.6: Bar Chart Showing Predictive Probabilities of Growth Slowdown for ASEAN Economies for the Period 2012–2017 (Based on Income Group-Specific Logistic Models)

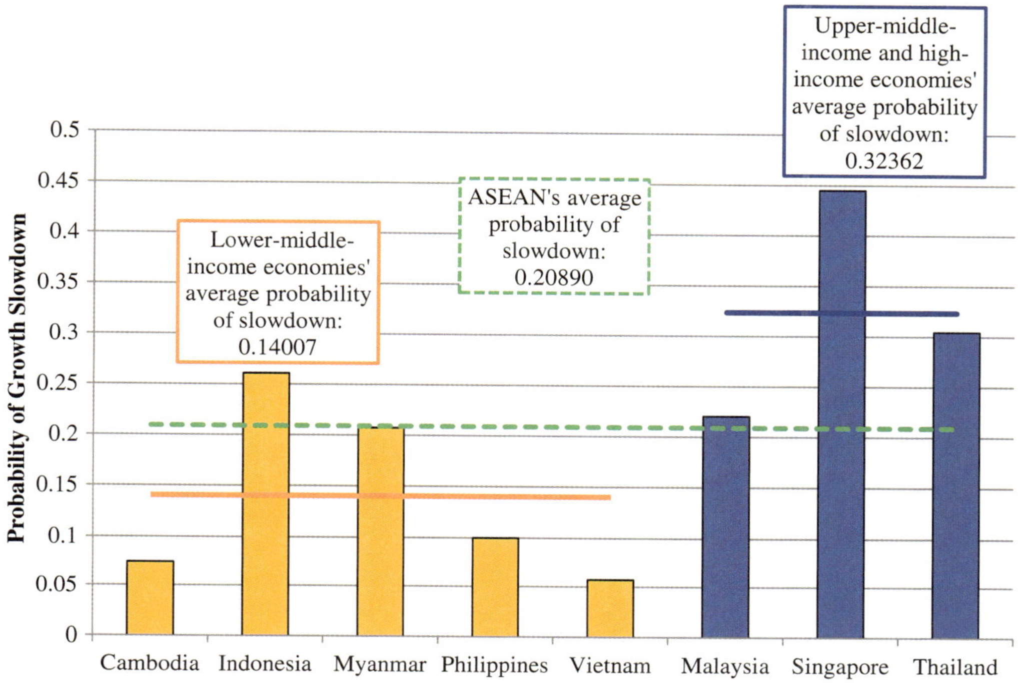

Notes: (i) Predictive probabilities for Brunei and Laos are not generated. This is because Brunei's GRDP per capita in 1990 PPP dollars are not available throughout the study period while Laos' GRDP per capita in 1990 PPP dollars are not available from 2009 onwards. (ii) Averages reported are simple averages
Source: Asia Competitiveness Institute

Table 3.14: Predictive Probabilities of Growth Slowdown for ASEAN Economies for the Period 2012–2017 (Based on Income Group-Specific Logistic Models)

Economy	Income Group Which Economy Belongs to in 2012	Probability of Experiencing Growth Slowdown during 2012–2017
Cambodia	Lower-middle-income	0.07425
Indonesia	Lower-middle-income	0.26102
Malaysia	Upper-middle-income	0.22063
Myanmar	Lower-middle-income	0.20748
Philippines	Lower-middle-income	0.10023
Singapore	High-income	0.44545
Thailand	Upper-middle-income	0.30479
Vietnam	Lower-middle-income	0.05736
	Average	0.20890

Notes: (i) Predictive probabilities for Brunei and Laos are not generated. This is because Brunei's GRDP per capita in 1990 PPP dollars are not available throughout the study period while Laos' GRDP per capita in 1990 PPP dollars are not available from 2009 onwards. (ii) Average reported is simple average.
Source: Asia Competitiveness Institute

3.7 Relative Strengths and Weaknesses for ASEAN Economies

Equipped with the knowledge of the general risk level of each economy experiencing growth slowdown at its respective level of development as illustrated by the predictive probability results in Section 3.6.3, it would be meaningful if we could pinpoint the relative strengths and weaknesses of each economy, thereby aid policy-makers to identify areas in which further improvement could be made to reduce the risks of growth slowdown. To this end, we compute the standardised score for each economy in terms of the determinants of growth slowdown for the income groups they belong to. Standardised scores are calculated for all determinants of growth slowdown with the exception of the control variable GRDP per capita.

Formally, the standardised score for determinant D of economy E which is in income group I is defined as $\textit{Standardised score}_{D,E,I} = \frac{X_{D,E,I} - \bar{X}_{D,I}}{SD_{D,I}}$, where $X_{D,E,I}$ is the value of determinant D of economy E which is in income group I, $\bar{X}_{D,I}$ is the mean value of determinant D for all economies within the income group I, and $SD_{D,I}$ is the standard deviation of determinant D for all economies within the income group I. The mean value of determinant D for all economies within the income group I is defined as $\bar{X}_{D,I} = \frac{1}{N}\sum_{e=1}^{N} X_{D,e,I}$, where N is the total number of economies within the income group I. The standard deviation of determinant D for all economies within the income group I is defined as $SD_{D,I} = \sqrt{\frac{1}{N}\sum_{i=1}^{N}\left(X_{D,E,I} - \bar{X}_{D,I}\right)^2}$. For all determinants except for old dependency ratio, a high value of $X_{D,E,I}$ would indicate a high $\textit{Standardised score}_{D,E,I}$. In contrast, we reverse score old dependency ratio so that the standardised score is low if the original value of the ratio is high. This is because unlike the other determinants, high old dependency ratio is associated with increasing likelihood of growth slowdown.

Constructed in the manner described above, the standardised scores reflect the gaps between the economy's performance and the average performance of other economies in the same income group. If the standardised score of an economy is zero, it means that the economy is an average performer within its income group. On the other hand, if the standardised score is negative, it implies that the economy is performing more poorly than others, while positive standardised score indicates better than average performance. The further away the standardised score is from zero, the further away is the performance of said economy from the average of that particular income group. For instance, a large negative standardised score means very poor performance, while a large positive standardised score denotes very strong performance.

Figures 3.7–3.14 are web charts displaying the standardised scores of ASEAN economies in terms of the determinants of growth slowdown (with the exception of GRDP per capita). The larger the area under each economy's line, the better its performance in the particular dimension considered. To provide a better sense of the relative strengths and weaknesses of each economy, we also benchmark their standardised scores against the median scores and maximum scores of the income group they belong to. All data used in generating these web charts are as of 2012. The dimensions/determinants chosen to be considered for each economy depend on the income group to which the economy belongs in the same year.

Cambodia

Lower-middle-income economy

Figure 3.7 shows the relative strengths and weaknesses of Cambodia which was a lower-middle-income economy in 2012 according to the income classification we adopt. As discussed in Section 3.6.1, four determinants are associated with growth slowdown in this particular income group, namely Old Dependency Ratio, Literacy Rate, FDI Inflows as Percentage of GRDP and Employment in Tertiary Industry as Percentage of Total Employment. The purple solid line shows the standardised score for Cambodia. The red dashed line represents the median score of all economies in the lower-middle-income group across ASEAN, Greater China, India and Indonesia, while the green dotted line denotes the maximum score of those economies.

Cambodia performed better than the median scores of the lower-middle-income group in terms of Old Dependency Ratio and FDI Inflows as Percentage of GRDP. However, Cambodia's standardised scores for these determinants were still some way below the maximum scores as achieved by Papua and Sulawesi Tengah, signalling possible areas for improvement. Meanwhile, Cambodia's most significant weakness seems to be Literacy Rate.[38] Its standardised score for this determinant was −1.0986, much lower than the median score of the lower-middle-income group at 0.4026. Thus, it is advisable for Cambodia to do more in improving access to basic

Figure 3.7: Cambodia's Strengths and Weaknesses

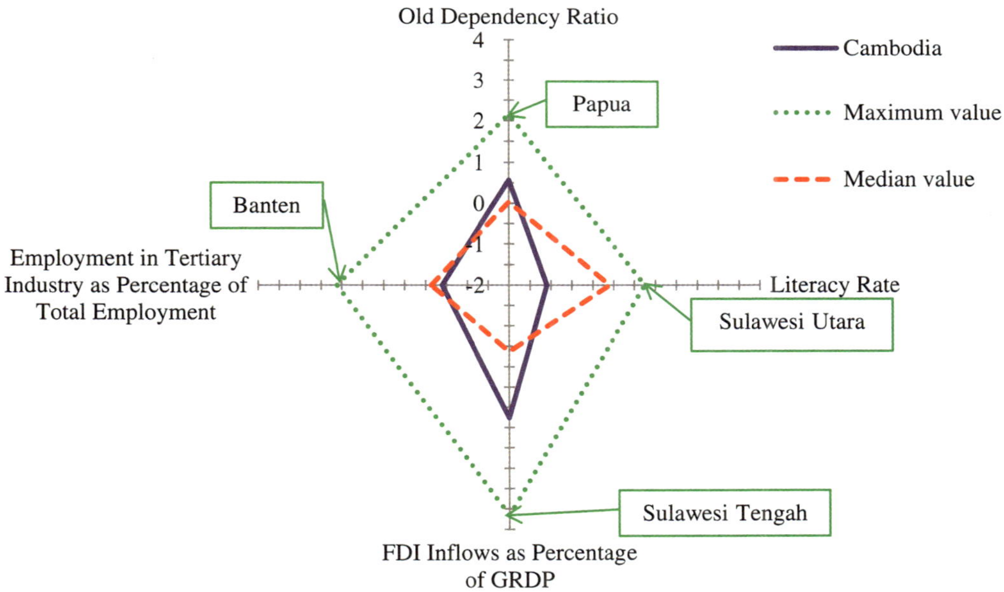

Source: Asia Competitiveness Institute

[38]As of 2012, Cambodia's literacy rate was 75.5 percent (*Source*: Euromonitor Passport).

education. In addition, Cambodia's labour share in tertiary industry was relatively low as compared to other lower-middle-income economies. The standardised score of Cambodia for Employment in Tertiary Industry as Percentage of Total Employment at –0.3938 was lower than the median score of the lower-middle-income group at –0.1334. Developing its tertiary industries is also a strategy policy-makers in Cambodia can consider to undertake.

Indonesia

Lower-middle-income economy

Figure 3.8 shows the relative strengths and weaknesses of Indonesia which was a lower-middle-income economy in 2012 according to the income classification we adopt. As discussed in Section 3.6.1, four determinants are associated with growth slowdown in this particular income group, namely Old Dependency Ratio, Literacy Rate, FDI Inflows as Percentage of GRDP and Employment in Tertiary Industry as Percentage of Total Employment. The purple solid line shows the standardised score for Indonesia. The red dashed line represents the median score of all economies in the lower-middle-income group across ASEAN, Greater China, India and Indonesia, while the green dotted line denotes the maximum score of those economies. Incidentally, the maximum scores for all four determinants were set by Indonesian sub-national economies. Thus, aside from showcasing Indonesia's strengths and weaknesses, Figure 3.8 also provides an interesting comparison of Indonesia as a national economy with some of its most high-performing sub-national lower-middle-income economies.

Figure 3.8: Indonesia's Strengths and Weaknesses

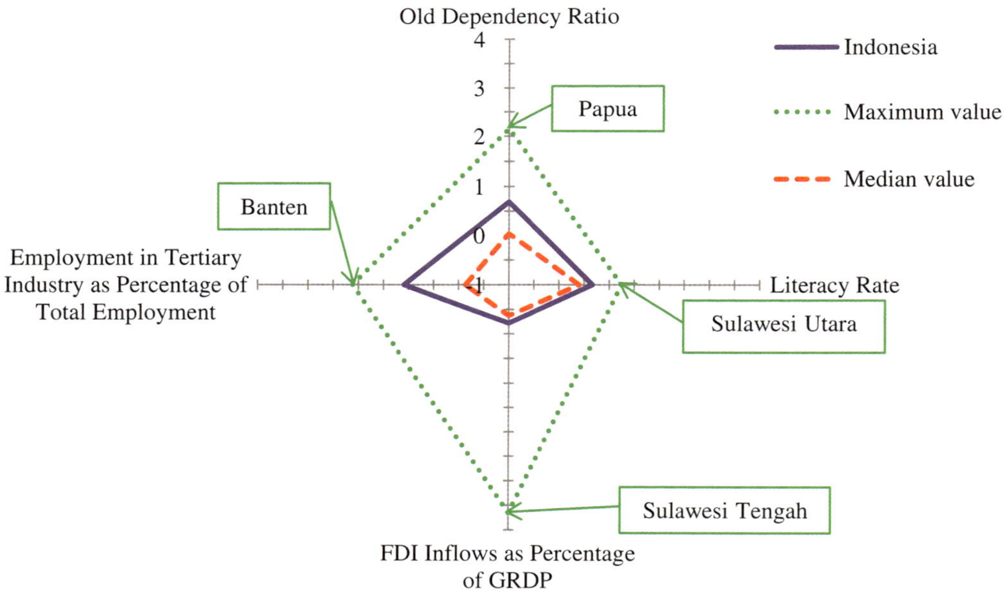

Source: Asia Competitiveness Institute

In general, Indonesia performed better than the median scores of the lower-middle-income group in all determinants considered. Nevertheless, there were still relatively big gaps between Indonesia's standardised scores and the respective maximum scores, signalling areas for improvement. Specifically, Indonesia's score for FDI Inflows as Percentage of GRDP stood at –0.2167, much lower than the maximum score of 3.6549 as achieved by Sulawesi Tengah. The performance gap between Indonesia as a national economy and Sulawesi Tengah suggests that Indonesia not only needs to step up its efforts to attract FDIs but must also seek to ensure that more of its sub-national economies can benefit from the inflows. FDI brings in much-needed capital, advanced technology and managerial expertise which will help Indonesia to achieve continued economic growth.

Malaysia

Upper-middle-income economy

Figure 3.9 shows the relative strengths and weaknesses of Malaysia which was an upper-middle-income economy in 2012 according to the income classification we adopt. As mentioned in Section 3.4.2, due to data constraint, we have combined the analysis of high-income economies with that of the upper-middle-income economies. Four determinants are associated with growth slowdown in this combined group of upper-middle-income and high-income economies, namely Openness to Trade, Literacy Rate, Secondary Industry Value-Added per Worker and Employment in Tertiary Industry as Percentage of Total Employment. The purple solid line shows the

Figure 3.9: Malaysia's Strengths and Weaknesses

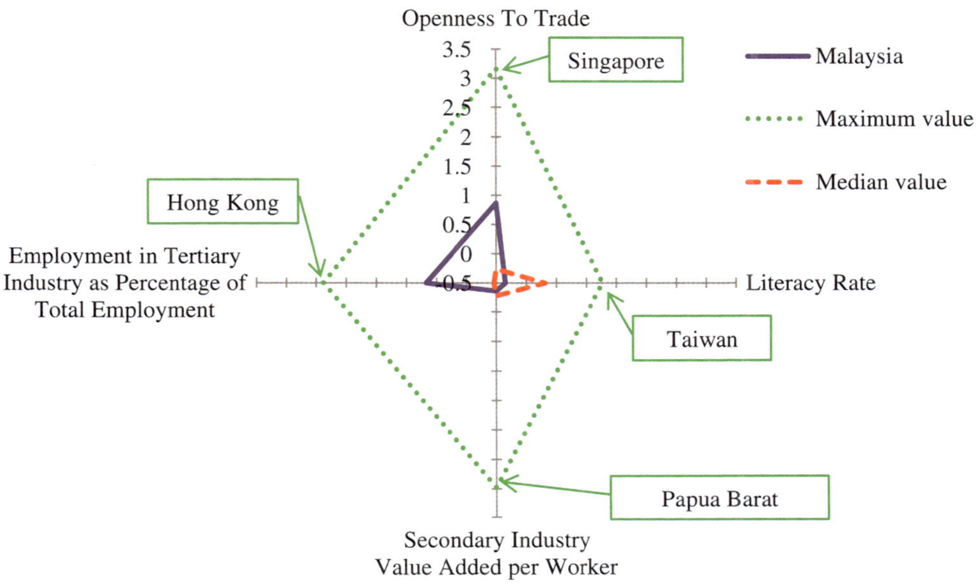

Source: Asia Competitiveness Institute

standardised score for Malaysia. The red dashed line represents the median score of all economies in the combined group of upper-middle-income and high-income economies across ASEAN, Greater China, India and Indonesia, while the green dotted line denotes the maximum score of those economies.

Malaysia performed better than the median scores of the combined group of upper-middle-income and high-income economies in terms of Openness to Trade and Employment in Tertiary Industry as Percentage of Total Employment. However, Malaysia's standardised scores for these determinants were still much smaller than the maximum scores as achieved by Singapore and Hong Kong, signalling possible areas for improvement. One notable weakness of the Malaysian economy was that productivity in its secondary industry was low. Malaysia's score for Secondary Industry Value Added per Worker is –0.3592 which was lower than the median score of the combined group of upper-middle-income and high-income economies at –0.2771. This suggests that Malaysia needs to do more in terms of productivity enhancement in order to mitigate the risks of slowing down.

Myanmar

Lower-middle-income economy

Figure 3.10 shows the relative strengths and weaknesses of Myanmar which was a lower-middle-income economy in 2012 according to the income classification we adopt. As discussed in Section 3.6.1, four determinants are associated with growth slowdown in this particular income group, namely Old Dependency Ratio, Literacy Rate, FDI Inflows as Percentage of GRDP and

Figure 3.10: Myanmar's Strengths and Weaknesses

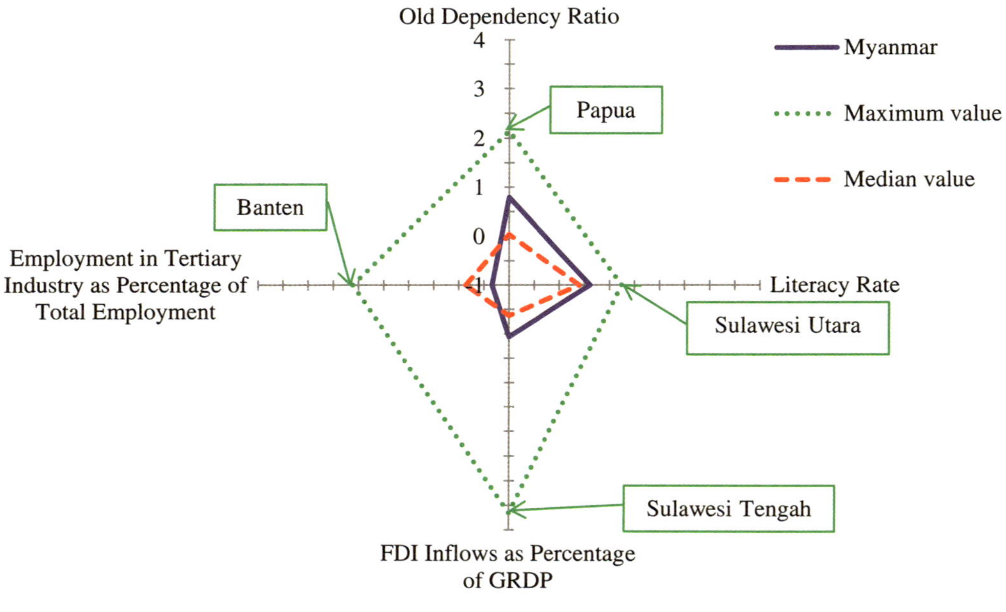

Source: Asia Competitiveness Institute

Employment in Tertiary Industry as Percentage of Total Employment. The purple solid line shows the standardised score for Myanmar. The red dashed line represents the median score of all economies in the lower-middle-income group across ASEAN, Greater China, India and Indonesia, while the green dotted line denotes the maximum score of those economies.

In general, Myanmar performed better than the median scores of the lower-middle-income group in all determinants considered except for Employment in Tertiary Industry as Percentage of Total Employment. Myanmar's standardised score for this determinant was –0.6578 which was lower than the median score at –0.1334. Thus, the economy may look to further develop its tertiary industries, especially the tourism sector which has great potential, but remains relatively underdeveloped. Furthermore, as Figure 3.10 demonstrates, though Myanmar's standardised scores for Literacy Rate and FDI Inflows as Percentage of GRDP were higher than the respective median scores, they were still much smaller than the maximum scores of the lower-middle-income group. As the country undergoes democratic transition, it is hoped that economic development will take priority and Myanmar will be able to enjoy sustained growth in the years to come.

Philippines

Lower-middle-income economy

Figure 3.11 shows the relative strengths and weaknesses of Philippines which was a lower-middle-income economy in 2012 according to the income classification we adopt. As discussed in Section 3.6.1, four determinants are associated with growth slowdown in this particular

Figure 3.11: Philippines' Strengths and Weaknesses

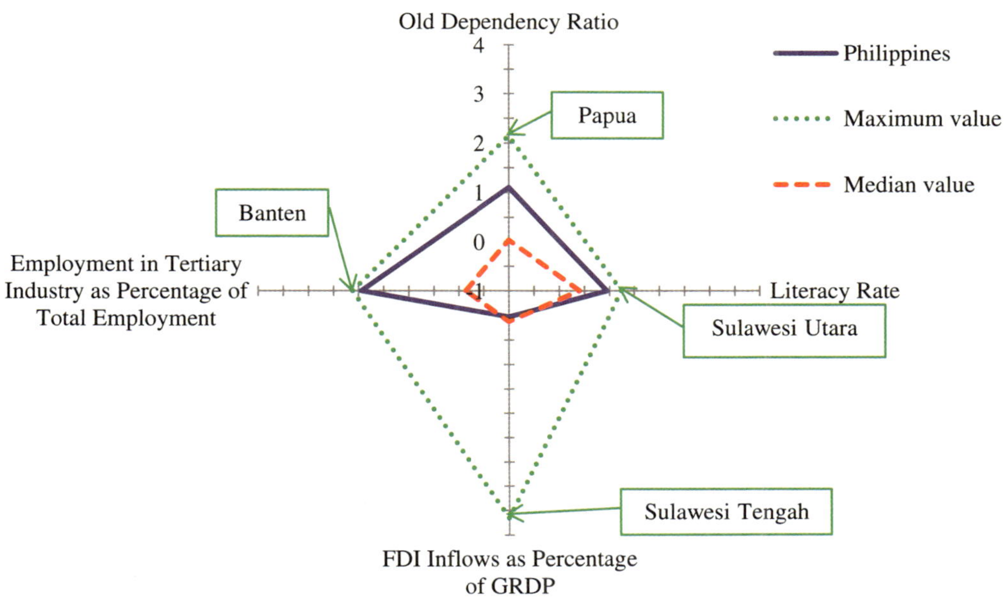

Source: Asia Competitiveness Institute

income group, namely Old Dependency Ratio, Literacy Rate, FDI Inflows as Percentage of GRDP and Employment in Tertiary Industry as Percentage of Total Employment. The purple solid line shows the standardised score for Philippines. The red dashed line represents the median score of all economies in the lower-middle-income group across ASEAN, Greater China, India and Indonesia, while the green dotted line denotes the maximum score of those economies.

In general, Philippines performed better than the median scores of the lower-middle-income group in all determinants considered except for FDI Inflows as Percentage of GRDP. In particular, Philippines' standardised scores for Literacy Rate and Employment in Tertiary Industry as Percentage of Total Employment, at 0.9498 and 1.9401, respectively, were relatively close to the maximum scores as achieved by Sulawesi Utara and Banten. This testifies to Philippines' achievement in widening access to basic education and illustrates the importance of the service sector to the Philippines' economy. However, Philippines' standardised score for FDI Inflows as Percentage of GRDP was –0.4737, lower than the median score of the lower-middle-income group at –0.3720. Thus, attracting FDI seems to be a weakness of the Philippines economy and it should step up its effort in this aspect.

Singapore

High-income economy

Figure 3.12 shows the relative strengths and weaknesses of Singapore which was a high-middle-income economy in 2012 according to the income classification we adopt. As mentioned in

Figure 3.12: Singapore's Strengths and Weaknesses

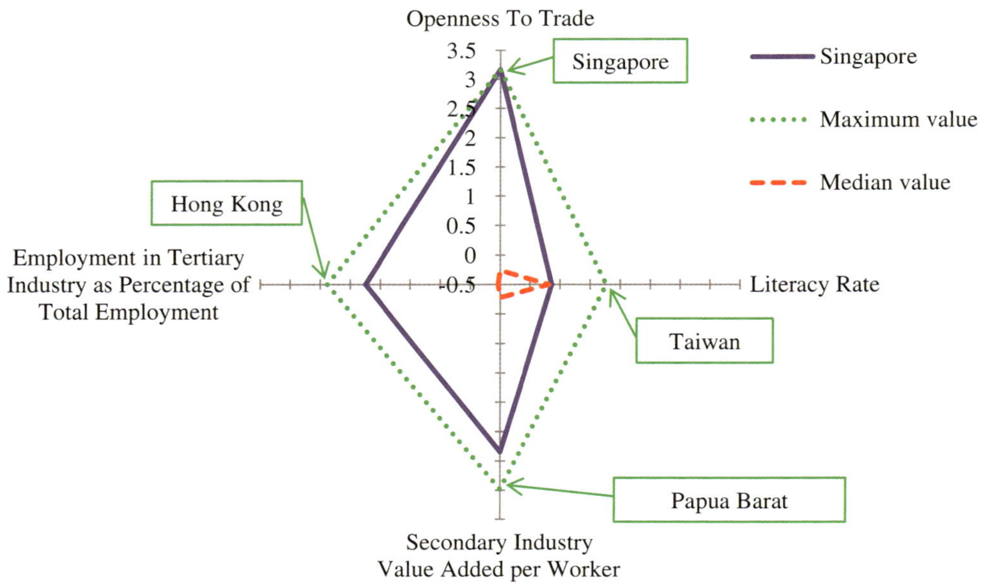

Source: Asia Competitiveness Institute

Section 3.4.2, due to data constraint, we have combined the analysis of high-income economies with that of the upper-middle-income economies. Four determinants are associated with growth slowdown in this combined group of upper-middle-income and high-income economies, namely Openness to Trade, Literacy Rate, Secondary Industry Value Added per Worker and Employment in Tertiary Industry as Percentage of Total Employment. The purple solid line shows the standardised score for Singapore. The red dashed line represents the median score of all economies in the combined group of upper-middle-income and high-income economies across ASEAN, Greater China, India and Indonesia, while the green dotted line denotes the maximum score of those economies.

In general, Singapore performed well in all determinants considered. At 3.1663, its standardised score for Openness to Trade was the maximum score of the combined group of upper-middle-income and high-income economies for this determinant. Furthermore, even though Singapore's standardised score for Secondary Industry Value Added per Worker and Employment in Tertiary Industry as Percentage of Total Employment were below the respective maximum scores as set by Papua Barat and Hong Kong, the economy still ranked second and third respectively in these dimensions. However, Singapore's standardised score for Literacy Rate at 0.3574 was only slightly higher than the median score of the combined group of upper-middle-income and high-income economies at 0.3131.[39] Going forward, boosting productivity still remains a key task for Singapore if it is to enjoy continued growth, especially given the economy's constraints in terms of labour force and natural resource endowments.

Thailand

Upper-middle-income economy

Figure 3.13 shows the relative strengths and weaknesses of Thailand which was an upper-middle-income economy in 2012 according to the income classification we adopt. As mentioned in Section 3.4.2, due to data constraint, we have combined the analysis of high-income economies with that of the upper-middle-income economies. Four determinants are associated with growth slowdown in this combined group of upper-middle-income and high-income economies, namely Openness to Trade, Literacy Rate, Secondary Industry Value Added per Worker and Employment in Tertiary Industry as Percentage of Total Employment. The purple solid line shows the standardised score for Thailand. The red dashed line represents the median score of all economies in the combined group of upper-middle-income and high-income economies across ASEAN, Greater China, India and Indonesia, while the green dotted line denotes the maximum score of those economies.

Relative to other upper-middle-income and high-income economies in ASEAN, Greater China, India and Indonesia, Thailand performed well in terms of Openness to Trade as its

[39] This is largely because literacy rates in upper-middle-income and high-income economies are in general high. In 2012, Singapore's literacy rate was 96.4 percent while the average literacy rate of the combined group of upper-middle-income and high-income economies was 95.03 percent (*Source*: Euromonitor Passport database and Asia Competitiveness Institute).

Figure 3.13: Thailand's Strengths and Weaknesses

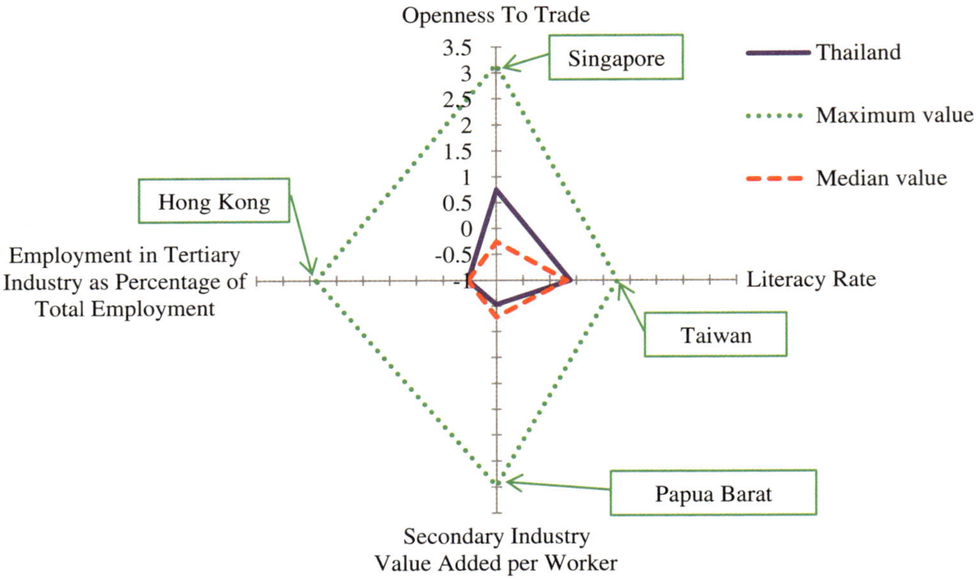

Source: Asia Competitiveness Institute

standardised score was above the median score for this determinant. Meanwhile, Thailand's score for Employment in Tertiary Industry as Percentage of Total Employment was also the median of the combined group of upper-middle-income and high-income economies for this determinant, indicating decent performance of the Thai economy in this aspect. However, similar to Malaysia, the main weakness of the Thai economy seem to be low productivity in its secondary industry. Thailand's standardised score for Secondary Industry Value Added per Worker was –0.5287, lower than the median score of the combined group of upper-middle-income and high-income economies at –0.2771. Thus, enhancing productivity should be one of the priorities for Thai policy-makers in order to reduce the risks of growth slowdown in the coming years.

Vietnam

Lower-middle-income economy

Figure 3.14 shows the relative strengths and weaknesses of Vietnam which was a lower-middle-income economy in 2012 according to the income classification we adopt. As discussed in Section 3.6.1, we found four determinants which are associated with growth slowdown in this particular income group, namely Old Dependency Ratio, Literacy Rate, FDI Inflows as Percentage of GRDP and Employment in Tertiary Industry as Percentage of Total Employment. The purple solid line shows the standardised score for Vietnam. The red dashed line represents the median score of all economies in the lower-middle-income group across ASEAN, Greater

Figure 3.14: Vietnam's Strengths and Weaknesses

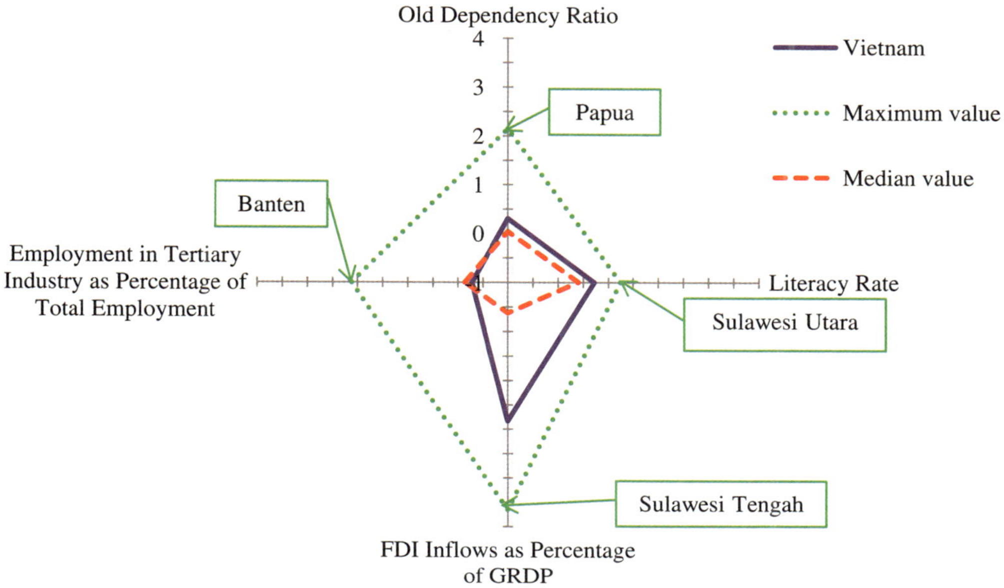

Source: Asia Competitiveness Institute

China, India and Indonesia, while the green dotted line denotes the maximum score of those economies.

Figure 3.14 shows that Vietnam has done particularly well in terms of attracting FDI as compared to other lower-middle-income economy. Its standardised score for FDI Inflows as Percentage of GRDP, at 1.8334, was higher than the median score of the lower-middle-income group (at –0.3720). Literacy Rate is another dimension in which Vietnam has performed commendably though there are rooms for improvement: its standardised score for this determinant was higher than the median but still some way below the maximum score as achieved by Sulawesi Utara.[40] However, relative to other lower-middle-income economies, Vietnam has low employment share in the tertiary sector. The economy's standardised score for Employment in Tertiary Industry as Percentage of Total Employment is only –0.2776, lower than the median score of the middle-income group at –0.1334. As pointed out in Section 3.6.1, the tertiary industry can be an important engine of continued economic growth, firstly because it directly creates more sustainable growth opportunities and secondly because high-value added service sectors such as research and development, financial services and consultancy can create positive spillovers for other sectors of the economy. Thus, it may be advisable for Vietnam to further develop its tertiary industry.

[40] Actual literacy rate for Vietnam in 2012 was 93.6 percent (*Source*: Euromonitor Passport).

3.8 Policy Implications and Concluding Notes

Over the past 50 years, robust economic growth across the 10 ASEAN countries has lifted millions out of poverty and raised the living standards of people in Southeast Asia. However, further development. The spectre of the middle-income trap has been discussed by many pundits given the persistence of external and domestic challenges to growth. Against this backdrop, our research is conducted to examine the growth slowdown likelihood in ASEAN, benchmarking them against Greater China economies and the sub-national economies in India and Indonesia. As differed from existing literature on middle-income trap and growth slowdown, we are more comprehensive and study all ASEAN economies for which data are available.

We found that despite a general increase in the level of GRDP per capita for the ASEAN economies since we started to track them in 1960, disparity still exists across economies. According to the income thresholds classification we adopt, there was only one ASEAN economy in the high-income group by 2014, namely Singapore. Conversely, Malaysia and Thailand attained the upper-middle-income status. The rest of the five economies are in the lower-middle-income group as of 2014.

By conducting both logistics and probit estimations as well as employing the BMA techniques, we found that growth slowdown in various income groups tend to be associated with different sets of determinants. Lower-middle-income economies are more likely to experience growth slowdown when they have higher levels of GRDP per capita, lower FDI Inflows as Percentage of GRDP, higher Old Dependency Ratio, lower Employment in Tertiary Industry as Percentage of Total Employment and lower Literacy Rate. On the other hand, growth slowdown in the combined group of upper-middle-income and high-income economies is associated with high GRDP per capita, low Openness to Trade, low Literacy Rate, low Employment in Tertiary Industry as Percentage of Total Employment and low Secondary Industry Value added per Worker. Clearly, there is no one-size-fits-all approach to growth and development. Policy-makers should therefore take into account the different challenges an economy may face at different development levels in the design and implementation of policies.

Having identified the underlying drivers of growth slowdown in each income group, we assess whether each ASEAN economy is prone to experience growth deceleration. Overall, we discovered that the ASEAN economies have a relatively optimistic near-future prospects. ASEAN economies only have a 21 percent chance of experiencing growth slowdown in the 2012–2017 period on average. ASEAN's low regional average probability of growth slowdown is even more impressive if set in comparison with the prospects of economies in Greater China and India.[41] Among the ASEAN economies, Singapore, which is the only high-income economy in the region, is the most likely to slow down. However, its probability of slowdown is still less than 0.5.

The outcomes from our analysis corresponds to the optimistic forecasts on ASEAN at which the economic bloc is projected to be the fourth largest single economy by 2030.[42] Despite the

[41] The average predictive probabilities of Greater China and India economies are 0.56872 and 0.43071, respectively.

[42] See J.P. Morgan's article on ASEAN https://www.jpmorgan.com/country/US/EN/cib/investment-banking/trade-asean-future and McKinsey's article on ASEAN http://www.mckinsey.com/industries/public-sector/our-insights/understanding-asean-seven-things-you-need-to-know (accessed on 25 March, 2017).

hopeful prospects, it is still important not to overlook any probability of slowdown in the near future. In particular, the prevailing global uncertainties may cause higher unpredictability in the domestic economy. Therefore, the ASEAN economies should continue to exploit their advantages and overcome their structural shortfalls in order to maintain the positive growth momentum. In this respect, our analysis which details relative strengths and weaknesses of each ASEAN economy provides an instructive roadmap for impactful policy-making. To forge ahead as a single entity, ASEAN has to recognise the disparities and differences among the member states and to tailor the policy directions accordingly. Besides, peer-learning both within and outside the bloc is imperative in formulating policies to combat the risk of growth slowdown.

References

Abbas, S. Ali, Nazim Belhocine, Asmaa ElGanainy, and Mark Horton. 2010. "A Historical Public Debt Database." IMF Working Paper No. 10/425, International Monetary Fund (IMF), Washington D.C.

Agenor, Pierre-Richard. 2015. "Caught in the Middle? The Economics of Middle-Income Trap", FERDI Working Paper No. 142, Fondation pour les études et recherches sur le développement international (FERDI), Clermont-Ferrand.

Aiyar, Shekhar, Romain Duval, Damien Puy, Yiqun Wu, and Longmei Zhang. 2013. "Growth Slowdowns and the Middle-Income Trap." IMF Working Paper No. 13/71. International Monetary Fund (IMF), Washington D.C.

Azariadis, Costas, and John Stachurski. 2005. "Poverty Traps." in *Handbook of Economic Growth*, edited by Philippe Aghion and Steven N. Durlauf, 1A: 295–384. Amsterdam: Elsevier.

Barro, Robert J., and Jong Wha Lee. 2013. "A New Data Set of Educational Attainment in the World, 1950–2010." *Journal of Development Economics* 104(C): 184–198.

Benkovskis, K., B. Bluhm, E. Bobeica, C. Osbat, and S. Zeugner. 2015. "An Empirical Analysis of Competitiveness Drivers Using Bayesian Model Averaging."

Bloom, David E., David Canning, and Jaypee Sevilla. 2003. "Geography and Poverty Traps." *Journal of Economic Growth* 8(4): 355–378.

Bluedorn, John, Rupa Duttagupta, Jaime Guajardo, and Petia Topalova. 2013. "Capital Flows Are Fickle: Anytime, Anywhere." IMF Working Paper No. 13/183. International Monetary Fund (IMF), Washington D.C.

Brock, William. A., and Steven Durlauf. 2001. "What Have We Learned from a Decade of Empirical Research on Growth? Growth Empirics and Reality." *The World Bank Economic Review* 15(2): 229–272.

Bulman, David, Maya Eden, and Ha Nguyen. 2014. "Transitioning from Low-Income Growth to High-Income Growth: Is There a Middle Income Trap?" The World Bank Policy Research Working Paper No. 7104, World Bank, Washington D.C.

Dehn, Jan. 2014. "The High Income Trap." *The Emerging View*, available at https://www. ashmoregroup. com/sites/default/files/article-docs/June14HighInco metrap.pdf (accessed on 25 March, 2016).

Eichengreen, Barry, Donghyun Park, and Kwanho Shin. 2012. "When Fast-Growing Economies Slow Down: International Evidence and Implications for China." *Asian Economic Papers* 11: 42–87.

Eichengreen, Barry, Donghyun Park, and Kwanho Shin. 2013. "Growth Slowdowns Redux: New Evidence on the Middle-Income Trap." NBER Economic Research Paper Series No. 18673, National Bureau of Economic Research (NBER), Massachusetts.

Felipe, Jesus. 2012a. "Tracking the Middle-Income Trap: What Is It, Who Is in It, and Why? Part 1." ADB Working Paper No. 306, Asian Development Bank (ADB), Manila.

Felipe, Jesus. 2012b. "Tracking the Middle-Income Trap: What Is It, Who Is in It, and Why? Part 2." ADB Working Paper No. 307. Asian Development Bank (ADB), Manila.

Flaaen, Aaron, Ejaz Ghani, and Saurabh Mishra. 2013. "How to Avoid Middle Income Traps? Evidence from Malaysia." The World Bank Policy Research Working Papers No. 6427, World Bank, Washington D.C.

Gill, Indermit Singh, and Homi Kharas. 2007. *An East Asian Renaissance: Ideas for Economic Growth.* Washington D.C.: The World Bank.

Gill, Indermit Singh, and Homi Kharas. 2015. "The Middle-Income Trap Turns Ten", The World Bank Policy Research Working Paper No. 7403, World Bank, Washington D.C.

González-Aguado, Carlos, and Enrique Moral-Benito. 2013. "Determinants of Corporate Default: A BMA Approach." *Applied Economics Letters* 20(6): 511–514.

Hausmann, Ricardo, Lant Pritchett, and Dani Rodrik. 2005. "Growth Accelerations. Journal of Economic Growth." *Journal of Economic Growth* 10(4): 303–329.

Hausmann, Ricardo, Jason Hwang, and Dani Rodrik. 2005. "What you export matters". NBER Economic Research Paper Series No. 11905, National Bureau of Economic Research (NBER), Massachusetts.

Hausmann, Ricardo, Francisco Rodríguez, and Rodrigo Wagner. 2006. "Growth Collapses." 136. CID Working Paper No. 146, Center for International Development (CID), Massachusetts.

Im, Fernando Gabriel, and David Rosenblatt. 2013. "Middle-Income Traps: A Conceptual and Empirical Survey." The World Bank Policy Research Working Paper No. 6594, World Bank, Washington D.C.

Jalan, Jyotsna, and Martin Ravallion. 2002. "Geographic Poverty Traps? A Micro Model of Consumption Growth in Rural China." *Journal of Applied Econometrics* 17(4): 329–346.

Jerzmanowski, Michal. 2006. "Empirics of Hills, Plateaus, Mountains and Plains: A Markov-Switching Approach to Growth." *Journal of Development Economics* 81(2): 357–385.

Kasenda, Daniel. 2015. "Can Asian Developing Countries Stuck In A "Middle-Income Trap" Learn From South Korea's Economic Development Experience?", GDN Working Paper No. 86, Global Development Network (GDN), Washington D.C.

Kyozuka, Tamaki. 2016. "ASEAN Bloc's Exports Drop for First Time in 6 Years." *Nikkei Asian Review*, 24 February, available at http://asia.nikkei.com/Politics-Economy/Economy/ASEAN-bloc-s-exports-drop-for-first-time-in-6-years (accessed on 25 February, 2016).

Maddison, Angus. 2010. "*Statistics on World Population, GDP and Per Capita GDP, 1-2008AD.*", available at http://www.ggdc.net/maddison/oriindex.htm (accessed on 11 August, 2015).

Neumann, Frederic. 2015. "Time to Talk about the High Income Trap." *Nikkei Asian Review*, 24 May, available at http://asia.nikkei.com/Viewpoints/Economeister/Time-to-talk-about-the-high-income-trap (accessed on 23 February, 2016).

Ohno, Kenichi. 2009. "Avoiding the Middle-Income Trap: Renovating Industrial Policy Formulation in Vietnam." *ASEAN Economic Bulletin* 26(1): 25–43.

Pritchett, Lant. 2000. "Understanding Patterns of Economic Growth: Searching for Hills among Plateaus, Mountains, and Plains." *The World Bank Economic Review* 14(2): 221–250.

Quah, Danny T. 1993. "Empirical Cross-Section Dynamics in Economic Growth." *European Economic Review* 37(2-3): 426–434.

Reddy, Sanjay, and Camelia Minoiu. 2008. "Real Income Stagnation of Countries 1960–2001." *The Journal of Development Studies* 45(1): 1–23.

Rhee, Changyong. 2012. "Indonesia Risks Falling Into the Middle-Income Trap." *Asian Development Bank Op-Ed/Opinion*, available at http://www.adb.org/news/op-ed/indonesia-risks-falling-middle-income-trap-changyong-rhee (accessed on 25 February, 2016).

Shimada, Gaku. 2015. "Kra Isthmus shortcut would mean big shifts in Southeast Asia", *Nikkei Asian Review*, 25 June, available at http://asia.nikkei.com/magazine/20150625-IS-ASIA-READY/Politics-Economy/Kra-Isthmus-shortcut-would-mean-big-shifts–in-Southeast-Asia?page=2 (accessed on 25 February, 2016).

Tan, Khee Giap, Xiao Lian and Teleixi Xie. 2016. "Growth Slowdown Analysis for Greater China Economies" *Journal of Economics and Development Studies*, 4(2): 129–144.

Tan, Khee Giap, Nguyen Trieu Duong Luu, Yoong, Sangiita Wei Cher. 2016. "An Empirical Investigation of Growth Slowdown Analysis for India's Sub-National Economies". ACI Technical Working Paper No. 06-2016, Asia Competitiveness Institute, Lee Kuan Yew School of Public Policy, National University of Singapore, June.

Tan, Khee Giap, Ahmad, Nursyahida Binte and Gopalan, Sasidaran. 2016. "Indonesian Sub-National Economies and Growth Slowdown: An Empirical Analysis." ACI Technical Working Paper No. 07-2016, Asia Competitiveness Institute, Singapore.

Tan, Khee Giap, Nguyen Trieu Duong Luu, Xiao Lian. 2017 (forthcoming). "Empirical Analysis of Growth Slowdown in ASEAN". *The Journal of Developing Areas.*

Tan, Khee Giap, Peng Wang, and Teleixi Xie. 2017 (forthcoming). *2016 Annual Update of Provincial and Regional Competitiveness Analysis for Greater China*. Singapore: World Scientific.

Tan, Khee Giap, Sasidaran Gopalan, Anuja Tandon, and Kong Yam Tan. 2017 (forthcoming). *2016 Annual Competitiveness and Growth Slowdown Analysis for Subnational Economies of India*. Singapore: World Scientific.

The Conference Board. 2015. "Output, Labour and Labour Productivity, 1950–2015, *Total Economy Database*, May 2015 Version." https://www.conference-board.org/data/economydatabase/index.cfm?id=27762 (accessed on 11 August, 2015).

Tran, Van Tho. 2013. "The Middle-Income Trap: Issues for Members of the Association of Southeast Asian Nations." *ADBI Working Paper* No. 421. Tokyo: Asia Development Bank Institute (ADBI).

Wei, Shang Jin. 2015. "PRC's Slowdown for Asia's Growth — Key Takeaways." *Asian Development Blog*, 25 July, available at http://blogs.adb.org/blog/prc-s-slowdown-asia-s-growth-key-takeaways (accessed on 25 February, 2016).

Woo, Wing Thye. 2012. "China Meets the Middle-Income Trap: The Large Potholes in the Road to Catching-Up." *Journal of Chinese Economic and Business Studies* 10(4): 313–336.

World Bank. 2014. *Indonesia Development Policy Review 2014 — Indonesia: Avoiding the Trap*, World Bank, Washington D.C.

Ye, Longfeng and Peter Robertson. 2016. "*Identifying prisoners of the middle-income trap*", available at http://www.voxeu.org/article/identifying-prisoners-middle-income-trap (accessed on 29 April, 2016).

Yusuf, Shahid, and Kaoru Nabeshima. 2009. "Can Malaysia Escape the Middle-Income Trap? A Strategy for Penang." World Bank Policy Research Working Paper No. 4971, World Bank, Washington D.C.

Zhang, Derong. 2014. "The Mechanism of the Middle Income Trap and the Potential Factors Influencing China's Economic Growth" *Frontiers of Economics in China* 9(3): 499–528.

Zhang, Longmei, and Damien Puy. 2015. "Growth Slowdown: Are Frontier and Developing Asian Economies Different?" in *Frontier and Developing Asia: The Next Generation of Emerging Markets*, edited by Alfred Schipke. Washington D.C.: International Monetary Fund (IMF).

Discussant Notes 3.1

Dr Darwin Marcelo

Infrastructure Economist, The World Bank Group

I have two sets of comments, one on the methods and models, and the other one on the results.

First, this is a very interesting research, addresses a very relevant question and includes a huge effort to prepare the data, especially because the numbers are at the sub-regional level. Last year, The World Bank worked together with the National University of Singapore and the Asia Competitiveness Institute (ACI) to obtain similar information at the national level. This process was very complicated, so what you have achieved here is remarkable.

On the methods and models, the search for slowdown episodes started with a window of five years. The selection of that window is rather arbitrary. A question I would ask to the researchers is what would have happened if you had a longer or shorter window. This is relevant because the number of episodes may change if the window is narrower or wider. When trying to explain the probability of occurrence of a slowdown episode, the window selection may affect the results. This window also has a direct effect on the time series presented. The study used a twenty-year dataset, but with a five-year window, 10 years of data are lost. The analysis detected a slowdown only for a period of 10 years, from 1998 to 2008. One may think that most slowdowns happened after 2008 and before 1998. Therefore, the selection of this window is very important, because it has two repercussions on the results of the model.

On the results, it would be useful if you can include the classification statistics, given that the whole point of the exercise is to make a prediction and assess the probability of a slowdown episode. Two indicators should have been presented; sensitivity and specificity. Sensitivity means the fraction of events that are correctly classified and specificity means fraction of non-events that correctly classified. This will give the reader an idea of how powerful the model is. Furthermore, given that the suggested probabilistic model is trying to predict the probability of occurrence of a slowdown event, it should also be contrasted against the observed results to give the reader an idea of how powerful the model is.

I also think that it is highly possible that observations are clustered at the country level because the units of observation are at the sub-regional level. This might lead to standard error bias, but more importantly, coefficient bias, which could lead to a wrong conclusion. Therefore, I suggest to perform a test to be completely sure that this kind of phenomenon (clustering at the country level) is not present. The intuition is that a country is exposed to the same macroeconomic environment. Observations may not be independent because they correspond to sub-regions within a country. All the sub-regions are exposed to the same macroeconomic factors and so they may be clustered.

The results are striking. For a country like Singapore, there is a very high probability of experiencing a slowdown event. And then, when we look at the sub-regional level there are many economies that have about 40 percent probability for facing a slowdown event.

Results suggest that the richer the sub-national region is, the higher the probability of a slowdown episode is. Again, what happens when you have clustering? You may have a region within a country that is getting richer and that has a high probability of facing a slowdown. But it may happen that all the regions inside a country grow at the same time because they are clustered at the country level. I would not consider the sub-regional levels as micro nations, I would consider the sub-region as a cluster inside a country. Again, regions are similar in terms of legislation, language, trade relations, national government, etc.

Finally, regarding the implications of the model, I have the following question: what is the space that governments have or what are the instruments that governments have to reduce the probability of a slowdown, especially when the country is a middle-income or high-income one? According to the model, one of the determinants of growth slowdown is the literacy rate. Well, increasing the literacy rate is very complicated when the nation is already well educated, as in the case of Singapore.

Discussant Notes 3.2

Dr Kirida Bhaopichitr

Research Director, Thailand Development Research Institute (TDRI), Thailand

Good afternoon everyone, I would like to thank the ACI, especially Professor Tan for inviting me here today. If you remember we had a similar conference last November, and I was also here. I can see the progress that has been made since then. I would like to congratulate the team for doing such comprehensive research, especially the young researchers from the ACI who have been putting in a lot of hard work. They have been crunching all these data for us to have a very comprehensive explanation of the slowdown that different countries in ASEAN and also the sub-national units in Indonesia as well as in China and India have been experiencing.

With the good work that the team has already done, I probably have more observations and questions than answers to offer to them. Let me start with some observations that I have on the results that they have presented.

The observations that I have are on the main page which shows the results. The paper claims that there are these important determinants, as you can say, of growth slowdown in each income group for the economies. The different explanations that the paper offers make up a 95-page PowerPoint of slides. For some of them, there may be more in-depth explanations than others. For those that I still have not understood, please allow me to ask some questions. I would like to focus on two of the main determinants: openness to trade and the old dependency ratio.

The paper claims that if upper- and middle-income countries had high openness to trade, then the probability of that country slowing down would be less. This conclusion was based on the negative sign in front of the coefficient for the openness to trade variable in the regression tables. In this new normal world where growth is slowing down around the world and world trade is also slowing down, I am not sure if this still holds. The chart on screen shows the latest data from the World Bank. The next one is the IMF world forecast. As evident from these charts, in this new normal world, one of the main characteristics is that world growth will slow down. This is because of volatility or what they now call VUCA which stands for Volatility, Uncertainty, Complexity and Ambiguity. There are a lot of uncertainties and one of the things that have also happened is trade consolidation. For instance, the US may have been using inputs from Asia to produce goods but they are consolidating the supply chain, meaning that they are producing more in Mexico or in Latin America. Even China is doing the same thing. They are trying to produce closer to home to reduce the costs of production and logistics.

Let us now look at how world growth data compares to world trade data. We observe that before the Lehman Brother Crisis in the US, when the world economy grew by 1 percent, world trade would roughly increase by two percent, so the relation is one to two. After the Crisis we see that that relationship has softened. Now, when world growth expands by percent, instead of world trade growing by two percent, it only grows by one percent. This has really affected countries that are open to trade, especially countries that are export-oriented like Thailand and Malaysia. To make a long story short, world growth is growing slower than before, and in addition to that, world trade is slowing even more. As such, countries that are open to trade may actually have higher probability of slowing down instead of having a lower probability of slowing down as the paper suggested. This is something that happens because the world changes so quickly. It is not that there is something wrong with the model, but it is just that with the new data coming out in recent years, we can see that the structure of world trade has changed. As a result, its impact on countries that are very open can be different.

In addition, I would like show you the example of Thailand. The TDRI has conducted a constant share analysis to decompose the different determinants of export growth. There are four main components: (i) export growth depends on growth in world trade, (ii) export growth depends on conditions in the country that we export to, (iii) export growth depends on the commodity that we actually export and (iv) export growth depends on competitiveness. As you can see, in the case of Thailand, the world trade effect is pretty significant. Hence, if world trade slows down, it will very much affect Thailand's exports. We also extend the analysis for other countries; and if the ACI is interested, we can partner on this research, not only at the country level but also the sub-national level.

Next, I would also like to make an observation about old age dependency ratio. The paper says when old age dependency in a country rises, the probability of a country slowing down would increase. That makes sense because if you have more old people and fewer working-age people, it reduces your economy's growth potential. However, the paper suggests that the effect is only significant for lower-middle-income countries. Is that because many of the middle-income countries are still very protective of their labor market? Singapore is aging but is already a high-income country, and it welcomes talents from overseas to supplement their workforce. In contrast, middle-income and lower income countries, like Thailand, do not welcome foreign talents. Clearly, the relationship between old age dependency ratio and the probability of growth slowdown may change if the underlying policies change. Being more open to immigrants, especially skilled workers, may help middle-income countries.

I also have a few questions. I like the paper because the model has yielded a lot of results. However, I would like the team to explain the reasons behind some of these results. One of the charts shows that upper-middle income and high-income economies in ASEAN have a higher probability of getting into a slowdown. I am wondering why this is the case. One possible explanation might be that these ASEAN countries are more open to trade, so now that trade is slowing down, the probability of economic growth slowdown has risen. However, this is probably not the reason because the data used in this paper is only until 2013. Hence, I am not sure why that is the case.

The second question is that when the research team takes into account all the economies and not just ASEAN, they found that the probability of lower-middle income economies slowing down is actually quite high. The graph is in a concave fashion which means that when we are at this level, the probability of you slowing down is higher than when you are in a high-income area. I'm not sure why that is the case. But if that is really the case, we can argue for the middle-income trap. If you are in the middle-income group, your chances of slowing down are much higher, so you can try to become high-income before you are trapped in there. This is a powerful result if it is going to prove the existence of a middle-income trap.

The last question concerns the chart that shows a comparison of Singapore with other countries in different dimensions. Now that we know that there are different reasons for why Singapore may grow at a slower rate, I'm also interested to know which determinants we should focus on if we want to reduce the probability of Singapore slowing down. Which bottleneck is the most problematic that we need to address first? I think such analysis is something useful which could be added into the paper. The authors may then suggest which policy should be implemented in order to reduce the probability of growth slowdown.

Chapter 4
Transitional Economies in ASEAN: Reform Progress, Challenges and Policy Options

4.1 Introduction

With expansion to 10 member states in the late 1990s, the concerted efforts by ASEAN towards deeper economic integration has gained wide attention globally. Currently standing as the seventh largest economy in the world, the regional bloc with its great untapped potentials could leap to the fourth largest economy by 2030 as remarked by the Laotian Prime Minister during the ASEAN Business and Investment Summit in 2016.[1] Among ASEAN, Singapore spearheaded growth with spectacular economic performance since the early 1960s, and it was classified as one of the Asian Tigers together with Hong Kong, South Korea and Taiwan. This remarkable performance was then replicated, albeit to a lesser degree, in Indonesia, Malaysia, Philippines and Thailand. Meanwhile, Brunei has been prospering from its rich natural resource endowments. On the other hand, the remaining four ASEAN members: Cambodia, Laos, Myanmar and Vietnam (CLMV) are growing with rapid expansion rates in recent years after they undertook progressive reform initiatives.

Besides geographical proximity, CLMV can be classified as a sub-group within ASEAN due to several common characteristics. First, they were the last to open up among all ASEAN countries. In fact, they only joined the association in the mid- and late-1990s. Second, decades of wars and conflicts after decolonisation has hampered economic development in CLMV, setting them back *vis-à-vis* their regional neighbours. To this day, CLMV remain transitional economies which, as shown in our competitiveness analysis in Chapter 2, lag behind the ASEAN-6. Third, notwithstanding rapid structural shifts towards manufacturing due to industrialisation efforts, agriculture remains an important engine of growth and source of employment in these countries. The shares of agriculture in Gross Domestic Product (GDP) in CLMV are greater than ASEAN-10's average though there are also heterogeneities as Vietnam has a much lower share than Cambodia, Laos and Myanmar.[2] Fourth, as this chapter shall elaborate, CLMV share a number of common challenges which hamper their growth and development.

ASEAN as an organisation recognises that the persistence of development gap among its members can hinder effective regional integration. As a result, it launched the Initiative for ASEAN Integration (IAI) strategic framework in 2000 to provide support for the CLMV countries. This has been followed up with specific Work Plans, with the most recent, the IAI Work Plan III, being adopted in 2016. In general, leaders in the more developed ASEAN countries

[1] See Moriyasu (2016).

[2] Based on data from the Asian Development Bank (ADB) and World Bank, in 2015, the shares of agriculture in GDP for Cambodia, Laos, Myanmar and Vietnam were respectively, 28.2 percent, 27.4 percent, 26.7 percent and 18.9 percent. Meanwhile, the average share for ASEAN-10 was 14.4 percent.

have expressed support for closing the development divide. Speaking at the ASEAN Tourism Forum on 18 January 2017, Singapore's Prime Minister Lee Hsien Loong remarked that, "... if ASEAN can build on what we have achieved, and deepen our cooperation across the board, all our peoples will benefit."[3] Such mindset of prosper thy neighbour to prosper thyself is welcoming and is indeed necessary to sustain the regional integration effort.

Nevertheless, while regional initiatives can play a part in bridging the development gap, equally important, if not more so, is the need for far-reaching domestic reforms among the CLMV countries. This chapter aims to study the reform progress in CLMV, highlighting achievements and identifying challenges so as to draw policy implications for the next phase of their development. The rest of the chapter is structured as follows. Sections 4.2 and 4.3 discuss the main development theories and development experiences of East Asian economies. Next, we review briefly the current reform progress in CLMV in Section 4.4. This is followed by Section 4.5 which examines the external factors that may affect the development in CLMV. Lastly, the chapter ends with a concluding note in Section 4.6.

4.2 Overview of Development Theories

Prior to examining the development progress of CLMV, it is important to first define development. There are divergent views on the definition of development, with the majority these days associating development primarily with economic growth as measured in GDP growth. One of these proponents is Dani Rodrik, who believes that economic growth is one of the most powerful solutions to poverty.[4] The argument is backed by negative correlation between economic growth and poverty in development experiences of multiple economies. The most evident poverty reduction over the last three decades can be witnessed in China where the proportion of population living in poverty dropped from 53 percent to 8 percent between 1981 and 2001.[5] China has not only achieved spectacular economic growth after opening up in 1978 but also lifted hundreds of millions of its people out of poverty.

To formulate development in terms of national income is convenient. It allows quantification of growth rate and objective analysis on the development progress. However, this oversimplified approach overlooks other social and political factors that affect the society. Current issues such as environmental sustainability, the rise of political extremism and the voice of the "We are the 99%" movement should not be overheard. Alternative views linked development to poverty, inequality and unemployment besides national income.[6]

Some economists brought this argument further and see development as freedom and the fulfilment of human potential.[7] The critical views on the current discourse of development has inspired the creation of the Human Development Index, which emphasises that human capabilities should be the ends of development while economic growth should only serve as a means to

---

[3] See *Channel News Asia* (2017).

[4] See Rodrik (2007).

[5] See Ravallion and Chen (2005).

[6] See Seers (1969).

[7] See Sen (1999).

achieve that ends. Acknowledging that development is about both material wealth and fulfilment of human capabilities, we next seek the answer of how some countries have developed faster than others. The discussion on this has been circling around the debate on the role of market versus state. The tension on whether development should be driven by market or state remains unsettled even to this day.

4.2.1 Market-oriented Development

Adam Smith's invisible hand theory has laid the cornerstone for the narrative on liberal market economy, which believes that individuals pursuing their self-interests in a free market will subsequently lead to optimal outcomes benefiting the society at large.[8] This argument which originated in the 18th century is still echoed by many modern economics scholars.[9] Not only so, it is still alive in many development policies and approaches practised today. One of these is the Washington Consensus which was widely adopted in developing countries, particularly in Latin America and Africa during the 1970s and 1980s.

Sharing common goals on promoting growth and reducing poverty, the International Monetary Fund (IMF)'s stabilisation policies and World Bank's structural adjustment policies are designed for developing the so-called Third World. The commonalities of the international financial institutions' policies which can be summed up as "Stabilise, Privatise and Liberalise" are later codified by Williamson (1990) and named as the "Washington Consensus". Developing countries, particularly Latin America and Sub-Saharan Africa, which fell into debt crises in the late 1970s or 1980s were prescribed to undertake the agenda of 10 policy suggestions under this Consensus.[10] Such policies ultimately aim to minimise state's intervention in the market and restore market's supremacy.

The proponents of market-oriented development generally believe that nothing can do better than the price mechanism in allocating and distributing limited resources efficiently. While recognising the reality of possible market failures, problems such as rent-seeking and information barrier make government a bigger evil. Or as argued by Hayek (1944), all government efforts in economic planning will lead to failure because only individuals know best about what they want.[11] Anchoring to such belief, the government's role is solely to create and enforce the right rules, and next to stand back from the market and let the economy flourishes by itself. Long list of failed state interventions in the market such as the collapse of the Soviet Union, the Khmer Rouge in Cambodia and the recent corruption scandals that resulted in Dilma Rousseff's and Park Geun-hye's fall from power in Brazil and South Korea seems to affirm what the proponents have argued.

---

[8] See Chapter 2 in Smith (1776).

[9] See Hayek (1944), Friedman (1962), Bauer (1969) and Sen (1999).

[10] See Williamson (1990) for further explanation on 10 broad sets of policy prescriptions under Washington Consensus. These include policies on public expenditure, tax reforms, exchange rate, trade liberalisation and privatisation of state enterprises, to mention a few.

[11] See Hayek (1944).

4.2.2 State-led Development

It is logical to adopt market-driven development approach if pervasive state intervention always brings more harms than benefits. However, a deeper inspection shows that this argument deviates from the historical evidence. By studying the European development since the 19th century, Polanyi argued that free market does not exist because market itself is a product of the state.[12] Not only so, the state has been playing an important role to protect the society from potential negative effects of the market such as environmental degradation and labour exploitation. Findings on several Western developed economies such as the United States (US), the United Kingdom (UK) and Germany are consonant with Polanyi's conclusion that the states' active intervention through implementation of protectionism approaches such as tariffs and subsidies had driven the development in these economies in their early stages.[13] List (1909) and Chang (2003) went further to argue that the developed economies are kicking away the ladder (interventionist and protectionist policies) they had used by imposing market liberalisation ideology onto the developing economies.[14]

The outcomes from more contemporary studies on Asian economies are also contradicting the *laissez-faire* argument. In-depth case studies on the remarkable growth experience of Taiwan and South Korea showed that their successful structural transformation can be attributed to states' protection of infant industries and state-directed resources allocation and mobilisation which are often argued as state's manipulation of the market mechanism.[15] Besides, it has been pointed out that the Washington Consensus did not deliver on its promises.[16] Neither Latin America nor Sub-Saharan Africa has duplicated the economic success of the West or the East Asian economies. Instead, these economies have become more vulnerable to volatility of the global market which led to higher capital flights and indebtedness, not to mention, worsened social welfare due to reduction in public expenditure.[17]

Neither a perfectly free-market economy nor a centrally planned economy exists in the real world. Even if they did, both are flawed. Price mechanism which is determined purely by market forces fails to capture negative and positive externalities, leading to the overprovision of socially harmful goods and underprovision of public goods. These market failures manifest in problems such as resources depletion, high mortality rate and poor access to education. In addition, the proponents of free market mechanism have oversimplified development by equating development with economic growth. In fact, development is multidimensional and can be defined by different approaches. On the other hand, state-led development is not perfect either. Public institution weaknesses such as bureaucratic red tape and information barrier may

---

[12] See Polanyi (1944).

[13] See List (1909), Gerschenkron (1962) and Chapter 2 of Chang (2003) for historical development of UK, US and Germany.

[14] See Chang (2002).

[15] See case study on Taiwan by Amsden (1989) and South Korea by Wade (1990) and Kohli (2004).

[16] See Rodrik (2006).

[17] See Gwynne and Kay (2000) and Boyce and Ndkrumanah (2001).

cause inefficiency in state-level decision making. In addition, the agenda for growth and development might be held hostage to political interests of politicians who are engaged in internal political struggles. Hence, both market and state should not have an absolute role in the development process. Instead, both should play complementary roles and provide checks and balances to one another. In sum, there is no one-size-fits-all approach. ASEAN transitional economies should draw on the diverse development experiences in the East and West, in the past and present, before choosing their own paths.

4.3 The Development Experiences of East Asian Economies: Lessons for CLMV

"East Asian Miracle", a term coined by a 1993 World Bank's report, has put the development experiences of the High-Performing Asian Economies (HPAEs) under the microscope.[18] HPAEs had achieved a spectacular growth for over three decades from the 1960s to the early 1990s with significant decline in inequality and improvement in human welfare. Besides that, what makes the East Asian development a miracle is the exceptionally high productivity growth and rapid technological catching-up, which allow swift structural transformation from agricultural-based economy to export-oriented manufacturing-led development.

According to the World Bank's report, 23 East Asian economies had grown faster than all other regions from 1965 to 1989.[19] Among these, eight Asian economies: Japan, the Four Asian Tigers (Hong Kong, Singapore, South Korea and Taiwan) and three newly industrialising economies (NIEs) of Southeast Asia (Indonesia, Malaysia and Thailand) stood out, being grouped as HPAEs due to their unusual rapid growth sustained over a relatively long period with equitable distribution and significantly improved welfare. More specifically, the average real growth rate in GDP per capita between 1965 and 1989 of these economies except Malaysia[20] exceeded four percent per annum whereas the average ratio of income shares of the richest 20 percent of the population to the poorest 20 percent was less than 10.

Such remarkable performance of stable and rapid growth with well distributed income was an exception to development experiences in other economies which were not able to achieve sustainable growth and at the same maintain low income inequality. Given the adverse distributive effect of globalisation, the development path of East Asian Miracle remains valid and even more relevant than ever in today's globalised world. With Japan, Four Asian Tigers and NIEs leading the way, ASEAN emerging economies such as CLMV show some positive signs of catching up as well.

---

[18] See World Bank (1993).

[19] *Ibid.*

[20] Although inequality in Malaysia was slightly higher than the rest, the remarkable poverty reduction from 37 percent in 1973 to less than 15 percent in Malaysia in 1987 made it stood out and be classified as one of the HPAEs.

4.3.1 The Flying Geese Pattern

The East Asian spectacular growth has evoked intense intellectual discussion and research. One of the major theoretical frameworks established is that the development trajectory of East Asian economies conform to the Flying Geese Pattern.[21] The model was used to explain the iterative process of industrialisation adopted by developing economies, where capital investment and development, as well as the rationalisation of production processes, evolved in a cascading fashion from a 'lead goose'.

The catching-up process involves a transfer of capabilities from developed to developing countries on a global basis since the Industrial Revolution in the West and follows a sequential order of M–P–X. At the early stage, the developing economies engage in primary sector and export primary commodities while importing (M) consumer goods from the advanced economies. The next stage begins as they withdraw from commodities dependency and adopt import-substitution policy by producing (P) consumer goods domestically. As the leading goose loses the cost competitiveness, the industry, particularly low-skilled labour-intensive manufacturing sectors, shift to the follower economies. With the investment and inflow of capital goods from the advanced economies to the less advanced economies, the followers manage to forge ahead to export-oriented industrialisation. They are now capable of producing consumer goods and exporting (X) them to the advanced economies.

Apart from the industrial transformation, there is a constant and dynamic discarding and relocating of labour-intensive and low value-added manufacturing industries in exchange for more sophistication and upgrading among the leading geese and followers. This corresponds to the metaphor of cascade used by the late Mr Lee Kuan Yew, founding Prime Minister of Singapore in one of his interviews[22]: "Then came the rapid spread of this industrialization process. It accelerated with the Plaza Accord in 1985, which pushed up the yen, then forced the Korean won and the Taiwanese dollar and the Singapore dollar up. This forced the relocation of Japanese industries to the newly industrialised economies, from these economies to the rest of Southeast Asia, then China, Vietnam and now Myanmar. This had a cascading effect."

Specifically within East Asia, there is scope for interchanging of the lead 'prime goose', namely the role historically played by Japan and increasingly by China. Chinese and Japanese industries relocate their production facilities to take advantage of cost efficiencies in the developing ASEAN countries or to better capture expansion opportunities with tax advantage given the various prevailing regional Free Trade Agreements (FTAs). This is in line with the "Made in China 2025" plan, which aims to shift China's manufacturing sector towards higher value-added, sophisticated industrial activities, and "away from simple, labour-intensive production" by the year 2025.[23] In particular, CLMV will be better able to use their abundant low-cost labour and natural resources to attract foreign direct investment (FDI) from multinational corporations (MNCs) to move up the flying geese model.

---

[21] See Akamatsu (1962).

[22] See Tanzer (1996), cited Ozawa (2009), p. 4.

[23] See Abe (2015) for details on manufacturing transformation in the "Made in China 2025" plan.

While the forerunner economies which have developed advanced and patented technologies continue to dominate the upper stream of the global value chain, it is imperative and challenging for the followers such as CLMV to breakthrough and leapfrog their predecessors. In this context, as the leading geese advance to the pursuits of more sophisticated production chain, they play a role in guiding the followers in terms of economic and technological advancement instead of kicking away the ladder they have used.

A word of caution pertains to how much and how long any export of 'dirty' (pollution-prone) industries should be tolerated, as they tend to be the ones relocated as well as labour-intensive industries. This is where the right policies of safeguarding finite resources, protecting both labour force and the environment must be heeded from the outset. While service sector will be gaining more weight in driving the economic growth and job creation as the economy develops, developing economies such as CLMV should therefore develop service sector in tandem with labour-intensive industries for a more resilient economic structure.

4.3.2 The East Asian Development Model

Numerous studies and researches have been conducted to examine the East Asian Miracle with the hope that the success can be emulated in other developing economies. While debate on the roles of state and market in leading to the East Asian success remains unreconciled, several determinants of the miracle have been identified. The basic economic strategy is explicit in the East Asian development approach, namely strategic infrastructure investment to unlock production bottlenecks as a prerequisite for economic take-off. Moreover, the success of the HPAEs can also be attributed to superior accumulation of capital, mainly driven by high private domestic investment and abundant human capital.[24] It serves to release production bottlenecks by strategically investing in comprehensively planned regional infrastructure and the rest of upgrading to follow. Undoubtedly, infrastructure, from transportation to energy, is a prerequisite condition for economic acceleration.

In economic parlance, the HPAEs shared a significant common feature in their initial labour-intensive and export-oriented focus, which accounted for "more than 50 percent of total manufactured exports from all developing countries" by the end of the 1980s despite their aggregate share of population of developing countries being less than 3 percent.[25] This was no accident, but a conscientious endeavour to assimilate their respective economies into the global trade regime via competitive export strategies. Trade as a growth engine facilitates specialisation and hence creates a more efficient allocation of natural resources based on the economy's comparative advantage.

Following from CLMV as the latest ASEAN entrants in joining the flying geese model, they simultaneously latch on to the HPAEs' development pattern of growing export-oriented economies by engaging in international trade. Asian state capitalism, as demonstrated in Japan Inc., Singapore Inc. and many government-led cases across Asia as government-driven modernisation

---

[24] See World Bank (1993) and Page (1994).

[25] See Chow and Kellman (1993).

and industrialisation, has shown itself to be a viable alternative.[26] It is in contrast to Western *laissez-faire* market development paths taken by historic first-mover countries of industrialisation. The policy-induced competitive advantage has enabled resource-deficit city-states of Hong Kong and Singapore and other HPAEs such as South Korea and Taiwan to make their great leaps since the 1960s by export-oriented trade despite their different governance structures, cultural heritage or geographical endowment.

To what extent that state intervention helps to create the East Asian Miracle is subject to considerable debate, which this book cannot do justice to. However, all parties are responsibly aware of how effective leadership and good governance at the helm play a paramount role in harnessing and promoting, especially infrastructure investment. The CLMV quad's attempt to leapfrog to catch up on industrialisation and supply chains must be leveraged on the experience of their East Asian counterparts, while the stronger economies which have comparative advantages in terms of capital, technology and competitive skills should play an active role in meeting pressing infrastructure bottlenecks for a balanced, sustainable and inclusive regional development.

4.4 Progress of Reforms in CLMV: Achievements, Challenges and Policy Implications

The admission of CLMV to ASEAN in the 1990s has fulfilled the vision of ASEAN-10, but it also made painfully clear the development gaps between CLMV and the other members. Three out of four CLMV countries, namely Cambodia, Laos and Myanmar are the poorest economies among ASEAN-10. They were also classified as Least Developed Countries (LDC) by the United Nations (UN).[27] This section chronicles the development experience of CLMV in modern history, especially the episodes of economic reforms over the past three decades. From this, we assess the reform progress in each country and identify key areas for improvement, drawing country-specific policy implications.

4.4.1 Cambodia

4.4.1.1 *Progress of Reforms in Cambodia*

The splendid view of the Angkor Wat in Cambodia tells the story of the legendary Angkor Empire to its visitors from all over the world. However, no less well-known is the country's turbulent modern history sketched by the standing mass graves in the killing fields of the Khmer Rouge regime. Cambodia has endured a brutal period of Cambodian genocide under the Khmer Rouge from 1975 to 1979. The revolution's aspiration of creating a new classless utopia had instead led the nation to a dark dystopia. The Khmer Rouge's socio-economic programme had almost completely destroyed the social, political and economic structures of the country.

---

[26] See Low (1998, 2004).

[27] The list of LDCs is accessible from the UN website, https://www.un.org/development/desa/dpad/least-developed-country-category/ldcs-at-a-glance.html.

By 1979, there was little to no industry left and the stock of human capital had been largely destroyed.[28]

Thus, after the downfall of the Khmer Rouge, the new Marxist regime, the People's Republic of Kampuchea (PRK) faced tremendous challenges. The PRK at first set up an economic system which recognised only three types of economic organisations: state, cooperative and family. Land ownership was nationalised, and industries were dominated by state-owned enterprises (SOEs) which were at first centrally managed.[29] However, despite these broad socialist characteristics, the PRK's economic system was in practice more market-oriented than the systems of its Indochinese neighbours Laos and Vietnam. Though collectivised farming remained the ideal of the government's agriculture policy, private plots were also given to households, and agricultural production became increasingly dominated by private producers in the 1980s.[30] Free markets for both agricultural produces and manufactured goods were also tolerated.

The mid- and late-1980s saw more market liberalisation reforms. After the Fifth Party Congress in 1985, the government legitimised the private sector as the fourth component of the economic system. As the country moved into a transition phase with its name changed to the State of Cambodia in 1989, the pace of reforms quickened. The government restored private property ownership, decollectivised agriculture and decentralised the management of SOEs. The state's official monopoly on foreign trade was abolished in 1987. Foreign investment law was promulgated in 1989, allowing the private sector to engage in trade.[31]

The new era of Cambodia commenced in 1993 with the election organised by the United Nations Transitional Authority in Cambodia. This election led to the restoration of the Kingdom of Cambodia and the adoption of multiparty democracy. Post 1993, the reform blueprint in Cambodia is largely aligned with the Washington Consensus agenda focusing on macroeconomic stabilisation, economic liberalisation and integration with the world economy.[32] Due to the heavy presence of international organisations such as the UN and the World Bank in driving the reforms in the early 1990s, liberalisation and decentralisation had progressed in a rather fast pace in Cambodia as compared to other transitional economies such as Myanmar. SOEs have largely been privatised and only economically viable ones were retained. According to one estimate, by 2011, 96 percent of all business establishments were private and they accounted for 90 percent of the number of persons engaged. For the state sector, these figures were 3 percent and 8 percent, respectively.[33]

Meanwhile, similar to the HPAEs and its Indochinese neighbours Laos and Vietnam, the development path taken by Cambodia has been steered by labour-intensive, export-oriented industrial development. Trade policies were liberalised and most quantitative restrictions were

---

[28] See Chhair and Ung (2013).

[29] See St John (2006).

[30] *Ibid.*

[31] See Chhair and Ung (2013).

[32] See Chheang and Wong (2012) and Hill and Menon (2013).

[33] See Chhair and Ung (2013).

eliminated. The government also provided incentives to attract FDI. Tax exemptions were given on imported intermediate inputs and on exports of finished goods.[34]

Economic reforms in Cambodia have happened through a series of five-year plan, guided by two overarching strategic frameworks: the Triangle Strategy and the Rectangular Strategy. The latter was the more recent, adopted to replace the former in 2004. It comprised four pillars: Growth, Employment, Equity and Efficiency, targeting at economic growth, job creation, poverty reduction and good governance. The Cambodian economy has made some important progress as a result of reforms. Figure 4.1 depicts the growth rate of real GDP and GDP per capita in Cambodia during the period of 1994–2015. High economic growth was maintained at an average of 7.7 percent real GDP growth for more than two decades from 1994 to 2015, an achievement comparable to those of the HPAEs. However, the drop in the real GDP growth rate to negative territory in 2009 due to the Global Financial Crisis (GFC) exposed the continued vulnerability of the Cambodian economy to the global market.

Figure 4.1: Real GDP and Real GDP Per Capita Growth Rates in Cambodia, 1994–2015

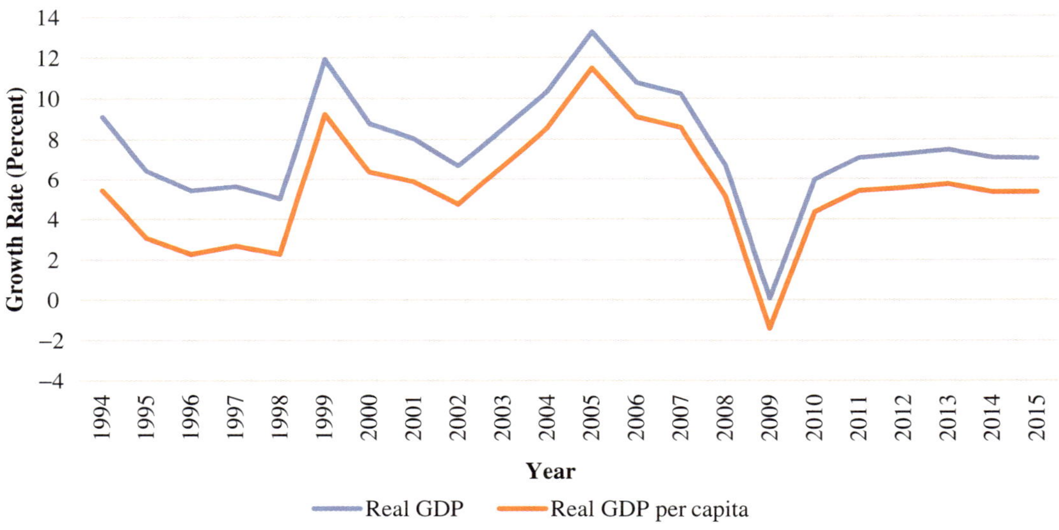

Source: World Bank, World Development Indicators

As noted in Section 4.3.2, multiple studies have shown that the spectacular growth and development in the HPAEs can be attributed to their high savings level, among other factors.[35] As can be seen from Figure 4.2, there was a rising trend of domestic savings level in Cambodia over time, though there were considerable fluctuations in the earlier years. The increased savings and narrower gap between savings and investment suggest a positive prospect of

[34] Chhair and Ung (2013).

[35] See Amsden (1989), Wade (1990), World Bank (1993) and UNCTAD (1994).

Figure 4.2: Share of Gross Domestic Savings and Share of Gross Fixed Capital Formation in Cambodia's GDP, 1993–2015

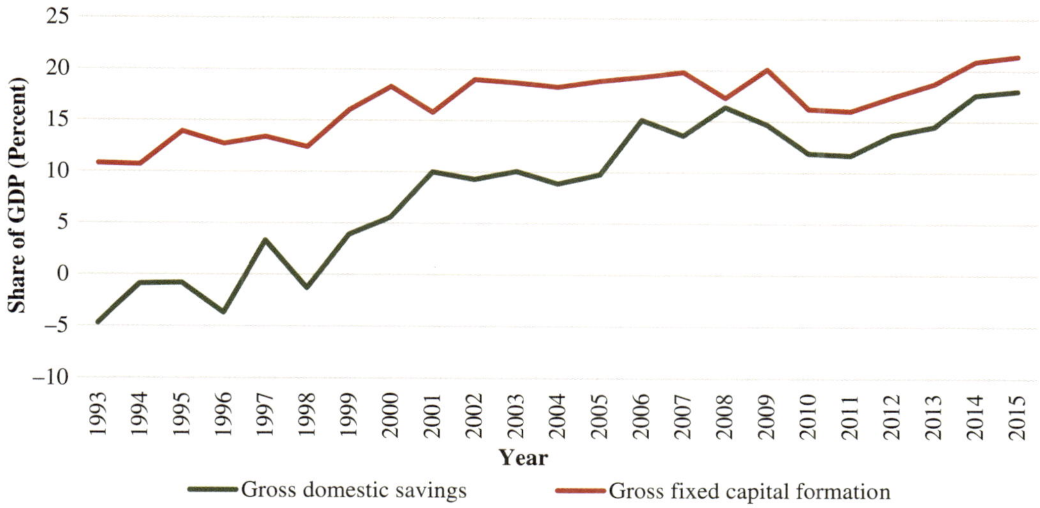

Source: World Bank, World Development Indicators

Figure 4.3: Sectoral Shares of Cambodia's GDP, 1981–2014

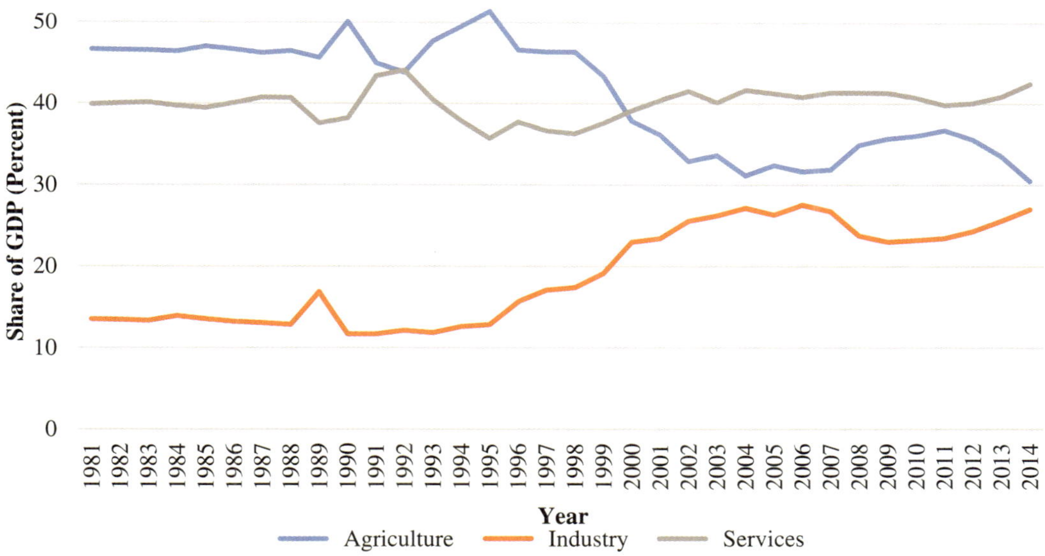

Source: United Nations Conference on Trade and Development

growth fuelled by the accumulated domestic savings, which is a more stable source of fund as compared to other sources such as foreign assistance.

Furthermore, similar to the experience of the HPAEs, the Cambodian economy has undergone structural transformation. Figure 4.3 depicts the breakdown of GDP by sectoral contribution. The clear pattern of convergence between industrial and agriculture sectors as shown in the figure implies an ongoing progress of structural transformation in Cambodia. In 1981, the agriculture sector was the primary source of national income, contributing to 46.6 percent of total GDP in Cambodia while industry only contributed to 13.5 percent of the total GDP. Industry has been growing steadily since then while the agriculture sector has declined in its importance and was displaced by service sector as the principal contributor to GDP in 2001.

The effectual transformation from an agrarian economy to an industrial and services-based economy can be attributed to the booming garment industry and tourism in Cambodia. Garment industry represented 14 percent of Cambodia's GDP, constituted 90 percent of recorded exports and more than 600,000 of direct and indirect jobs in 2010.[36] The abundant supply of unskilled young labours and generous quota set by the expired Multi-Fibre Arrangement led to a leap of garment exports from 28 million US dollars in 1995 to 3.4 billion US dollars in 2012. Meanwhile, blessed with both natural and cultural heritage sites, the tourism sector made the second largest contribution to Cambodia's GDP. The number of international tourists increased significantly from 0.1 million tourists in 1993 to 4.5 million tourists in 2014 and generated a revenue of about 2.7 billion US dollars in 2014 as compared to 0.1 billion US dollars in 1995. The contribution of the tourism sector to Cambodia's economy is expected to rise steadily in the future given its robust growth over the years.[37]

Besides economic decentralisation, Cambodia also carried out trade liberalisation and economic integration. The reform outcome is pronounced as shown in Figure 4.4. Export spurted from near zero in 1981 to the peak of 68.6 percent of total GDP in 2006. Export growth is primarily fuelled by the thriving export-oriented garment industry. Nonetheless, Cambodia is also highly dependent on import of raw materials for the garment industry. As a result, the gap between exports and imports remained relatively wide over the period. One point to note is that opening up the market also increased the vulnerability of the domestic economy. The slump in demand for Cambodian garment exports from the US as a result of the GFC caused a sharp drop in the country's export earnings in 2009.

Economic integration and liberalisation also brought in FDI, another key element which had driven the rapid growth in the HPAEs. As shown in Figure 4.5, FDI in Cambodia experienced a steady growth after 2004. In more than two decades, FDI inflows have multiplied from 300 million US dollars in 1992 to 1.7 billion US dollars in 2015. Although FDI sees a downward trend after 2013, the positive aggregate increase in FDI over the years indicates growing confidence among the investors in the prospect of Cambodian economy.

As mentioned, the social structure in Cambodia was shattered under the collectivisation policy during the Khmer Rouge's rule. Despite the shortfall of official data, the regime is believed to have caused the deaths of about two million people, including three quarters of the educated.[38] According to the UN's estimation, most of the best educated Cambodians were either killed or

[36] See Ear (2013).

[37] See Tanaka (2016).

[38] See Kluttz (2015).

Figure 4.4: Shares of Imports and Exports in Cambodia's GDP, 1981–2014

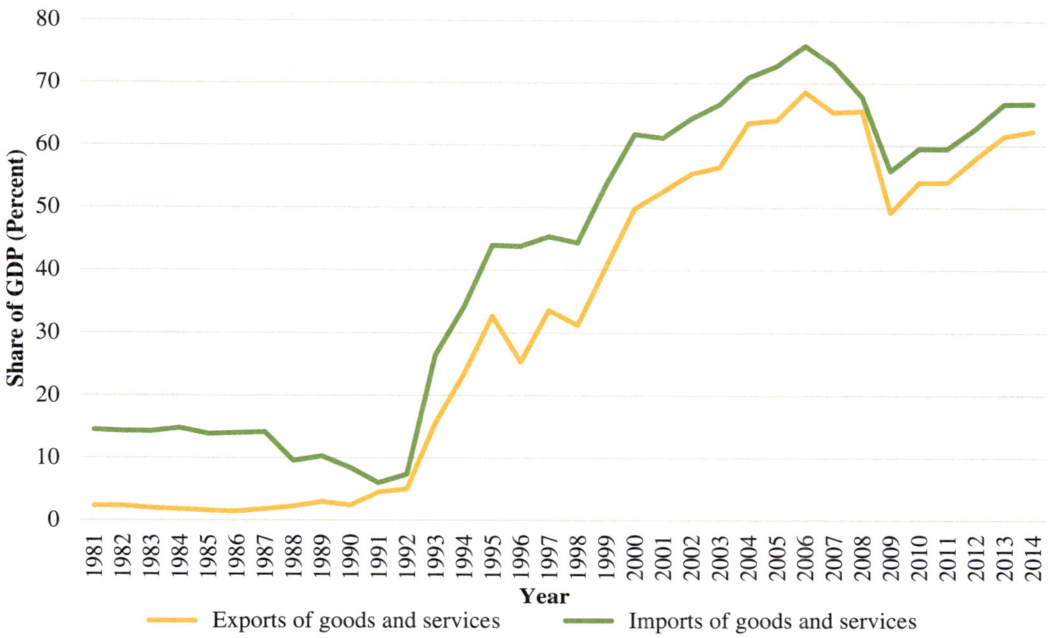

Source: United Nations Conference on Trade and Development

Figure 4.5: FDI Inflows to Cambodia at Current Prices Million US Dollars, 1992–2015

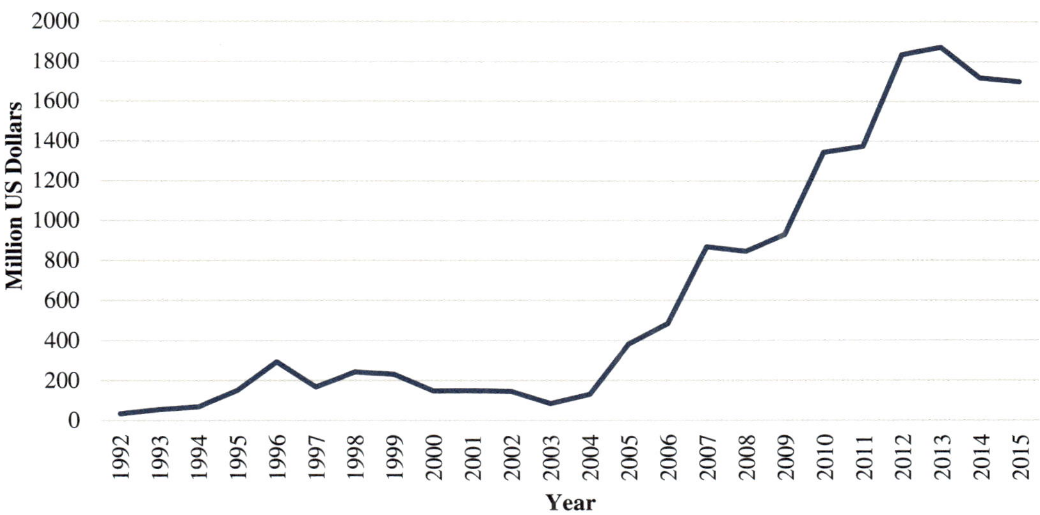

Source: United Nations Conference on Trade and Development

had fled the country as they were seen as a threat by the Khmer Rouge.[39] Health and education facilities were also mostly destroyed during the wars. After years of reforms with great support from international organisations and non-governmental organisations (NGOs), the social sector in Cambodia has experienced a revival, even though the country's records in terms of education and healthcare remain spotty.

For education, a number of policies were implemented to rebuild the abandoned formal education under the Khmer Rouge regime. More schools were built across the country, school fees were minimised through subsidisation and foreign aid, and campaigns targeting parents were implemented to instil the importance of education. The efforts seem to bear fruit as Cambodia achieved a near universal primary school enrolment rate of 94.7 percent in 2014 as compared to 82.8 percent in 1997 according to the World Bank's data. Nevertheless, more remains to be done as the country's adult literacy rate only stood at 78.4 percent in 2015, the lowest among CLMV, according to the UNESCO Institute for Statistics (UIS). In addition, problems remain in terms of the quality of education. After the Ministry of Education implemented policies to crack down on rampant cheating and bribing in school exams, the national exam passing rate plummeted from 87 percent in 2013 to 25 percent in 2014.[40] This implies that majority of the total students graduated in the past might not have actually reached the qualification benchmark. In this context, other achievements should be interpreted with caution. For instance, greater access to higher education with 200,000 students admitted in 2013 as compared to about 10,000 in 1997 may seem optimistic, but it might mask a serious problem about the quality of education.[41]

Similarly, the record of the health sector is also spotty. According to UIS, the infant mortality rate has plunged from 87.5 to 24.6 per 1,000 live births between 1985 and 2015, which indicates a betterment of healthcare standards in Cambodia. Nevertheless, there is a continued lack of physicians, which reflects the broader problem of skilled labour shortage in the economy. The ratio of physicians to population was 1:10,000 in 1983 and it has not improved much even after almost three decades with only two physicians serving 10,000 people in 2012 according to data from the World Bank.

The reforms progress in Cambodia has not only led to tremendous economic growth; growth has also been pro-poor as shown in the significant reduction of poverty rate. According to World Bank's Poverty Assessment Report, Cambodia is one of the world's best performers in poverty eradication as the economy overachieved the Millennium Development Goal (MDG) by halving the poverty rate from 52.2 percent to 20.5 percent of the population between 2004 and 2011.[42] The significant poverty reduction can be attributed to the adoption of the East Asian development model which focused on the development of labour-intensive manufacturing industry as the key engine for economic growth. In addition, improved agricultural productivity, particularly in rice production, which is facilitated by enhancement in road access, improved irrigation and increased access to market information, also contributed to the poverty reduction in Cambodia.

---

[39] See United Nations (1992).

[40] See Channyda and Taguiam (2015).

[41] See Ford (2013).

[42] See Sobrado *et al.* (2014).

4.4.1.2 *Meeting Challenges and Seizing Opportunities*

As seen in the previous discussion, Cambodia is on a general positive trajectory. Past growth has been robust and the country's industrialisation effort is gathering pace. Increased domestic savings can be channelled towards productive investment, and Cambodia also has tremendous potentials for tourism. On the social development front, the country has made great strides over the past 30 years in recovering from the scars of the Khmer Rouge regime. Accessibility to healthcare and education has been improved while millions have been lifted out of poverty. Nevertheless, challenges remain.

First, poor governance and weak institution are still the main hurdles to development. As shown in ACI's competitiveness analysis in Chapter 2, nine out of 24 weakest indicators for Cambodia come from the Government and Institutional Settings environment.[43] Even though the state plays a relatively passive role in driving economic reforms in Cambodia,[44] low credibility and accountability within the governing institutions may deter investment from potential investors and cause economic loss. Moreover, owing to poor governance, large foreign aid infusions were misused and did not reach the intended beneficiaries.[45] More worrisome, poor governance may also propagate social inequality as social mobility tends to be determined by wealth instead of merit. Such patronage mechanism is leveraged by the rich elites to climb higher while leaving the poor further behind.

Decades of conflicts in Cambodia had led to massive destruction in terms of socio-economic setting as well as the physical landscape. Due to the financial constraints, the Cambodian government has been highly dependent on foreign aids to finance the reconstruction and recovery progress since the early 1990s. Official Development Assistance (ODA) received by Cambodia contributed to an average of 9 percent of total GDP for over two decades from 1993 to 2014 as shown in Figure 4.6. While foreign assistance is indeed essential for the reconstruction, the large scale of aid infusions had also caused distortions in the economy, which were also termed as "Dutch disease" effects in some studies.[46] First, the robust foreign aid sector in Cambodia had siphoned scarce talent from the public and private sectors, causing talent gap in the economy and public administration.[47] Second, aid dependence may also be associated with the deterioration of fiscal capacity.[48] This is manifested in one of the IMF's studies which found a significant negative association between foreign aid and domestic tax revenues particularly in low-income countries with weak institutions.[49] While the contribution of net ODA received by Cambodia has dropped to its lowest in 2014 at 4.8 percent of GDP, the unintended consequences of aid dependence including brain drain and weak fiscal capacity need to be rectified.

---

[43] See Chapter 2 for a detailed discussion.

[44] *Ibid.*

[45] See Ear (2007).

[46] See Ear (2007) and Godfrey *et al.* (2000), cited Ear (2007).

[47] See Ear (2007).

[48] *Ibid.*

[49] See Benedek *et al.* (2012).

Figure 4.6: Share of Net ODA Received in Cambodia's GDP, 1993–2014

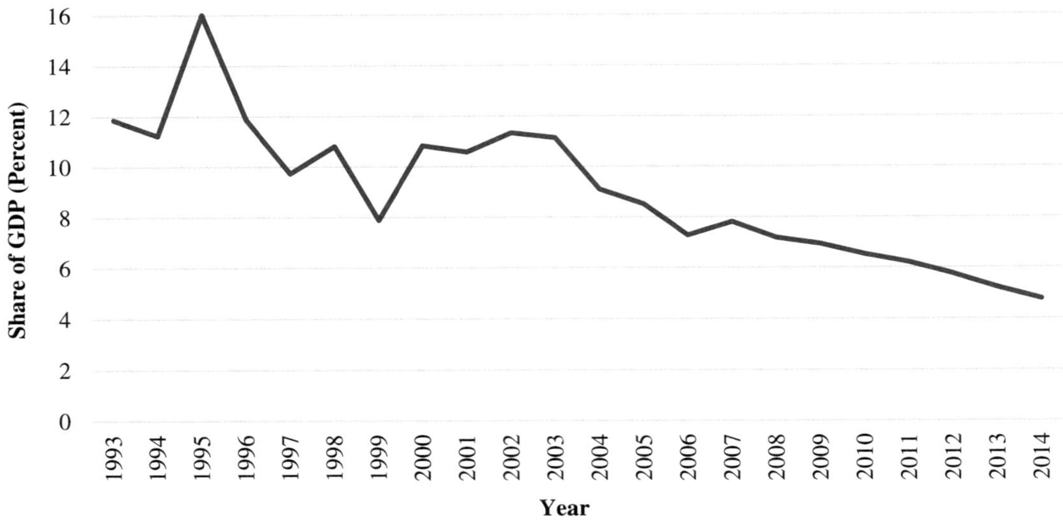

Source: World Bank, World Development Indicators

Moreover, the Cambodian economy still lagged behind in connectivity enhancement in terms of the road, rail and waterway as remarked by the Director-General of the Ministry of Public Works and Transport Investment.[50] In addition, infrastructure development has been concentrated in urban areas including Phnom Penh, Siem Reap and Sihanoukville where major economic activities, namely tourism and the garment industry are located. In contrast, the infrastructure serving the rural poor is still inadequate, and this leads to unbalanced development between rural and urban areas.[51] Apart from the logistics connectivity, basic amenities such as water supply and sanitation remain a huge concern in Cambodia. As identified by the World Bank, merely 21 percent and 42 percent of the total population have access to piped water supply and improved sanitation respectively as of 2015. The low accessibility and quality of infrastructure in Cambodia including power, water and sewage, telecommunications and transport need to be upgraded given its significant impacts to economic development and welfare improvement.[52]

While the performance of poverty eradication in Cambodia is applauded, poverty assessment by the World Bank found that the impressive poverty reduction is fragile as the income of many people who escaped absolute poverty had increased merely from 1 US dollar per day to 2–4 US dollars per day according to the same poverty assessment report.[53] That implies that a slight shock can easily push these vulnerable people back to poverty. In addition, 90 percent of the poor

[50] See Cambodia Development Resource Institute (2016) and Parikh (2016).

[51] See Sobrado *et al.* (2014) and Parikh (2016).

[52] See World Bank (2002).

[53] See Sobrado *et al.* (2014).

are concentrated in the countryside, implying a large rural–urban divide in Cambodia.[54] More worrisome, the reduced inequality in Cambodia as depicted by declining Gini coefficient does not stand to scrutiny according to the same World Bank report. In fact, the gap between the rich and the poor had widened in absolute terms.

As mentioned earlier, the labour-intensive manufacturing sector has been the key engine of economic growth in Cambodia, of which the export-oriented garment industry has been playing a substantial role since the mid-1990s. The garment industry had not only contributed to the export revenue in Cambodia but also led to poverty reduction and gender equality.[55] This is because majority of the garment factory workers are female and they were paid a minimum monthly wage of 45 US dollars (above the poverty line of 30 US dollars) as imposed in the US–Cambodia Bilateral Textile Agreement. Nonetheless, that might not be the case now with the expiration of bilateral agreement in 2004. Cambodian garment industry is now more commonly associated with sweatshops and labour rights abuses according to a report by Human Rights Watch.[56]

In addition, the garment industry constitutes the lion share of exports. Overdependence on this industry, which mainly involves low-skilled labour and a minimum level of technology, is unsustainable and does not contribute much to the industrial upgrading.[57] According to data from the World Bank, a mere 0.76 percent of total manufactured exports from Cambodia in 2015 were high-technology products,[58] which has highlighted the need to revamp the manufacturing sector. Nevertheless, Cambodia's effort to move up the value chain may also be hampered by poor education quality. High unemployment among college graduates[59] points to the persistence of mismatches between graduates' skills and industry needs.

4.4.1.3 *Policy Implications for Cambodia*

Going forward, Cambodia needs to improve the credibility, accountability and transparency of the government to reduce the associated economic and social costs. Strengthening good governance and improving institutional capacity have been codified as key areas in Cambodia's Rectangular Strategy. A concrete step was made to fulfil these goals with the promulgation of the first Anti-Corruption Law in 2010. However, more should be done. According to the latest Corruption Perceptions Index released by Transparency International, Cambodia was ranked 156 out of 176 countries in 2016, the worst performer among all ASEAN economies.[60] The rise of opposition party and civil society expressing their dissatisfaction through demonstrations such as the most notorious civilians' fight against land grab of Boeung Kak Lake and garment factory labour strikes sent a clear signal of the immediate need in improving governance.[61]

---

[54] See World Bank's country overview, https://www.worldbank.org/en/country/cambodia/overview#1.

[55] See Yamagata (2006).

[56] See Kashyap (2015).

[57] See Rasiah (2009) and Lee and Duong (2010).

[58] See World Development Indicators database of the World Bank.

[59] See Ford (2013).

[60] See Transparency International (2017).

[61] See Kry (2014).

Meanwhile, lessons from the flying geese paradigm point to the need of education reforms in order to produce the talent pool which is essential for catching-up. Labour equipped with technical knowledge is critical for vertical upgrading from low-end manufacturing to more sophisticated industries. The partnership between Cambodian government and one of the tech giants, Microsoft shows that the reforms have been initiated to prepare the economy for the fourth Industrial Revolution.[62] Education and training focusing on science, technology, engineering and mathematics — collectively known as the STEM fields — should be the focal point in pushing Cambodia forward in a tech-driven economy.

As industrial upgrading is pursued, the service and agriculture sectors should not be neglected. With regard to services, Cambodia can learn from the experience of Malaysia to further develop its tourism industry by investing in infrastructure, especially airport and port facilities, enhancing government expenditure in tourism promotion activities and maintaining socio-political stability.[63] Moreover, for diversification, other service industries such as financial and logistics should also be fostered. Meanwhile, despite a declining share in total GDP, the agriculture sector remains critical for Cambodia as it employed almost half of the total labour force as of 2012.[64] Hence, enhancing agricultural productivity is vital for food security and rural–urban balanced development.

As mentioned earlier, Cambodia's overdependence on foreign aid has led to the deterioration of fiscal capacity, especially in terms of tax revenue mechanism in Cambodia.[65] While the adoption of Revenue Mobilisation Strategy in 2014 had seen an improvement in tax administration and contributed to tax revenue gains from 13.7 percent of total GDP in 2014 to 14.6 percent in 2015, the forecast by the IMF[66] has projected a rising fiscal pressure in Cambodia resulting from the expanding public expenditure. More worrisome, the external debt-to-GDP ratio in Cambodia has been rising steadily since 2008. The external debt stock of Cambodia has increased from 23.8 percent of GDP in 2008 to 51.6 percent in 2015.[67] Although Debt Sustainability Analysis by the IMF [68] shows a low risk of debt distress in Cambodia, debt sustainability remains vulnerable to external shocks and weak fiscal position. With a decline in ODA support over the years (see Figure 4.7), it is apparent that the government has to continue its effort in building a stable revenue mechanism and tax administration for maintaining its fiscal sustainability.

Finally, as remarked by the Cambodian Prime Minister, Hun Sen during the annual Cambodia Outlook Conference in 2016, the infrastructure constraints have impeded economic integration in Cambodia. He also highlighted the urgent need to push for infrastructure investment in Cambodia.[69] While the policies outlined in the National Strategic Development Plan

---

[62] See *Microsoft Asia News Center* (2016).

[63] See Tan, Gopalan and Ye (2016) for an empirical investigation of the drivers of growth for the Malaysian tourism industry.

[64] See Joosu-Palu (2015).

[65] See Ear (2007).

[66] See IMF (2016).

[67] See World Development Indicators database of the World Bank.

[68] See IMF (2016).

[69] See Parikh (2016).

2014–2018[70] had demonstrated the government's ambitious plan in developing physical infrastructure including road networks, railways, ports and airports, the masterplan also pointed out the financial constraints faced by the government. Being one of the founding members for the Asian Infrastructure Investment Bank (AIIB), Cambodia is on the right trajectory and should continue its efforts in leveraging the international and regional partnerships in order to overcome the development bottlenecks. In addition, the Country Engagement Plan released by the World Bank in 2016 targeting at improving the road system and water supplies among others has also echoed the main thrust of infrastructure development set out in the National Strategic Development Plan.[71]

4.4.2 Laos

4.4.2.1 *Progress of Reforms in Laos*

Formerly a part of French Indochina, Laos gained its independence in 1953, the same year as Cambodia. Being the only landlocked country in ASEAN, Laos has a relatively low profile in the international scene. Nevertheless, Laos was soon drawn into the Vietnam War, the residual effects of which still affect the daily life of Laotians these days. Approximately 80 million unexploded ordnances or 30 percent of total bombs dropped are still causing 300 causalities annually and contaminated 25 percent of villages, leaving large areas of non-arable land.[72] As Laos restored peace and stability in 1975, the country was placed under the governance of the Lao People's Revolutionary Party, which still remains as one of the last one-party regimes in today's world.

In general, economic development in Laos since 1975 can be divided into two phases. The first phase (1976–1985) was under a command economy, while the second phase (1986 and onwards) sees the transition of Laos towards a market-based system. After decades of conflicts and warfare, reconstruction and state building were the main priorities set by the government in the first phase. Two major development plans, namely the One-Year Plan (1976–1977) and the Three-Year Plan (1978–1980) were formulated in order to rebuild the war-torn economy. Major land collectivisation was implemented across the country to promote sharing of land and other production means, and consequently to boost agricultural production.[73] Nonetheless, the policy outcomes did not turn out as expected. The collectivised land and village-based agriculture cooperatives as well as state farms which were established had brought minimal impacts on agricultural development.[74] On the contrary, declining agricultural productivity and rising opposition among the peasants eventually forced the government to suspend the policy in the late 1980s.[75]

The Three-Year Plan was succeeded by the first Five-Year Plan (1981–1985), which emphasised on improving agricultural production, education, external economic assistance, state

[70] See Ministry of Planning of Cambodia (2014).

[71] See World Bank (2016a).

[72] See National Regulatory Authority (2017).

[73] See St John (2006).

[74] *Ibid.*

[75] See Vandergeest (2003) and Ducourtieux, Laffort and Sacklokham (2005).

governance, and infrastructure development including sanitary, transportation and telecommunication. Similar to its predecessors, the plan had failed to deliver satisfactory outcomes in the targeted areas, particularly in the agriculture sector.[76] After multiple rounds of experiments which did not seem to bear fruit, the government had finally decided to take a bolder move by changing the course from a centrally planned to a market-based economic system.

The Laotian government announced its New Economic Mechanism (NEM) in 1986 with the aim of transforming the economy. The second Five-Year Plan (1986–1990) saw a gradual withdrawal of the state from the economy and also marked the departure from a centrally planned economy to a market-oriented economy in Laos. Price and exchange rate controls were lifted, and domestic markets and international trade were liberalised. SOEs were privatised, the banking system restructured and private sector's participation in the economy was encouraged.

Figure 4.7: Real GDP and Real GDP Per Capita Growth Rates in Laos, 1985–2015

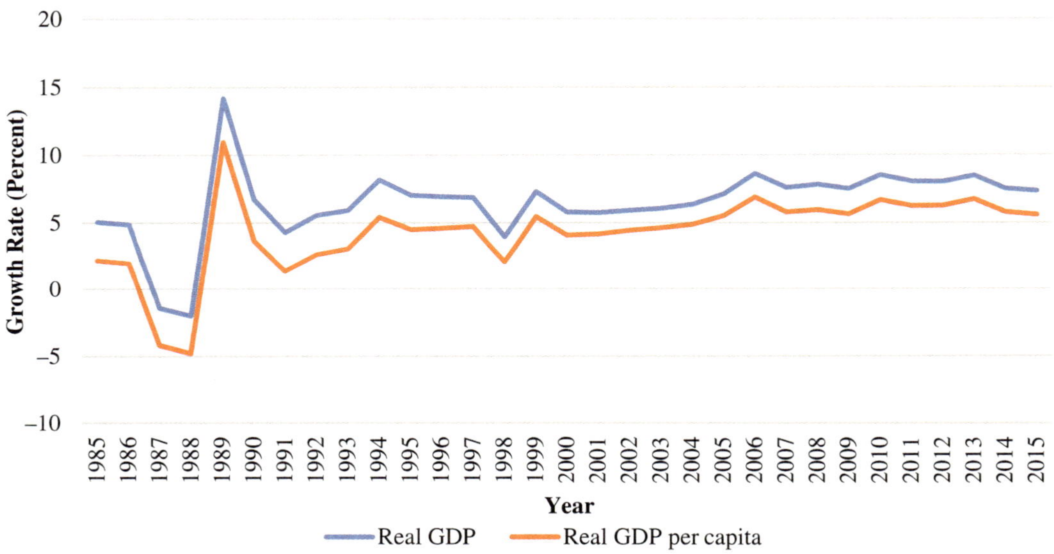

Source: World Bank, World Development Indicators

The ambitious reforms had a rough start due to the serious drought that hit the agricultural production in 1987 and 1988. As a consequence, real GDP had plummeted to negative growth rates of –1.4 percent and –2.0 percent respectively in 1987 and 1988.[77] Nonetheless, inflows of foreign assistance led to a rapid recovery, and the economy managed to achieve an average of 7.2 percent real GDP growth between 1989 and 2015 as shown in Figure 4.7. Real GDP per capita growth also tracked the patterns of real GDP growth between 2000 and 2014, suggesting a better living standard of the people provided there is equitable distribution of growth. After a

[76] See Stuart-Fox (1986).

[77] See World development indicators database of the World Bank.

Figure 4.8: Shares of Gross Domestic Savings and Gross Fixed Capital Formation in Laos' GDP, 2000–2015

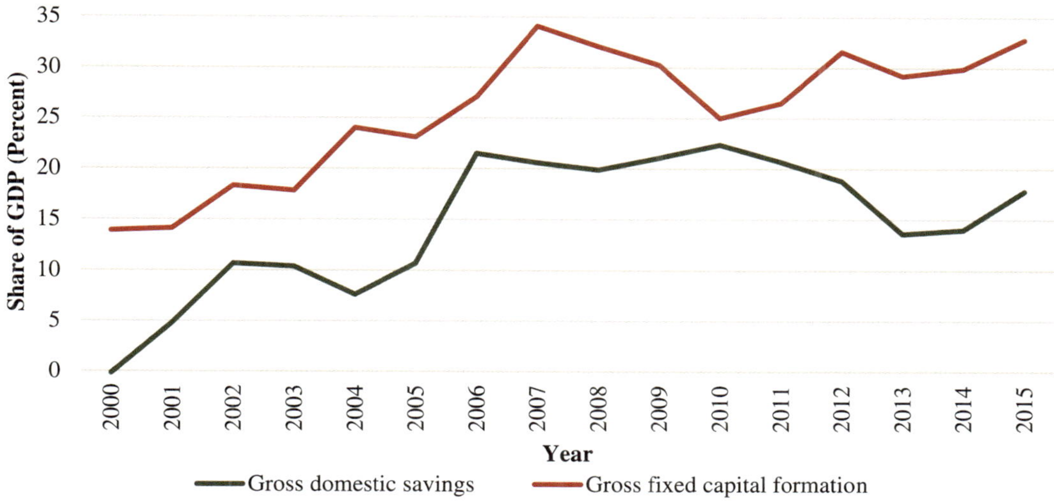

Source: World Bank, World Development Indicators

dip in growth rate due to the Asian Financial Crisis (AFC), real GDP growth stayed relatively constant and showed a sign of slowdown after 2013.

Figure 4.8 shows the level of domestic savings and investment in Laos during the period of 2000–2015. As can be seen, the domestic savings level in Laos was virtually zero in 2000. This suggests that the investment was largely financed by foreign capital through direct investment or foreign assistance. After 2000, the savings level in Laos has improved remarkably and reached 18 percent of total GDP in 2015. Nonetheless, policy-makers should stay precautious given the evident gap between domestic savings and investment of about 15 percent in 2015.

During the early years of reforms in Laos, the agriculture sector had remained the most prioritised sector, absorbing the highest proportion (20 percent) of total public expenditure as laid out in the second Five-Year Plan.[78] However, there has been a structural shift. Figure 4.9 illustrates the share of GDP by sector of origin in Laos between 1989 and 2014. The share of agriculture has declined over time, and in 2004, it was overtaken by the service sector as the primary contributor to GDP. In the meantime, the manufacturing sector has also gained in importance although its share in GDP has dropped after 2012.

Figure 4.10 shows the external trade performance of Laos between 1984 and 2014. Imports surged between 1986 and 1989 as Laos was compelled to import rice from neighbouring countries due to its low rice yields following severe droughts. As the NEM was implemented, trade flows in terms of both imports and exports increased. Persistent trade deficits, whereby imports always constitute a significantly higher share of GDP than exports, is a cause for concern which should not be overlooked.

---

[78] See Ng (1987).

Figure 4.9: Sectoral Shares of Laos' GDP, 1989–2014

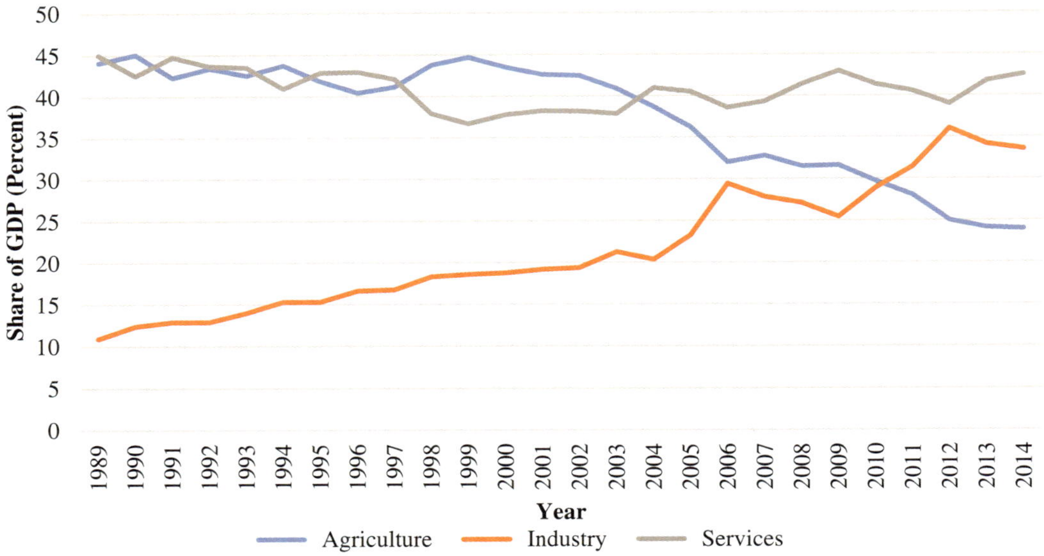

Source: United Nations Conference on Trade and Development

Figure 4.10: Shares of Imports and Exports in Laos' GDP, 1981–2014

Source: United Nations Conference on Trade and Development

Figure 4.11: FDI Inflows to Laos at Current Prices Million US Dollars, 1992–2015

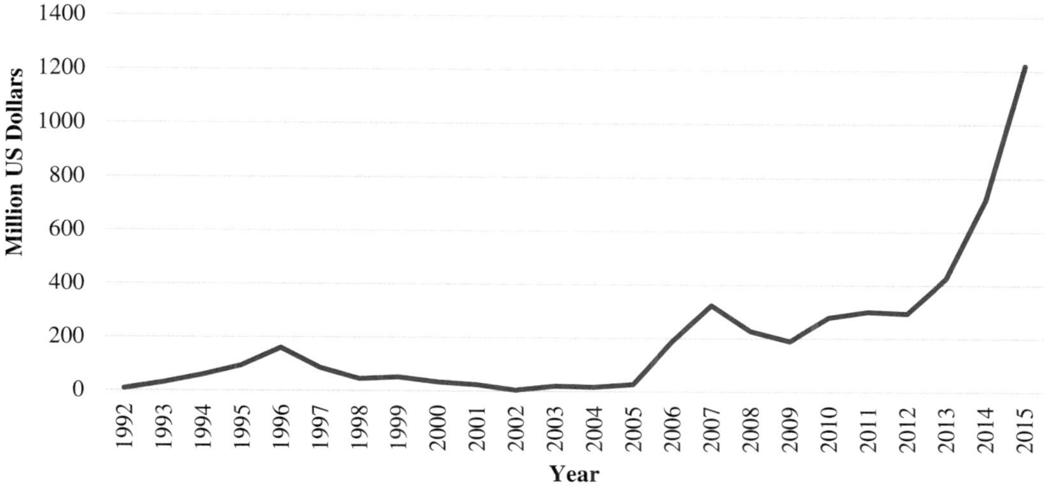

Source: United Nations Conference on Trade and Development

In terms of FDI attraction, Laos has demonstrated little improvement in attracting foreign capital even after embarking on market-oriented reforms. As can be seen in Figure 4.11, FDI remained below 400 million US dollars for two decades between 1992 and 2012, albeit with a slight bounce in 2005 and onwards. FDI only has gained in momentum since 2013. By 2015, FDI inflows to Laos exceeded 1.2 billion US dollars (see Figure 4.11). The development experience of HPAEs has demonstrated the importance of FDI in driving the economic growth. Hence, Laos has to continue the current momentum of FDI growth to invigorate its reforms progress.

Apart from economic development, the reforms also set priorities in public administration improvement, living standard betterment and infrastructure development. The development in the education sector was shown in the rise of net primary school enrolment rate from 65.2 percent in 1988 to 92.7 percent in 2015 according to UIS. Nevertheless, literacy rate of the adult population is still relatively low, having only increased from 60.3 percent in 1995 to 79.9 percent in 2015. Meanwhile, better access to health services has significantly reduced the infant mortality rate from 120.6 to 50.7 per 1,000 live births between 1986 and 2015. However, more remains to be done as the infant mortality rate in Laos is still the highest among the CLMV countries. Furthermore, similar to Cambodia, Laos also faces a shortage of doctors as the ratio of physicians to population has remained stagnant at 2:10,000 since 1990.[79]

Remarkable growth also brought about significant reduction in poverty in Laos. The MDG's first goal of eradicating extreme poverty was achieved ahead of the 2015 deadline. According to

[79] See World development indicators database of the World Bank.

the UN, Laos' national poverty rate was halved from 46 percent in 1992 to 23 percent in 2013. On the contrary, inequality in Laos has worsened despite significant poverty reduction.[80] Its Gini coefficient rose from 34.3 to 37.9 from 1992 to 2012 according to World Bank data.

4.4.2.2 *Meeting Challenges and Seizing Opportunities*

Laos is one of the fastest growing economies in East Asia and the Pacific region.[81] Positive progress has also been made in achieving the MDGs including poverty alleviation, hunger reduction, and health and education improvement. However, notwithstanding the advancement in many socio-economic dimensions, Laos has not graduated from its LDC status since 1971. The prevailing challenges must be overcome in order to achieve the goal of graduating from LDC status by 2020.[82]

Being the most heavily bombed country in the world per capita,[83] Laos had a tougher start than its peers. Four decades after the Vietnam War, unexploded ordnances still leave many in danger. Human casualties aside, the enormous number of unexploded bombs have also contaminated large areas of land in all provinces and impeded the development of the agriculture sector. More worrisome, Laos is an agrarian society with 80 percent of total employed workforce engaged in agricultural production as of 2015 according to the data by the International Labour Organisation (ILO). The wide area of contaminated and non-arable land will indeed hamper agricultural development and more importantly threaten the livelihood of the society. While the former US President Obama had pledged 90 million US dollars in funding the bombs clearance mission during his visit to Vientiane in 2016,[84] the complete clearance of unexploded bombs will not be achieved any time soon. Furthermore, the poor conditions of the agriculture sector are exacerbated by the state of the country, which is highly prone to natural disasters including cyclone, drought and flooding. The impacts of natural disasters most of the time tend to fall on the vulnerable rural agricultural communities, threatening their food security and livelihood.[85]

The higher level of vulnerability against natural hazards among the rural population also highlighted the predicament of rural–urban disparities in Laos. As the increase in Gini coefficient from 34.3 in 1992 to 37.9 in 2012[86] has shown, inequality in Laos has deteriorated despite a rapid growth in GDP over the years, making Laos the most unequal economy among CLMV. More importantly, in-depth studies have found that the worsened inequality in Laos is characterised by the widening rural–urban divide.[87] The growth outcomes have concentrated in the hands of the few in urban areas, leaving the marginalised rural poor behind. More worrisome, the rural-urban divide is not manifested in income level alone but also in education and healthcare as well. For instance, a report by World Food Programme found there was still about 55 percent of

[80] See Warr, Rasphone and Menon (2014).

[81] See World Bank's country overview, http://www.worldbank.org/en/country/lao/overview#1.

[82] See Ministry of Planning and Investment of Laos (2016).

[83] See Kiernan and Owen (2015).

[84] See Labott (2016).

[85] See Center for Excellence in Disaster Management and Humanitarian Assistance (2014).

[86] See World Development Indicators database of the World Bank.

[87] See Chareunsy (2012).

children from rural ethnic minorities who suffered from stunted growth in 2015.[88] While there was positive outcome in reducing the hungry poor, Laos is still struggling with the persistence of disparities between rural and urban areas.

The inequality problem in Laos is exacerbated by the poor infrastructure in Laos. Laos was ranked at 152nd out of total 160 countries in the World Bank's 2016 Logistics Performance Index (LPI), the lowest in Southeast Asia. In particular, Laos had performed most weakly in terms of the infrastructure dimension (ranked 155th) among all other components included in the index. Being one of the most sparsely populated economies in Asia, more than half of the total population in Laos lives in rural areas[89] dispersed in over 10,000 villages.[90] Without a comprehensive logistics network, connectivity within the country is constrained, which in turn resulted in unbalanced development.

Similar to Cambodia, the list of weakest indicators for Laos as identified by the ACI competitiveness analysis[91] also underlined the weak fiscal capacity of the economy. Laos is among the highest per capita aid recipient and is highly dependent on external sources for growth and development.[92] Figure 4.12 demonstrates the amount of ODA received by Laos for the period

Figure 4.12: Share of Net ODA Received in Laos' GDP, 1984–2014

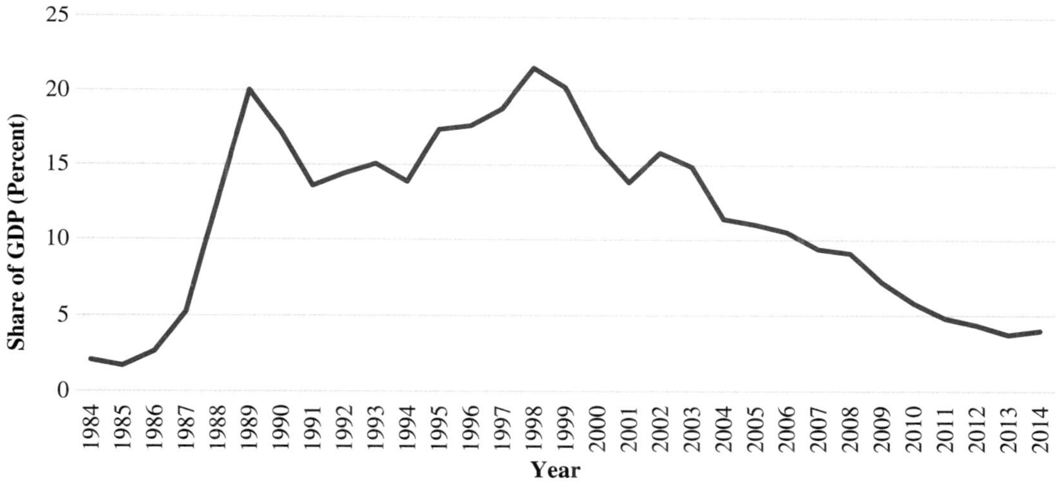

Source: World Bank, World Development Indicators

between 1984 and 2014. While the proportion of ODA received dropped to merely 4 percent in 2014 as compared to its peak at 22 percent of total GDP in 1998, heavy dependence on extensive foreign assistance in the past may leave Laos unprepared to fill in the vacuum left by the withdrawal of ODA[93] since 2002 and consequently may put Laos on the brink of sovereign default.

[88] See World Food Programme (2017).

[89] According to World Bank data, rural population in 2015 constitutes 61 percent of total population.

[90] See the country overview of Laos, http://www1.wfp.org/countries/lao-peoples-democratic-republic.

[91] See Chapter 2 for a detailed discussion.

[92] See St John (2006).

[93] See World Bank (2016b).

As noted by IMF during the consultation with Laos in 2016, Laos' fiscal position is weak and vulnerable due to widening fiscal deficit and growing external debt. The fiscal deficit is projected to increase from 2.7 percent of nominal GDP in 2015 to 5.9 percent in 2016 owing to bloating current expenditure and weak tax revenue gains. Furthermore, the stock of external debt saw a steady growth from 45.5 percent of nominal GDP to 51.7 percent between 2011 and 2015.[94]

Although Laos is a landlocked country, it is blessed with rich natural resources which have been driving economic growth. The mining and hydropower sectors have been the key engines of growth for the country.[95] While growth in the mining sector is projected to stall due to depleting mineral deposits as well as volatile commodities prices, the power sector with an expected expansion rate of 7 percent will remain an important source of government revenue.[96] While Laos has benefited tremendously from its natural endowment, it must beware of the "resource curse", where the overdependence on natural resources will eventually suppress productivity growth and negatively impact long-term development. In addition, if not properly managed, the exploitation of natural resources will create tremendous environmental costs.

4.4.2.3 *Policy Implications for Laos*

As compared to other transition economies, Laos is located in a less strategic geographical location. The landlocked geographical setting coupled with infrastructure constraint have caused bottlenecks to Laos' development progress. Moreover, economic integration into the regional and global markets is impaired by poor connectivity. This makes infrastructure development a policy priority for Laos. Enhancing intra-country and inter-country connectivity through construction of transport infrastructure including land and air transport will help to overcome the geographical disadvantage of the landlocked economy and aid in achieving more balanced development.

The government has taken steps to overcome the geographical impediments as reflected in the implementation of Master Plan on Communication and Transport in 2011. Among others, development of physical road linkage within the country is one of the priorities in the plan.[97] While progress has been made, more still need to be done, particularly in overcoming the financing gaps. Policy-makers should gear up the development progress by leveraging on regional cooperation as well as bilateral economic relations. For instance, the partnerships with Chinese investors in several infrastructure and hydropower projects have eased the financial constraints in infrastructure development and should therefore be promoted.[98]

Besides road transport, the government should also seek to develop the Information and Communications Technology (ICT) sector. As the broad-based transformational impact of ICT

---

[94] See IMF (2017).

[95] See OECD (2013) and World Bank (2016b).

[96] See World Bank (2016b).

[97] See Oraboune (2008).

[98] See World Bank (2016b) and http://www.investlaos.gov.la/index.php/news-and-events?start=4.

on the livelihoods of the poor has been widely recognised, the utilisation of technology in overcoming the geographical barrier should be promoted in Laos. Moreover, the global economy has embarked on the Fourth Industrial Revolution driven by the advancement of technology. There is no doubt that technology will be playing a bigger role in the future economy. Laos has witnessed improvement in ICT penetration as the percentage of households with internet rose from 3.4 percent to 11.4 percent between 2010 and 2015.[99] Nevertheless, the rate of internet access still remains low and more should be done.

Policy-makers should also steer education reforms towards the goal of producing a workforce which is resilient to future structural changes. Echoing the point on the importance of ICT, the education sector in Laos should be revamped in line with the future market demands. School syllabus has to be revised to equip the students with knowledge in the field of ICT and eventually to groom a pool of tech-savvy labour force. For instance, the collaboration between Ministry of Agriculture and Forestry and Wetlands Alliance, a Swedish funded organisation which deployed ICT in teaching and learning process has successfully produced a pool of well-trained workforce.[100] Such initiative should be endorsed and strengthened in Laos.

In addition, Laos is vulnerable in terms of its fiscal capacity. Inflows of foreign aid, on the one hand, had supported war reconstruction and rebuilding in Laos after 1975. On the other hand, it is a low-hanging fruit which provides no incentive for the government to seek for other fiscal resources. With respect to the double-edged sword effect of foreign aid, it is apparent for the government to strike a balance between aid dependence and fiscal governance. More worrisome, the shrinking external assistance and bloating public spending, which are coupled with decades of trade deficit have put Laos on risk of fiscal default. As emphasised by the IMF, Laos should pursue fiscal consolidation to strengthen its fiscal position and achieve fiscal sustainability.[101] It is encouraging to see that the revision of the State Budget Law in 2015 and the formulation of the Long-term Fiscal Development Strategy which aims to enforce fiscal discipline in Laos have set a positive tone for future fiscal reforms.[102]

In terms of the overall development strategy, policy-makers in Laos should seek to achieve economic diversification and move up the value chain. As discussed in Section 4.4.2.2, exploiting natural resources for economic growth may hamper the economy's capacity in the long run and entail negative trade-offs in terms of the environmental costs. Thus, the service sector and high value-added manufacturing should be developed as a means for diversification. At the same time, policy-makers should also seek to develop the agriculture sector. With limited arable land, improving agricultural productivity growth is paramount. In addition, the low resilience of agricultural productions to weather fluctuations and natural disasters, particularly droughts, is a cause for concern. Thus, modernising the agriculture sector through introduction of new crops and construction of irrigation systems to mitigate vulnerability is also a key priority in Laos.

[99] See International Telecommunication Union (2015, 2016).

[100] See Haddawy (2011).

[101] See IMF (2017).

[102] See World Bank (2016b).

4.4.3 Myanmar

4.4.3.1 *Progress of Reforms in Myanmar*

Myanmar has caught global attention since the early 2010s after undertaking a series of political, economic and administrative reforms. Its economic prospects seem promising in light of the government's commitment to market-oriented reforms and further economic integration. Moreover, the lifting of sanctions has seen MNCs and international investors flocking to this transitional economy.

After gaining independence from the British in 1948, the newly elected government had progressively pursued a number of national plans including Two-Year Plan (1948–1950), Eight-Year Plan (1952–1960) and Four-Year Plan (1961–1964). While free trade policy is not something alien under almost one and a half centuries of British colonisation, Myanmar switched its course with the implementation of import substitution policy and restrict exports to only rice exports. Nonetheless, the promising targets laid out in the national plans remain unrealised due to poor planning and mismanagement by the state. The over-reliance on rice export backfired as the international price of rice dipped from 60 pounds sterling per ton in 1953 to 35 pounds sterling per ton in 1960.

Against the backdrop of disintegrating unity and economic downturn, the army took over the government in 1962 and nationalisation was implemented throughout the country. Major economic activities were brought under public ownership. However, the outcome of the command economy policies did not turn out as expected.[103] Besides relatively low economic growth as compared to post-1988,[104] savings and investment rate were also low, contributing to less than 15 percent of GDP by 1988.[105] The isolationist policies also led to shortage of essential goods in the market, which in turn fostered the black market trade activities.[106]

Interestingly, economic deterioration did not affect social development in Myanmar. On the contrary, there was notable improvement in education and healthcare between 1960 and 1980 (see Table 4.1). Evident leaps can be observed in terms of literacy rate, primary school enrolment, life expectancy, infant mortality, safe water access and ratio of physicians to population.

Nevertheless, as the economy slumped, riots arose among workers and students to express their discontent over increasing living costs and high unemployment. As a result, the military regime was forced to roll out reforms in the late 1970s. The state started to relax the inward-looking policy and encourage more participation of private sector in the economy. Price caps which were imposed on paddy and other crops were eliminated. Additionally, the isolationist policy was aborted with acceptance of foreign aids from the international community.

---

[103] See Thein (2004).

[104] According to World Development Indicators, Myanmar grew at an average growth rate of 4.3 percent in real GDP terms between 1968 and 1987. After reforms in 1988, the real GDP grew at an average of 8.0 percent between 1988 and 2015.

[105] See Thein (2004).

[106] *Ibid.* Despite lack of official data, black market activities were estimated to have contributed to 50–85 percent of total official trade in the mid-1980s.

Table 4.1: Comparison of Socio-economic Indicators in Myanmar between 1960 and 1980

Indicator	Myanmar's Performance 1960	Myanmar's Performance 1980	Average Performance of 33 Low-Income Countries 1980
Adult literacy rate (percent)	60	70	50
Enrolment in primary school (percentage of age group)	56	84	94
Life expectancy at birth (years)	44	54	28.5
Infant mortality rate (per 1,000)	129	101	94
Access to safe water (percentage of population)	—	35	31
Population per 10,000 physician (persons)	0.6	1.9	1.7

Source: Thein (2004)

Nonetheless, mounting budget deficit which was financed through money printing had built up pressure on the public administration. The brewing trouble that had emerged since the 1970s was initially buffered by the acceptance of foreign assistance and some reforms policies. The reforms, however, were not sufficient to stop the collapse of the domestic fiscal and monetary systems. The demonetisation without any compensation in 1987 was the last straw that broke the camel's back and sparked the political upheaval in 1988.[107]

The State Law and Order Restoration Council, which later was renamed as the State Peace and Development Council, took over the government in September 1988 with the mission of transforming the close-to-bankrupt economy. The council adopted a market-oriented approach after taking into account the lessons from its predecessor. The reforms saw gradual withdrawal of state intervention in several aspects including external trade, price controls on rice and other major crops, and the banking and financial sector. The reforms also sought to encourage more private sector participation and entrepreneurship in the economy. In accordance with the privatisation agenda, a Privatisation Commission was established in 1995 to oversee the privatisation of inefficient SOEs which were identified as one of the main contributing factors to economic stagnation.[108]

The market-oriented policies continued under the new leadership of President Thein Sein, who was elected in 2010. The newly formed government brought the reform to a whole new level with the initiation of second phase of economic liberalisation in 2011. A series of reforms including outward-looking policy, good governance and further reduction of state's intervention in the market were carried out. The moderate reformist president also announced the release of political prisoners and the nominal abolishment of media censorship which was enforced since 1962. The international community was pleased with the progressive reforms and rewarded

[107] See Thein (2004).
[108] See Odaka (2016).

Figure 4.13: Real GDP and Real GDP Per Capita Growth Rates in Myanmar, 1985–2015

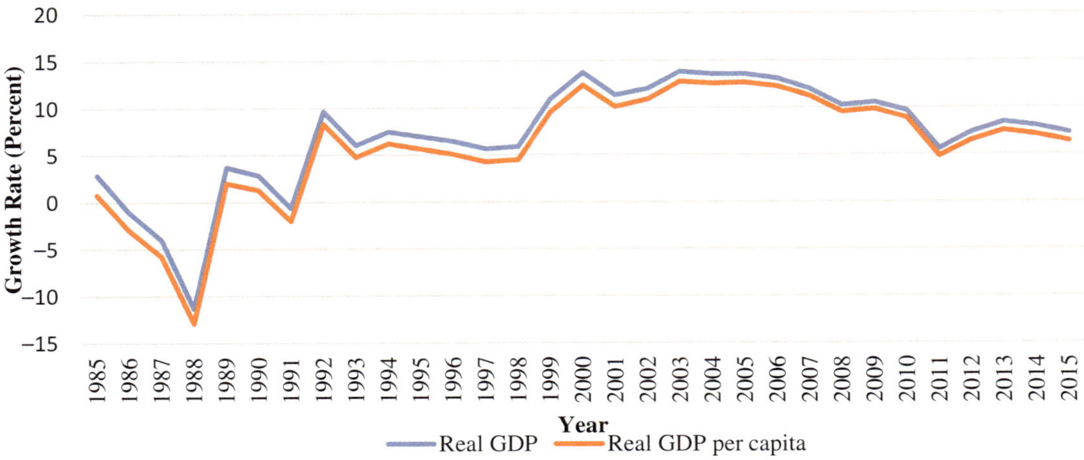

Source: World Bank, World Development Indicators

Figure 4.14: Shares of Gross Domestic Savings and Gross Capital Formation in Myanmar's GDP, 1990–2015[109]

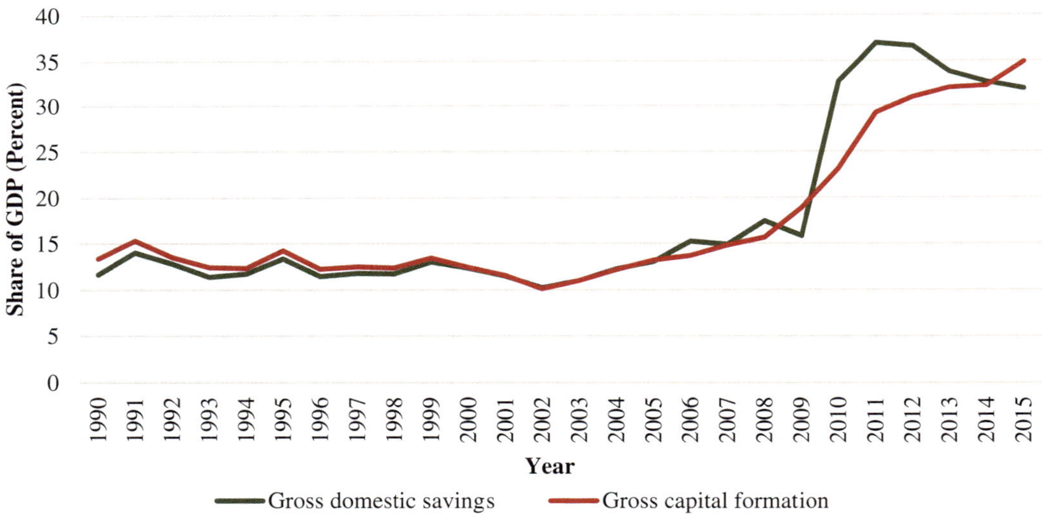

Source: Asian Development Bank

Myanmar with significant debt relief. Sanctions imposed by the United States and European Union were also eased or lifted. As a consequence of the progressive reforms, Myanmar's economy witnessed a quick recovery after the big "V" dip in 1988 (see Figure 4.13). Between 1989 and 2015, real GDP grew at an impressive rate 8.7, percent in average.

[109] As shown in Figure 4.14, gross capital formation was rising consistently even after Asian Financial Crisis and GFC.

Figure 4.15: Shares of Imports and Exports in Myanmar's GDP, 1981–2014

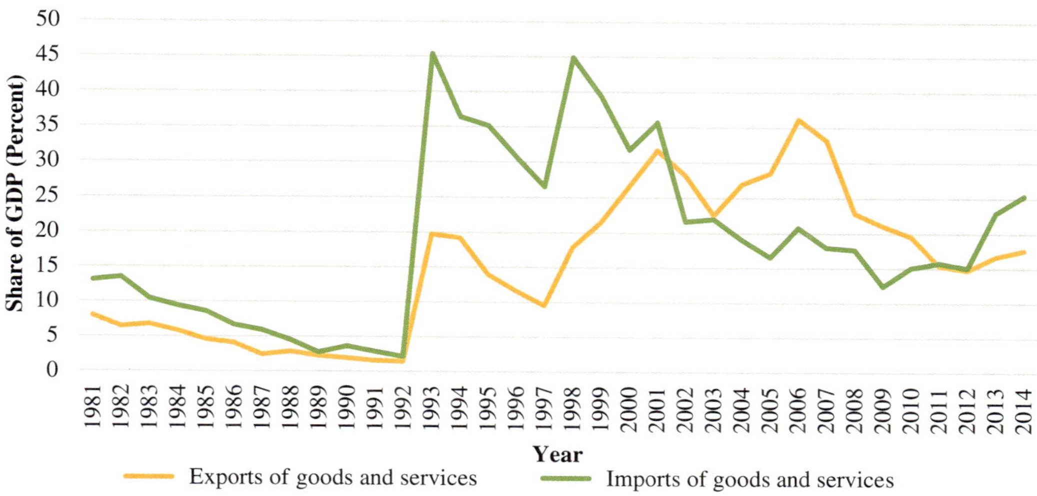

Source: United Nations Conference on Trade and Development

However, savings and investment remained low since 1990 and only gained momentum after 2009 as shown in Figure 4.14. Myanmar's case is unique because domestic savings was almost on par with investment at the early stage of reforms. The low dependence on foreign capital might have reduced the vulnerability of the domestic economy and shielded Myanmar from the impacts of the AFC and the GFC (see Figure 4.14).[110]

Strengthening economic integration which is part of the reform agenda, also saw some positive outcomes. The contribution of external trade to GDP in 2014 almost tripled that in 1984 (see Figure 4.15). Greater participation in the global economy also brought in more foreign capital in terms of FDI as illustrated in Figure 4.16 despite a high volatility of flows after 2002. In general, FDI has increased from 149 million US dollars to 2.8 billion US dollars between 1992 and 2015.

The determination of the government in driving structural transformation is evident in the establishment of the Myanmar Industrial Development Committee, the Myanmar Industrial Development Bank and industrial zones aiming at inviting more investments from the private sector and foreign investors. The efforts did yield positive outcomes as shown in Figure 4.17. Myanmar has undergone transition from an agriculture-based economy to an industrial and service-based economy. The contribution of the agriculture sector to the economy began to shrink after 1999 while the shares of industry and the service sector in Myanmar's GDP are becoming more significant as the reforms progress.

For social development, education has improved in terms of quality and accessibility.[111] The number of schools and tertiary education institutions as well as teaching staffs have increased.

---

[110] Data of Gross Fixed Capital Formation are not available. Gross Capital Formation is used instead.

[111] See Thein (2004).

Figure 4.16: FDI Inflows to Myanmar at Current Prices Million US Dollars, 1992–2015

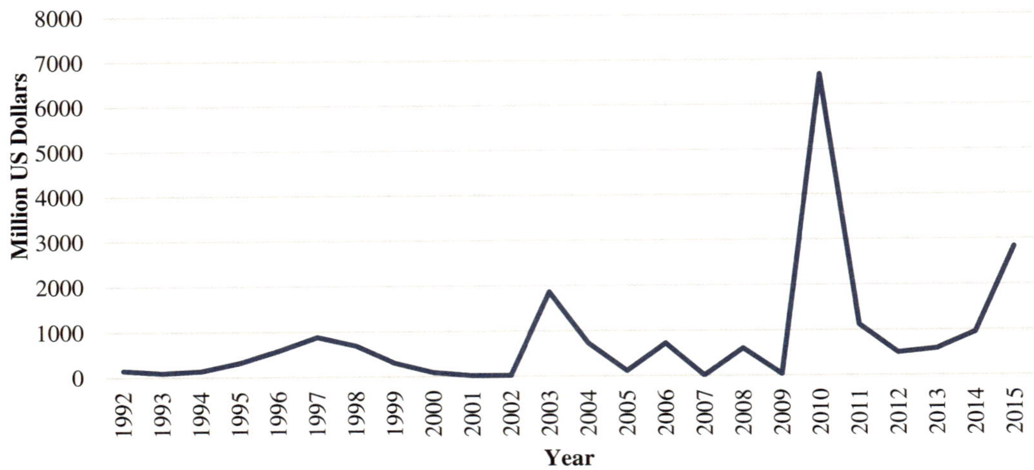

Source: United Nations Conference on Trade and Development

Figure 4.17: Sectoral Shares of Myanmar's GDP, 1981–2015

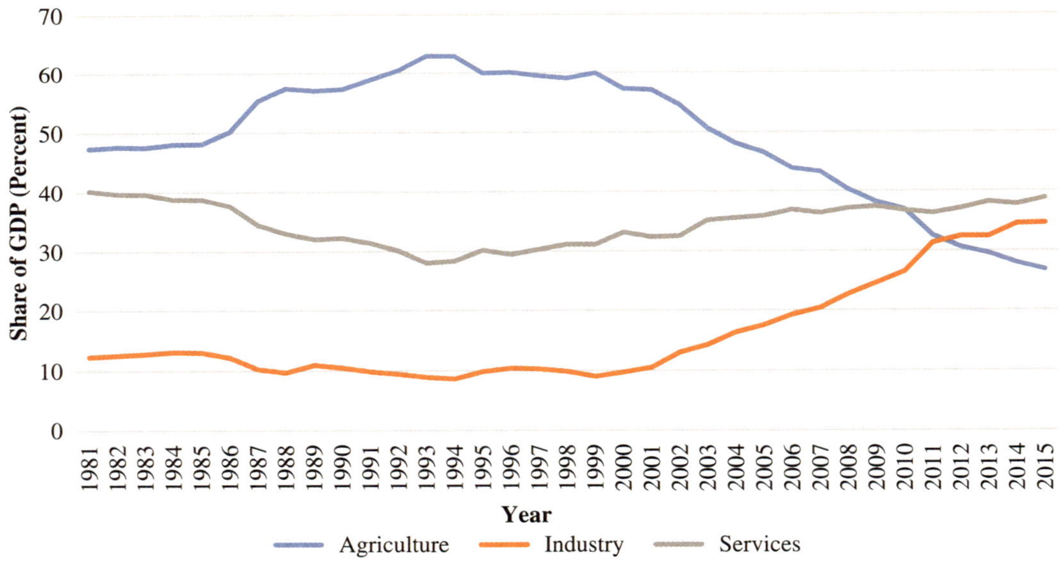

Source: United Nations Conference on Trade and Development

The quality of education was also upgraded through the revision of school syllabus and the introduction of computer literacy since primary school. Myanmar's literacy rate went up to 93.1 percent in 2015, one of the highest among the transition economies according to UIS. The special emphasis on improving the accessibility to health services in the rural areas is also worth highlighting. Infant mortality rate dropped from 101 per 1,000 live births in 1980 to 39.5 in 2012 while ratio of physician to population rose from 2:10,000 in 1980 to 6:10,000 in 2012, the second highest among CLMV.[112] However, the poverty rate in Myanmar was still high with about a quarter of the population living in poverty in 2010.[113]

4.4.3.2 *Meeting Challenges and Seizing Opportunities*

As discussed in the previous section, economic reforms in Myanmar have led to positive outcomes in both economic and social aspects as reflected in multiple indicators. Robust economic growth is coupled with rising savings, deepened economic integration and sectoral transition. Furthermore, the health and education development in Myanmar is also one of the highest among CLMV. While maintaining the current momentum of reforms, it is essential to identify and overcome the prevailing challenges in order to propel the country forward.

Firstly, good governance and political stability are the fundamental building blocks for a prosperous economy. However, such an enabling environment is still in its infant stage in Myanmar. Ethnic insurgencies are a cause for concern as they may deter investment and discourage business activities. While Myanmar has been making progress towards resolving the internal conflicts through dialogues, the intensified communal tensions particularly in the Rakhine state may pose a new threat to public governance. In addition, bureaucratic capacity is in need of improvement and reform. As pointed out by a study by the Asian Development Bank (ADB),[114] the militarisation of the bureaucracy in the former military regime has resulted in a bloated and inefficient public sector. As identified by the United Nations Development Programme (UNDP), immense legislative reform will be another central challenge for Myanmar.[115] Past instances of being on the verge of bankruptcy in the mid-1970s and in 1987[116] also underscore the need to strengthen the country's weak fiscal capacity.

Secondly, Myanmar has not fully utilised opportunities arising from economic integration to realise its potentials. Myanmar has been one of the forerunners among the CLMV to engage in regional and global partnerships, namely ASEAN and the World Trade Organisation (WTO).[117] However, Myanmar remained the least open among the four economies. In 2014, total trade flows in Myanmar accounted for less than half of its GDP (see Figure 4.15), while the total trade flows in Cambodia, Laos and Vietnam constituted almost or more than 100 percent of their GDP, respectively (see Figures 4.4, 4.10 and 4.21, respectively).

Thirdly, although Myanmar has reduced state intervention in the economy, the residual effects of the former command economy have not been erased. In particular, the patron-client relationship between the government and business actors persists. The prevalence of monopolies has created a non-level playing field which hinders economic development. This problem is

---

[112] See World Development Indicators database of the World Bank.

[113] See ADB (2016).

[114] See Hendrix and Noland (2015).

[115] See UNDP (2013a).

[116] See Thein (2004).

[117] Myanmar joined WTO and ASEAN in 1995 and 1997, respectively. It is also the only economy among CLMV which had signed General Agreement on Tariffs and Trade in 1948.

recognised by policy-makers in Myanmar, as evident in the remarks by the Minister of Planning and Finance Kyaw Win during a meeting at the Union of Myanmar Federation of Chambers of Commerce and Industry on 13 June 2017 in Yangon: "Why is our country not developed? What I find first of all is that it is due to monopoly. I believe it is a key reason behind the country's underdevelopment".[118] Moreover, the SOEs in Myanmar are also characterised by inefficiency and lack of financial transparency.[119] While the privatisation of inefficient SOEs was one of the key priorities of the Thein Sein's government, the outcomes of SOE reforms were not impressive, and rent-seeking remained rampant in the economy.[120]

Fourthly, the shortage of skilled labour is another obstacle for Myanmar. Despite the efforts on education reforms, which were reflected in the doubling of budget allocation towards education between fiscal years 2011–2012 and 2012–2013,[121] the economy still lagged behind in terms of higher education as well as technical and vocational education and training. For instance, it was reported by the ADB that as many as 25 percent of total primary school graduates do not enter secondary school.[122] The shortage of skilled labour will become a great barrier as Myanmar speeds up its economic integration and reforms.

Finally, infrastructure development remains a challenge. Besides national transport system including road, railways and waterways, Myanmar also faces challenges in access to electricity and telecommunication. The road density in Myanmar is the lowest among CLMV, faring at 40 km per 1,000 km^2 in 2011.[123] Similarly for telecommunication, Myanmar is the weakest among CLMV with only one fixed telephone subscription per 100 people and 0.3 fixed broadband subscriptions per 100 people in 2015.[124]

4.4.3.3 *Policy Implications for Myanmar*

As discussed in the previous section, enforcement of good governance is one of the biggest barriers to effective reform and development in Myanmar. In recognition of the limitations on the constitution framework which was established in 2008,[125] the Constitutional Review Joint Committee was set up in 2013 to improve the accountability and capacity of all three branches of government, namely judiciary, legislative and executive. The initiative of strengthening good governance can be complemented with the partnerships with international organisations. For instance, the collaboration between the government and UNDP in the three-year Country

[118] See http://www.elevenmyanmar.com/local/myanmar-underdeveloped-due-monopolies-union-minister

[119] See ADB (2012) and Rieffel (2015).

[120] *Ibid.*

[121] In fiscal year 2011–2012, 3.8 percent of national budget was allocated on education. This rose to 6.3 percent in fiscal year 2012–2013. See ADB (2012).

[122] See ADB (2012).

[123] See ADB (2011).

[124] See World Development Indicators database of the World Bank: fixed broadband subscription per 100 people in CLV was 0.5, 0.5 and 8.1, respectively, while fixed telephone subscription per 100 people in CLV was 1.6, 13.7 and 6.3, respectively, in 2015.

[125] See UNDP (2013a).

Programme Action Plan has provided funding and technical support for governance improvement and capacity building.[126]

While the debt write-offs by the Paris Club[127] in 2013 has indeed helped to relieve the fiscal burden of the government, the narrow tax base and low tax revenue in Myanmar has led the IMF to call for fiscal reforms.[128] Fiscal consolidation policies including rationalisation of public spending and establishment of efficient tax mechanism merit particular attention. In addition, the long standing social unrest in Myanmar has elevated economic uncertainties and discouraged economic activities. Thus, the government should continue the efforts in establishing peaceful resolution of civil disputes by fostering dialogue among the conflicting parties.

As studies on government-linked companies in Malaysia have shown, the political patronage practised has led to market inefficiencies and worsened social inequality.[129] The same outcomes can also be observed in Myanmar in which SOEs have impeded economic development.[130] In acknowledgement of the great extent of negative impacts that resulted from inefficient SOEs and monopolies, a new Competition Law is put in place in 2017. While the commitment of the government in creating a level playing field is applauded by many market players, a significant level of political will is required to sustain the efforts in disentangling the intertwining interests among former military, government and business actors. Apart from curbing the abuse of market dominance by the SOEs and monopolies, the privatisation initiatives and SOEs reforms initiatives which had been implemented under the leadership of former President Thein Sein should be broadened and expedited.[131]

In addition, as pointed out by Gerschenkron (1962), being a latecomer allows a faster catching-up process by riding on the forerunners' experience. Myanmar should utilise its advantages as a latecomer and continue its momentum in catching up with other forerunners. Central to this effort is the need to improve Myanmar's human capital. In collaboration with a number of international partners such as British Council, the United Nations International Children's Emergency Fund (UNICEF) and the World Bank, the government has initiated a Comprehensive Education Sector Review in 2012, which set the path for education reforms.[132] The education system should be revamped with a focus on equipping students with technical skills to meet industrial needs.

At the same time, infrastructure development must be prioritised. The development of comprehensive road networks and telecommunication infrastructure will contribute to better national and regional linkages. Nonetheless, as with most developing economies, financial constraints

---

[126] See UNDP (2013b).

[127] As defined in the official website, http://www.clubdeparis.org/, the Paris Club is an informal group of official creditors whose role is to find coordinated and sustainable solutions to the payment difficulties experienced by debtor countries.

[128] See IMF (2015).

[129] See Amsden (1989) and Gomez and Jomo (1999).

[130] See Rieffel (2015).

[131] *Ibid.*

[132] See UNICEF (2012).

may limit the scope and scale of public investment in Myanmar. In this context, policy-makers should leverage on the rising trend of Public–Private Partnerships in financing infrastructure projects as advocated by the World Bank.[133]

4.4.4 Vietnam

4.4.4.1 *Progress of Reforms in Vietnam*

The fall of Saigon on 30 April 1975 marked the end of the Vietnam War as the country was unified under the Vietnamese Communist Party (VCP).[134] The Fourth Party Congress in December 1976 resolved to "turn Vietnam into a socialist country with modern agriculture and industry within 20 years".[135] The VCP adopted the Second Five-Year Plan (1976–1980) which prioritised agriculture development and investment in heavy industry. Meanwhile, a grand socialist transformation programme was implemented throughout the South where the state collectivised agriculture and nationalised industry and commerce.

Vietnam soon faced serious economic difficulties. Agricultural production fell, and the country began to suffer from food shortages. Economic development was hampered by loss of human capital, both through the Vietnam War and as a result of mass exodus of refugees following the communist victory. Approximately one million people had fled Vietnam by October 1982, among whom tens of thousands were professionals, intellectuals, technicians and skilled workers.[136] In addition, the war with and the occupation of Cambodia, as well as the resultant border war with China in 1979, only compounded the challenges. These conflicts not only placed tremendous strains on the Vietnamese economy but also isolated the country, reducing the flow of foreign aids to Vietnam.

The early 1980s saw the implementation of some early measures of reforms, largely due to bottom–up pressures from the ground.[137] The Third Five-Year Plan (1981–1985), as aptly described by Riedel and Turley (1999), was an "awkward compromise". Though the VCP reaffirmed its goal of achieving a complete socialist transformation of the South, it acknowledged that at least for a definitive period of time, private ownerships have to be tolerated, either in the form of private enterprises or state–private joint enterprises. The household economy was also encouraged to develop, though households' economic activities must be consistent with the plans of the co-operatives.[138]

In agriculture, the Party Secretariat's Directive No. 100 CT/TU of 1981 (Directive 100 for short) stipulated the widespread adoption of the end-product contract system (*khoan san pham*) which had been experimented on in some localities. Under this system, the peasants were

[133] The overview of Public–Private Partnerships can be found in the official World Bank webpage, http://www.worldbank.org/en/topic/publicprivatepartnerships/overview#1 .

[134] From 1951 to 1976, the VCP was officially named the Workers Party of Vietnam (*Dang Lao Dong*). Its name was changed back to the Vietnamese Communist Party at the Fourth Party Congress in December 1976.

[135] See Pham, Bui and Thanh (2007).

[136] See Federal Research Division (1989: 149).

[137] See Riedel and Turley (1999) and Pham, Bui and Thanh (2007).

[138] See Vo (1990: 131).

contracted to farm lands owned by the cooperatives. If output surpassed the pre-set quotas, the peasants were allowed to keep the surplus to consume, sell on the private domestic market or sell to the government at "negotiated prices". Changes in the incentive system resulted in improvement in agricultural production. Nevertheless, the results were limited. From 1983, the peasants returned parts of the lands operated under the end-product contact system as they tended to receive only 16–17 percent of the contract outputs after meeting all their obligations to the co-operatives, which were not sufficient to cover production expenses.[139]

The reform era of the Vietnamese economy officially began in 1986. The Sixth Party Congress announced the *Doi Moi* (Renovation) Policy, which ushered in the transformation of the centrally planned economy to a "socialist-oriented market economy", a type of market-based mixed economy where state planning through five-year plans is still executed and SOEs play a major role. Rationing and price controls were abolished for many commodities. In 1987, the Law on Foreign Investment were promulgated, sanctioning foreign investment in the country.

In April 1988, the Politburo's Resolution No. 10/NQTU on the "Renovation of economic management in agriculture" (Resolution 10 for short) took the end-product contract system a long way forward by recognising the household as the basic production unit in agriculture. It leased out farm lands to households for longer duration of 15 years as compared to three years under Directive 100 and gave the households total autonomy in their farming activities. Coupled with the 1988 Land Law, Resolution 10 marked the start of the decollectivisation of agriculture. As a result, it helped liberalise huge resources in the rural economy, and Vietnam became a rice exporter in 1989.[140] Throughout 1988 and 1989, more measures were implemented to encourage the development of the private sectors. SOEs were also accorded more autonomy in setting their business plans. However, as the reforms progressed, state budget suffered from huge deficits which were financed by printing more money, resulting in hyperinflation which reached more than 700 percent in 1986. It was not until 1989 and the early 1990s that inflation was back under control.[141]

In the next phase of its development since 1990, Vietnam has intensified its efforts to integrate into the global economy, especially after the collapse of the Soviet Union in 1991. Similar to the HPAEs, an export-oriented industrialisation strategy was adopted. The withdrawal of troops from Cambodia paved the way for the restoration of relations with the ASEAN countries, culminating in Vietnam becoming the seventh member of ASEAN in 1995. Trade embargo with the US was also lifted in 1995, and in 2007, Vietnam became a member of the WTO.

After 30 years of economic reforms, Vietnam has made some tremendous progress. Figure 4.18 tracks the real GDP growth rate and real GDP per capita growth rate of the country from 1986 to 2015, the latest data year. Over the period, real GDP has grown at about 6.5 percent annually on average while GDP per capita has averaged an annual growth rate of almost 5 percent. This is on par with the performance of the HPAEs. Furthermore, as Figure 4.18 demonstrates,

[139] See Vo (1990: 134).

[140] See Pham, Bui and Thanh (2007).

[141] *Ibid.*

Figure 4.18: Real GDP and Real GDP Per Capita Growth Rates in Vietnam, 1986–2015

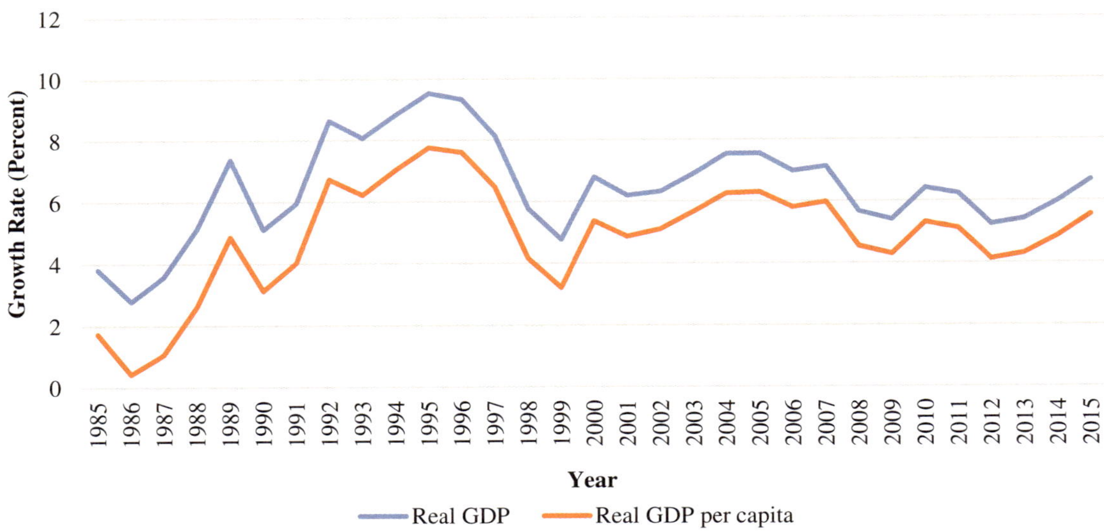

Source: World Bank, World Development Indicators

Figure 4.19: Share of Gross Domestic Savings, 1985–2015 and Share of Gross Fixed Capital Formation in Vietnam's GDP, 1994–2015

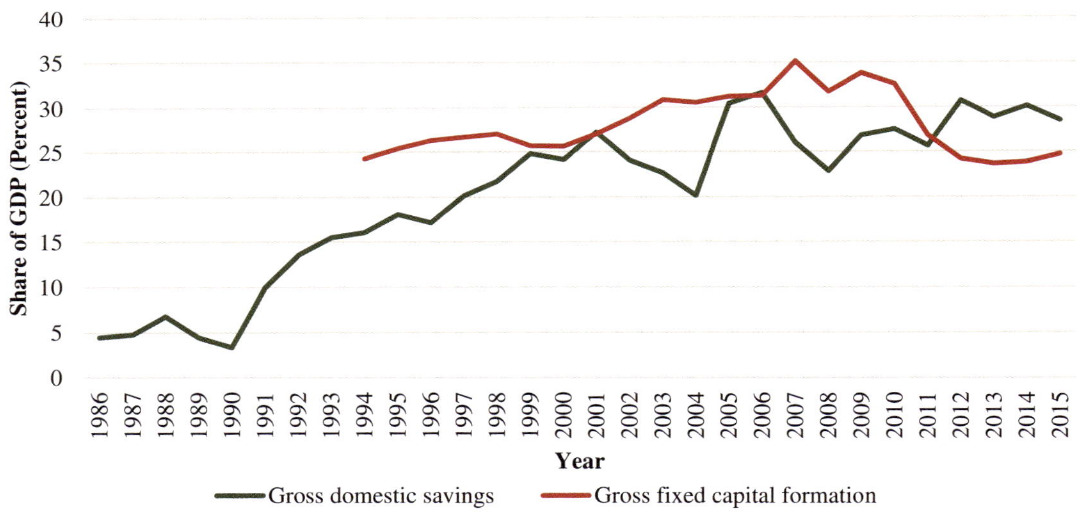

Source: World Bank, World Development Indicators

the Vietnamese economy has exhibited resiliency during the GFC as it still maintained positive growth in both real GDP and GDP per capita over 2008–2009 and the drop in growth rates were relatively modest as compared with that during the AFC.

Much savings have also been accumulated in the economy. As shown in Figure 4.19, the share of gross domestic savings in GDP has risen over the years, from 4.4 percent in 1986 to

28.5 percent in 2015, though there were considerable fluctuations between 2001 and 2009. Meanwhile, gross fixed capital formation has consistently increased in absolute terms, at an annualised real growth rate of 9.1 percent between 1994 and 2005.[142] Nonetheless, its share in GDP has declined since 2010. That domestic savings are now higher than gross fixed capital formation may indicate that there are ample resources to meet Vietnam's future investment needs. However, this is provided that savings can be channelled to productive investment through an efficient financial system.

Furthermore, Vietnam has been transformed from an agrarian economy to an industrial and service-based economy. Figure 4.20 plots the share of each sector in GDP over the period of 1976–2014. The share of agriculture in total GDP started to decline in 1988, and it was overtaken by the service sector as the most dominant sector in the economy in 1993. Nevertheless, agriculture remained important as it still constituted more than 18 percent of GDP in 2014. Meanwhile, industrialisation has resulted in the share of the secondary sector to pick up since 1992. By 2014, industry made up 38.5 percent of Vietnam's GDP, as compared to 43.4 percent from services.

Figure 4.20: Sectoral Shares of Vietnam's GDP, 1976–2014

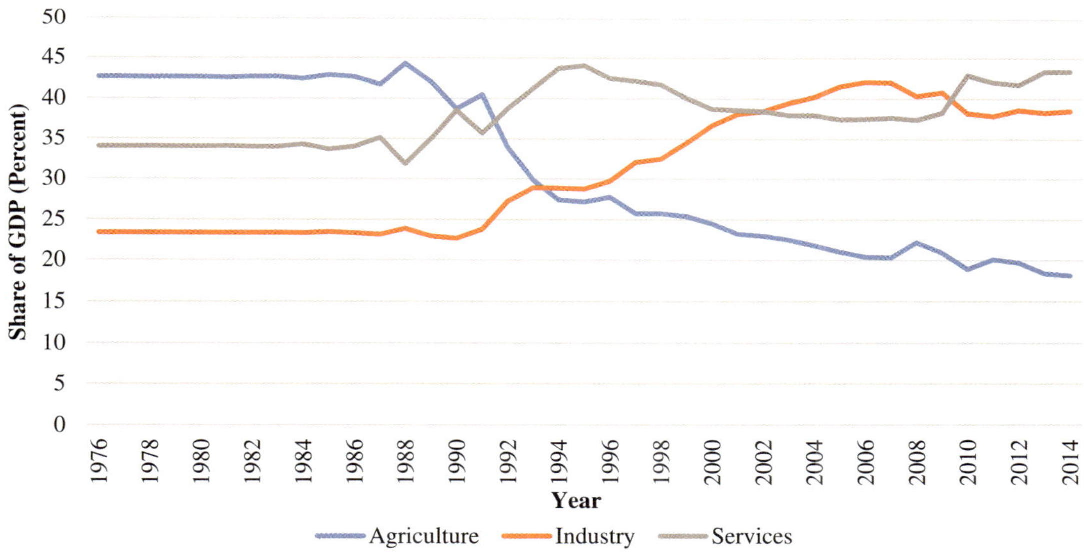

Source: United Nations Conference on Trade and Development

Vietnam has also fully embraced trade liberalisation and economic integration. Vietnam is currently involved as either a signatory or a negotiating party in 16 bilateral and multilateral FTAs. As compared to other ASEAN countries, Vietnam has more FTAs than not just Cambodia, Laos and Myanmar but also Brunei and the Philippines.[143] The importance of trade to the

[142] Based on data from the World Development Indicators by the World Bank.

[143] The number of FTAs which each ASEAN country is currently involved in is available at https://aric.adb.org/fta-country (accessed on 23 March 2017).

Figure 4.21: Shares of Imports and Exports in Vietnam's GDP, 1986–2015

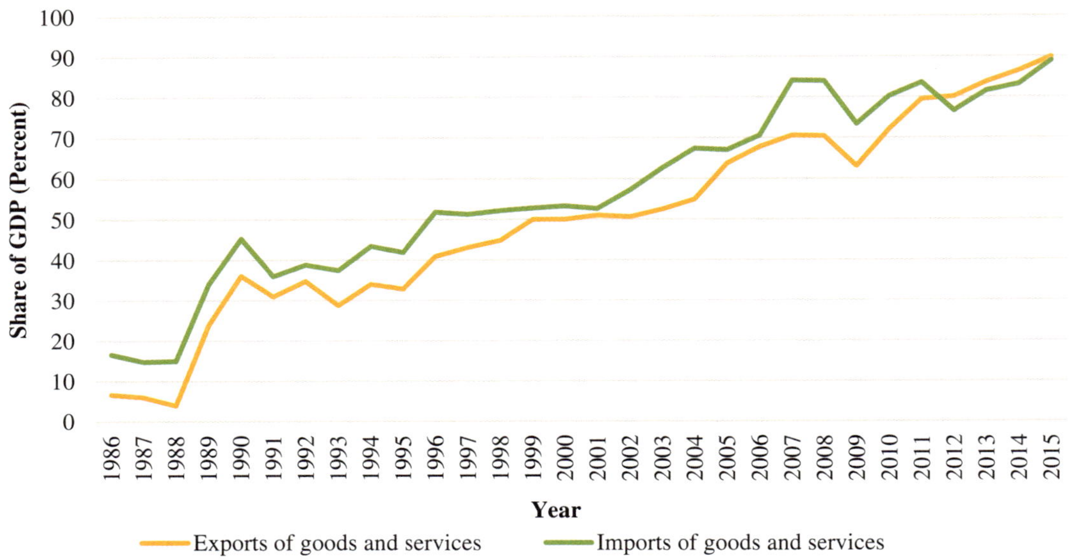

Source: World Bank, World Development Indicators

Vietnamese economy can be clearly seen in Figure 4.21. Both exports and imports picked up after 1989 to reach 89.8 percent and 89 percent of GDP respectively in 2015. Thus, as of 2015, trade constituted more than 178 percent of Vietnam's GDP, making it the second-most trade-dependent economy in ASEAN after Singapore.

More encouraging is the fact that as the country pursues economic integration, the technological content of its exports has improved over time. As shown in Figure 4.22, the share of high-technology exports in total manufactured exports has jumped from a mere 0.1 percent in 1997 to 26.9 percent in 2014. The sharpest increase has taken place since 2008.

Vietnam's advancement in high-technology exports is closely linked to the presence of MNCs such as Samsung and Intel in the country. Overall, Vietnam has proven to be an attractive destination for investors, especially after it joined the WTO. As shown in Figure 4.23, FDI inflows multiplied from –0.01 million US dollars in 1976, which indicates divestment out of the country, to 11.8 billion US dollars in 2015. As manufacturing in China matures and labour cost rises, it is expected that more MNCs will shift southward to Vietnam, facilitating its rise as the next manufacturing hub.

Throughout its reforms, Vietnam has retained a strong emphasis on social development. For education, the government's approach changed with the launch of *Doi Moi*. Education was viewed as a necessary investment for development rather than as part of the "ideology-cultural revolution" as before.[144] The country has achieved some equitable outcomes in terms of basic

[144] See World Bank and Ministry of Planning and Investment of Vietnam (2016: 85).

Figure 4.22: Share of High-Technology Exports in Total Manufactured Exports in Vietnam, 1997–2014

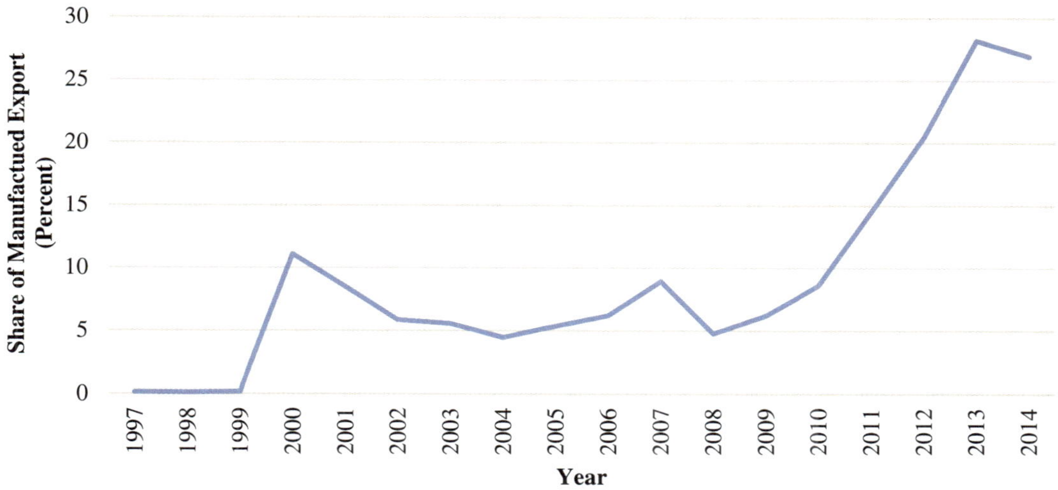

Source: World Bank, World Development Indicators

Figure 4.23: FDI Inflows to Vietnam at Current Prices Million US Dollars, 1976–2015

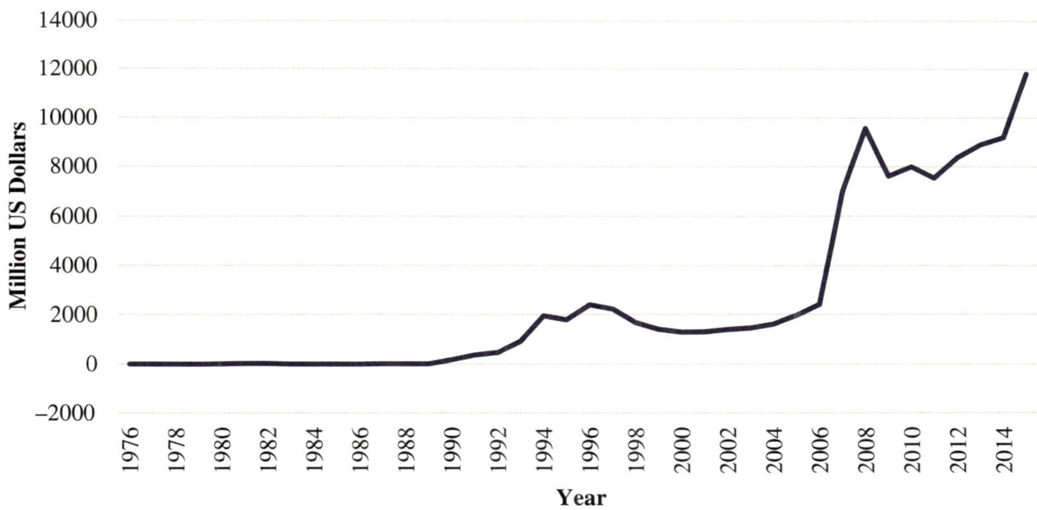

Source: United Nations Conference on Trade and Development

literacy and numeracy. According to data from the World Bank, Vietnam's adult literacy rate in 2015 was 94.5 percent, the highest among the CLMV countries. Nevertheless, it should be noted that Vietnam started at an advantage as its literacy rate in 1979 was already 83.8 percent, one of the highest in Southeast Asia.[145]

[145] Data are from the World Bank, World Development Indicators.

In terms of healthcare, Vietnam performs exceptionally well in basic care. Its infant mortality rate dropped steadily from 50.9 per 1,000 live births in 1976 to 17.9 per 1,000 live births in 2015. Life expectancy in Vietnam was 75.6 years as of 2014, the third highest in ASEAN after Brunei and Singapore. Moreover, Vietnam's ratio of physician per 10,000 population has also improved dramatically from 2.4 per 10,000 in 1980 to 11.9 per 10,000 in 2013.[146] Meanwhile, the country has made great strides in terms of poverty reduction. As strong economic growth propelled the country from the low-income to the lower-middle-income group,[147] more than 30 million people were lifted out of poverty over the past two decades.[148] Extreme poverty where people live below 1.90 constant 2011 prices Purchasing Power Parity dollars has virtually been eliminated.[149]

Nonetheless, major social development issues remain. Overcrowding, outdated facilities and the prevalence of "out-of-pockets payments" are perennial problems plaguing Vietnam's public hospitals.[150] Furthermore, there is a lack of access to quality care in the provincial-level public hospitals as patients tend to flock to national-level hospitals in the major metropolises for treatment, resulting in overcrowding. In addition, though it has been relatively contained in the past, inequality is on the rise. Oxfam and World Bank researches have pointed to the rise in the number of superrich individuals (those with more than 30 million US dollars) and inequalities in opportunities where girls, ethnic minorities and the poorest are disproportionately excluded as the two most worrisome trends with regard to inequality in Vietnam.[151]

4.4.4.2 *Meeting Challenges and Seizing Opportunities*[152]

After 30 years since the launch of *Doi Moi*, Vietnam has transformed from a backward low-income economy to a dynamic middle-income economy with tens of millions lifted out of poverty. The reforms have mobilised production factors from agriculture to manufacturing and services and have enabled economic activities to flourish. At the same time, Vietnam's economic development is closely linked to its integration into the world economy. Trade and FDI have become important engines of growth. Going forward, FDI can be expected to increase as MNCs relocate their production facilities southward from China. This will serve to deepen Vietnam's participation in the global value chains and facilitate its rise as a key manufacturing hub in Asia. Moreover, natural endowments in terms of scenic landscapes and fertile lands conducive to the cultivation of rice, tropical fruits and cash crops also bless Vietnam with tremendous potential to become a top tourist destination and a major agriculture producer in the world.

However, despite the country's potentials, there are worrying signs that Vietnam's actual growth momentum might have fizzled out. Over the period of 2008–2015, Vietnam's real GDP

---

[146] Data on infant mortality, life expectancy and physician accessibility are collected from the World Bank, World Development Indicators.

[147] See Chapter 3 for a detailed discussion.

[148] See World Bank (2013).

[149] See World Bank and Ministry of Planning and Investment of Vietnam (2016: 284).

[150] See *The Economist* (2014).

[151] See Lefur (2017).

[152] This section builds on Tan, Nguyen and Luu (2016).

growth has slowed to 5.9 percent from an average of 7.2 percent between 1990 and 2007. Furthermore, as Chapter 2 has shown, Vietnam has not caught up to the ASEAN-6 in terms of overall competitiveness. More worryingly, there has also been no discernible improvement in its competitiveness score since 2011.

The economy is plagued by many structural weaknesses. Central among these is the continued dominance of the inefficient state sector. Despite three decades of economic reforms, market distortions in favour of SOEs remain widespread. SOEs tend to occupy the majority of land allocated for business activity and are often granted a considerable portion of new land provided by the government for business rental. Another area where favouritism is salient is in access to credit. SOEs are still able to obtain bank loans even when their asset size or profitability do not meet the banks' lending criteria.[153] In terms of market access, while the government usually offers important market opportunities for firms to grow and become competitive through state contracts, eligibility criteria for bidding such contracts are clearly biased towards SOEs. Consequently, the majority of public contracts have been awarded to SOEs.[154]

Easy access to business resources reduces the incentives to improve productivity and engage in industrial upgrading. Many SOEs are thus inefficiently run. They also tend to invest in non-core, low-hanging fruit business activities which are speculative in nature. Such investment ultimately results in losses, even leading to the eventual failures of some SOEs. High-profile default cases of large SOEs such as Vinashin and Vinalines are just the tip of the much bigger iceberg of poor governance, corporate graft and misallocation of resources which are rampant in the ailing state sector.

Meanwhile, the competitiveness of the domestic private sector leaves much to be desired. Foreign corporations have often complained about the lack of reliable local suppliers, which is a testament to the wide capability gap between the FDI sector and the local sector. Technological transfers between FDI enterprises and domestic firms remain limited. Furthermore, as Chapter 2 has pointed out, corporate governance in Vietnam is still problematic. Notwithstanding the development of the legal and regulatory framework for investor protection, weaknesses remain in terms of poor disclosure, outdated accounting standards, lack of internal control mechanisms and limited accountability of firm management. In fact, current practices in many public enterprises fall far short of what is required in the revised Corporate Governance Regulations, which also highlights the government's difficulties in enforcing the rule of law.

The third area of shortcoming is the poor quality of Vietnam's human capital. Strong economic performance in the past has been achieved on the back of a large, young, literate and low-cost workforce. Such a model is not sustainable, especially given the shrinking demographic dividends and disruptive technological changes which are happening around the world. As such, only by upgrading labour skills and labour productivity can Vietnam maintain healthy growth and successfully industrialise. Nonetheless, skill mismatches are currently prevalent in the labour market. Firms still find it hard to hire skilled workers to fill available vacancies, especially

---

[153] See Taussig, Nguyen and Nguyen (2016).

[154] See Nguyen and Freeman (2009).

managers, executives and technicians. Moreover, the degree of soft skills development and the workforce's proficiency in conversational English also leave much to be desired.

Finally, infrastructure bottlenecks represent a particularly pressing challenge to Vietnam's economic development. According to an assessment by the Economic Research Institute for ASEAN and East Asia in 2015, 37 percent of the country road network was in average condition while 20 percent was rated as "poor to very poor". Rapid urbanisation strains the transport systems in the countries' largest metropolises, resulting in frequent traffic congestions. Meanwhile, despite significant investment in energy generation capacity, blackouts and insufficient supply during peak load periods are still expected to increase as energy demand is projected to continue to outstrip supply.[155] It is crucial to alleviate these infrastructure bottlenecks which hamper production, commerce and investment if Vietnam is to take off.

4.4.4.3 *Policy Implications for Vietnam*

As evident from the discussion above, a top priority for Vietnam is to quicken the pace of the SOE reform and move towards a rule-based, transparent and competitive economic environment. The promulgation of the third Enterprise Law and the launch of a new round of SOE restructuring in 2005 raised new hopes for private sector development. Nonetheless, the progress has been notably slow. For instance, as of the first quarter of 2015, only 29 SOEs were equitised out of the target of 289 for the whole year.[156] More should be done, and it is important for Vietnam to engage strategic investors with industry expertise in the process. At the same time, SOEs' special privileges which have resulted in market distortions at the expense of private enterprises must be eliminated. It is also exigent that Vietnam puts in place fundamental market institutions required for local enterprises to develop, streamline bureaucracy and improve bureaucratic capabilities to enhance ease of doing business.

To help develop the capacity of domestic enterprises, measures to support and upgrade best-performing local firms, as well as pair them up with MNCs should be put in place. Tax incentives could be introduced to foreign firms engaging in technology transfer with local suppliers. For better governance, incentives for firms to uphold accountability to investors should be introduced. For example, the rankings of the Corporate Governance Scorecard could be made public for investors to monitor the listed firms as well as for the firms to improve their management.

To upgrade the labour force, education and technical training should be revamped in alignment with industry needs. Collaboration between higher-learning institutes, industry associations and companies is thus vital. In particular, apprenticeship *a la* the German model should be encouraged. At the same time, curriculum should also seek to develop soft skills and language skills. Finally, governments should play an active role in nudging workers to upgrade their skills throughout the course of their careers so that they can stay relevant with market demands.

With regard to infrastructure, as with other developing economies, overcoming the financing gap is the main challenge to Vietnam's infrastructure development strategy. The World Bank

---

[155] See Duong (2015).

[156] See World Bank (2015).

estimated that Vietnam's investment requirement over the next several decades could reach tens of billion US dollars a year.[157] State budget is unlikely to be able to meet this demand while funding from official development assistance may be scaled down as the economy develops. In this context, it is important that Vietnam leverages on its cooperation with multilateral development banks including the World Bank, the ADB and the AIIB to partly cover the financing gap. At the same time, allocation and management of infrastructure funding must be made more efficient in order to reduce wastages. Finally, Vietnam should look to encourage more private sector participation in infrastructure development through Public–Private Partnership. In 2015, the government issued Decree 15 which provided a single transparent legal framework for investment according to this model. This is a step in the right direction, and the effort to facilitate Public–Private Partnership investment should be intensified.

In its next phase of development, it is also important that Vietnam leverages on its strength to ensure a vibrant and diversified economic structure. Vietnam should aim to become both a manufacturing hub and an excellent regional centre for services, with a modern, highly productive agriculture sector. In addition, a more balanced pattern of growth must also be achieved where business and investment are expanded not just in the South, but also the North and the Central parts of Vietnam.

4.5 The Development of CLMV in the Regional and Global Context

Decades of conflicts and political instability post-decolonisation had hampered economic development in CLMV. It was not until the late-1980s that the momentums of reforms in these countries intensified. While each among CLMV adopts different development trajectories in varied pace, all long for the same goal of growth and development. The reforms of CLMV in general can be encapsulated as a transition from centrally planned to market-oriented economy, driven by export-oriented industrialisation and integration into the world economy. The transitional economies soon emerge as the new darlings of investors, being regarded as the new frontier of growth in Southeast Asia after the HPAEs.

In the global context, Myanmar was the first to join the WTO in 1995 and was also the only one among CLMV which had signed the General Agreement on Tariffs and Trade in 1948. Two years after joining WTO, Myanmar joined ASEAN in the same year as Laos. On the other hand, Cambodia, Laos and Vietnam started by integrating in the regional level before their accessions to the WTO. Being in a regional bloc has equipped CLMV with stronger bargaining power when it comes to trade negotiations. ASEAN, in particular, has opened a gateway to the global market for CLMV through partnerships with other economies including Japan, South Korea, China, European Union, to name a few. More than half of the total FTAs applied in CLMV ride on the ASEAN's partnership with other economies. For instance, six out of eight FTAs enforced in Laos are associated with ASEAN.[158] With ongoing negotiations of trade

[157] See World Bank and Ministry of Planning and Investment of Vietnam (2016).

[158] See https://aric.adb.org/fta-country for a comprehensive listing of bilateral and plurilateral FTAs which CLMV are engaged.

agreements and partnerships, cross-border cooperation will continue to act as a catalyst for the future development of CLMV. Nevertheless, the adverse impacts of globalisation should also be acknowledged and addressed.

4.5.1 Harmonising Domestic Reforms to Mitigate Vulnerability and Ensure Inclusivity

"New Normal" or "growth slowdown" have become the new buzzwords in the aftermath of the GFC. Almost a decade has passed, but the residual effects of the crisis can still be felt today. Recovery from the crisis has been slow in many industrial countries, particularly the US and UK, with prospects of sluggish economic growth[159] and persistently high unemployment rate of over 7 percent on average between 2010 and 2015 as compared to an average rate of 5 percent between 2000 and 2007 before the GFC.[160]

Over the years, China has emerged as a key driver of global economic growth with an average annual GDP growth of 10 percent between 2001 and 2011. It comes as no surprise when the drop in China's growth rate to 7.9 percent in 2012,[161] the lowest rate since 2000 and the continuous fall in the following years, has created concerns about a sustained Chinese slowdown and its potential adverse spillover effects. While the ASEAN countries have been benefiting from globalisation, integration into the global economy also heightens their vulnerability to global volatility. Being the single largest trading partner of ASEAN, having contributed 15.2 percent of total trade in 2015, China's slowdown may create some negative ripple effects in ASEAN.[162] In particular, CLMV are more vulnerable as they depend more heavily on China in terms of trade flows.[163] The challenges for CLMV are further compounded by rising economic uncertainties after the election of Donald Trump and Brexit in 2016.

More fundamentally, while trade liberalisation has indeed resulted in aggregate gains, it may also have adverse distributive effects. Workers in industries where there is a lack of comparative advantage may lose out, especially if they cannot find transition to other sectors. As an example, recent empirical studies show that employment in export-competing industries in the US has been adversely affected by China's rise as an export powerhouse. More importantly, such losses have not been offset by gains in non-tradable sectors, export-oriented industries and industries which use imported inputs.[164] In turn, China may have to grapple with similar problems as the US regarding the transition of its workforce in the near future as manufacturing matures and labour cost rises. At the end of the day, the need for structural transformation is ubiquitous and will come to pass in all economies.

It is for this reason that we have continuously emphasised in Section 4.4 the importance of fostering a balanced economic structure even as CLMV continue to ride the export-oriented

---

[159] See El-Erian (2010).

[160] See World Development Indicators database of the World Bank.

[161] Data on nominal GDP growth obtained from World Development Indicators database of the World Bank.

[162] See ASEANStats, http://data.aseanstats.org/.

[163] See Salidjanova, Koch-Weser and Klanderman (2015).

[164] See Autor, Dorn and Hanson (2013, 2015).

manufacturing wave. Measures to develop a modern, high value-added service sector must be put in place so as to prepare the economy for future transition. Governments have a crucial role in facilitating an appropriate regulatory framework which fosters competitive and efficient service markets. Additionally, investment in infrastructure is essential for service industries to grow, specifically in the case of logistics, information and tourism. Besides the long-term benefits, a well-balanced economic structure is also important in the short run. It affords the economy some diversification to mitigate the adverse impacts of slowdown in external demands for manufactured goods.

Fostering micro, small, and medium enterprises (MSMEs) is another key step to realise inclusive growth in the age of globalisation. MSMEs form the large part of the enterprise population in many countries and constitute an important source of employment. For instance, in Vietnam, employment by MSMEs made up 46 percent of the total number of workers in all enterprises as of 2012, accounting for more than five million jobs.[165] To develop MSMEs, policy-makers, especially those in developing countries, should not rely solely on direct interventions through grants and tax breaks which are costly and possibly ineffective. Instead, the government should seek to play a facilitative role, adopting market-based initiatives aimed at developing MSMEs' capacity. MSMEs usually miss out on opportunities arising from FDI because overseas investors and prospective business partners lack information about them. Therefore, policy-makers should look to profile MSMEs to amend such information asymmetries. Similarly, in order to address MSMEs' weaknesses, the government should facilitate dialogue between MSMEs and industry captains to promote cross-learning.

4.5.2 Deepening Integration to Revitalise Reform Momentum

The challenges associated with globalisation as discussed in the previous section by no means serve to imply that CLMV should turn their back on economic integration. Indeed, the achievements of reforms in these countries so far were brought about by their participation in the global economy. Going forward, deepening integration will continue to be vital in invigorating reforms in CLMV for economic development in the following ways.

Firstly, by linking up with their regional neighbours in ASEAN to form a single market and production base, CLMV will be able exploit the advantages of economies of scale and demographic dividends and at the same time mask the weaknesses of development gaps by complementing each other in an intra-regional economic network. Furthermore, the benefits of larger market access and cost competitiveness offered by a regional bloc will also provide more incentives for the investors and hence increase its attractiveness as a FDI host. The increased inflows of foreign capital can therefore be mobilised to complement the shortfall of domestic capital. In addition, shortage in skilled workforce faced by CLMV can be relieved through cross-border talents and knowledge sharing, which ultimately will contribute to industrial upgrading from low-end manufacturing to a more sophisticated and knowledge-based level.

Secondly, FDI inflows will also directly fuel investment in infrastructure development in CLMV. This is best illustrated in, among others, the recent ground-breaking ceremony of

[165] See Ministry of Planning and Investment of Vietnam (2014).

China–Laos railway in December 2016. The railway constructions which cost about 6 billion US dollars, 70 percent of which funded by Chinese investors and 30 percent by Laos can hardly be realised without the foreign investment.[166] As discussed extensively in Section 4.4, CLMV tend to fall into the deadlock of infrastructure constraints and financial shortfalls which FDI can help alleviate. Strengthened economic integration in parallel with the incorporation of inclusivity agenda will ensure a mutually beneficial regional partnership to all economies.

Thirdly, deepening economic integration will reduce the cross-border barriers among CLMV and their neighbouring economies, which in turn may intensify the competition in the region. For instance, the concentration of FDI in Vietnam can serve to nudge CLM towards attending to their unfavourable investment climate. FDI in Vietnam leaped to almost 10 billion US dollars in 2007 and continued to rise to close to 12 billion US dollars in 2015. CLM, on the other hand, demonstrated little improvement in attracting investment as their FDI remained at around two billion US dollars after more than two decades of reforms.[167] While there may be some diversion effects resulting from regional integration, the resultant competitive pressure will not only reveal the weakness within the economy but may also act as an enabling factor for CLMV to overcome their inertia and push forward necessary structural changes.

In sum, for transitional economies like CLMV that are facing bottlenecks in domestic reforms, deepened economic integration will enable them to revitalise the reform progress. Against the backdrop of rising vulnerability and dampened reform momentum, integration initiatives including ASEAN Economic Community (AEC), Regional Comprehensive Economic Partnership (RCEP), One Belt, One Road Initiative (OBOR) come timely to propel CLMV as well as the ASEAN-6 forward. The following sections will discuss each initiative in detail.

4.5.2.1 *The ASEAN Economic Community*

Regional integration in ASEAN has become increasingly economically driven especially after the AFC in 1997. The ASEAN Free Trade Area was instituted by the end of the 2000s with significant tariff reduction and elimination in ASEAN-6 though CLMV have yet to fulfill their commitments. In addition, ASEAN also forged new and closer economic ties with other economies with the establishment of new partnerships including ASEAN+1, ASEAN+3 and ASEAN+6.

ASEAN has taken regional economic integration to new heights with the official establishment of the AEC on 31 December 2015. Since its conception, the AEC is widely regarded as a highly ambitious project which aims to transform ASEAN into (i) a single market and production base, (ii) a highly competitive economic region, (iii) a region of equitable economic development and (iv) a region fully integrated into the global economy.[168] As shown by an empirical projection,[169] the full realisation of the AEC may raise ASEAN's aggregate real GDP by 69.4 billion US dollars, or 5.3 percent as compared to the baseline scenario. Gains for CLMV are also

---

[166] See *Xinhua* (2016).

[167] See UNCTAD Data Centre.

[168] See ASEAN Secretariat (2015).

[169] The projection here is based on the simulation studies by Rashid *et al.* (2009) and Petri, Plummer and Zhai (2010).

substantial as these economies may see a 4.3 percent increase in real GDP on average. In particular, exports in CLMV are projected to increase by 55.4–101.1 percent of the baseline.

Thus, the AEC is welcomed as an economic catalyst which may propel ASEAN forward as the fourth largest economy and hence place ASEAN at the centre of the global economic landscape. However, despite its official establishment in 2015, many key initiatives in the AEC blueprint remains unfulfilled. One noteworthy missed target is the establishment of the ASEAN Single Window (ASW). The ASW, comprising 10 National Single Windows (NSWs), is envisaged to expedite customs clearance, reduce transaction costs and thus facilitate a more seamless intra-regional flow of goods. Despite an extended deadline set in 2015, Cambodia, Laos and Myanmar are still in the progress of developing their NSWs, causing setbacks to the establishment of a fully functional ASW.[170]

The ASEAN leaders do acknowledge that the prevailing development gap in multiple dimensions including socio-economic, infrastructure, human resources and institutional capacity between CLMV and the rest may lead to emergence of a two-tier ASEAN, which will obstruct regional integration.[171] In order to tackle this, IAI was launched in 2000 with the objective of bridging the development divide. Financial and technical support dedicated to CLMV under IAI is a concrete step taken to overcome the infrastructure and financial constraints in CLMV's reforms progress, which in turn, help promote economic activities and trade flows. The Master Plan on ASEAN Connectivity 2025 also complements the IAI in strengthening regional integration through a focus on regional connectivity improvement, which is also a critical enabling factor to facilitate cross-border economic development.

The spirit of prosper-thy-neighbour advocated by Malaysia's former Prime Minister, Mahathir Mohamad after the AFC and Singapore's Prime Minister Lee Hsien Loong is echoed in the IAI.[172] Special assistance and technical support will be directed to CLMV under this initiative to ensure that growth outcomes of AEC are equitably shared. However, while the flexibility conditions agreed among the 10 member states have given CLMV more time to meet their integration commitments, they have also hindered the full realisation of free trade flows within ASEAN, especially in terms of eliminating non-tariff barriers. In light of this, CLMV should shoulder their obligations by speeding up their progress towards fulfilling the integration agenda.

4.5.2.2 *The Regional Comprehensive Economic Partnership*

The United States' withdrawal from the Trans-Pacific Partnership (TPP) was among the first few executive orders signed by President Trump on his first day in office. As TPP is now effectively off the table, the signatories have started seeking other alternatives. Malaysia, for instance, is looking at bilateral trade deals with other TPP signatories such as Mexico and Peru, while Singapore is turning to other regional integration initiative such as the RCEP.[173] With the

[170] See http://asw.asean.org.

[171] See ASEAN Secretariat (2016a).

[172] See Yean and Teng (2007).

[173] See Soon (2017) and Damodaran (2017).

impending rise of protectionism and the reversal of globalisation in the West, RCEP has now become more relevant than ever for ASEAN to strengthen economic integration in the global arena.

RCEP was introduced by ASEAN at the 19th Summit in Bali in November 2011 with the goals of untangling the spaghetti bowl effect of existing ASEAN+1 FTAs as well as deepening economic integration between ASEAN and its six FTA partners including China, Japan, South Korea, India, Australia and New Zealand. The RCEP negotiation is conducted in parallel with its main objectives of achieving a modern, comprehensive, high-quality and mutually beneficial economic partnership agreement for all participating economies.[174] The six prospective partners are growing in their significance as a source of FDI in ASEAN. In 2015, FDI from these countries accounted for 30 percent of total FDI inflows to ASEAN, or 40 billion US dollars in absolute terms. For CLMV, of the 17.4 billion US dollars worth of FDI inflows observed in 2015, a large proportion comes from the six ASEAN's FTA partners, especially Japan and China.[175]

While TPP is more ambitious in terms of its standards and regulations harmonisation, the RCEP is more pragmatic and practical in allowing the prospective members to participate in accordance to their needs for market access and acceptable levels of commitment. The RCEP's coverage includes trade in goods, trade in services, investment, intellectual property, competition, dispute settlement, and economic and technical cooperation. The last component, economic and technical cooperation, which is not part of the TPP, reflects the development orientation of the RCEP and the acknowledgement of the diverse economic circumstances of member countries.[176] The less demanding commitments required and potential benefits from technical cooperation certainly makes RCEP a more appealing option for CLMV.

RCEP negotiations were formally initiated in November 2012 and have gone through 15 rounds of negotiation thus far. Time-consuming negotiation is an inevitable feature of any plurilateral or multilateral partnership. The mega regional partnership, RCEP is not an exemption. Fifteen rounds of underway negotiations have yet to lead to a conclusion due to the difficulties in reaching a consensus among 16 member states in contentious issues. While there are existing FTAs between ASEAN and these six economies, to merge these respective FTAs into a single comprehensive agreement is not an easy task. The RCEP negotiations are further impeded by the same problem faced in the establishment of ASEAN Community, namely the development gap among ASEAN member states. ASEAN is leading the RCEP negotiation as a single bloc, and hence the disparities in the level of economic development among ASEAN member states pose critical challenges to harmonisation of domestic rules and policies. While a flexibility clause has been built into the RCEP framework, which helps protect disparate national interests and thus resolve deadlocks, it might compromise the main objective of establishing a high-quality partnership and reduce the cooperation to the "lowest common denominator".

---

[174] The guiding principles for negotiating RCEP are accessible from http://dfat.gov.au/trade/agreements/rcep/Documents/guiding-principles-rcep.pdf.

[175] See ASEAN Secretariat (2016b).

[176] See Tan *et al.* (2017).

Although RCEP is smaller in size as compared to TPP, the partnership will be covering 30 percent of the global economy should it conclude and get ratified. That means there are immense opportunities for international trade and investment that ASEAN could benefit from. CLMV should also tap into this for a new source of foreign investment which will not only bring in economic benefits but also allow infrastructure and skills upgrading, which are the common pain points of CLMV. RCEP negotiations have sped up especially after the end of TPP.[177] The leaders of the member states including Indonesia, China and Malaysia have called for the conclusion of the agreement in 2017.[178] The realisation of the ASEAN-led RCEP will fill the vacuum left from the TPP failure and also help ingrain ASEAN centrality in the Asia Pacific. More importantly, it is the stepping stone for ASEAN towards deeper economic integration and paves the way for a larger and more ambitious initiative, the Free Trade Area of the Asia Pacific. Hence, RCEP should not be seen as an end but rather a means to revitalise growth and reforms in CLMV.

4.5.2.3 *The One Belt, One Road Initiative*

The idea of the Silk Road Economic Belt was first proposed during China's President Xi Jinping visit to Kazakhstan in September 2013. The idea was reiterated a month later when President Xi visited Indonesia. Concrete steps have been taken subsequently with the adoption of the proposal, which is officially termed as One Belt, One Road or Belt and Road Initiative, as one of the key policy priorities of the Chinese Central Committee. Formulation of OBOR gained momentum after the endorsement of 57 economies in establishing the AIIB. Unlike other economic partnership agreements which lay out the commitments of each member, OBOR is not defined explicitly in black and white. The potential stakeholders can only acquire clues about the initiative from the reports of China's State Council and National Congress, and speeches of Chinese leaders on multiple occasions. It was not until March 2015 during the Boao Forum that an action plan revealing the principles, framework, and cooperation priorities and mechanisms was announced by President Xi.

The OBOR will be covering the continents of Africa, Asia and Europe, which accounts for more than 60 percent of world population and 30 percent of world GDP.[179] Against the backdrop of rising uncertainties in the global landscape, OBOR has set five cooperation priorities: (i) Policy coordination; (ii) Facilities connectivity; (iii) Unimpeded trade; (iv) Financial integration; and (v) People-to-people bonds.[180] In sum, the global initiative has gone beyond economic integration and includes the elements of mutual social, political and cultural interests.

International scholars and pundits have reacted differently to the initiative. Putting the unresolved debate aside, OBOR is significant for CLMV given its priority in infrastructure development, which is also the main feature distinguishing OBOR from other international cooperation initiatives. The connectivity vision which is the main driver of OBOR envisages a common

---

[177] See *The Strait Times* (2016).

[178] See Ng (2016), Suokas (2016) and *The Straits Times* (2016).

[179] See Huang (2016).

[180] See Tian (2015).

prosperity built on an efficient and integrated network of land, sea and air. As the discussion in Sections 2.3 and 4.4 have pointed out, infrastructure inadequacy has been the main stumbling block of reforms in CLMV. Therefore, the establishment of OBOR could not be timelier.

According to the estimation by the Asian Development Bank Institute, Asia's overall infrastructure financing need between 2010 and 2020 amounted to about 8 trillion US dollars, or an average of 730 million US dollars per year.[181] The creation of the AIIB and the Silk Road Fund under OBOR will certainly add to the current financing options which usually come from the limited national budget or international organisations such as World Bank and ADB. Nonetheless, an aggregate of 140 billion US dollars capital base from both AIIB and the Silk Road Fund is still far from the estimated financing need. More still needs to be done to fill the financing gap and to ensure the financial viability and sustainability of the massive infrastructure development projects. As the OBOR initiative acknowledges the central role of infrastructure in generating inclusive growth, ASEAN must leverage on their positions as founding members of the AIIB to shape its policy agenda and channel this new infrastructure funding mechanism towards fostering intra-ASEAN connectivity and bridging the development gap between CLMV and ASEAN-6.

4.6 Concluding Notes

ASEAN started off with only five members in 1967, namely Indonesia, Malaysia, Philippines, Singapore and Thailand. In fact, the *raison d'être* for the establishment of ASEAN was primarily politically driven during the height of the Cold War. There was a collective thirst for regional peace and stability against the backdrop of territorial dispute between Malaysia and Philippines, the separation of Singapore from Malaysia and the battles against communist insurgencies in Malaysia and Indonesia. The need for reconciliation among the member states had provided impetus to the inauguration of ASEAN.

At its inception, no one would have foreseen that the regional partnership would potentially emerge as the fourth largest economy by 2030. The member states of ASEAN can be generally categorised into two sub-groups, ASEAN-6 as the forerunner and CLMV as the latecomer. The two sub-groups are different in terms of accession dates as well as their development stages. In order to achieve inclusive development and a cohesive partnership, ASEAN-6 has to shoulder more responsibility in leading CLMV to forge ahead. This chapter seeks to shed light on the development approaches and the trajectory taken by the East Asian economies, which may serve as beacons for the transitioning CLMV.

While the debate on the roles of market and state in the economy remains unsettled, the main insight we can derive from the analysis of development theories and experience of East Asian economies is that there is indeed no universal path for growth and development. More importantly, neither market nor state can monopolise the development process. Instead of emulating other economies, CLMV should navigate along the development spectrum and opt for what suits them the most.

[181] See Chapter 5 in Asian Development Bank Institute (2009).

The prolonged conflicts and civil wars in CLMV after independence had caused lagged development in the economies as compared to their more developed ASEAN counterparts such as Malaysia and Singapore, which gained their independence later than CLMV. As we take stock of the reforms progress in CLMV, we realised that the reforms in these countries adhere to the Washington Consensus, namely the mantra "Stabilise, Liberalise and Privatise", in varying degree. CLMV have shifted from the centrally planned approach to a market-oriented mechanism since the late 1980s. Economic growth in the four countries have picked up soon after they embarked on the reforms process. Furthermore, by tracking several economic indicators, we found that CLMV's approach is in line with the experiences of the HPAEs. Their economic development has been driven by high levels of savings, export-oriented manufacturing as well as enhanced trade and FDI flows as a result of economic integration.

However, while the positive progress resulting from the reforms is indisputable, the sustainability of economic growth remains questionable. This is due to several reasons. Firstly, CLMV still exhibit major structural weaknesses including huge infrastructure spending needs, poor human capital quality, prevalence of market distortions and weak enterprises' capacity. Secondly, despite successful structural transformation from agriculture-based to industrial and service-based economies, a closer inspection shows that growth is still steered by low-end industries leveraged on the demographic dividends of the young economies. The flying geese paradigm underlying the East Asian Miracle has demonstrated that the hierarchical relocation of low-end industry is unpreventable due to the diminishing cost competitiveness resulting from rising labour cost. CLMV must therefore improve their industrial productivity and capability, and subsequently shift their manufacturing structure from low-end to high-end industry in order to sustain the growth momentum. Finally, the over-reliance on external sources, especially international assistance, has impeded the development of fiscal capacity in CLM, especially in Cambodia and Laos. As the transitional economies are undergoing reforms which may require massive amounts of capital to be mobilised, fiscal reforms are much needed.

Besides economic growth, social development in CLMV also calls for more attention. According to the Kuznets curve theory, rising inequality may be an inevitable phenomenon at the early stage of economic development, but the society will eventually benefit from the trickle-down effect as the economy grows. The theory, however is contested by some economists.[182] Rising inequality in CLMV should not be neglected and the state has to be more active in income redistribution before the problem escalates into a bigger issue. Besides rising inequality, CLMV also share other common challenges in stepping up the quality of education and healthcare. We also found that institutional reforms have lagged behind economic reforms. The problems of poor governance and weak institutions have led to rampant corruption and ineffective government. Going forward, policy-makers should take into account all the prevailing challenges and incorporate them in policy design and implementation.

[182] See Piketty (2014) and Dabla-Norris *et al.* (2015) who have presented evidences of rising inequality as the economy grows. The trickle-down effect anticipated does not happen by the market economy principles.

The competitiveness analysis by ACI which identified the weakest indicators in CLMV may serve as an instructive roadmap for CLMV to forge ahead.[183]

As CLMV become increasingly integrated in the international market, the economies will be exposed to more external risks which are beyond their control. For instance, the residual effects from the GFC and the rise of protectionism in the US and Europe has caused mounting unpredictability in the global economy. With limitation in mitigating the vulnerability, it is therefore important for CLMV to establish an effective risk management mechanism. Concerted efforts can be made by harmonising the domestic reforms, which consequently allow risk sharing among the economies. Despite the risks, it remains imperative to integrate in the global economy by engaging in international cooperation initiatives such as AEC, RCEP and OBOR, which in turn will contribute to the domestic reform momentum.

Finally, another point worth highlighting is the solidarity of ASEAN as a single bloc. The development gap within ASEAN has been a great concern since the late 1990s which provided impetus to the implementation of IAI. Nonetheless, a two-tier ASEAN seems to surface as the gap between CLMV and ASEAN-6 remains large. Hence, inclusivity should be considered as a core element in ASEAN's development agenda in order to ensure the cohesiveness and solidarity within ASEAN. In this context, IAI needs to become more prominent with more progressive policies to support the transition process of CLMV and subsequently to bridge their gap with the ASEAN-6. At the same time, geopolitical challenges from the territorial disputes in the South China Sea must be managed so as to preserve ASEAN unity.

References

Abe, Tetsuya. 2015. "Plan laid out to become manufacturing powerhouse by 2025." *Nikkei Asian Review*, 6 March, available at http://asia.nikkei.com/print/article/79569 (accessed on 15 March 2017).

Akamatsu, Kaname. 1962. "A Historical Pattern of Economic Growth in Developing Countries." *The Developing Economies* 1(1): 3–25.

Amsden, Alice. 1989. *Asia's Next Giant: South Korea and Late Industrialization*. Oxford: Oxford University Press.

ASEAN Secretariat. 2015. *ASEAN Economic Community Blueprint 2025*. Jakarta: ASEAN Secretariat.

ASEAN Secretariat. 2016a. *Initiative for ASEAN Integration (IAI) Work Plan III*. Jakarta: ASEAN Secretariat.

ASEAN Secretariat. 2016b. *ASEAN Investment Report 2016*. Jakarta: ASEAN Secretariat.

ADB. 1999. *Key Indicators of Developing Asian and Pacific Countries 1999*. Manila: Asian Development Bank (ADB).

ADB. 2010. *Key Indicators for Asia and the Pacific 2010*. Manila: Asian Development Bank (ADB).

ADB. 2011. *Key Indicators for Asia and the Pacific: Towards Higher Quality Employment in Asia*. Manila: Asian Development Bank (ADB).

ADB. 2012. *Myanmar in Transition: Opportunities and Challenges*. Manila: Asian Development Bank (ADB).

[183] See Chapter 2 for a detailed discussion.

ADB. 2014. *Myanmar: Unlocking the Potential. Country Diagnostic Study*. Manila: Asian Development Bank (ADB).

ADB. 2016. *Key Indicators for Asia and the Pacific 2016*. Manila: Asian Development Bank (ADB).

Asian Development Bank Institute. 2009. *Infrastructure for a Seamless Asia*. Tokyo: Asian Development Bank Institute.

Autor, David H., David Dorn and Gordon H. Hanson. 2013. "The China Syndrome: Local Labour Market Effects of Import Competition in the United States". *American Economic Review* 103(6): 2121–2168.

Autor, David H., David Dorn and Gordon H. Hanson. 2015. "The China Shock: Learning from Labour Market Adjustment to Large Changes in Trade". NBER Working Paper No. 21906, National Bureau of Economic Research (NBER), Massachusetts.

Bauer, Peter T. 1969. "Dissent on Development." *Scottish Journal of Political Economy* 16(3): 75–94.

Benedek, Dora, Ernesto Crivelli, Sanjeev Gupta, and Priscilla Muthoora. 2012. "Foreign Aid and Revenue: Still a Crowding Out Effect?" IMF Working Paper No. 12/186, International Monetary Fund (IMF), Washington D.C.

Boyce, James and Leonce Ndkrumana. 2001. "Is Africa a Net Creditor? New Estimates of Capital Flight from Severely Indebted Sub-Saharan African Countries, 1970–96". *The Journal of Development Studies* 38(2): 27–56.

Cambodia Development Resource Institute. 2016. *2016 Cambodia Outlook Conference Briefing Note*, available at https://www.cdri.org.kh/webdata/policybrief/ob16.htm (accessed on 22 February 2017).

Chang, Ha-Joon. 2002. *Kicking Away the Ladder: Development Strategy in Historical Perspective*. London: Anthem.

Chang, Ha-Joon. 2003. *Rethinking Development Economics*. London: Anthem.

Channels News Asia. 2017. "ASEAN can Work Together to Increase Tourism Numbers, Says PM Lee." 18 January, available at http://www.channelnewsasia.com/news/singapore/asean-can-work-together-to-increase-tourism-numbers-says-pm-lee/3447638.html (accessed on 24 January 2017).

Cheng, Leonard. K. 2016. "Three questions on China's 'Belt and Road Initiative'." *China Economic Review* 40: 309–313.

Chens, Ching-Yaw, Phyra Sok, and Keomony Sok. 2008. "Evaluating the Competitiveness of the Tourism Industry in Cambodia: Self-assessment from Professionals." *Asia Pacific Journal of Tourism Research* 13(1): 41–66.

Center for Excellence in Disaster Management and Humanitarian Assistance. 2014. *Lao PDR Disaster Management Reference Handbook*. Hawaii: Center for Excellence in Disaster Management and Humanitarian Assistance.

Channyda, Chhay and Sarah Taguiam. 2015. "Exam crackdown to intensity." *The Phnom Penh Post*, 12 May, available at http://www.phnompenhpost.com/national/exam-crackdown-intensify (accessed on 20 February 2017).

Chareunsy, Andrea K. 2012. "Social Hierarchy and the Inequalities of Access: Evidence from Rural Southern Laos." *Journal of Contemporary Asia* 42(2): 276–297.

Chhair, Sokty and Luyna Ung. 2013. "Economic History of Industrialization in Cambodia." WIDER Working Paper No. 2013/134, United Nations University — World Institute for Development Economics Research (UNU–WIDER), Finland.

Chheang, Vannarith. 2008. "The Political Economy of Tourism in Cambodia." *Asia Pacific Journal of Tourism Research* 13(1): 281–297.

Chheang, Vannarith and Yushan Wong. 2012. Cambodia–Laos–Vietnam: Economic reforms and regional integration. CICP Working Paper No. 48, Cambodian Institute for Cooperation and Peace (CICP), Phnom Penh.

Chow, Peter C.Y. and Mitchell H. Kellman. 1993. *Trade — The Engine of Growth in East Asia.* New York: Oxford University Press.

Dabla-Norris, Era, Kalpana Kochhar, Frantisek Ricka, Nujin Suphaphiphat, and Evridiki Tsounta. 2015. "Causes and Consequences of Income Inequality: A Global Perspective." IMF Staff Discussion Note No. 15/13, International Monetary Fund (IMF), Washington D. C.

Damodaran, Rupa. 2017. "Bilateral trade deals 'more realistic' option: Mustapa." *New Straits Times*, 16 February, available at https://www.nst.com.my/news/2017/02/213034/bilateral-trade-deals-more-realistic-option-mustapa (accessed on 20 February 2017).

Ducourtieux, Olivier, Jean Richard Laffort, and Silinthone Sacklokham. 2005. "Land Policy and Farming Practices in Laos." *Development and Change* 36(3): 499–526.

Duong, Thi Nhi. 2014. "Vietnam Country Report". In *Financing ASEAN Connectivity*, edited by Fauziah Zen and Michael Regan. Jakarta: Economic Research Institute for ASEAN and East Asia (ERIA).

Ear, Sophal. 2007. "The Political Economy of Aid and Governance in Cambodia." *Asian Journal of Political Science* 15(1): 68–96.

Ear, Sophal. 2013. "Cambodia's Garment Industry: A Case Study in Governance." *Journal of Southeast Asian Economies* 30(1): 91–105.

El-Erian, Mohamed A. 2010. *Navigating the New Normal in Industrial Countries.* Washington, D. C.: Per Jacobsson Foundation.

Federal Research Division. 1989. *Vietnam: A Country Study.* Washington DC: Federal Research Division, Library of Congress.

Friedman, Milton. 1962. *Capitalism and Freedom.* Chicago: University of Chicago Press.

Ford, David. 2013. "Cambodian higher education — Subprime degrees?" *International Higher Education* 70: 15–16.

Gerschenkron, Alexander. 1962. *Economic Backwardness in Historical Perspective*, Cambridge, Massachusetts: Harvard University Press.

Gomez, Edmund Terence and K. S. Jomo. 1999. *Malaysia's Political Economy: Politics, Patronage and Profits.* Cambridge: Cambridge University Press.

Gwynne, Robert and Cristóbal Kay. 2000. "Views from the Periphery: Futures of Neoliberalism in Latin America." *Third World Quarterly* 21: 141–56.

Haddawy, Peter. 2011. "ICT for Poverty Reduction in Lao PDR." *UN Chronicle* 48(3), October, available at https://unchronicle.un.org/article/ict-poverty-reduction-lao-pdr (accessed on 22 March 2017).

Hayek, Friedrich. 1944. *The Road to Serfdom.* London: Routledge.

Hendrix, Cullen and Marcus Noland. 2015. "Myanmar: Cross-Cutting Governance Challenges." ADB Economics Working Paper Series No. 428, Asian Development Bank (ADB), Manila.

Hill, Hal and Jayant Menon. 2013. "Cambodia: Rapid Growth with Weak Institutions." *Asian Economic Policy Review* 8(1): 46–65.

Huang, Yiping. 2016. "Understanding China's Belt & Road Initiative: Motivation, framework and assessment." *China Economic Review* 40: 314–321.

IMF. 2015. *Myanmar: Staff Report for the 2015 Article IV Consultation-Debt Sustainability Analysis.* Washington D. C.: International Monetary Fund (IMF).

IMF. 2016. *Cambodia: Staff Report for the 2016 Article IV Consultation-Debt Sustainability Analysis.* Washington D. C.: International Monetary Fund (IMF).

IMF. 2017. "IMF Executive Board Concludes 2016 Article IV Consultation with the Lao People's Democratic Republic." *IMF News*, 15 February, available at https://www.imf.org/en/News/Articles/2017/02/15/PR1750-Lao-IMF-Executive-Board-Concludes-2016-Article-IV-Consultation (accessed on 22 March 2017).

International Telecommunication Union. 2015. *Measuring the Information Society Report.* Geneva: International Telecommunication Union (ITU).

International Telecommunication Union. 2016. *Measuring the Information Society Report.* Geneva: International Telecommunication Union (ITU)

Joosu-Palu, Tiina. 2015. "Cambodian Agriculture in Transition: Opportunities and Risk." *The World Bank*, 19 August, available at https://www.worldbank.org/en/news/feature/2015/08/19/cambodian-agriculture-in-transition-opportunities-and-risks (accessed on 18 March 2017).

Kashyap, Aruna. 2015. *Work Faster or Get Out: Labor Rights Abuses in Cambodia's Garment Industry.* New York: Human Rights Watch.

Kiernan, Ben and Taylor Owen. 2015. "Making More Enemies than We Kill? Calculating U.S. Bomb Tonnages Dropped on Laos and Cambodia, and Weighing Their Implications." *The Asia-Pacific Journal* 3(13).

Kohli, Atul. 2004. *State-Directed Development: Political Power and Industrialization in the Global Periphery.* Cambridge: Cambridge University Press.

Kluttz, Jenalee. 2015. "Re-evaluating the Relationship between Education and Child Labour using the Capabilities Approach: Policy and Implications for Inequality in Cambodia." *Theory and Research in Education* 13(2): 165–179.

Kry, Suyheang. 2014. "The Boeung Kak Development Project: For Whom and For What? Poor Land Development Practices As A Challenge For Building Sustainable Peace In Cambodia." *Cambodia Law and Policy Journal* 3: 1–42.

Labott, Elise. 2016. "Obama announces $90 million to clear Laos' unexploded bombs." *CNN*, 6 September, available at http://edition.cnn.com/2016/09/06/asia/laos-obama-aid-package/ (accessed on 22 March 2017).

Lee, Joosung and Vathana TE Duong. 2010. "Analysis of the Cambodia's Garment Industry and Catch up Strategy." *Asian Journal of Technology Innovation* 18(1): 97–123.

Lefur, Babeth. 2017. "Vietnam inequality challenges — next generation of Doi Moi?" *Tuoi Tre News*, 12th January, available at http://tuoitrenews.vn/society/38983/vietnam-inequality-challenges-next-generation-of-doi-moi (accessed on 23 March 2017).

List, Friedrich. 1909. *National System of Political Economy*, London: Longmans, Green, and Co.

Low, Linda. 1998. *Political Economy in a City-state: Government-made Singapore.* Singapore: Oxford University Press.

Low, Linda, Ed. 2004. *Developmental States: Relevancy, Redundancy or Reconfiguration?* New York: Nova Science.

Microsoft Asia News Center. 2016. "Microsoft partners Cambodian Ministry of Education, Youth and Sport to accelerate digital transformation in education to empower educators." 25 November available at https://news.microsoft.com/apac/2016/11/25/microsoft-partners-cambodian-ministry-of-education-youth-and-sport-to-accelerate-digital-transformation-in-education-to-empower-educators/#sm.000020ljswcc5dpasxw19el3natso#hzHiXYf4YHe4VgWm.97 (accessed on 16 February 2017).

Ministry of Planning of Cambodia. 2014. *National Strategic Development Plan 2014–2018*.

Ministry of Planning and Investment of Laos. 2016. *8th Five-Year National Socioeconomic Development Plan* (2016–2020).

Ministry of Planning and Investment of Vietnam. 2014. *White Paper: Small and Medium Enterprises in Vietnam 2014*. Hanoi: Statistical Publishing House.

Moriyasu, Ken. 2016. "ASEAN to become world's No. 4 economy by 2030 - Laos PM." *Nikkei Asian Review*, 5th September, available at http://asia.nikkei.com/Politics-Economy/Policy-Politics/ASEAN-to-be-worlds-4th-largest-economy-in-2030 (accessed on 20 February 2017).

National Regulatory Authority. 20.17. "UXO Problem.", available at http://www.nra.gov.la/uxoproblem.html (accessed on 15 February 2017).

Ng, Fintan. 2016. "RCEP negotiations likely to be substantially concluded by end-2017." *The Star*, 9 December available at http://www.thestar.com.my/business/business-news/2016/12/09/rcep-negotiations-likely-to-be-substantially-concluded-by-end2017/ (accessed on 20 February 2017).

Ng, Shui Meng. 1987. "Laos in 1986: Into the Second Decade of National Reconstruction." *Southeast Asian Affairs* 1987: 177–193.

Nguyen, Van Thang and Nick J. Freeman. 2009. "State-owned enterprises in Vietnam: are they 'crowding out' the private sector?" *Post-Communist Economies* 21(1): 227–247.

Odaka, Konosuke. 2016. *The Myanmar Economy: Its Past, Present and Prospects*. Japan: Springer.

Oraboune, Syviengxay. 2008. "Infrastructure Development in Lao PDR", In *International Infrastructure Development in East Asia – Towards Balanced Regional Development and Integration*, edited by Kumar, Nagesh. Jakarta: Economic Research Institute for ASEAN and East Asia (ERIA).

Ozawa, Terutomo, 2009. *The Rise of Asia: The 'Flying-Geese' Theory of Tandem Growth and Regional Agglomeration*. Cheltenham: Edward Elgar Publishing.

Page, John 1994. "The East Asian Miracle: Four Lessons for Development." *NBER Macroeconomics Annual* 9: 219–282.

Parikh, Tej. 2016. "Prime Minister Pushes Infrastructure Investment". *The Cambodia Daily*, 8th March, available at https://www.cambodiadaily.com/business/prime-minister-pushes-infrastructure-investment-109578 (accessed on 22 March 2017).

Peou, Chivoin. 2016. "Negotiating Rural-urban Transformation and Life Course Fluidity: Rural Young People and Urban Sojourn in Contemporary Cambodia." *Journal of Rural Studies* 44: 177–186.

Petri, Peter, Michael Plummer, and Fan Zhai. 2010. "The Economics of the ASEAN Economic Community." Brandeis Working Papers No. 13, Brandeis University, Department of Economics and International Businesss School, Massachusetts

Pham, Quang Ngoc, Trinh Bui and Duc Nguyen Thanh. 2007. "Economic performance of Vietnam, 1976–2000: New evidence from input-output model". Depocen Working Paper No. 2007/13, Development and Policies Research Center (Depocen), Hanoi.

Piketty, Thomas. 2014. *Capital in the Twenty-First Century.* Cambridge, Massachusetts: Harvard University Press.

Polanyi, Karl. 1944. *The Great Transformation: The Political and Economic Origins of Our Times.* Boston: Farrar & Rinehart.

Rashid, Zakariah, Fan Zhai, Peter A. Petri, Michael G. Plummer and Chia Siow Yue. 2009 "Regional Market for Goods, Services and Labor" in *Realizing the ASEAN Economic Community: A Comprehensive Assessment,* edited by Michael G. Plummer and Chia Siow Yue. Singapore: ISEAS Publishing.

Rasiah, Rajah. 2009. "Can Garment Exports from Cambodia, Laos and Burma be Sustained?" *Journal of Contemporary Asia* 39(4): 619–637.

Ravallion, Martin, and Shaohua Chen. 2007. "China's (uneven) Progress against Poverty." *Journal of Development Economics* 82(1): 1–42.

Riedel, James, and William S. Turley. 1999. "The Politics and Economics of Transition to an Open Market Economy in Viet Nam". OECD Development Centre Working Paper No. 152, OECD Development Centre, Paris.

Rieffel, Lex. 2015. "Policy Options for Improving the Performance of the State Economic Enterprise Sector in Myanmar." ISEAS Working Paper Series No. 2015/01. Institute of Southeast Asian Studies (ISEAS), Singapore.

Rodrik, Dani. 2006. "Goodbye Washington Consensus, Hello Washington Confusion? A Review of the World Bank's Economic Growth in the 1990s: Learning from a Decade of Reform." *Journal of Economic Literature* 44(4): 973–87.

Rodrik, Dani. 2007. *One Economics, Many recipes: Globalization, Institutions, and Economic Growth.* Princeton: Princeton University Press.

Salidjanova, Nargiza, Iacob Koch-Weser and Jason Klanderman. 2015. *China's Economic Ties with ASEAN: A Country-by-Country Analysis.* Washington D. C.: US–China Economic and Security Review Commission.

Seers, Dudley. 1969. "The Meaning of Development." IDS Communication No. 44. Brighton, UK: Institute of Development Studies.

Sen, Amartya. 1999. *Development as Freedom.* New York: Alfred A. Knopf.

Smith, Adam. 1776. *An Inquiry into the Causes of the Wealth of Nations.* London: Methuen & Co., Ltd.

Sobrado, Carlos, Samsen Neak, Sodeth Ly, Aldaz-Carroll Enrique, Elisa Gamberoni, Francisco Arias-Vazquez, Tsuyoshi Fukao, Simeth Beng, Timothy Johnston, Miguel San Joquin, Lucilla Bruni, Richard de Groot. 2014. *Where have all the poor gone?: Cambodia poverty assessment 2013.* Washington DC: The World Bank.

Soon, WeiLun. 2017. "Singapore says TPP cannot come into effect, turns to other regional trade initiatives." *Business Times*, 24 January available at http://www.businesstimes.com.sg/government-economy/singapore-says-tpp-cannot-come-into-effect-turns-to-other-regional-trade (accessed on 20 February 2017).

Suokas, Janne. 2016. "China wants to conclude RCEP trade talks in 2017." *Gbtimes*, 27 December available at http://gbtimes.com/business/china-wants-conclude-rcep-trade-talks-2017 (accessed on 20 February 2017).

St John, Ronald Bruce. 2006. "The Political Economy of Laos: Poor State or Poor Policy?" *Asian Affairs* 37(2): 175–191.

Stuart-Fox, Martin. 1986. "Laos in 1985: Time to take stock." *Southeast Asian Affairs* 13(165): 165–181.

Tan, Khee Giap, Sasidaran Gopalan, and Ye Ye. 2016. "Drivers of Growth in the Travel and Tourism Industry in Malaysia: A Geweke Causality Analysis". *Economies* 4(3): 1–15.

Tan, Khee Giap, Le Phuong Anh Nguyen and Trieu Duong Luu Nguyen. 2016. "Make or Break for Vietnam in the TPP Era". Policy Brief, Asia Competitiveness Institute, Singapore.

Tan, Khee Giap, Le Phuong Anh Nguyen, Sasidaran Gopalan and Nguyen Trieu Duong Luu. 2017. *2015 Annual Competitiveness Analysis, Agricultural Productivity and Development Vision for ASEAN-10*. Singapore: World Scientific.

Taussig, Markus D., Chi Hieu Nguyen, and Thuy Linh Nguyen. *From Control to Market: Time for Real SOE Reform in Vietnam?* Singapore: Centre for Governance, Institutions and Organisations (CGIO).

The Economist. 2014. "Healthcare in Vietnam: Limping Along." 20 December available at http://www.economist.com/news/asia/21618894-ordinary-folk-are-sick-and-tired-their-public-hospitals-limping-along (accessed on 23 March 2017).

The Strait Times. 2016. "RCEP talks speed up amid TPP failure." 7 December, available at http://www.straitstimes.com/asia/se-asia/rcep-talks-speed-up-amid-tpp-failure (accessed on 20 February 2017).

Thein, Myat. 2004. *Economic Development in Myanmar*. Singapore: Institute of Southeast Asian Studies (ISEAS)

Tian, Shaohui. 2015. "Full Text: Vision and actions on jointly building Belt and Road". *Xinhua*, 28 March available at http://news.xinhuanet.com/english/china/2015-03/28/c_ 134105858.htm (accessed on 21 February 2017).

Tanaka, Kiyoyasu. 2016. "Forecasting Inbound Tourists in Cambodia." IDE Discussion Paper No. 601, Institute of Developing Economies (IDE), Chiba.

Transparency International. 2017. *Corruption Perceptions Index 2016*. Berlin: Transparency International.

UNICEF. 2012. "Comprehensive Education Sector Review in Myanmar Sets the Path for Improving Quality of Education". 8 November, available at https://www.unicef.org/myanmar/reallives_19891.html (accessed on 23 March 2017).

United Nations. 1992. *The Secretary-General's Consolidated Appeal for Cambodia's Immediate Needs and National Rehabilitation*. Cambodia: United Nations Transitional Authority in Cambodia (UNTAC).

UNCTAD. 1994. *Trade and Development Report*. Geneva: United Nations Conference on Trade and Development (UNCTAD).

UNDP. 2013a. *Democratic Governance in Myanmar: Current Trends and Implications*, available at http://www.undp.org/content/dam/myanmar/docs/Publications/DemoGov/UNDP_MM_DG_Democratic GovernanceSummary.pdf (accessed on 22 March 2016).

UNDP. 2013b. "UNDP Myanmar opens a new chapter of partnership". 9 April, available at http://www.undp.org/content/undp/en/home/presscenter/pressreleases/2013/04/09/undp-myanmar-opens-a-new-chapter-of-partnership.html (accessed on 24 March 2017).

Vandergeest, Peter. 2003. "Land to Some Tillers: Development-induced Displacement in Laos." *International Social Science Journal* 55(1): 47.

Vo, Nhan Tri. 1990. *Vietnam's Economic Policy Since 1975*. Singapore: Institute of Southeast Asian Studies (ISEAS).

Wade, Robert. 1990. *Governing the Market: Economic Theory and the Role of Government in East Asian Industrialization*. Princeton: Princeton University Press.

Warr, Peter, Sitthiroth Rasphone and Jayant Menon. 2015. "Two Decades of Rising Inequality and Declining Poverty in the Lao People's Democratic Republic." ADB Economics Working Paper No. 461, Asian Development Bank (ADB), Manila.

Williamson, John, Ed. 1990. *Latin American Adjustment: How Much Has Happened*. Washington D.C.: Institute for International Economics.

World Bank. 1993. *The East Asian Miracle: Economic Growth and Public Policy.* New York: Oxford University Press.

World Bank. 2002. *Private Solutions for Infrastructure in Cambodia-A Country Framework Report.* Washington DC: World Bank.

World Bank. 2009. *China — From Poor Areas to Poor People: China's Evolving Poverty Reduction Agenda — An Assessment of Poverty and Inequality*. Washington, DC: World Bank.

World Bank. 2013. "Poverty Reduction in Vietnam: Remarkable Progress, Emerging Challenges." 24 January available at http://www.worldbank.org/en/news/feature/2013/01/24/poverty-reduction-in-vietnam-remarkable-progress-emerging-challenges (accessed on 23 March 2017).

World Bank. 2015. "Vietnam's Growth Strengthens despite Mixed Progress on Structural Reforms." 20 July available at http://www.worldbank.org/en/news/press-release/2015/07/20/vietnams-growth-strengthens-despite-mixed-progress-on-structural-reforms (accessed on 23 March 2017).

World Bank and Ministry of Planning and Investment of Vietnam. 2016. *Vietnam 2035: Toward Prosperity, Creativity, Equity, and Democracy*. Washington DC: The World Bank.

World Bank. 2016a. "New Country Engagement Plan for Cambodia Outlines More World Bank Group Support to Help Reduce Poverty". 19 May available at http://www.worldbank.org/en/news/press-release/2016/05/19/new-country-engagement-plan-for-cambodia-outlines-more-world-bank-group-support-to-help-reduce-poverty (accessed on 22 March 2017).

World Bank. 2016b. *Lao Economic Monitor FY15-16*. Washington DC: World Bank.

World Food Programme. 2017. *WFP Lao PDR Country Brief.* Rome: World Food Programme.

Xinhua. 2016. "Construction of China-Laos railway officially commences". 25 December available at http://english.gov.cn/news/international_exchanges/2016/12/25/content_281475524680610.htm (accessed on 20 February 2017).

Yamagata, Tatsufumi. 2006. "The Garment Industry in Cambodia: Its Role in Poverty Reduction through Export-Oriented Development." IDE Discussion Paper No. 62. Institute of Developing Economies (IDE), Chiba.

Yean, Tham Siew and Kwek Kian Teng. 2007. "Prosper-Thy-Neighbour Policies: Malaysia's Contributions after the Asian Financial Crisis." *Journal of Southeast Asian Economies* 24(1): 72–97.

Chapter 5
Positioning Singapore for the Waves of Change: Building Deep Capabilities for the Future Economy

5.1 Introduction

Known as one of the Four Asian Tigers, Singapore is the most competitive economy in ASEAN as shown in Chapter 2 of this book. Despite the turbulences during the aftermaths of the Asian Financial Crisis (AFC) in 1997 as well as the 2007/08 Global Financial Crisis (GFC), the city-state has been undergoing steady growth and development. With the latest real Gross Domestic Product (GDP) growth of 2.9 percent[1] in the second quarter of 2017, the Singapore's economy has shown some signs of rebound against the backdrop of global growth slowdown since the GFC. An optimistic outlook is also reflected in the Ministry of Trade and Industry (MTI)'s projection which narrowed the 2017 GDP growth forecast from between one to three percent announced earlier this year to between two and three percent (MTI 2017). However, downside risks remain given the social-economic uncertainties generated from rising protectionist sentiments in the developed Western economies, especially after the triumph of the "Leave" camp in the Brexit vote and Donald Trump's ascension to the United States (US)' Presidency in 2016.

Indeed, rising global uncertainties are a common challenge for the ASEAN countries, which have been pursing export-led growth strategies. With the establishment of the ASEAN Economic Community (AEC) in 2015 and the adoption of the Master Plan on ASEAN Connectivity 2025, ASEAN has continued to demonstrate its determination in deepening economic integration, both within and outside Southeast Asia. Nevertheless, high interconnectivity with the global economy also means that the regional association is now more vulnerable to unpredictable changes in the global landscape. This is especially true for Singapore, one of the most open economies in the world.

However, good policy-making entails adeptly navigating the immediate risks while not losing sight of the potential long-term challenges. In this respect, policy-makers must prepare for reforms to address ageing population and technological disruptions. For both Singapore and its ASEAN neighbours, these are the two major trends which will shape their economic performances in the long run.

5.1.1 The Social and Economic Implications of Ageing Population

With the acceleration of population ageing worldwide and particularly in developed economies (United Nations 2015), it is essential for policy-makers to prepare for the inevitable economic and social implications which follow. Singapore with a population size of 5.6 million people

[1]According to MTI's press release on 11 August 2017 which can be assessed at, https://www.mti.gov.sg/ResearchRoom/SiteAssets/Pages/Economic-Survey-of-Singapore-Second-Quarter-2017/PR_2Q17.pdf.

(as of 2016)[2] is not an exception. Improved longevity resulted from advancements in healthcare and rising living standards has led to increased life expectancy at birth from 65.7 years to 82.6 years between 1960 and 2015.[3] However, this has been coupled with decreasing fertility rate from 5.8 births per woman to 1.2 births per woman over the same period. The disproportionate growth rates between the older population and the new births in Singapore have led to rising old-age dependency ratio. As shown in Figure 5.1, the old-age dependency ratio in Singapore is growing at the fastest rate among 10 ASEAN economies and is projected to reach 61 dependents per 100 working-age persons in 2050. This indicates that the labour force will have to support a higher number of elderlies.

Figure 5.1: Trends and Forecasts of Old-Age Dependency Ratio (Ratio of Population Aged 65 and Above Per 100 Population of Aged 15–64) in ASEAN-10, 1990–2050

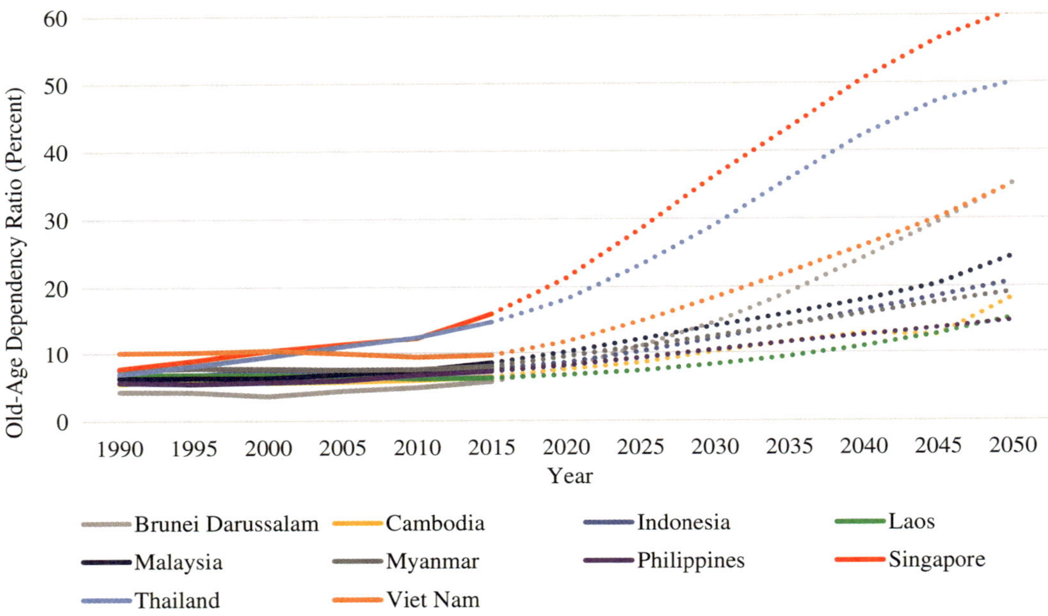

Source: World Population Prospects, United Nations

Socially, such a demographic transition will call for improvements in healthcare which should effectively target both prevention and care for the older population who have different needs from other age groups (Beard *et al.* 2012). Furthermore, aging population also pose new challenges to public finances, as social spending needs are expected to increase while the base of tax-paying workers will shrink. With the number of people aged 65 and above in Singapore projected to rise from 12 percent of the population in 2015 to 34 percent in 2050, it is high time for policy-makers to re-evaluate healthcare and fiscal policies with a view of adapting them to the inevitable demographic change.

[2] Latest data from the Department of Statistics, Singapore.

[3] Based on World Development Indicators database of the World Bank.

On the economic front, with fewer people of working age, the pool of productive labour will shrink. A smaller working-age population also means less domestic resources for productive investments as this group tends to save while the older population tends to dissave. As a result, the future growth momentums may be impeded (Bloom, Canning and Fink 2011). In response, the Singapore government has tried to encourage people to work longer. The Retirement and Re-employment Act, which was implemented in 2012, extends the re-employment age to 67 for Singaporeans and permanent residents. This has led to an increase in labour force participation among the elderlies, which may help to ameliorate the supply pressure in the labour market. According to the Singapore's Department of Statistics, the labour participation rate of the residents aged 65 years and over has come to its highest level of 26.5 percent since 1998. However, the key long-term solution to combat the anticipated decline in labour force is to improve labour productivity. This has been a policy priority of the Singapore government for the past few years. However, the country's efforts in boosting productivity have only yielded mixed results and more needs to be done.

5.1.2 Opportunities and Challenges Arising from Technological Shifts and Disruptions

In addition to ageing population which has profound impacts on economic growth, the recent technology surge commonly known as the Fourth Industrial Revolution is another trend which will shape Singapore's economic future. The fusion of technological shifts across digital, physical and biological fields is expected to alter the way we live and how the economy works (Schwab 2015). Indeed, the unprecedentedly rapid pace of technological improvement and the magnitude of its impacts on entire systems will create both challenges and opportunities for all economies including Singapore.

On the one hand, some pundits have expressed concerns about the unintended consequences of technological transformation. The technological surge may yield a lot of benefits in the economy. However, distributional issues remain a challenge. As termed by Brynjolfsson and McAfee (2014), the 'Great Decoupling' in the US and other developed economies, the phenomenon where these economies experience growth in GDP and productivity yet suffer from widening income inequality, is partially caused by the technological revolution. This is because following the automation and digitalisation of industries, many low-skilled jobs have been displaced by computers and machines while demand for high-skilled labour is on the rise. With high proportion of jobs at stake given the emergence of robotics and AI technology, there is even emergence of new discourse in implementing universal basic income with ongoing pilot studies in countries like Finland and Netherlands (Manjoo 2016; Coppola 2017; The Economist 2017). Moreover, in order to cultivate future-ready labour force, the traditional education system needs to be revamped in order to empower individuals with relevant skill sets for the future market.

On the other hand, the penetration of technology in our day-to-day life which ranges from ordering taxis to paying bills has made life more convenient than ever. Technological innovation has also led to advancements in transportation and communication which fuel economic activities across borders. Furthermore, the adoption of technology in the supply chains including research and development, production, distribution, sales and marketing has led to productivity and efficiency gains in the economy. Moving forward, the emerging technological leaps in multiple domains including artificial intelligence (AI), big data, the Internet of Things, and robotics are expected to open new avenues for growth and consequently create new types of jobs.

Businesses will also be exposed to new opportunities and challenges under the Fourth Industrial Revolution. For instance, due to technological advancements, the process of buying and selling is no longer constrained to a physical store but can now be completed via a smart phone or computer. Moreover, consumers are better informed than ever with easy access to more information via the Internet. Given these disruptions, business-as-usual is no longer an option if firms are to survive and thrive on the acceleration of technological change. Firms have to think of new ways in doing business to ensure that they are future-ready and continue to drive the competitiveness of the economy.

In particular, small and medium enterprises (SMEs) need to be encouraged to innovate and develop their digital capacity. SMEs is an important engine of growth and a source of employment creation for many economies. For instance, they made up 99 percent of Singapore's total business establishments in 2015.[4] However, due to resource constraints or lack of incentives, SMEs are not always in the position to capitalise on technological innovations to improve their productivity and efficiency. This in turn causes them to become less competitive and lag further behind multinational corporations, which is a cause for concern.

The initiative of Smart Nation and the recommendations by the Committee on the Future Economy (CFE) in Singapore show that the country is at the forefront in responding to the Fourth Industrial Revolution. The five key areas (also known as the 'five futures') of the CFE recommendations focusing on corporate capabilities and innovation, growth industries and markets, connectivity, city, and jobs and skills is a comprehensive framework which covers different stakeholders including firms, industry players and individuals. On top of that, the Enterprise Future Initiative (EFI) launched by the Asia Competitiveness Institute (ACI) at the Lee Kuan Yew School of Public Policy (LKYSPP), National University of Singapore (NUS) in 2017, which is in line with the Skills Future Initiative (SFI), illustrates the commitment of both government and academic in assisting SMEs to uplift their productivity and monitor the management efficiency in coping with the waves of technological transformation.

5.2 Building Deep Capabilities for the Future Economy[5]

This chapter benefits from the insights by the Minister for Finance of Singapore, Mr Heng Swee Keat. In this Section, we present his speech on "Building Deep Capabilities for the Future Economy" delivered at the Economic Society of Singapore (ESS) Annual Dinner on Wednesday, 2 August 2017. Drawing on comprehensive observations about the current challenges and

---

[4] Based on data from Singstat.

[5] This section includes a reprint with permission of the speech on "Building Deep Capabilities for the Future Economy" by Mr Heng Swee Keat, Minister for Finance of Singapore at the Economic Society of Singapore (ESS) Annual Dinner on Wednesday, 2 August 2017 at 2005hrs at the Mandarin Orchard Singapore Grand Mandarin Ballroom.

envisioning the future trends, Mr Heng sets out a clear roadmap with specific policy recommendations in preparing Singapore for the future economy. The policy issues discussed in Mr Heng's speech are not only applicable to Singapore, but also relevant for other ASEAN economies looking to transition successfully into the future.

5.2.1 Creating Value amid Change

When I last spoke at an ESS Annual Dinner, I touched on the effects of the GFC, structural changes in the global economy and how we should respond. That was only four years ago (2013), and global uncertainty has risen significantly since. The rise of ISIS and the increase in terrorist incidents worldwide, North Korea's missile tests, Brexit, the US' withdrawal from the Trans-Pacific Partnership are just some examples. In some advanced economies, political support for globalisation has given way to nationalism. The future is uncertain — a complex configuration of both short-run challenges and long-run trends. Even as we address the immediate pressure points, we should anticipate the long-term changes. Let me identify some of these.

First, our population is ageing. This means higher healthcare expenditures, and a decline in our domestic labour force, which will affect our growth rates. Other economies, including China, Japan, Korea and the European Union (EU), are facing the same. In comparison, there are many other countries in Asia with youthful populations. Whether this will translate to a population dividend depends on how well they educate and develop their people, and if new technology trends will enhance or diminish this advantage.

The second change is the global slowdown of productivity growth and the impact of technology. Economists have been grappling with the Solow paradox — you can see the computer age everywhere but in the productivity statistics. Various explanations have been put forth to explain the global slowdown in productivity growth, including: the rising importance of the domestic services industries; under-investment in capacities and structures; the slow and patchy diffusion of best practices; and the lack of competitive pressures to channel resources to their most productive use.

There are also different views about the impact of technological progress on productivity and jobs. On one side, Robert Gordon, studying the total factor productivity (TFP) in the US economy over the past century, concluded that technological advancements in recent decades, including the rise of Information and Communications Technology (ICT), have paled in comparison to the five Great Inventions that drove substantial growth from 1870 to 1970 — electricity, urban sanitation, chemicals and pharmaceuticals, the internal combustion engine, and modern communication. Recent technology just has not lifted growth and productivity as much as past advancements have.

On the other side are the techno-optimists. Erik Brynjolfsson and Andrew McAfee advocate for the potential of digitalisation and automation. For example, they see large economic potential of online platforms, citing Tom Goodwin's observation that large companies — like Facebook, Airbnb, Alibaba and Uber — do not own or make the underlying assets from whose value they profit. Others call data the new oil, perhaps even more valuable and powerful. Klaus Schwab describes the Fourth Industrial Revolution as a confluence of emerging technology breakthroughs, not just in ICT, but also in materials science, biotechnology, energy storage and others, which interact across different domains. It is not certain what the overall impact of technology will be. What is certain is that the countries that are prepared for technological change will be at the greatest advantage.

A third trend is the rise of emerging economies. Attention was previously on the Brazil, Russia, India and China (BRIC) economies. More recently, the limelight is on Asia, which hosts two of the strongest growing economies, China and India. Studies suggest that the shift in the world's economic centre of gravity to Asia may be accelerating. The IMF's latest forecast places Asia at the top of the global growth league table. Though there are other trends to consider, each of these alone will have profound impact on a small, open economy like Singapore's.

We won't feel the full effects of these trends tomorrow, and no one can predict the future. But we can prepare. When the CFE considered these trends and discussed possible responses, there were some who sought to bet on new growth industries, new technologies and new markets to go into. But in a fast-changing, unpredictable world, there are no short-cuts. What we need is a certain shift in orientation — a readiness for change, and a willingness to try, learn, and try again.

Last year, I met the Chief Executive Officer (CEO) of a food company that was doing well, along with several of his competitors in the industry. He told me, "Years back, an official told us that we were in a sunset industry. We wanted to prove him wrong. We worked hard, we worked together. There's no sunset industry, only sunset thinking!" I applaud his fighting spirit. I've continued to reflect on the food manufacturing sector's experience. Whether a firm or an industry will succeed is not pre-ordained — it depends on our mindset and how we build competitive advantage.

Our economy's competitiveness and ability to create good opportunities for our people rests on a set of inter-related factors. First, we need to maintain *macroeconomic stability*, and have a well-functioning financial system that channels savings to productive uses. We have done this well in recent years, keeping inflation at bay through effective monetary policy, while maintaining fiscal prudence. Our financial system has also continued to innovate to meet the evolving demands of the modern economy.

Second, we need strong *microeconomic foundations* that allow resources to be allocated efficiently across firms and individuals, in an equitable and sustainable way. We have, and must, continue to make our regulations more pro-business, tweaking them to encourage innovation and risk-taking, while protecting the interests of our people.

And third, we must encourage our individuals, firms and industries to build *deep capabilities*, so that they can achieve sustainable competitive advantage to adapt and thrive in their fields. This third factor, capabilities, is what I will focus on today. At their core, the recommendations of the CFE are about keeping our economy globally connected, and building deep capabilities — both horizontal capabilities across the economy, and vertical ones within each industry. By bringing all key stakeholders together to create Industry Transformation Maps (ITMs) and to build capabilities, we can better address the challenges and opportunities in each industry, and the entire economy. While we cannot predict the future, strong corporate and human capabilities give us the best chance of riding the waves of changes ahead.

5.2.2 Our Firms: Creating Value through Firm-specific and Industry-wide Capabilities

Let me start with our firms. Firms need two main types of capabilities to be competitive, particularly in a time of change:

i. Distinctive, firm-specific capabilities, to differentiate themselves from their competitors.
ii. Industry-wide capabilities that benefit all firms within a sector.

5.2.2.1 *Firm-specific Capabilities*

First, firm-specific capabilities. A competitive firm creates unique value for its customers, in cost-effective ways. There is no formula for this. Every company must develop its own. But there are some broad areas that we heard about during the CFE's industry consultations:

i. Human capital;
ii. Innovation, including the use of technology; and,
iii. Internationalisation.

I will speak more on human capital later. Let me first discuss innovation. The ability to innovate new products, services, processes or business models that create new value gives companies a competitive edge.

In recent times, the rapid growth of some start-ups has captured public imagination. Innovation is often associated with start-ups. But large companies need as much, if not more, innovative capacity. Beyond in-house development of new products and services, companies are also setting up corporate venture funds and incubators, so as to discover, work with, and invest in promising start-ups. We see this in the pharmaceutical industry, where large companies are licensing drugs developed by smaller start-ups. Also in Silicon Valley, where promising tech start-ups get acquired by larger players.

The value chain for innovation is changing — some start-ups may choose to develop themselves fully, while others may partner established companies to commercialise their innovations. ST Engineering has launched a corporate venture capital unit, and started an open innovation lab called Innosparks in Launchpad @ one-north. In time, companies can make use of the Global Innovation Alliance (GIA) to extend their innovation networks overseas — in fact, as part of our GIA efforts, BLOCK71 Jakarta was officially opened just last week.

Another way to innovate is to use technology. Firms can adopt existing technology to improve productivity, or adapt technology to change their business models and disrupt industries. Others may invent technology and create intellectual property (IP). We should encourage a variety of approaches to innovation, including the use of technology, and create some flexibility in our regulatory frameworks, like regulatory sandboxes, to allow new things to be tried.

Another important corporate capability is the ability to internationalise. Technological advancements and trade liberalisation have reduced distances and extended companies' reach to resources and customers. Companies need local market insights and outreach capabilities to tap on the larger potential markets that emerge as a result. Technology allows big and small firms alike to expand into the region and the world. From start-ups like Carousell to large enterprises like CapitaLand, Singapore firms are already doing so. There is Government support for firms to internationalise.

5.2.2.2 *Industry-wide Capabilities*

Beyond firm-specific capabilities, industry-wide capabilities also matter. Companies can cooperate to help build these. A few years back, I visited a company in Switzerland that was training about 100 students to operate complex machinery. But the company needed only 60 new recruits. The remaining 40 would go to their competitors. Now, why would a company train for its competitors? The CEO explained that there would be an industry-wide shortage of talent otherwise — a shortage would affect them all. It was a lesson in competing and cooperating at the same time.

In Singapore too, industry leaders have taken encouraging steps. You may be familiar with the TechSkills Accelerator (TeSA), which trains ICT professionals. About two years back, members of the Singapore Infocomm Technology Federation (SITF) and the Singapore Computer Society (SCS) told me they were facing a shortage of strong ICT talent. I asked them, "Would you be willing to work together? Government can help provide resources, but, as industry, you know best what skills are relevant." They said yes, and competitors worked actively together with our agencies to form and run TeSA. I was impressed by this. Over 10,000 professionals have benefitted from TeSA's programmes. And companies can hire from a deeper pool of talent with relevant skills. I look forward to seeing TeSA achieve even more.

Our Trade Associations and Chambers (TACs) are also important in building industry-wide capabilities. So I am glad that they, too, are actively collaborating. For example, more than 20 TACs will share facilities and resources at the Singapore Chinese Chamber of Commerce and Industry's (SCCCI) Trade Association Hub, which will officially open soon. Some industry leaders have asked me if our economic agencies can also improve our coordination, to provide more integrated support, in areas such as helping companies to build capabilities and to internationalise. We are studying these.

Indeed, collaboration is the spirit of the ITMs. Each ITM gathers the stakeholders — companies, TACs, unions, research institutes, training providers and Government agencies — to formulate and implement strategies to develop the industry and its capabilities. The different capabilities cannot be considered in isolation. Each industry will need a different configuration of capabilities. By bringing all stakeholders together, we can implement changes more effectively. Beyond each single industry, we should also explore developing capabilities across different industries. This is why we formed six clusters of related ITMs.

To sum up, to compete in the Future Economy, our companies will need firm-specific and industry-wide capabilities. To develop firm-specific capabilities, companies should invest in internationalisation, innovation and smart technology use and development. To develop industry-wide capabilities, companies can look beyond their individual pursuits, and collaborate with others, both within their industry and across industries, for mutual benefits.

Contrary to the classical view, the marketplace is not an arena where companies are pitted against each other in atomistic competition. Instead, it is a journey across a complex terrain, where, at points, we will have to rely on our distinctive strengths to progress, and, at others, we can work together to advance. There is great potential for collective gain through collaboration, among partners along the value chain and even among erstwhile rivals, if we look for the right opportunities. We need to think about multiplying effectiveness, because it is not a zero-sum game.

Indeed, aside from Ronald Coase's seminal work, the role of firms in coordinating resources, both internally and through their interactions with other firms and the wider economy, has not received enough academic attention. Perhaps the members of the ESS can take a closer look at this, especially in the Singapore context.

On our part, the Government will foster conducive macro- and microeconomic conditions for all companies to excel. Ultimately, firms and industries must take the lead to create value for their customers, by building strong capabilities.

5.2.3 Our People: Creating Value through Lifelong Development of Relevant Capabilities

Let me now speak about the capabilities of our people. Factors like the reconfiguration of global supply chains, shifts in consumption patterns, and technological advances are changing the nature of jobs and the skills we need for work, along with how businesses operate. So corporate and human capabilities must go hand-in-hand, growing in tandem to drive our industry transformation. This is why Jobs and Skills form an important pillar of every ITM. These changes will affect *what* we learn, *how* we learn and *when* we learn.

First, *what we learn* should help us realise our potential, and build foundations for further learning. Part of this involves learning skills that are relevant to society and the economy. Along with domain-specific skills, some general ones, like the ability to work with digital tools and data, will increase in economic significance. Others, like social skills and emotional intelligence, will remain important in making us effective members of society. We should harness technology to create more value. If we can use AI to automate more routine cognitive tasks, for instance, we can then focus on developing the uniquely human skills, like creativity or open-ended problem solving, that will enable us to do higher-value work.

Next, to keep up with fast-changing skills requirements, *how we learn* should expand to include learning from all sources and in different settings. Learning does not have to happen in a classroom — it can also happen via new technologies, like online platforms, or new modalities, like on-the-job training or overseas attachments, which can help to integrate theoretical understanding with practical application.

Third, *when we learn* need not be confined to the first two decades of our lives. As we all live and work longer, we cannot expect to cram all that we need to know for our entire lives within the first twenty-odd years of our lives. Instead, we should learn throughout life, through on-the-job experience interspersed with bouts of more intense, modular full-time training.

If we are to change *what*, *how*, and *when* we learn, individuals, institutes of learning, and industry must change our habits and practices significantly. Individuals will have to shift from "learning, then doing" to "lifelong learning *and* doing". Instead of just learning before starting work, we should embrace a lifelong cycle of learning and doing. Throughout our careers, we learn the skills that we need for our jobs, hone them by using them at work, and then, as the economy evolves, learn a new set of skills and in turn put those to use. It is a virtuous cycle of learning and doing. In Mandarin, there is a phrase: "活学活用，学以致用" — living and learning, learning and doing, are deeply integrated.

We must each take ownership, and be proactive about lifelong learning and doing throughout our lives. This is what the SkillsFuture movement is about. We should also take up opportunities to broaden our experience beyond our shores. Initiatives like the GIA, for instance, can help us to understand overseas contexts better.

Institutes of learning also have a role. For instance, Ministry of Education (MOE) has the 21st Century Competencies Framework, to help students in our schools develop competencies like responsible decision-making and critical and inventive thinking, encouraging them to become self-directed learners who can keep up learning and throughout their lives. Our educational institutions are placing a greater emphasis on skills application and hands-on learning at all levels. Examples include the Applied Learning Programmes in our secondary schools, the Skills Future Earn and Learn Programmes in our polytechnics and Institute of Technical Education (ITE), and the various work-learn programmes in our autonomous universities.

The Singapore Institute of Technology's (SIT) Integrated Work-Study Programme (IWSP) gives students real-world experience through 8–12 months of relevant on-the-job training with partner companies. The results are promising. 84 percent of the first batch of Accountancy students received priority job offers from the partner companies, and two were even able to start in a position above entry-level! Almost all of the rest found employment within three months of graduation. I understand that the second batch has also done well. Employers also benefit. They get 8–12 months to assess potential employees, and a head-start in training them. We should continue to encourage such close collaboration between our educational institutions and industry partners, to tighten the link between learning and working.

Increasingly, our educational institutions also encourage students to gain overseas exposure, through programmes like the NUS Overseas Colleges, the Polytechnics' Overseas Student Internship Programme, and ITE's Global Education Programme. Our universities, Polytechnics and ITE have all embarked on making courses available online. The Nanyang Technological University (NTU) has announced that it would convert some 1,500 courses in five years, about 50 percent of their pre-employment training (PET) courses. NUS has partnered Coursera to launch several Massive Open Online Courses. The rest are making progress to make available modules online, to support new modes of learning for full-time and part-time students. MOE's Student Learning Space will also use the latest digital tools and modalities of learning to improve educational outcomes.

What about industry players? It is encouraging to see that many companies are building up their human capital, as part of their overall business strategy, and reaping significant benefits from this investment. Firms are integrating the development of their people with the redesign of their company processes. For example, in upgrading its Singapore plant into a smart factory, Panasonic upgraded employees' skills to remain relevant in a smart factory. As a result, the median salary of their local staff has increased by 35 percent. Many companies operate as "in-house approved training organisations" which provide industry-validated training to their own staff. Examples include Wing Tai, SATS and McDonald's. Firms that are far-sighted in building corporate capabilities are those that anticipate future skills needs, and invest in developing their people. I am a firm supporter of such efforts. These firms can collaborate with our educational institutions through various work-study programmes, or work with Government agencies.

Industry-wide, there is collaboration on human capital development. Today, there are companies who deliver training programmes, not just for their own needs, but for the broader industry. Examples include Ascott and the PBA Group. The Supply Chain and Logistics Academy is an example of an industry-driven effort that trains supply chain professionals across different companies, through experiential workplace learning. I encourage further collaboration.

In sum, as jobs and skills requirements change, we will need to transform what we learn, how we learn and when we learn. Individuals, institutes of learning, and industry will have to work closely together and use new modalities to tighten the link between learning and doing. This will maximise the potential for both corporates and people to make the most of the opportunities ahead.

5.2.4 Concluding Notes

Allow me to conclude. The world is facing major structural changes. Singapore is well-placed to manage these changes, and make the most of the opportunities they bring — we have strong tripartite relations, sound macro-economic and micro-economic foundations, and strong physical and virtual connections to the world. If our companies and our people continue to build strong capabilities, we can make the most of these advantages, to create unique value for the world and our people. There is no playbook to follow. What we need is the right mindset — to be proactive, dare to take risks, and learn from our failures, and recognise that this is a continuous journey of upgrading. And we will have to work together — in a national effort where we each have a role.

I look forward to our people embracing "lifelong learning and doing". I look forward to our companies developing distinctive capabilities, while actively collaborating for shared benefits. I look forward to our TACs playing a leadership role in building industry-wide capabilities, to benefit all within their sectors. I look forward to our educational institutions continuing to innovate to bring out the best in our people, and exploring how to better integrate work and study to make "lifelong learning and doing" a way of life for Singaporeans. And I look forward to all of us coming closer together, preparing for and riding change with optimism and confidence, with the courage to experiment, and the humility to learn from others and from our failures, so that we can make the most of the changes ahead, and create good opportunities and good lives for our people.

Let us all work together to build our Future Economy. Let us compete fairly, but collaborate generously, and seek to be greater than the sum of our parts. And let us support one another, especially those of us who are less advantaged, so that we can all advance together. I hope that the ESS too, with your economic expertise, will contribute actively to these efforts. Thank you.

References

Beard, J., S. Biggs, D. Bloom, L. Fried, P. Hogan, A. Kalache, and J. Olshansky. 2012. "Global Population Ageing: Peril or Promise?" *PGDA Working Paper 89*. Geneva: World Economic Forum.

Bloom, D., D. Canning, and G. Fink. 2011. "Implications of Population Aging for Economic Growth." *NBER Working Paper 16705*. MA: NBER.

Brynjolfsson, E. and A. McAfee. 2014. *The Second Machine Age: Work, Progress, and Prosperity in a Time of Brilliant Technologies*. New York: W. W. Norton & Company.

Coppola, F. 2017. Top Economists Endorse Universal Basic Income. *Forbes*, 31 August, available at https://www.forbes.com/sites/francescoppola/2017/08/31/top-economists-endorse-universal-basic-income/#399ed78215ae (accessed on 31 August, 2017).

Heng, Swee Keat. 2017. Speech at the Economic Society of Singapore (ESS) Annual Dinner on "Building Deep Capabilities for the Future Economy". Singapore, 2 August.

Lee, Jeong-Dong, A. Heshmati. 2009. "Introduction." In. *Productivity, Efficiency, And Economic Growth In The Asia-Pacific Region*, edited by Lee, J. D., A. Heshmati, 1–9. Heidelberg: Physica-Verlag.

Manjoo, F. 2016. "A Plan in Case Robots Take the Jobs: Give Everyone a Paycheck". *The New York Times*, 2 March, available at https://www.nytimes.com/2016/03/03/technology/plan-to-fight-robot-invasion-at-work-give-everyone-a-paycheck.html?mcubz=1 (accessed on 3 September, 2017).

Ministry of Trade and Industry. 2017. Press release on "MTI Narrows 2017 GDP Growth Forecast to '2.0 to 3.0 Per Cent'." Singapore. 11 August.

Schwab, Klaus. 2015. "The Fourth Industrial Revolution: What It Means, How to Respond." *Foreign Affairs*, 12 December, available at https://www.foreignaffairs.com/articles/2015-12-12/fourth-industrial-revolution (accessed on 30 August, 2017).

The Economist. 2017. If Universal Basic Income Took Off: Giving Money to Everyone. 3 July, available at http://worldif.economist.com/article/13518/giving-money-everyone (accessed on 31 August, 2016).

United Nations. 2015. *World Population Ageing 2015*. New York: United Nations.

Chapter 6
Concluding Remarks and Future Research Agenda

6.1 Summary of Key Findings

With this compendium on *2016 Annual Competitiveness Analysis And Growth Slowdown Analysis For ASEAN-10*, the Asia Competitiveness Institute (ACI) at the Lee Kuan Yew School of Public Policy (LKYSPP), National University of Singapore (NUS) presents not only our latest competitiveness ranking and simulation analysis for the 10 ASEAN member states but also studies of various economic issues, with a view of contributing to policy formulation in the region for continued prosperity and balanced development. At the same time, the shock election of Donald Trump to the Presidency of the United States (US) and the victory of the "Leave" campaign during the Brexit referendum in 2016 has served to underscore the fact that the development of human societies is driven by not only economic but also sociological and political forces acting in conjunction with one another. In a region as diverse as Southeast Asia, we cannot ignore the influence of identities on humans' affairs.

The book benefits from the insights of Mr George Yeo, Former Minister for Foreign Affairs of Singapore, who provided a thoughtful and timely reflections on the nature of human beings' identities and their continued relevance for policy-making in **Chapter 1** of the book. As Mr Yeo pointed out, each of us has multiple identities which run deep. These identities have endured the cycles of history and in the age of globalisation, their role in shaping human societies will only become greater. Technological changes are causing fragmentation and undermining traditional institutions. At the same time, the digital revolution has also helped to connect people with similar identities or interests, forming neural networks around the globe. Such networks create new challenges for governance at both the national and international levels. The force of identity can be seen most clearly in the aftermath of the Soviet Union's collapse, when the new countries which were held by a deeper sense of identity remained stable while others like Yugoslavia broke up into small pieces. In the Middle East, it was the US' underestimation of the depth of the Sunni–Shiite divide which led to civil war and external interference in Iraq and Syria. More recently, the support for Brexit expressed popular frustration with European institutions which have become so complicated that they no longer enjoy the affection of ordinary people. Similarly in the US, loss of faiths in institutions contributed to the election of Trump.

Southeast Asia is the most culturally diverse region in the world. There are not only considerable differences between the 10 member states of ASEAN but at the sub-national level, these countries are also not homogeneous. As such, there can only be peace in the region if diversity is acknowledged and respected, with institutions built based on the acceptance of diversity. ASEAN countries should never impose their views upon one another but seek to influence each other positively. Based on these values, ASEAN has kept the peace between its members for the past 50 years. Furthermore, the association is slowly but steadily inculcating in Southeast Asians a sense of ASEAN citizenry. Nevertheless, going forward, a stable regional order also requires ASEAN to continue to engage all major powers and manage territorial disputes in the South China Sea. Singapore, as the most *ASEAN-ised* country of all the 10 members, has an important role to play in fostering ASEAN unity and ensuring that ASEAN remains a neutral platform friendly to all powers.

Chapter 2 presents our 2016 annual update on ACI's competitiveness ranking and simulations for the 10 ASEAN member states which was conducted through a comprehensive and rigorous methodological framework. Overall Competitiveness is defined along four environments: (i) Macroeconomic Stability, (ii) Government and Institutional Setting, (iii) Financial, Businesses and Manpower Conditions, and (iv) Quality of Life and Infrastructure Development. Amalgamating various data sources for 121 indicators over the period from 2000 to 2013, our competitiveness analysis indicates wide variations not only in levels of economic development but also paces of catching-up within the bloc.

In general, the Overall Competitiveness ranking of ASEAN-10 was relatively stable throughout the study period. Singapore and Malaysia remained the two best-performing economies in ASEAN, followed by Thailand at third and Brunei at fourth between 2000 and 2013. Indonesia has been surging firmly ahead of Vietnam and Philippines at fifth, particularly in the Economic Vibrancy sub-environment. Philippines and Vietnam were in a neck-to-neck competition for most of the study period, as were Cambodia and Laos since 2005. In 2013, Philippines was ranked sixth, one place higher than Vietnam for the third consecutive year while Cambodia was ranked eighth, barely edging Laos which was ranked ninth. Myanmar remained rooted to the bottom of the ranking throughout the 2000–2013 period. In fact, the gap in the standardised score between Myanmar and the closest-ranked economy has widened over the years. This underscores the magnitude of the challenges awaiting Myanmar's fledgling democratically elected government as it looks to unlock the country's potentials and usher in economic development.

The persistence of the development gap in ASEAN is evident in the fact that the composition of the top four has remained unchanged for 14 consecutive years. In addition, the pace of catching-up also varies among countries. For instance, Cambodia and Laos have been rising with marked improvements in many aspects of competitiveness while the catching-up momentum of Vietnam seems to have run out of steam since 2010. Among the top four, Thailand risks being overtaken by Brunei as it has experienced a mild decline in standardised score since 2007 while the latter's performance has been consistent.

Through economic integration, synergies between economies at different stages of development can be harnessed for increased overall regional competitiveness. Regional integration may also serve as a catalyst for bridging the development divide. Nevertheless, the fruits of integration can only be enjoyed by all members if individual economies pursue their domestic reforms in earnest to address their economic malaises while strengthening their capabilities. Our annual competitiveness analysis and simulation offers an instructive roadmap for such pursuits.

In fact, the post-simulation results for Cambodia, Laos, Myanmar and Vietnam (CLMV) are impressive, indicating that improved competitiveness is totally feasible with the right solutions. *Ceteris paribus*, if each economy improved on its top 20 percent weaknesses to catch up with the regional average, Laos would jump two places from ninth to seventh while Cambodia and Vietnam would climb one place from seventh to sixth and ninth to eighth, respectively, in terms of Overall Competitiveness. Moreover, while Myanmar's post-simulation ranking would still remain at 10th, the gap between its standardised score and that of other ASEAN members would narrow considerably.[1]

Chapter 3 explores the issue of potential growth slowdown in ASEAN. Over the past 50 years, robust economic growth across the ASEAN economies has lifted millions out of poverty and created a growing middle class. Nevertheless, challenges remain and further development is not guaranteed. Pundits have expressed concern about whether growth will be derailed in the future and ASEAN economies will be caught in the so-called "middle-income trap". Against this backdrop, our research contributes to the policy discourse by empirically identifying the determinants of growth slowdown at each level of development or income group. Moreover, based on our econometric models, we also compute the likelihood that ASEAN economies would experience growth slowdown over the period 2012–2017.

According to the classification criteria we adopt, there was only one ASEAN economy in the high-income group by 2014, namely Singapore. Malaysia and Thailand have attained upper-middle-income status while Cambodia, Indonesia, Myanmar and Vietnam were lower-middle-income economies.[2] However, there are signs of concern as Malaysia and Thailand have not been able to graduate to the high-income group despite becoming upper-middle-income economies since 1996 and 2003, respectively. Meanwhile, by 2014, Indonesia and Philippines had spent around 30 and 40 years in the lower-middle-income group, respectively. For ASEAN economies to continue to progress, mitigating the risk of growth slowdown is paramount.

Pooling observations from the ASEAN economies, Greater China economies as well as sub-national economies in India and Indonesia, we found that growth slowdown in various income groups tend to be associated with different sets of determinants. For instance, lower-middle-income economies are more likely to experience growth slowdown when they have higher level of Gross Domestic Product (GDP) per Capita, lower Foreign Direct Investment (FDI) Inflows as Percentage of GDP, higher Old Dependency Ratio, lower Employment in Tertiary Industry as Percentage of Total Employment and lower Literacy Rate. On the other hand, growth slowdown in the combined group of upper-middle-income and high-income economies is associated with high GDP per Capita, low Openness to Trade, low Literacy Rate, low Employment in Tertiary Industry as Percentage of Total Employment, and low Secondary Industry Value added per Worker.

Next, we assess whether each ASEAN economy is prone to experiencing growth slowdown over the period of 2012–2017. Overall, we discovered that the prospects for the ASEAN economies are relatively optimistic. On average, they only have a 21 percent chance of

[1] Myanmar's pre-simulation score was −1.6116. After the simulation, its score would have risen to −1.0834. See Chapter 2 for more details.

[2] The income classification criteria is based on the economy's GDP per capita in 1990 Purchasing Power Parity dollar. Data for Brunei are not available. Data for Laos are only available until 2008, when Laos was still a low-income economy. See Chapter 3 for more details.

experiencing growth slowdown between 2012 and 2017. This low regional average probability is even more impressive if set in comparison with the prospects of economies in Greater China and India. Among the ASEAN countries, Singapore as the sole high-income economy is the most likely to slow down. However, its probability of slowing down is still less than 50 percent.

Despite the hopeful prospects, the ASEAN economies cannot afford to become complacent. They are still plagued by significant domestic weaknesses which hinder the full realisation of their potentials. Moreover, the prevailing global socio-economic uncertainties have caused higher unpredictability for the domestic economy. Peer-learning is imperative in formulating policies to combat the risk of growth slowdown. The framework which we have developed allows the ASEAN economies to benchmark their performances in the relevant policy dimensions against each other as well as the other Asian developing economies. Thus, relative strengths and weaknesses of each economy can be identified, and necessary reforms can thus be implemented to sustain the positive growth momentums.

Chapter 4 seeks to provide some insights on the reform progress in the transitional economies of CLMV by highlighting their achievements as well as identifying prevailing challenges. While the ongoing debate on the roles of market and the state in the economy remain unreconciled, they share a common ground about the importance of development in leading to the betterment of the society. As a matter of fact, there is no universal approach to growth and development. Nonetheless, CLMV should not overlook the development experiences of other economies especially of the East Asian miracle which may provide insights to their own development trajectory. This will allow CLMV to leverage on their second-mover advantage to forge ahead.

Both the West and the High-Performing Asian Economies (HPAEs) have undertaken a similar development path as encapsulated in the flying geese paradigm. It involved an iterative process of industrialisation, where capital investment as well as industrial production evolved in a cascading fashion from a 'lead goose' to the followers. CLMV, harnessing on their demographic dividends, have offered attractive environment to host FDI as depicted in the rising FDI inflows in CLMV. However, the constant and dynamic discarding and relocating of such industries serve as a nudge for industrial upgrading and economic diversification in CLMV.

While being the new entrants to the flying geese model, CLMV have also adopted the East Asian development strategy of growing export-oriented industries which is boosted by the intensification of economic integration in CLMV. Aside from international trade, high capital accumulation marked another important element of East Asian model. A number of indicators examined in this chapter such as gross domestic savings and trade flows indicated that CLMV are following the trajectory taken by the HPAEs. After the restoration of peace and stability, CLMV have witnessed a positive progress in economic growth and social development following a series of market-oriented reforms. Overall, the reforms in CLMV are characterised by greater participation of private sectors and withdrawal of the states from the economy in a varying degree. Real GDP growth has spurred to a higher level as compared to pre-reforms period. Structural transition can also be observed in CLMV as depicted in the shrinking share of agriculture and growing significance of industry and the service sector in GDP. Furthermore, social dimensions also saw remarkable development. Health and education in the economies have improved with more people gaining access to basic health services and education.

Nevertheless, while positive progress has been made in both social and economic dimensions, some challenges remain and merit particular attention. Among these, infrastructure bottlenecks represent a pressing challenge to CLMV as they hamper investment and business activities. CLMV also lagged in good governance as reflected in the low transparency and weak fiscal capacity. Furthermore, shortage of skilled labour is another pain point which needs to be addressed. By taking into account these predicaments which have hindered the reforms progress, we also seek to shed light on policy formulations for future development, as shall be discussed in more detail in Section 6.2.2.

Finally, deepening integration will continue to be vital in closing the development gap. By linking up with their regional neighbours in ASEAN to form a single market and production base, CLMV will be able to exploit the advantages of economies of scale and demographic dividends and, at the same time, to mask the weaknesses of development gaps by complementing each other in an intra-regional economic network. Furthermore, competitive pressure resulting from economic integration will not only reveal the weakness within the economy but may also act as an enabling factor for CLMV to overcome their internal inertia and push forward necessary structural changes. Thus, against the backdrop of rising vulnerability and dampened reforms momentum, integration initiatives including the ASEAN Economic Community (AEC), the Regional Comprehensive Economic Partnership (RCEP), and the One Belt, One Road Initiative (OBOR) also called the Belt & Road initiative — may serve to invigorate economic reforms in CLMV.

Chapter 5 centres on the comprehensive discussion by Mr Heng Swee Keat, Minister for Finance of Singapore, on the challenges faced by Singapore as it transitions into the future economy. The insights derived from this Chapter are not only applicable to Singapore, but also relevant for other ASEAN economies in the next phase of their development. As pointed out by Mr Heng, while it is indeed important for policy-makers to confront the immediate challenges caused by rising global uncertainties, they must not overlook other upcoming trends in long-term planning. Among the key unfolding challenges are ageing population and rapid technological advancements, both of which will have profound social, political and economic implications on an economy as open as Singapore. Developing capacity to remain competitive and preparing for the unknown should therefore be the priorities for the city-state. This requires a two-pronged approach targeting at both micro and macro levels.

At the macro level, maintaining a well-functioning financial system as well as sustaining a stable fiscal position are key in creating a favourable environment for the economy to flourish. This has to be complemented with an efficient allocation of resources for businesses and people to strive at the micro level. Beyond that, building capabilities for firms and individuals which are relevant to the future economy is essential to address the challenges as well as to grab new opportunities that arise. That also means that the government efforts in fostering conducive micro and macroeconomic conditions have to go in tandem with the initiatives among the firms and individuals in cultivating strong capabilities. Finally, being one of the forerunners and the only developed economy in ASEAN, Singapore plays a paramount role in setting the pace for the region amid the shifting landscape of the global economy.

6.2 Policy Implications

6.2.1 Mitigating the Risk of Growth Slowdown

The empirical analysis on growth slowdown in Chapter 3 illustrates that there is no one-size-fits-all approach to growth and development. Economies in different income groups face different sets of challenges. Nonetheless, our analysis also highlights three major common themes. Firstly, developing human capital is paramount for growth. Literacy rate, which reflects basic human capital formation, is a significant determinant of growth slowdown across all income groups. Therefore, ensuring universal access to basic education is a critical first step, especially in Cambodia and Laos where literacy rates were still low as compared to other countries in Southeast Asia. At the same time, secondary and tertiary education, as well as vocational training, should also be extended in coverage and improved upon so as to equip the workforce with the necessary skills to participate in higher value-added industries.

Secondly, it is important to have a vibrant and balanced economic structure where both manufacturing and services are developed in tandem. Our econometric models show that the likelihood of growth slowdown among middle-income and high-income economies is negatively associated with the share of the workforce engaged in tertiary industries. Though ASEAN economies, particularly Vietnam and Indonesia, may now ride the wave of export-led manufacturing, aging population and disruptive technological changes will erode their comparative advantage in manufacturing in due course. Thus, to ensure that growth is sustainable, service industries must be developed as a key growth engine and a source of employment creation.

As noted in Tan and Luu (2017), the development of the service sector is not a natural progression achieved solely through market forces. Governments have an important role to play in facilitating an appropriate regulatory framework which fosters competitive and efficient service markets. Additionally, investment in infrastructure is essential for service industries to grow, specifically in the case of logistics, information and tourism. One area where government intervention can have a real impact is the Information Communication Technology (ICT) sector. ICT serves to make other services tradable and it also has large positive spillover effects on other sectors of the economy. Policy-makers can facilitate the development of the ICT sector through market liberalisation and upgrading the telecommunication and broadband networks.

Thirdly, productivity enhancement is necessary for continued economic growth. Our analysis in Chapter 3 demonstrates that improving labour productivity is a common challenge for the upper-middle-income and high-income economies in ASEAN including Malaysia, Thailand and Singapore. For the other ASEAN countries, raising productivity is also of utmost importance as competition based on low labour cost is a race to the bottom which is ultimately unsustainable. In this context, improving human capital through encouraging skill-deepening in the labour force is vital. As echoed in the speech by Mr Heng Swee Keat in Chapter 5, educational institutions also play a role in nurturing competent human capital. Programmes to foster innovation and to incentivise firms to adopt productivity-enhancing technologies should also be implemented. Moreover, policy-makers should seek to promote closer linkages between multinational corporations (MNCs) and local businesses, especially small and medium enterprises (SMEs), so as to ensure that FDI results in technological transfers to the domestic economy.

6.2.2 Narrowing the Development Divide

Coming to its 50th anniversary in 2017, ASEAN's success is deemed a miracle.[3] Starting as a cooperation among five founding members seeking for reconciliation in 1967, ASEAN has expanded to a bloc with 10 member states standing as the seventh largest economy in the world. Being the most culturally diverse region, ASEAN has to muddle through the challenges brought by a multicultural setting as well as the prevailing socio-economic gaps between CLMV and ASEAN-6 as highlighted in Chapters 2 and 4. While ASEAN has set a major milestone with the establishment of the AEC in 2015, concerted efforts are still needed in order to fully realise the key targets laid out in the AEC blueprint.

The road towards a prosperous, sustainable and globally integrated economic community will be challenging in the absence of inclusive growth and development. Thus, economic convergence between CLMV and ASEAN-6 has to be expedited so that the opportunities arising from an integrated regional grouping will be fully capitalised. In this context, CLMV have to revitalise their reforms momentum to address their various outstanding structural weaknesses.

In particular, they must step up investment in infrastructure, including land, air and sea transportation, power and water supplies as well as ICT services. To meet the funding need, it is crucial that policy-makers facilitate greater private involvement in infrastructure development, such as through the Public–Private Partnership model. Bridging the financing gap would also require the implementation of comprehensive fiscal reforms to improve the governments' fiscal capacity, particularly among Cambodia, Laos and Myanmar. In addition, good governance and capacity building should be promoted at every level of governance so as to reduce wastages from inefficiency and corruption.

Meanwhile, improving human capital is another key area, especially if CLMV want to ride the wave of FDI relocation from China to Southeast Asia. Synergies between education and training institutions and the industry must be fostered so as to reduce skill mismatches in the labour market. Moreover, the education systems in CLMV need to be revamped in parallel with the Fourth Industrial Revolution and a knowledge-based economy. More emphasis should also be placed on developing proficiency in English as a business language to enable the workforce to fully participate in the global economy.

Central to future reform agenda for CLMV, however, is the need to reassess the development model. Over the past 30 years, export-oriented manufacturing on the back of low labour cost has led to economic growth and broad-based employment creation in CLMV, enabling them to gear up the convergence with other ASEAN economies. Nevertheless, as discussed in Section 6.2.1, this model is not indefinitely sustainable. While CLMV may still benefit from such development

[3] See Mahbubani (2017) and Mahbubani and Sng (2017).

model for some time to come, their cost competitiveness will eventually diminish with shrinking demographic dividends and rapid technological innovations. In fact, the window for manufacturing-led growth for CLMV, and ASEAN in general, may be shorter than that for China.

Part and parcel of the future development strategy in CLMV is the need to stay nimble and not become overdependent on a particular sector or industry. Industrial upgrading through technological transfers between the FDI sector and the local sector must be promoted so that the economy may steadily move up the value chain. Furthermore, economic diversification should be a key priority. Even as CLMV strive to become the next manufacturing hubs, policies must be in place to develop the service sector. As the experience of the ASEAN-6 has shown (see Table 6.1), the service sector grows in significance as a source for employment creation and economic growth as the economy matures. On average, the services sector in ASEAN-6 in 2015 accounted for 60.8 percent of total employment and 53.8 percent of GDP.

At the same time, agriculture remains a vital economic sector in CLMV. On average, the agriculture sector accounted for 48.5 percent of total employment in 2015 as depicted in Table 6.1. However, the large share of employment is not proportionate to the contribution to GDP at only 25.3 percent on average. This gap signifies that there is still a lot of room for improvement in terms of agriculture productivity in CLMV. Modernising the agriculture sector is important as it opens up another avenue of growth through competitive agro-based industries. Moreover, as Section 6.2.3 will discuss in more detail, improving agricultural productivity is also vital, given the rapid urbanisation in these countries, and more broadly across Southeast Asia.

At the regional level, policy-makers across ASEAN should continue to pursue concerted efforts aimed at narrowing the development gap. Financial and technical support dedicated to CLMV in overcoming their capacity constraints, such as the Initiatives for ASEAN Integration (IAI), will help catalyse the reforms progress and convergence with the other ASEAN member economies.

Table 6.1: Sectoral Shares of Total Employment and GDP in ASEAN-10, 2015

	Share of Total Employment (Percent)			Share of GDP (Percent)		
Economy	**Agriculture**	**Industry**	**Services**	**Agriculture**	**Industry**	**Services**
Brunei	0.6	19.0	80.4	1.1	60.2	38.7
Cambodia	44.1	19.5	36.4	28.2	29.4	42.3
Indonesia	32.9	22.2	44.9	14.0	41.3	44.7
Laos	79.6	3.9	16.5	27.4	30.9	41.7
Malaysia	12.5	27.5	60.0	8.6	39.6	51.8
Myanmar	26.2	14.0	59.9	26.7	34.5	38.7
Philippines	29.2	16.2	54.7	10.3	30.8	58.9
Singapore	0.3	17.1	82.6	0.0	26.4	73.6
Thailand	35.3	22.4	42.3	9.1	35.7	55.1
Vietnam	44.0	22.3	33.7	18.9	37.0	44.2

Source: Asian Development Bank, International Labour Organisation and World Bank

Regional connectivity should also be enhanced. In this context, an immediate goal is the successful completion of the Master Plan on ASEAN Connectivity 2025.

6.2.3 Managing the Urban Transition

Shifts in the employment structure from agriculture to manufacturing and services will continue to quicken the speed of growth of cities in the region. Over the past half-century, urbanisation in Southeast Asia has steadily progressed, fuelled in part by rural–urban migration as people leave their farms for the factories clustering around major cities in search of better economic opportunities.[4] In 1950, a mere 15.5 percent of the total population across ASEAN-10 lived in cities. By 2014, this figure has risen to 47.1 percent, or 294 million people in absolute term. Furthermore, according to the United Nations' projections, more than half of ASEAN's denizens would reside in cities by the end of this decade.[5]

Table 6.2: Urban Population at Mid-Year and Urban Population as Percentage of Total Population in ASEAN-10, 2014

Economy	Urban Population at Mid-Year, 2014 (Million People)	Total Population at Mid-Year, 2014 (Million People)	Urban Population as Percentage of Total Population, 2014 (Percent)
Brunei	0.3	0.4	76.9
Cambodia	3.2	15.4	20.5
Indonesia	134.0	252.8	53.0
Laos	2.6	6.9	37.6
Malaysia	22.3	30.2	74.0
Myanmar	18.0	53.7	33.6
Philippines	44.5	100.1	44.5
Singapore	5.5	5.5	100.0
Thailand	33.1	67.2	49.2
Vietnam	30.5	92.5	33.0
ASEAN-10	294.0	624.8	47.1

Source: United Nations' World Urbanisation Prospects, the 2014 revision

Among the ASEAN members, ASEAN-6 are currently more urbanised than the CLMV countries, with Singapore, Brunei and Malaysia leading the region in terms of the percentage of urban dwellers in total population (see Table 6.2). Nevertheless, the gap is shrinking fast. As shown in

[4]This is of course not to say that rural–urban migration is the sole driver of urbanisation. Inter-city migration, cross-border migration, natural growth of the urban population and administrative reclassification all contribute to the growth of cities in Southeast Asia and more broadly the whole of Asia. See UN Habitat (2015: 29–34).

[5]All population estimates and projections are based on the United Nations' World Urbanisation Prospects, the 2014 revision. The data are accessible at https://esa.un.org/unpd/wup/CD-ROM/ (accessed on 14 March, 2017).

Figure 6.1: Urban Population as Percentage of Total Population in ASEAN-10, 1985, 2000, 2015, 2030 and 2050

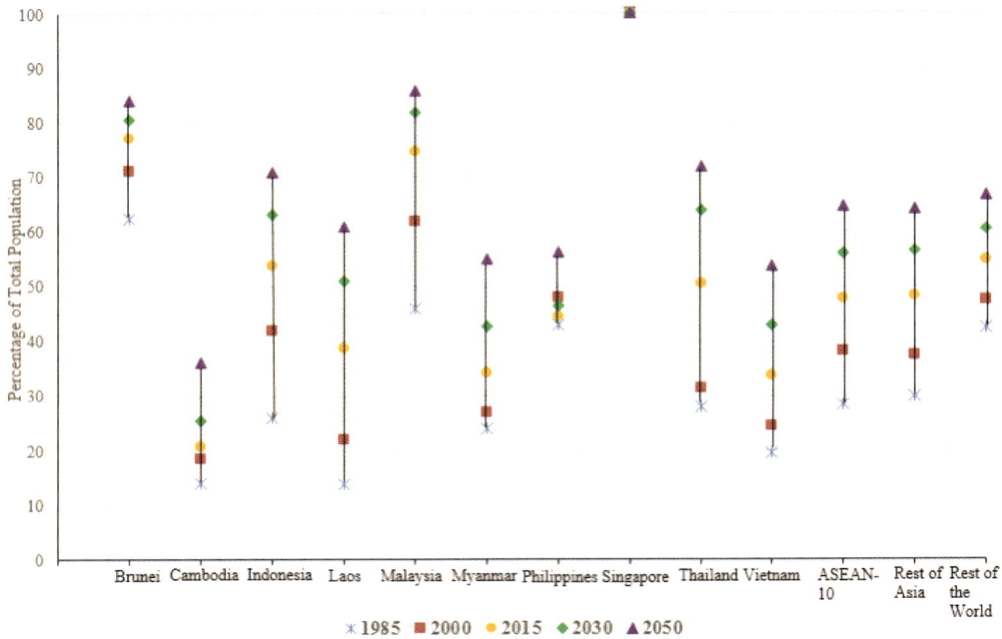

Note: Data in 2015, 2030 and 2050 are projections by the United Nations.
Source: Asia Competitiveness Institute based on data from the United Nations' World Urbanisation Prospects, the 2014 revision

Figure 6.1, the percentage of urban population has risen sharply for most countries over the past 15 years (2000–2015). This trend is expected to continue, especially for CLMV and Thailand. By 2050, the urban population across ASEAN-10 would swell by more than 200 million to reach 507 million people, or 64.5 percent of the total population.

Thus, raising urban living standards and quality of life must become a key priority for policy-makers in ASEAN. Central to achieving this goal is the need to improve the liveability of cities while keeping them affordable for the general populace. A liveable city is one which provides ordinary residents with good jobs, high-quality and accessible public services as well as a safe and clean living environment. Meanwhile, keeping city life affordable not only entails managing the cost of living, especially the costs of housing, transport, healthcare and education. It is also about ensuring robust and broad-based growth in ordinary residents' wages such that their purchasing power may rise over time. Failure to achieve these objectives may have dire consequences. Public dissatisfaction with the living conditions, fear for personal safety and anxieties about future economic prospects may help fuel anti-establishment populism or emigration, especially that of the skilled workforce, which would result in braindrain.

According to our researches, major cities in ASEAN have relatively low cost of living for ordinary residents as compared to cities in other parts of the world. Nevertheless, aside from Singapore, ordinary residents' purchasing power and the liveability of these cities are also low. Figures 6.2 to 6.6 illustrate these observations.

Figure 6.2 plots ACI's Cost of Living Index for Ordinary Residents against the Overall Liveability Score for 47 cities covered by both our Cost of Living, Wages and Purchasing Power research and the Global Liveable City Index (GLCI) study. The higher the Cost of

Figure 6.2: Scatterplot of Cost of Living Index for Ordinary Residents against Score for Overall Liveability

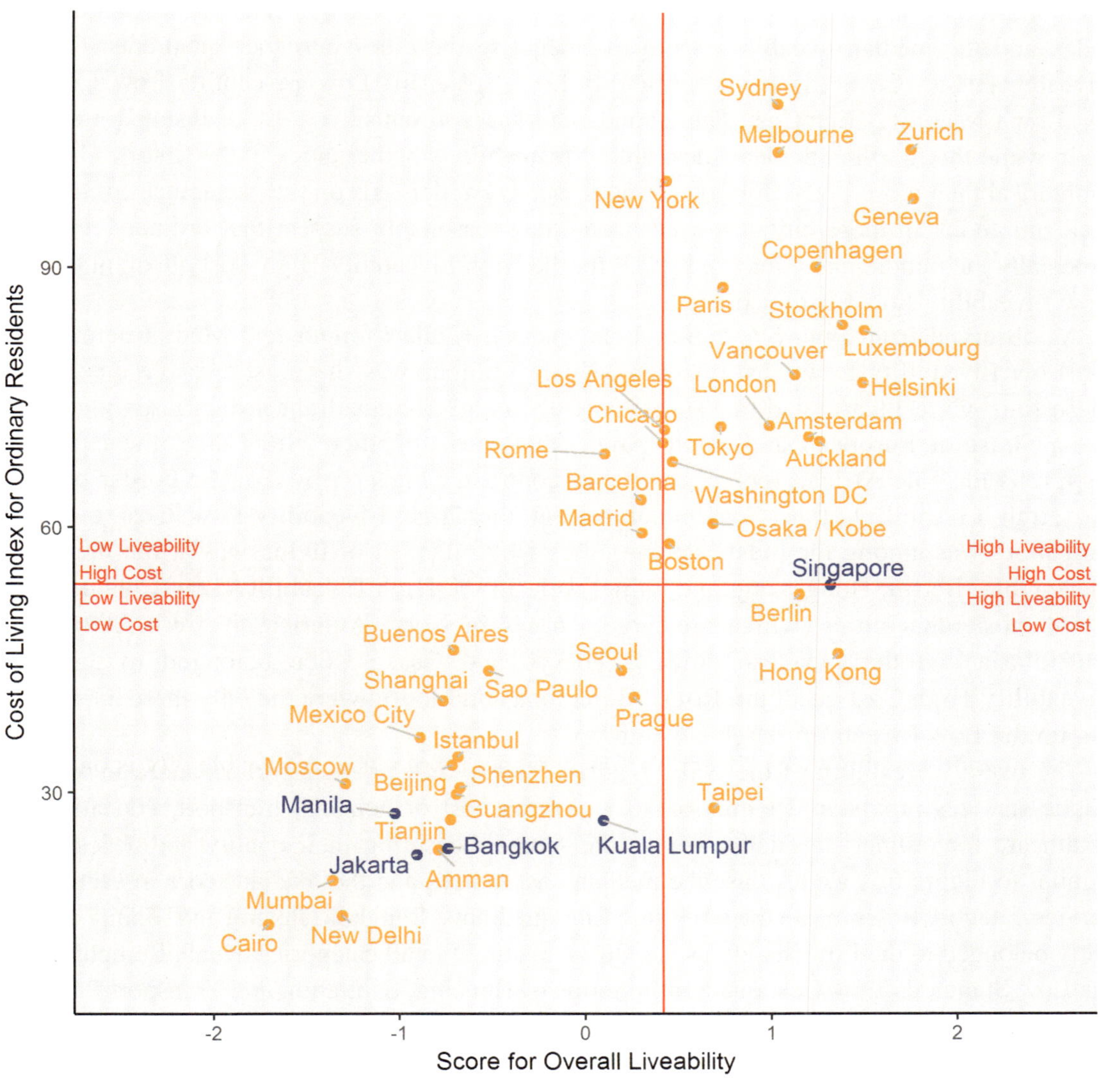

Notes: Based on 2013 data. The vertical and horizontal red lines represent respectively the median Score for Overall Liveability and the median Cost of Living Index for Ordinary Residents of the 47 cities in the analysis.
Source: Tan *et al.* (2017, forthcoming)

Living Index, the more expensive the city is for ordinary residents. Similarly, the higher the Overall Liveability Score, the more liveable the city is. Cost of living is measured based on a basket of goods and services consisting of 10 consumption categories whereas liveability is defined according to five environments: (1) Economic Vibrancy and Competitiveness, (2) Environmental Friendliness and Sustainability, (3) Domestic Security and Stability, (4) Socio-Cultural Conditions, and (5) Political Governance. More details can be found in Tan *et al*. (2017, *forthcoming*) and Tan, Nie, and Baek (2017, *forthcoming*). Figures 6.2–6.6 reflect indices computed based on 2013 data.

Among the 47 cities plotted are the capitals of ASEAN-5, namely Bangkok, Jakarta, Kuala Lumpur, Manila and Singapore. In Figure 6.2, we also use the median value of the cost of living index and the median liveability score to categorise the cities into four quadrants: (i) High Liveability-High Cost, (ii) High Liveability-Low Cost, (iii) Low Liveability-Low Cost and (iv) Low Liveability-High Cost. The second quadrant represents the most ideal state for a city to be in while the fourth is the least desirable. Meanwhile, whether cities in the first quadrant are more ideal than those in the third quadrant or *vice versa* depends on the preferences of ordinary residents living in those cities. However, one may reasonably suspect that ordinary residents, especially the middle-class, may in fact prefer the High Liveability-High Cost quadrant over the Low Liveability-Low Cost quadrant.

As observed from Figure 6.2, Bangkok, Jakarta, Kuala Lumpur and Manila belonged to the Low Liveability-Low Cost quadrant. Kuala Lumpur was the most liveable city among these four while Jakarta had the lowest cost of living. The quadrant in fact largely contains Asian, Eastern European and South American cities, together with Cairo, the capital of Egypt, as the sole African representative. In contrast, Singapore was at the border between the High Liveability-High Cost quadrant and the High Liveability-Low Cost quadrant. Singapore was among the most liveable cities while its cost of living was at the median of the sample. Berlin, Hong Kong and Taipei were in the High Liveability-Low Cost quadrant while most other cities, which are largely cities in North America, Western Europe and Australasia and the Japanese cities of Tokyo and Osaka–Kobe belonged to the High Liveability-High Cost quadrant. Rome, Barcelona and Madrid were the only three cities making up the Low Liveability-High Cost group.

The overall liveability of the ASEAN cities largely reflects their performances in terms of public services provision. Figures 6.3–6.5 plot the cost of housing, transport, education and healthcare for ordinary residents against the scores measuring their quality and accessibility. Similar to Figure 6.2, we also use the median cost indices and the median score in each public service category to segregate the cities into four quadrants. Bangkok, Jakarta and Manila consistently belonged to the Low Standards-Low Cost quadrant in all categories. Kuala Lumpur was in the Low Standards-Low Cost quadrant in terms of Housing, Sanitation and Transport Provision and Healthcare Provision (see Figures 6.3 and 6.5) although as shown in Figure 6.4, it was in the High Standards-Low Cost quadrant in terms of Education Provision. Meanwhile, Singapore showcased its strength in providing high quality education at comparatively low cost for ordinary residents (see Figure 6.4). Its standards of Housing, Sanitation and Transport Provision were also

Figure 6.3: Scatterplot of Housing Rents, Utilities and Transport Cost Index for Ordinary Residents against Score for Public Service Standards in terms of Housing, Sanitation and Transport Provision

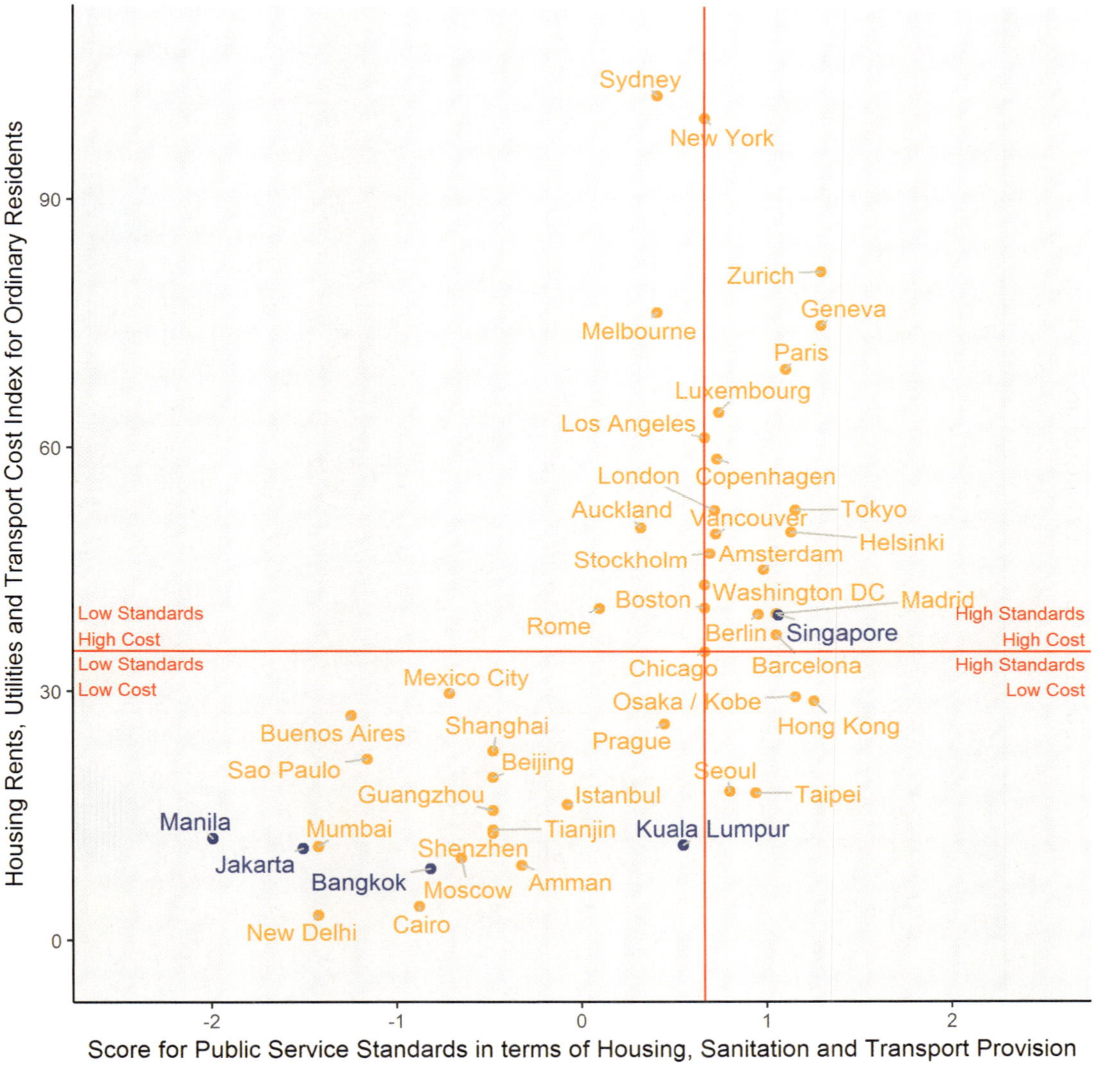

Note: Based on 2013 data. The vertical and horizontal red lines represent respectively the median Score for Public Service Standards in terms of Housing, Sanitation and Transport Provision and the median Housing Rents, Utilities and Transport Cost Index for Ordinary Residents of the 47 cities in the analysis.
Source: Tan *et al*. (2017, forthcoming)

high while the cost for ordinary residents in these respects was only slightly higher than the median cost (see Figure 6.3). Nevertheless, there is also room for improvement for the city-state. As Figure 6.5 demonstrates, Singapore was near the border of the Low Standards-Low Cost quadrant and the Low Standards-High Cost quadrant. This underlines the need for Singapore to

Figure 6.4: Scatterplot of Education Cost Index for Ordinary Residents against Score for Public Service Standards in terms of Education Provision

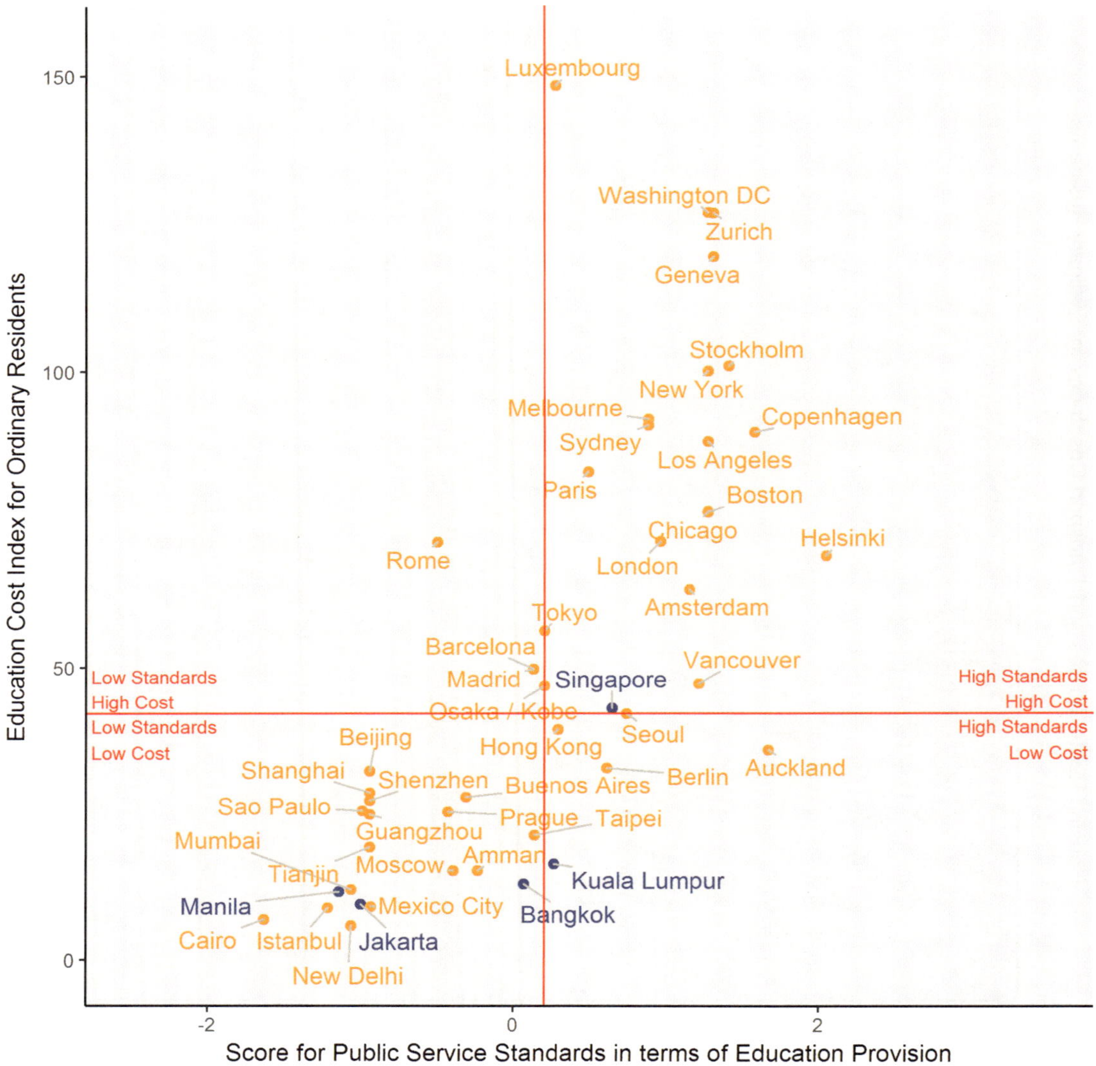

Note: Based on 2013 data. The vertical and horizontal red lines represent respectively the median Score for Public Service Standards in terms of Education Provision and the median Education Cost Index for Ordinary Residents of the 47 cities in the analysis.
Source: Tan *et al*. (2017, forthcoming)

improve the accessibility to healthcare as well as managing healthcare cost inflation, especially given its ageing population.

Next, Figure 6.6 provides an assessment of the purchasing power of ordinary residents relative to liveability in the ASEAN cities *vis-à-vis* their global counterparts. The vertical axis tracks the Purchasing Power Index for Ordinary Residents: the higher the index value, the higher the

Figure 6.5: Scatterplot of Health Cost Index for Ordinary Residents against Score for Public Service Standards in terms of Healthcare Provision

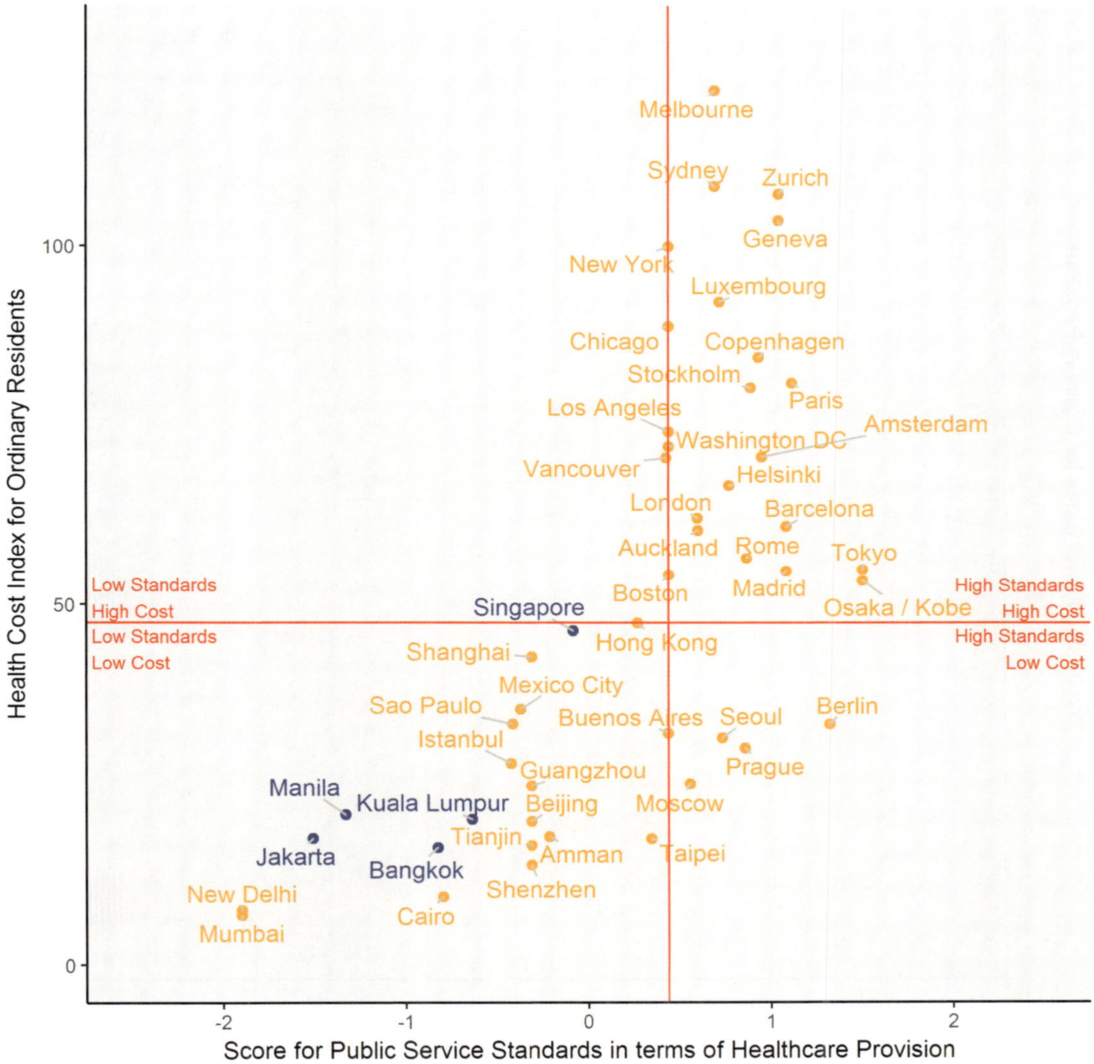

Note: Based on 2013 data. The vertical and horizontal red lines represent respectively the median Score for Public Service Standards in terms of Healthcare Provision and the median Health Cost Index for Ordinary Residents of the 47 cities in the analysis.
Source: Tan *et al.* (2017, forthcoming)

purchasing power of ordinary residents. This index is constructed by dividing a wage index reflecting the average wage of ordinary residents to the cost of living index used in Figure 6.2.[6] The horizontal axis tracks the Score for Overall Liveability. Median index values and scores were again used to distinguish the figure into four quadrants: (i) High Liveability-High

[6] See Tan *et al.* (2017, *forthcoming*) for more details.

Figure 6.6: Scatterplot of Purchasing Power Index for Ordinary Residents and Score for Overall Liveability

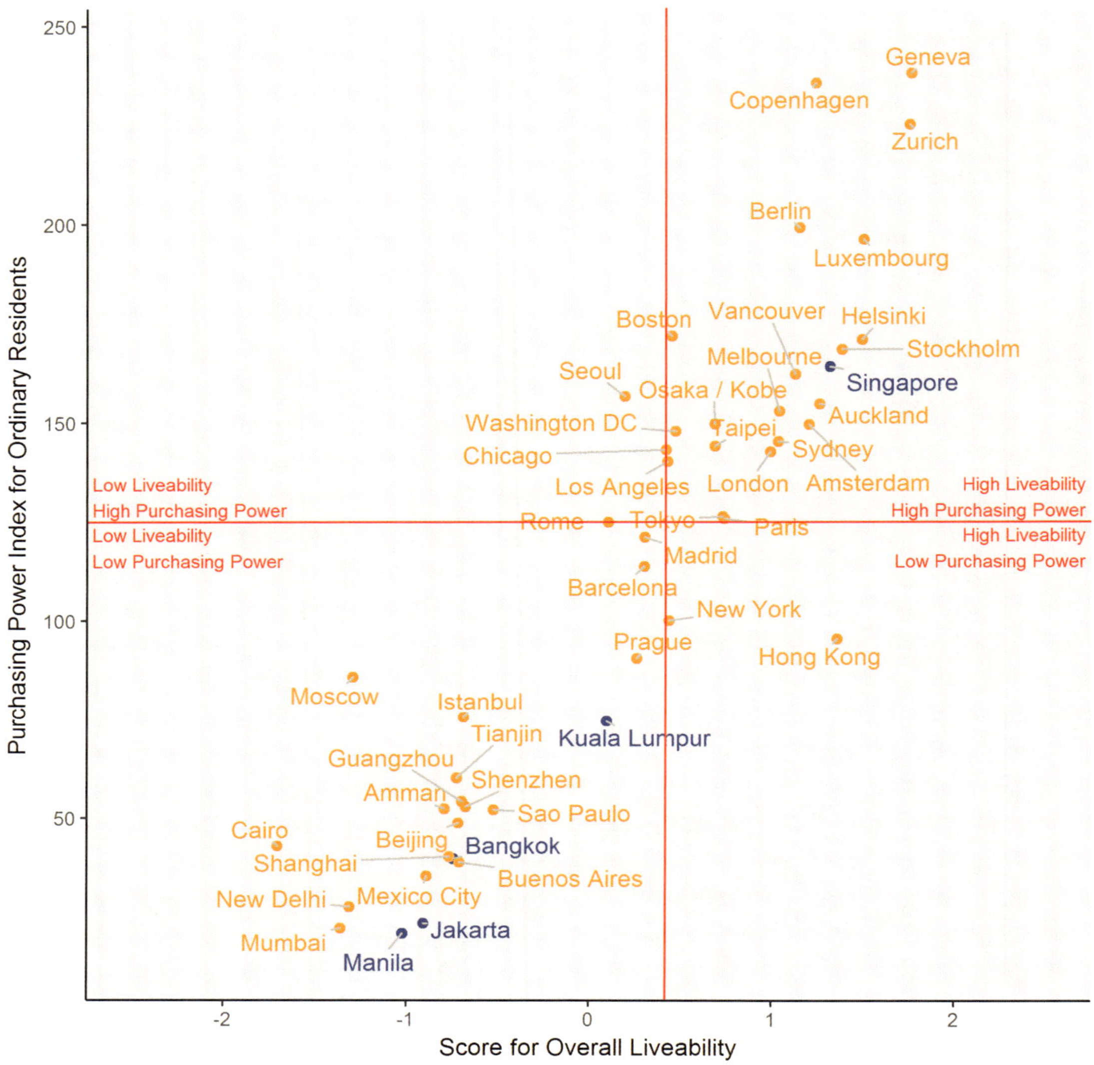

Note: Based on 2013 data. The vertical and horizontal red lines represent respectively the median Score for Overall Liveability and the median Purchasing Power Index for Ordinary Residents of the 47 cities in the analysis.
Source: Tan *et al*. (2017, forthcoming)

Purchasing Power, (ii) High Liveability-Low Purchasing Power, (iii) Low Liveability-Low Purchasing Power and (iv) Low Liveability-High Purchasing Power. In this case, the first quadrant is the most ideal state for a city to be in while the third is the least desirable.

As evident in Figure 6.6, Bangkok, Kuala Lumpur, Jakarta, and Manila were in the Low Liveability-Low Purchasing Power quadrant. Ordinary residents in Kuala Lumpur have the highest purchasing power among the four. Meanwhile, Singapore was in the most ideal High

Liveability-High Purchasing Power quadrant. Cities in this quadrant were mostly in Australasia, North America and Western Europe, with Tokyo, Osaka–Kobe, Taipei and Singapore, the only Asian, and in fact non-Western, representatives. Asian, African, Eastern European and South American cities largely belonged to the Low Liveability-Low Purchasing Power quadrant. Hong Kong provides an interesting divergent case as it belonged to the High Liveability-Low Purchasing Power quadrant.

The discussion above clearly highlights some major weaknesses of cities in Malaysia, Philippines, Jakarta and Bangkok. It also underscores the need for deeper thinking on urban development in these countries. Low liveability which manifests in air pollution, traffic congestion, lack of green cover and underprovision of public services is partly the result of conscious policy choices in the past to prioritise economic growth at the expense of the living environment. These symptoms may also be indicative of the lack of foresight in urban planning. As the economy develops and the people become better off, there will be increasingly louder clamour for a shift in policy priorities with more emphasis on liveability. Therefore, urban development strategies need to be recalibrated. At the same time, policy-makers must strive to ensure that the fruits of economic growth translate into robust wage growth for ordinary residents. Otherwise, they will end up in a situation similar to Hong Kong, where despite the relatively low cost, purchasing power for ordinary residents are low because of low and stagnant wages. These policy implications are also relevant to the CLMV countries as they seek to close the development gap with their more developed counterparts in ASEAN.

ASEAN policy-makers should make full use of their second-mover advantage where they can draw policy lessons in planning, administration and management of cities from more developed cities. In fact, cross-country learning does not have to be *vis-à-vis* the Western countries. As our research has shown, there are also successful Asian examples where ordinary residents are able to enjoy high liveability, low cost of living and high purchasing power such as Singapore and Taipei.

At the same time, sustainable urban development is not only about the cities, but it also requires the development of the rural areas. This is in fact one of the key concepts underpinning the United Nations' New Urban Agenda which was adopted at the Habitat III conference in Quito, Ecuador in 2016.[7] In particular, ensuring food security through improving agricultural productivity and forging urban–rural linkages are important policy priorities for the ASEAN countries.

As discussed in great detail in Chapter 3 of our previous book on *2015 Annual Competitiveness Analysis, Agricultural Productivity and Development Vision for ASEAN-10*, decades of industrialisation and urbanisation efforts present both opportunities and challenges to the agricultural sector in Southeast Asia. On the one hand, urbanisation benefits farmers with both new markets and higher prices. On the other hand, reallocation of land and labour out of agriculture intensifies the risk of food shortages, the brunt of which would fall on city dwellers. The global food crisis between 2007 and 2008 has highlighted the region's continued vulnerability to agricultural shocks

[7] See FAO (2016).

as ASEAN member states, comprising both net food importers and net food exporters, resorted to concurrent, uncoordinated export bans and extreme import orders, exacerbating the situation.[8]

In this context, enhancing agricultural productivity in ASEAN is paramount. Fostering agricultural productivity growth is of central importance to achieving food security and also for competitiveness and inclusive economic growth. As a region endowed with vast fertile land, diverse topography and abundant labour, ASEAN has the potential to become the food basket of Asia, besides being a highly integrated and competitive manufacturing and service hub. Malaysia may serve as an informative case study for its peers in ASEAN. As one of the most urbanised countries in ASEAN, Malaysia also tops the region in Total Factor Productivity growth in agriculture.[9] Lessons can be gleaned from the Malaysian development experience, especially in terms of developing a competitive agribusiness industry, promoting close partnership between government agencies, agribusiness firms and research institutes, integrating smallholders into agro-based value chains and providing infrastructure, credit and extension services.

Finally, strengthening urban–rural linkages through improved connectivity is crucial in easing the migration pressure on cities and preventing the emergence of deep urban–rural divide in ASEAN countries. Better public transport, enhanced ICT networks and greater availability of money transfer services to facilitate remittances will enable rural dwellers to participate in the urban economy and derive extra income from off-farm works. Last but not least, expanding education in the rural areas plays a major role in alleviating rural poverty and helps promote convergence between the countryside and the cities.

6.2.4 Navigating Geopolitical Challenges

Further development can only be realised in a stable external environment. As such, for continued peace and prosperity, it is vital that ASEAN countries adroitly manage geopolitical challenges arising from great powers' competition in Southeast Asia. The most important geopolitical relationship for Southeast Asia is that between the world's pre-eminent power, the US and the world's foremost emerging power, China. That China is rising is an indisputable fact. The country has become the second biggest economy in the world and it is now one of the largest trading partners of many countries, including the US. Buoyed by its growing economic strength, China

[8] Falling global stocks of rice and other grains, adverse weather and soaring oil prices in 2007 and 2008 led to a surge in prices of rice and other foodstuffs in many parts of the world including ASEAN. The initial policy responses to the global food crisis in ASEAN varied according to whether the country in question was a net exporter or a net importer of food. While the former, notably Thailand and Vietnam, raised export taxes and placed restrictions on exports, the latter such as Malaysia, Indonesia and Philippines reduced import restrictions and tariffs while trying to secure food supplies in the international market. In 2008, Vietnam, Cambodia and Laos banned export of rice although Cambodia subsequently abolished the policy to take advantage of high international food prices. Malaysia and Philippines, in contrast, resorted to "panic" buying from Thailand and Vietnam, respectively, at the peak of the crisis. See Asian Development Bank (2008) for analysis on the underlying causes of the 2007–2008 global food crisis and Chandra and Lontoh (2010) for details on policy responses in ASEAN countries.

[9] See Tan *et al.* (2017, Chapter 3) for more details.

has also undertaken a sweeping modernisation of its armed forces, with one of the priorities being the development of a first-class navy.[10]

Unlike the relationship between the US and the Soviet Union during the Cold War, current US–China relations are complex and highly interdependent.[11] The two countries are closely linked with one another as well as with the rest of the world through trade, investment and production networks. The scope of their relationship has also widened to include cooperation on global issues such as counter-terrorism, climate change and nuclear proliferation. However, while Beijing and Washington have sought to manage their ties — in President Xi Jinping's word, to build a "new type of great power relations"[12] — competition and rivalry remain an intrinsic character of the relationship.

In Southeast Asia, US–China competition may manifest itself in the benign form of charm offensives, whereby each power seeks to cultivate economic and diplomatic ties with countries in the region. Nonetheless, their competition may also be fractious. The prime example for this is the ongoing geopolitical tussles in the South China Sea where China holds conflicting territorial claims with some ASEAN members. The situation has heated up in recent years with China and other claimants undertaking unilateral actions to assert sovereignty and the US conducting Freedom of Navigation Operations to assert its navigation and overflight rights.

Traditionally, ASEAN countries have resisted the pressures to choose sides in their relationships with the great powers. Instead, they have pursued a mix of hedging strategies aimed at preserving autonomy and a fallback position should external circumstances change.[13] This is indeed the course of action that all ASEAN countries should continue to take. There are several reasons for why it is the case.

Firstly, a strategy of choosing sides entails the risk of becoming subservient. When small and medium-sized states gravitate towards the great powers, there will be pressure to align themselves even further to their benefactors, sometimes even at the expense of their national interests.[14] Secondly, choosing sides does not necessarily guarantee security or prosperity. The Sino-Soviet split and the US–China rapprochement in the late 1960s-early 1970s demonstrate all too well the unpredictability of great power relations. The complexity of US–China relations today only add to this ambiguity, which makes prematurely alienating either power by choosing the other strategically unwise. Finally, ASEAN risks "devolving into a house divided against itself"[15] if member states begin to choose sides between the US and China. ASEAN has already had a taste of this type of challenge in 2012 when, for the first time in the history of the bloc, ASEAN's foreign ministers failed to produce a joint communiqué at the ASEAN Summit due to Cambodia's opposition to the inclusion of references to the South China Sea issue, ostensibly out of deference to China's interests.

---

[10] See *The Straits Times* (2017).

[11] See Kausikan (2016) and Liow (2017).

[12] See Li and Xu (2014).

[13] See Kuik (2016).

[14] See Liow (2017).

[15] See Mahbubani (2015: 140).

Furthermore, there are great uncertainties in the current strategic landscape. President Trump's rhetoric on "America first" both during the election campaign and after his inauguration, culminating in the decision to withdraw the US from the Trans-Pacific Partnership, has casted doubts on the depth of future US engagement in Asia. Yet, at the same time, President Trump has articulated a rather hawkish position on China. Given uncertainties about the trajectory of US–China relations and their relative roles in Asia under the Trump administration, it becomes even more pertinent for the countries in Southeast Asia to act in such a way which preserves the most room for manoeuvre. For some countries, this may entail recalibrating their foreign policy postures towards the two powers. Malaysia and in particular the Philippines have made such adjustments by seeking warmer ties with China. [16]

Equally important is the need to maintain unity within ASEAN. ASEAN remains an indispensable organisation to ensure cohesion and peaceful relations in a region divided by a wide array of cultures, languages, religions and political systems. In addition, ASEAN provides a mechanism to mitigate external pressures on the member countries, thereby contributing to the preservation of their autonomy. ASEAN countries must thus coalesce and deepen regional integration under the three pillars of the ASEAN Community vision, namely political and security cooperation, economic integration and social–cultural exchanges.

In addition, the members of ASEAN must speak with one voice in articulating ASEAN's common interests in global forums and initiatives, especially APEC and the China-led OBOR, and in shaping the governance structure and operational guidelines for new global institutions such as the Asia Infrastructure Investment Bank where all 10 ASEAN economies are members. On the South China Sea, ASEAN should push for the conclusion of the Code of Conduct (COC) with China while emphasising peaceful resolution of the dispute. There has been progress on this front as China and ASEAN have finally agreed on a first draft of the COC.[17]

Lastly, ASEAN should continue to engage both the US and China in ASEAN-led multilateral forums such as the ASEAN Regional Forum, the East Asia Summit and the ASEAN Defence Minister's Meeting Plus. While multilateralism has its limitations as the most important interactions between the US and China will always be bilateral,[18] it provides ASEAN countries with the best chance to influence the great powers' competition which plays out in Southeast Asia and more broadly the Asia-Pacific. In the same vein, ASEAN should further engage and deepen ties with other powers which have a prominent role in maintaining a stable regional order, particularly Japan, India, Australia and Russia.

6.3 Future Research Agenda

Building on ACI's strengths in evidence-based quantitative policy analysis, our research agenda for future publications on ASEAN may include at least the following policy areas: (i) an empirical analysis of the nexus between exchange rate movements and FDI inflows, and (ii) analysing the relative importance of domestic and external engines of growth for ASEAN countries.

[16] See Heydarian (2016).

[17] See Channel News Asia (2017).

[18] See Kausikan (2016).

6.3.1 Nexus between Exchange Rate Movements and FDI Inflows to ASEAN Economies

The literature has long recognised the importance of FDI inflows in accelerating economic growth in developing countries through supplementing domestic capital, transfer of skills and technology as well as upgrading human capital.[19] In addition, a growing strand of economic literature notes that FDI inflows also enable countries to participate in global and regional value chains and enhance their exports.[20] ASEAN members are significant recipients of global FDI. In fact, sustained inflows of FDI continue to be emphasised as a key driver of growth in ASEAN as the regional bloc took economic integration to a new height with the formal establishment of the AEC on 31 December 2015. As stipulated in the AEC blueprint, "a free and open investment regime is key to enhancing ASEAN's competitiveness in attracting FDI," which in turn will "promote and ensure dynamic development of ASEAN economies."[21]

Past research suggests that a host of 'pull' factors ranging from skill endowments to robust institutions and locational advantages (to name just a few) help determine the extent of FDI flows into a country. Other determinants may include exchange rate movements and its volatility. In theory, exchange rate movements may have wealth effects, demand effects and cost-competitiveness effects on FDI inflows. Nevertheless, the directions of the effects depend on whether FDI is export-oriented or domestic market-oriented in nature. Furthermore, factors such as market expectations of exchange rate movements may also confound the analysis.

ACI's future research will seek to empirically establish the relationship between exchange rate movements and its volatility on FDI flows into ASEAN countries. Such study will be of great interest to policy-makers, especially given the current context. The gradual normalisation of monetary policy in the US has begun and it has generated fears of a repeat of the 'taper tantrum' which battered emerging markets in 2013. While ultra-loose monetary policies in the form of quantitative easing resulted in currency appreciations due to massive capital inflows, the tapering of the same through interest rate hikes might reverse the flow of capital, resulting in currency depreciations. The ebbs and flows of international capital will undoubtedly create a variety of challenges concerning monetary and exchange rate management in ASEAN, with significant bearing on trade and foreign investments into these countries.

6.3.2 Econometric Analysis on Domestic and External Engines of Growth for ASEAN Economies

The world economy appears to enter into turbulent times once again. Nearly eight years have passed since the Global Financial Crisis, but global economic growth is yet to be back on track. Furthermore, there have been worries over the process of 'deglobalisation' of trade and financial flows, which is further fuelled by events such as Brexit and the election of Donald Trump on a platform of protectionism in 2016. Socio-economic uncertainties in the West threaten to jeopardise

[19] See, for example, Borensztein, De Gregorio, and Lee (1998), Herzer (2012) and Iamsiraroj (2016).

[20] See Gangnes and Assche (2010).

[21] See ASEAN Secretariat (2008: 12).

a pickup in global economic growth, with potentially adverse consequences for Asian economies. The causes for concern are only compounded by the ongoing slowdown in China, the second largest economy in the world and a major driver of growth after the Global Financial Crisis.

Extending our research in 2014 which investigated the external engines of growth for ASEAN countries,[22] we will empirically examine both domestic and foreign growth engines through Error Correction Models (ECM). The ECM framework helps in separating the key drivers of long-run common trends from dependent trends. The main focus will be on structural shifts over the past 35 years: how different domestic and external engines might have changed in relative importance as drivers of economic growth in ASEAN countries. Aside from GDP growth, employment creation may also be examined.

The research will offer insights into important policy issues, contributing to budget discussion and the formulation of long-term growth strategies in ASEAN. For instance, the analysis will enable us to assess the domestic stimulus required to sustain growth if global growth continues to be weak. We may also shed light on the policy measures among ASEAN countries which can help maintain a more balanced external engine dependence, as well as policies which may increase intra-ASEAN linkages and resilience.

References

ASEAN Secretariat. 2008. *ASEAN Economic Community Blueprint*. Jakarta: ASEAN Secretariat.

Asian Development Bank. 2008. *Food Prices and Inflation in Developing Asia: Is Poverty Reduction Coming to an End?* Manila: Asian Development Bank.

Borensztein, E., De Gregorio Jose, and Lee Jong-wha. 1998. "How Does Foreign Direct Investment Affect Economic Growth?" *Journal of International Economics* 45(1): 115–35.

Chandra, Alexander C, and Lucky A. Lontoh. 2010. *Regional Food Security and Trade Policy in Southeast Asia*. Winnipeg: International Institute for Sustainable Development.

Channel News Asia. 2017. "China says first draft of South China Sea code of conduct framework ready", 8 March, available at http://www.channelnewsasia.com/news/asiapacific/china-says-first-draft-of-south-china-sea-code-of-conduct/3577984.html (accessed on 21 March, 2017).

FAO. 2015. "UN HABITAT III to address urban — rural linkages that prevent and reduce food waste and food loss". Food and Agriculture Organisation of the United Nations (FAO), 2 July, available at http://www.fao.org/save-food/news-and-multimedia/news/news-details/en/c/297114/ (accessed on 25 March, 2017).

Gangnes, Byron, and Ari Van Assche. 2010. "Global Production Networks in Electronics and Intra-Asian Trade." LICOS Discussion Paper No. 257, LICOS Centre for Institutions and Economic Performance, Leuven.

Herzer, Dierk. 2012. "How Does Foreign Direct Investment Really Affect Developing Countries' Growth?" *Review of International Economics* 20(2): 396–414.

Heydarian, Richard Javad. 2016. "Are US allies in Southeast Asia defecting to China?" *Al Jazeera*, 8 November, available at http://www.aljazeera.com/indepth/opinion/2016/11/malaysia-philippines-relations-china-161107101018957.html (accessed on 21 March, 2017).

[22] See Tan, Abeysinghe, and Tan (2014).

Iamsiraroj, Sasi. 2016. "The Foreign Direct Investment-Economic Growth Nexus." *International Review of Economics and Finance* 42: 116–33.

Kausikan, Bilahari. 2016. *Dealing with an Ambiguous World Lecture III: ASEAN & US–China Competition in Southeast Asia*. IPS-Nathan Lectures on 30 March 2016 at Auditorium 1, Town Plaza, Singapore.

Kuik, Cheng-Chwee. 2016. "How Do Weaker States Hedge? Unpacking ASEAN states' alignment behavior towards China". *Journal of Contemporary China* 25(100): 500–514.

Li, Cheng, and Lucy Xu. 2014. "Chinese Enthusiasm and American Cynicism over the 'New Type of Great Power Relations'". China–US Focus, 4 December, available at http://www.chinausfocus.com/foreign-policy/chinese-enthusiasm-and-american-cynicism-over-the-new-type-of-great-power-relations/ (accessed on 21 March, 2017).

Liow, Joseph Chinyong. 2017. "S-E Asia doesn't have to take sides". *The Straits Times*, 4 February, available at http://www.straitstimes.com/opinion/s-e-asia-doesnt-have-to-take-sides (accessed on 12 March, 2017).

Mahbubani, Kishore. 2015. "ASEAN as a Living, Breathing Modern Miracle". *CIRSD Horizons* (2): 136–148.

Mahbubani, Kishore. 2017. "How fear, luck and golf brought ASEAN together". *The Straits Times*, 18 March, available at http://www.straitstimes.com/opinion/how-fear-luck-and-golf-brought-asean-together (accessed on 21 March, 2017).

Mahbubani, Kishore and Jeffery Sng. 2017. *The ASEAN Miracle: A Catalyst for Peace*. Singapore: NUS Press.

Tan, Khee Giap, Nguyen Le Phuong Anh, Sasidaran Gopalan, and Luu Nguyen Trieu Duong. 2017. *2015 Annual Competitiveness Analysis, Agricultural Productivity and Development Vision for ASEAN-10*. Singapore: World Scientific.

Tan, Khee Giap, Tongxin Nie, and Shinae Baek. 2017 (*forthcoming*). *2015 Greater China Liveable Cities Index: Ranking Analysis, Simulation and Policy Evaluation*. Singapore: World Scientific.

Tan, Khee Giap, Nguyen Trieu Duong Luu, Diviya Chandran, and Kong Yam Tan. 2017 (forthcoming). *2016 Annual Indices for Expatriates and Ordinary Residents on Cost of Living, Wages and Purchasing Power for World's Major Cities*. Singapore: World Scientific.

Tan, Khee Giap, and Nguyen Trieu Duong Luu. 2017. "APEC 2017: Springboard for economic initiatives from Vietnam". *Jakarta Post*, 31 January, available at http://www.thejakartapost.com/news/2017/01/31/apec-2017-springboard-economic-initiatives-vietnam.html (accessed on 12 March, 2017).

Tan, Kong Yam, Tilak Abeysinghe, and Khee Giap Tan. 2014. "Shifting Drivers of Growth: Policy Implications for ASEAN-5". *Asian Economic Papers* 14(1): 157–173.

The Straits Times. 2017. "China to step up patrols to create first class navy". 10 March, available at http://www.straitstimes.com/asia/east-asia/china-to-step-up-patrols-to-create-first-class-navy (accessed on 12 March, 2017).

UN Habitat. 2015. *The State of Asian and Pacific Cities 2015: Urban Transformations, Shifting from Quantity to Quality*. Nairobi: United Nations Human Settlements Programme (UN Habitat).

Appendices

Appendix 1

Distinguished Speaker's Speech at the Asia Competitiveness Institute (ACI)–World Bank ASEAN Economic Forum, 9 September 2016

The ASEAN Community and ASEAN Competitiveness

Tan Sri Rastam Mohd Isa

Chairman and Chief Executive, Institute of Strategic and International Studies (ISIS), Malaysia

Introduction

I wish to thank ACI, in particular Associate Professor Tan Khee Giap for inviting me to this Forum. I am very pleased that the Institute of Strategic and International Studies (ISIS) Malaysia has been made one of ACI's partners related to the analysis of competitiveness. We signed a Memorandum of Understanding to collaborate on 26 November 2015.

I welcome the release of the 2016 Annual Update on ACI's Competitiveness Ranking and Simulations of the ASEAN-10. I look forward to participating in the discussion on the subject later this morning.

It is quite fitting that this Forum is held one day after the ASEAN Summits are concluded in Vientiane. Matters discussed and decided by the ASEAN Leaders among themselves and between them and the leaders of ASEAN's partners could serve as a useful backdrop for us in looking at some of the issues pertinent to the discussion at this Forum.

ASEAN is a successful regional organisation. Some people may not agree. They see ASEAN as still weak. They fear that ASEAN could at any time succumb to pressure from the major powers. They also see ASEAN as too elitist, the "ASEAN Way" of doing things as too slow and cumbersome, and the countless declarations, communiques, visions, plans and programmes of action mainly as repetitive rhetorical statements.

As ASEAN commemorates its 50th anniversary in 2017, it can look back to many successes. There are also some setbacks. ASEAN has declared itself a community, as of January 2016, at the 26th ASEAN Summit held in Kuala Lumpur in November 2015. It has also adopted a new "Vision 2025" and is busy working to translate that vision into real action and implementable programmes. The Leaders have reaffirmed in Vientiane their commitment to translate that vision into reality.

Global and Regional Strategic, Political and Economic Environment

The ASEAN Community has been established amidst global political and economic uncertainties. There are indeed some similarities between the present situation and the days when the Bangkok Declaration was adopted in 1967. The world is presently facing a period of strategic, political and economic doldrums, concern and uncertainty. Yet Southeast Asia is stable and much of that stability is owed to the spirit of ASEAN cooperation and regionalism.

The global economic situation continues to elicit concern. Low oil prices have affected many economies. Slow growth in China and elsewhere and a strong US dollar against most other currencies could have a prolonged effect on trade, investment and tourism for the ASEAN countries. Continuing conflict and tension in the Middle East and North Africa, the global threat of terrorism and violent extremism, especially the kind promoted by the Islamic State (IS), and the massive migration and refugee issues facing Europe and other parts of the world would inevitably have an impact on ASEAN.

There are other major issues which require attention: climate change, food security and new pandemic diseases which include the latest spread of the Zika virus in Southeast Asia. Increasingly governments in ASEAN would also have to deal with greater demands for freedom, democracy and human rights as well as cope with the tremendous influence of technology, in particular information technology, on communication, commerce and human interaction.

ASEAN is experiencing a relatively peaceful environment within the region of Southeast Asia amidst an interesting mixture of calm and tension in the Asia-Pacific region. Conflict among member states have been minimised with some serious efforts being made to resolve outstanding problems, although some intractable territorial claims and disputes remain. The differences between the United States and China over the South China Sea, China's increasing assertiveness on the issue and the threat of greater militarization in the area continue to be a source of major concern.

ASEAN will have to deftly manage and balance its relations with both the leading superpowers, the US and China. Any effort by them to influence either through pressure or persuasion on ASEAN as a group or on individual member states could make it difficult for ASEAN to decide on important issues, thus putting further strain and challenge on ASEAN solidarity, unity and cohesion.

In spite of the global economic slowdown, there is still comparatively high economic growth and prosperity in ASEAN and its two large neighbours, China and India. They, together with the United States, Japan and Korea are important partners for the success of the ASEAN Economic Community (AEC). All these countries have links to ASEAN or ASEAN members, in one way or another, through the East Asia Summit (EAS), APEC, the yet to be concluded Regional Comprehensive Economic Partnership Agreement (RCEP) and the Trans-Pacific Partnership Agreement (TPPA).

The establishment of the AEC should increase the prospects for further expansion of the ASEAN economies through increased trade, greater flow of investments and wider connectivity and interaction. With a population of 625 million people and a combined Gross Domestic Product (GDP) of 2.5 trillion US dollars, the ASEAN Community would become a formidable economic powerhouse in the future. ASEAN is now the seventh largest economy in the world and the third largest market. ASEAN, according to Nielsen, had a middle class comprising 190 million people in 2012 and the number is set to double to 400 million by 2020, even surpassing the number in the United States. Therefore it is urgent that the ASEAN member states work towards increasing their competitiveness level through the AEC.

The ASEAN middle class is growing quite rapidly to become one of the major drivers of growth and development in the ASEAN countries. But with a rising middle class juxtaposed against an aging population in some countries, ASEAN will face issues such as educational and skills gaps, labour problems, brain drain and intra-regional migration, which would have to be tackled head-on in the not so distant future.

New and emerging issues are posing a greater challenge to ASEAN unity and cohesion. They would increasingly test ASEAN's ability and willingness to respond and act collectively to deal with them. Such issues include human trafficking and migration, globalised terrorism and violent extremism, climate change and the environment and energy and food security. At some point in the future ASEAN would also have to deal with the issue of water security for member states.

The ASEAN countries would have to meet, in a more rational and matured fashion, the challenge of new technologies: disruptive, IT, social media. These would have a tremendous impact on the competition for and management of the political, economic and socio-cultural spaces and on the issue of governance in all member states. ASEAN governments have to be sensitive to these developments and react to them in a manner that does not infringe upon constitutional and individual rights. Indeed this development has already brought a greater demand for participation among the people through civil society and non-governmental organizations to make ASEAN a truly people-oriented and people-centred organization.

ASEAN as a Rules-based Community

With the ASEAN Charter being adopted in 2008 and the ASEAN Community being declared in 2015, ASEAN has evolved into a rules-based organization, developing its own norms and values which are increasingly observed and respected by member states as well as others. The adherence to rules and norms is important for ASEAN to progress as a community.

With the establishment of the ASEAN Community, a case can be made for the need to have the 'ASEAN Way' pick up more pace and steam for the sake of the peoples of ASEAN. In this regard, the principle of consensus in ASEAN decision making should also be reviewed to allow for quick decisions and early implementation of plans and programmes. Quite importantly also, ASEAN needs to ensure the continued relevance of ASEAN centrality within ASEAN, among the member states and among ASEAN's partners.

It is increasingly acknowledged that the resolution of many issues nowadays requires the involvement of all stakeholders: governments, private sector, legislators, non-governmental organisations (NGOs) and civil society organisations (CSOs), think tanks, people. As we move beyond ASEAN's fifty years, there should be a lesser role for governments and more stakes for the others.

Challenges and Opportunities Ahead

Moving forward into its next half century, ASEAN has to continue to confront the challenges that could impact on ASEAN's continued relevance, viability and vitality and seize on the opportunities that could sustain the momentum of growth, progress and prosperity.

First, ASEAN has to face the challenge of preserving ASEAN centrality, solidarity, unity and cohesion. ASEAN's Vision 2025 talks much about ASEAN centrality in its external relations. While this is important in keeping the external partners engaged, ASEAN needs to also address the issue of ASEAN centrality among members. Member states must be able to balance the Community's interest with their respective national interests while not sacrificing ASEAN solidarity and unity.

Second, ASEAN has to be dexterous in handling the impact of major power relations on the Community. This would not mean only in respect of China-US relations or even competition, but also with regard to the role and interests of others including Japan, India, Australia and Russia.

Third, ASEAN needs to be continuously sensitive to the global strategic and economic environment and landscape. It is important that ASEAN develops its own forecasting and projecting capabilities for 2025 and beyond, through the ASEAN Secretariat and other relevant ASEAN bodies.

Fourth, ASEAN must be able to ensure the successful elaboration and implementation of Vision 2025 and the community blueprints and adapt to future strategic and security demands. ASEAN should also be prepared to adjust and deploy additional financial resources and human capital to meet the ASEAN goals. These goals would serve to complement national plans and programmes.

Fifth, ASEAN has to be ready to face the challenge of changing values and expectations in all the member states and deal with many issues of internal, regional and global governance. The relatively young ASEAN population will have stronger demands and higher expectations as each member state prospers and people are exposed to better economic opportunities.

Sixth, while ASEAN seeks to grow and prosper, the member states will have to deal with future issues of competition for resources: water, food, energy. This could cause intra-Community friction and conflict that should be addressed through cooperative measures starting from now.

Seventh, ASEAN inevitably would be faced with the challenge of population: growth, aging, rural-urban ratio and migration. This could place severe political and socio-economic pressures on member states internally and community-wide. The issue of intra-regional migration and mobility will have to be tackled simultaneously with that of narrowing the development gap.

Conclusion

The success of the ASEAN Community should be a priority for all ASEAN member states. But success cannot be achieved if the right ingredients for it are not recognised and observed by everyone based on the continued commitment to regional integration among ASEAN member states and ASEAN's partners.

The ASEAN Community should provide the enabling environment for the member states to grow their economies and develop according to their domestic needs and conditions. The creation of a single market under the AEC and greater cooperation under the political-security and socio-cultural pillars should offer a better setting for the member states to become more competitive.

The vision of the founding fathers should continue to be the guide for ASEAN even as various visions and blueprints are being elaborated and implemented. The goal of a people-oriented and people-centred ASEAN Community should not owe its achievement to documents and declarations alone. It should embody the true spirit of cooperation and community building and preservation.

Appendix 2

Distinguished Speaker's Speech at the Asia Competitiveness Institute (ACI)–World Bank ASEAN Economic Forum, 9 September 2016

ASEAN Competitiveness and Productivity in a Fast-changing World

Dr Gilberto M. Llanto

President, Philippine Institute for Development Studies (PIDS), Philippines

Minister Ong Ye Kung, Provost Tan Eng Chye, Dean Mahbubani, Prof. Tan Khee Giap, ladies and gentlemen, a pleasant good morning!

First of all, please allow me to thank you for inviting me to this important Forum. It is a great honor for me to speak in this Forum and learn from the presentations and discussions that we will have today. Before I proceed, let me acknowledge and congratulate the ACI its significant contribution to efforts to strenghten national and local competitiveness, which is a critical building block for a strong ASEAN Economic Community.

The ASEAN faces many critical challenges, which will entail the improvement of the region's competitiveness and productivity amid a fast-changing world. The policy responses to those challenges could be specific to a particular ASEAN member-state but there are challenges that will call for close policy coordination and collaboration among ASEAN member-states. A graphic example of the latter type of challenge could be a regional pandemic or a natural disaster that transcends national boundaries and, thus, requires cross-border policy responses and interventions.

Since the 2008 global financial crisis, several challenges that have stretched the capacity of nation-states to handle have emerged. Among these are uncertainties driven by low commodity prices, the debt crisis in Europe, Brexit, the slowdown of the Chinese economy, the refugee crisis, the effects of climate change, and the political instability in different parts of the globe — all of which dampen global economic activity.[1] Moreover, the further widening of income inequality amid growth is cultivating discontent among the poor and marginalized. This, combined with an ascendant middle class in search of meaningful jobs and political influence, is threatening to break

[1] See various reports of BBC News: http://www.bbc.com/news/37055873; http://www.bbc.com/news/business-37006911; http://www.zerohedge.com/news/2016-08-08/weak-chinese-trade-data-confirms-global-slowdown-imports-tumble.

down economic and political structures and restrict open and competitive markets, which are the very forces that have ironically brought peace and prosperity to many countries around the globe.

However, in our part of the world, we have a reason to be proud of. Our dynamic ASEAN countries have shown their mettle in addressing those challenges. Indeed, they present a contrasting picture to the other parts of the global economy. The World Economic Forum and the IMF, among others, reported that the combined Gross Domestic Product (GDP) of ASEAN member-states registered a strong growth in the second quarter of 2016, with Indonesia, the Philippines, and Viet Nam leading the pack. The smaller economies of the region — Myanmar, Laos, and Cambodia — are expected to contribute to ASEAN growth further in 2016. I note the increasing percentage share of ASEAN to world GDP, from 2.6 percent in 2009 to 3.2 percent in 2014. In contrast, Japan's share to world GDP declined from 8.4 percent in 2009 to 6 percent in 2014.[2]

Likewise, the ASEAN Secretariat has reported encouraging trends in the region notwithstanding the weak economy of China, its third largest trading partner. The growth rates of intra-ASEAN and extra-ASEAN trade indicate the vibrancy of ASEAN member-states. In 2014, intra-ASEAN trade accounted for 24.1 percent of the total trade in ASEAN. The remaining 75.9 percent accounted for extra-ASEAN trade. This has been the trend in the past several years according to the ASEAN Secretariat. Meanwhile, foreign direct investment (FDI) inflows in the ASEAN reached 136.2 billion US dollars in 2014, an increase of 18.5 billion US dollars (16 percent) from 2013. In 2014, Singapore was the major recipient of FDI in ASEAN, with inflows amounting to 72 billion US dollars. Meanwhile, Viet Nam led the CLMV countries, with 9.2 billion US dollars of FDI inflows. In 2014, FDI inflows in ASEAN were about 5.3 percent of its GDP; extra-ASEAN made up 4.3 percent while intra-ASEAN accounted for 0.9 percent.[3]

The challenges I have mentioned continue to be daunting challenges, which our individual economies and the ASEAN member-states collectively have to deal with. Today, let me expound about a new challenge, which is more disruptive than what we have known before and one that promises an entirely new wave of productivity and growth for the world.

I am referring to the Fourth Industrial Revolution brought to our attention by Prof. Klaus Schwab in the World Economic Forum, which he describes as a revolutionary shift "characterized by a fusion of technologies that is blurring the lines between the physical, digital, and biological spheres."[4] Prof. Schwab talks about "profound shifts across all industries, marked by the emergence of new business models, the disruption of incumbents and the reshaping of production, consumption, transportation and delivery systems. . . [where there will be] new ways of using technology to change behaviour and our systems of production and consumption."[5] This is

---

[2] These figures are from the World Development Indicators and the ASEAN Secretariat.

[3] *Source*: ASEAN Secretariat.

[4] https://www.weforum.org/focus/the-fourth-industrial-revolution/.

[5] *Source*: Schwab (2016, pages 1 and 2), Schwab, Klaus (2016) *The Fourth Industrial Revolution*. https://www.amazon.com/Fourth-Industrial-Revolution-Klaus-Schwab/dp/1944835008/ref=sr_1_1?ie=UTF8&qid=1479801291&sr=8-1&keywords=klaus+schwab+the+fourth+industrial+revolution.

happening very quickly because "a convergence of technology forces is changing the industrial ecosystem."[6]

To contextualize what this Fourth Industrial Revolution means and the technologies it requires, let us take a look at a recent study done by the McKinsey Global Institute[7] on the new trends in global manufacturing. McKinsey Global Institute starts off by saying that as countries become wealthier, the share of manufacturing's output from labor-intensive tradables declines. The trend is toward more sophisticated and technology-driven goods and services. There is a shift of global demand toward developing economies, especially to those with an expanding middle class. For instance, McKinsey says that the demand for automobiles in developing economies has surpassed the demand in advanced economies, and sales are growing nearly four times as quickly. Moreover, the United Nations Industrial Development Organization projects that "globally, the emergence of middle and upper classes in the developing countries is expected to dramatically shift market concentration." This new breed of consumers will demand more sophisticated, modern, and technologically-oriented products, driven by the so-called Internet-of-Things that is starting to redefine modern living.

This begs the question then of how we can prepare ASEAN's industry, manufacturing, and services, and its workforces to capitalize on the opportunities laid down by the Fourth Industrial Revolution in order to sustain and deepen ASEAN's growth. As ASEAN prospers, it will shed more of its labor-intensive manufacturing and low-skilled jobs, and move up the technology, production, and consumption ladder. The Fourth Industrial Revolution is driven by new and emerging technologies but not every country is ready and equipped to take advantage of those technologies. In the new unfolding world of the future, talent more than capital will be the critical factor of production according to Prof. Schwab. In this regard, there will be a huge demand for high-skilled professionals and workers and a greater need for collaboration and cooperation with the private sector and civil society. Collaboration and cooperation are words easily said and the challenge is to foster a governance framework that will tease out the creative ideas and action from various sectors and to make these converge toward greater competitiveness and productivity.

I have no doubt in my mind that the more dynamic countries in East and Southeast Asia will be able to harness the technologies and capabilities to benefit from the opportunities arising from the Fourth Industrial Revolution. The time is now for ASEAN to develop more strategic and collaborative growth and investment strategies. There will be growing talent shortages and higher demand for high-skilled workers. However, there would not be enough low-skilled jobs according to McKinsey Global Institute; this may have negative ramifications on the region considering that the ASEAN workforce is partly characterised by low-skilled and unskilled labor. Clearly, this is another challenge that requires close policy coordination and collaboration among ASEAN member-states to address.

What is needed is a more certain environment that recognises and rewards innovation, skill development, flexible work and production systems, and talent. The ASEAN member-states

---

[6]Aidan Quilligan (2015) "The Fourth Industrial Revolution when Digital Technology meets the Shop Floor" http://cwbackoffice.co.uk/Presentation/PrestigiousLecture_11.02.15_AidanQuilligan_TheFourthIndustrialRevolution.pdf.
[7]McKinsey Global Institute (2012) "Manufacturing the future: the next era of global growth and innovation".

should strive to remove regulatory barriers to growth, invest in education and skill development, support research and development, and invest in the necessary physical, technical, and scientific infrastructure. In this light, I would like to underscore the important role played by the ACI in helping build the infrastructure for competitiveness and productivity of ASEAN member-states that will enable them to exploit various opportunities offered by the Fourth Industrial Revolution. We are fortunate that the ACI has started to establish a network of like-minded research and policy institutions in the region toward this goal.

Thank you and good day!

Appendix 3

Distinguished Speaker's Speech at the Asia Competitiveness Institute (ACI)–World Bank ASEAN Economic Forum, 9 September 2016

Dr Nguyen Dinh Cung

President, Central Institute for Economic Management (CIEM), Vietnam

Good morning ladies and gentlemen, and distinguished guests. I prepared quite a long presentation, but when I arrived here, I changed my mind. Today I will address two major challenges that ASEAN has to overcome.

Vietnam joined ASEAN in 1995, and since then, we've recognised that the organisation has played a vital role in both the development of individual states, and our region. However, for ASEAN's further development, and in order to strengthen its position, especially with respect to its centrality, there are several challenges we need to overcome.

Firstly, the rule making process in ASEAN is currently based on consensus. This is time consuming, and relies heavily on compromise. As a result, our final decisions are quite different from our original intentions for the region. Furthermore, the consensus rule makes room for third parties to intervene into ASEANs affairs. As such, I think reforming ASEAN's decision making process is the first challenge we have to overcome.

The second challenge is to bridge the gap between the advanced economies and less developed economies. This is essential in improving ASEAN's competitiveness. To achieve this, the less developed countries need far reaching and robust domestic reforms. I believe that these reforms play a decisive role in overcoming this challenge. I am unsure about other countries but in Vietnam, implementing such policies will pose a challenge.

Presently, a problem that Vietnam faces is the misallocation of resources. This arises from the administrative intervention of state. Further reforms require enabling the market to play a decisive role in the mobilisation and allocation of resources. However, with such reforms come changes in authority, function, and power. As such, there is much resistance to them and the implementation of reforms is challenging. Despite this we need to follow through, not only for the competitiveness of Vietnam, but the development of our region.

Finally, while domestic factors are decisive in implementing reforms, cooperation among the countries is very important as well. In this case, I think that Singapore can play a significant role, perhaps in providing a framework for less developed countries to make reforms. Furthermore, policy forums are very important and useful and as such I would like to see some similar ACI's activities in Vietnam to inspire the public to improve the competitiveness of Vietnam. So, thank you very much.

Appendix 4
Competitiveness Analysis of ASEAN-10 Economies, 2000–2013

List of Indicators

No.	Indicator	Unit	Reversed Indicator*
1	**Macroeconomic Stability**		
1.1	**Economic Vibrancy**		
1.1.01	Gross Domestic Product	US Dollars, Constant 2000 Prices	
1.1.02	Real GDP Growth	Percentage Change Per Annum	
1.1.03	GDP Per Capita	US Dollars, Constant 2000 Prices	
1.1.04	Output Agriculture (Value Added)	US Dollars, Constant 2005 Prices	
1.1.05	Output Industry (Value Added)	US Dollars, Constant 2005 Prices	
1.1.06	Output Services (Value Added)	US Dollars, Constant 2005 Prices	
1.1.07	Gross Domestic Savings	Percentage of GDP	
1.1.08	Gross Fixed Capital Formation	Percentage of GDP	
1.1.09	Inflation	Percentage Change Per Annum	R
1.1.10	Money Supply Growth (M2)	Percentage Change Per Annum	R
1.2	**Openness to Trade and Services**		
1.2.01	Current Account Balance	Percentage of GDP	
1.2.02	Exports of Goods and Services	US Dollars, Current Market Prices	
1.2.03	Imports of Goods and Services	US Dollars, Current Market Prices	
1.2.04	Openness to Trade	Ratio	
1.2.05	International Tourism Receipts	US Dollars, Current Market Prices	
1.3	**Attractiveness to Foreign Investors**		
1.3.01	Foreign Direct Investment Inflows	US Dollars, Current Market Prices	
1.3.02	Foreign Owned Companies	Survey Data	
1.3.03	Corporate Income Tax	Percentage of Profit	R
1.3.04	Lack of Discrimination Against Investors	Survey Data	
1.3.05	Levelness of Playing Field	Survey Data	
1.3.06	Transparency of Processes for Investors	Survey Data	
1.3.07	Business Impact of Rules on FDI	Survey Data	

(Continued)

(Continued)

No.	Indicator	Unit	Reversed Indicator*
2	**Government and Institutional Setting**		
2.1	**Government Policies and Fiscal Sustainability**		
2.1.01	Government Revenue (Including Grants)	US Dollars, 2000 Constant Prices	
2.1.02	Tax Revenue	US Dollars, 2000 Constant Prices	
2.1.03	Tax Revenue/Government Revenue	Percentage	
2.1.04	Government Consumption Expenditure	Percentage of GDP	
2.1.05	External Debt	US Dollars, Current Market Prices	R
2.1.06	International Reserves	US Dollars, Current Market Prices	
2.1.07	Net Foreign Assets	US Dollars, Current Market Prices	
2.1.08	International Monetary Fund Credit	US Dollars, Current Market Prices	R
2.1.09	Budget Balance	Percentage of GDP	
2.1.10	Tax Burden	Percentage of GDP	R
2.1.11	Money Supply (M2)	Percentage of GDP	
2.1.12	Deposit Interest Rate	Percentage	
2.1.13	Lending Rate	Percentage	R
2.1.14	Interest Rate Spread	Percentage	R
2.1.15	Exchange Rate Appreciation	Annual Average Percentage Change (Local Currency Unit per US Dollar)	R
2.2	**Institutions, Governance and Leadership**		
2.2.01	Quality of Government Policies	Survey Data	
2.2.02	Government Effectiveness	Survey Data	
2.2.03	Government Environmental Protection Policies	Percentage of Total Territorial Area	
2.2.04	Quality of Central Bank/Monetary Authority	Survey Data	
2.2.05	Government Stability	Survey Data	
2.2.06	Government Responsiveness	Survey Data	
2.2.07	Quality of Political Leadership	Survey Data	R
2.2.08	Political System Risk	Survey Data	R
2.2.09	Legislature/Parliament (Functioning of Government System)	Survey Data	
2.2.10	Strength of Auditing and Reporting Standards	Survey Data	
2.2.11	Institutional Sophistication	Survey Data	
2.2.12	Bureaucracy/Red Tape	Survey Data	

(Continued)

(*Continued*)

No.	Indicator	Unit	Reversed Indicator*
2.2.13	Lack of Corruption	Survey Data	
2.2.14	Lack of Cronyism	Survey Data	
2.2.15	Lack of Market Distortion due to State-Ownership	Survey Data	
2.3	**Competition, Regulatory Standards and Rule of Law**		
2.3.01	Corporate Governance	Survey Data	
2.3.02	Quality of Regulatory Environment	Survey Data	
2.3.03	Transparency of Government	Survey Data	
2.3.04	Monopolies and Cartel	Survey Data	
2.3.05	Policy Towards Private Enterprise Rating	Survey Data	
2.3.06	Ease of Starting Business	Number	R
2.3.07	Barriers to Trade	Survey Data	
2.3.08	Intellectual Property Rights Protection	Survey Data	
2.3.09	Regional Competitiveness	Survey Data	
2.3.10	Quality of Judiciary	Survey Data	
2.3.11	Effectiveness of Legal System	Survey Data	
2.3.12	Integrity of Legal System	Survey Data	
2.3.13	Quality of Police	Survey Data	
2.3.14	Political Change	Survey Data	
3	**Financial, Businesses and Manpower Conditions**		
3.1	**Financial Deepening and Business Efficiency**		
3.1.01	Claims on Private Sector	Annual Growth as Percentage of Broad Money	
3.1.02	Domestic Credit to Private Sector	Percentage of GDP	
3.1.03	Quality of Banking and Financial System	Survey Data	
3.1.04	Domestic Credit Provided by the Financial Sector	Percentage of GDP	
3.1.05	Listed Domestic Companies	Number	
3.1.06	Market Capitalisation	US Dollars, Current Market Prices	
3.1.07	Total Value of Stocks Traded	Percentage of GDP	
3.1.08	Sovereign Debt Risk	Number	R
3.1.09	Quality of Stock Market Regulatory Authority	Survey Data	

(*Continued*)

(Continued)

No.	Indicator	Unit	Reversed Indicator*
3.2	**Labour Market Flexibility**		
3.2.01	Labour Force	Number	
3.2.02	Unemployment Rate	Percentage	R
3.2.03	Cost of Production Labour	US Dollars, Current Market Prices	R
3.2.04	Availability of Scientists and Engineers	Survey Data	
3.2.05	Cost of Management Staff	US Dollars, Current Market Prices	R
3.2.06	High Quality Management Staff	Survey Data	
3.2.07	Extent of Staff Training	Survey Data	
3.2.08	Labour Market Rating	Survey Data	
3.3	**Productivity Performance**		
3.3.01	Agriculture, Value Added Per Worker	US Dollars, 2005 Constant Prices	
3.3.02	Industry, Value Added Per Worker	US Dollars, 2005 Constant Prices	
3.3.03	Services, Value Added Per Worker	US Dollars, 2005 Constant Prices	

4	**Quality of Life and Infrastructure Development**		
4.1	**Physical Infrastructure**		
4.1.01	Population	Number	
4.1.02	Local Road System	Survey Data	
4.1.03	Rail Facilities	Survey Data	
4.1.04	Airport Facilities	Survey Data	
4.1.05	Port Facilities	Survey Data	
4.1.06	Electric Power	Survey Data	
4.1.07	Access to Water	Percentage of Population	
4.1.08	Access to Sanitation	Percentage of Population	
4.2	**Technological Infrastructure**		
4.2.01	Telecommunications System	Percentage of GDP	
4.2.02	Telephone Main Lines	Number Per 100 Persons	
4.2.03	Internet Subscribers	Number Per 100 Persons	
4.2.04	Cellular Mobile Telephone Subscribers	Number Per 100 Persons	
4.2.05	Networked Readiness Index	Survey Data	
4.2.06	Personal Computers	Number Per 100 Persons	
4.2.07	Information and Communication Technology (ICT) Expenditure	Percentage of GDP	

(Continued)

(Continued)

No.	Indicator	Unit	Reversed Indicator*
4.3	**Standard of Living, Education and Social Stability**		
4.3.01	Literacy Rate	Percentage	
4.3.02	Primary Schooling	Percentage	
4.3.03	Secondary Schooling	Percentage	
4.3.04	University and Post-Graduate Education	Percentage	
4.3.05	Human Development Index	Composite Statistic	
4.3.06	Health Expenditure	Percentage of GDP	
4.3.07	Urban Population	Percentage of Total Population	
4.3.08	Urban Population Growth	Percentage Per Annum	
4.3.09	Public Security and Safety	Survey Data	
4.3.10	Freedom of Press	Survey Data	R
4.3.11	Freedom of Speech	Survey Data	
4.3.12	Access to Print Media	Number	
4.3.13	Freedom of Religion	Survey Data	
4.3.14	Religious Unrest	Survey Data	
4.3.15	Labour Unrest	Survey Data	
4.3.16	Social Unrest	Survey Data	
4.3.17	Labour Activism	Survey Data	R
4.3.18	Daily Organic Water Pollutant Emissions	Kilogram Per 100 Persons	R
4.3.19	Air Quality	Micrograms Per Cubic Metre	R
4.3.20	Traffic Congestion	Number of Vehicles Per Kilometre of Road	R

Note: * R indicates that the indicator is a reversed indicator.

Source: Asia Competitiveness Institute

Appendix 5
Competitiveness Analysis — The Algorithm

A step-by-step description of the ranking process is described below for N economies, M practical indicators and C environments, with each environment comprising S sub-environments.

(1) Compute the mean value of practical indicator j ($j = 1, \ldots, M$),

$$\bar{X}_j = \frac{1}{N}\sum_{i=1}^{N} X_{ij}$$

where X_{ij} represents the value that economy i ($i = 1, \ldots, N$) takes for practical indicator j.

(2) For each practical indicator j ($j = 1, \ldots, M$), calculate its standard deviation (SD),

$$SD_j = \sqrt{\frac{1}{N}\sum_{i=1}^{N}\left(X_{ij} - \bar{X}_j\right)^2}$$

(3) Compute the standardised value of indicator (SVI) that each economy i ($i = 1, \ldots, N$) takes under each of the practical indicators j ($j = 1, \ldots, M$),

$$SVI_{ij} = \frac{X_{ij} - \bar{X}_j}{SD_j}$$

(4) Compute the 'ranked' standardised value of indicator (RSVI) that each economy i ($i = 1, \ldots, N$) takes under each of the practical indicators j ($j = 1, \ldots, M$):

$$RSVI_{ij} = \begin{cases} SVI_{ij}, & \textit{if a higher value is better} \\ -SVI_{ij}, & \textit{if a lower value is better} \end{cases}$$

(5) For each of the practical indicators j ($j = 1, \ldots, M$), a ranking can be obtained for economies: economies with a higher value of RSVI for indicator j are ranked ahead of those with a lower value.

(6) For each economy i ($i = 1, \ldots, N$), calculate the RSVI for each sub-environment k ($k = 1, \ldots, S$) belonging to environment l ($l = 1, \ldots, C$),

$$Raw\_RSVI_{i,lk} = \frac{1}{y_{lk}} \sum_{p=1}^{y_{lk}} RSVI_{i,j_{lk,p}}$$

$$Mean\_RSVI_{lk} = \frac{1}{N} \sum_{i=1}^{N} Raw\_RSVI_{i,lk}$$

$$SD\_RSVI_{lk} = \sqrt{\frac{1}{N} \sum_{i=1}^{N} \left(Raw\_RSVI_{i,lk} - Mean\_RSVI_{lk} \right)^2}$$

$$RSVI_{i,lk} = \frac{Raw\_RSVI_{i,lk} - Mean\_RSVI_{lk}}{SD\_RSVI_{lk}}$$

where y_{lk} is the total number of practical indicators under sub-environment k of environment l and ($RSVIi,jlk,1$, . . . , $RSVIi,jlk,ylk$) are the RSVIs for economy i that make up sub-environment k of environment l.

(7) For each economy i ($i = 1, \ldots, N$), calculate the RSVI for each environment l ($l = 1, \ldots, C$),

$$Raw\_RSVI_{i,l} = \frac{1}{S_l} \sum_{k=1}^{S_l} RSVI_{i,lk}$$

$$Mean\_RSVI_{l} = \frac{1}{N} \sum_{i=1}^{N} Raw\_RSVI_{i,l}$$

$$SD\_RSVI_{l} = \sqrt{\frac{1}{N} \sum_{i=1}^{N} \left(Raw\_RSVI_{i,l} - Mean\_RSVI_{l} \right)^2}$$

$$RSVI_{i,l} = \frac{Raw\_RSVI_{i,l} - Mean\_RSVI_{l}}{SD\_RSVI_{l}}$$

where ($RSVIi,l1$, . . . , $RSVIi,lS$) are the RSVIs for the S sub-environments under each environment l.

(8) Overall score of economy i ($i = 1, \ldots, N$),

$$Raw\_R_i = \frac{1}{C}\sum_{l=1}^{C} RSVI_{i,l}$$

$$Mean\_R = \frac{1}{N}\sum_{i=1}^{N} Raw\_R_i$$

$$SD\_R = \sqrt{\frac{1}{N}\sum_{i=1}^{N}\left(Raw\_R_i - Mean\_R\right)^2}$$

$$R_i = \frac{Raw\_R_i - Mean\_R}{SD\_R}$$

Economies with a higher *Ri* are ranked ahead of those with lower value of *Ri*, and the economy with the highest *Ri* is the most competitive economy.

Step (5) provides the ranking of each economy for each individual practical indicator. To achieve this ranking, Step (4) adjusts the value of the SVIs so that a higher value will lead to a better ranking in terms of 'competitiveness'. Depending on the nature of the indicator in question, a higher or lower value may reflect a more 'competitive' economy. Take, for instance, the practical sub-indicators 'Gross Domestic Product (GDP)' and 'Unemployment Rate'. A higher GDP but a lower 'unemployment rate' suggests better economic performance which makes an economy more 'competitive'. In most cases where a higher value is better (e.g. GDP), the SVIs of regions are considered, and those with a higher SVI value will have a better ranking. However, for indicators where the inverse is true (e.g. Unemployment Rate), the 'negative SVI' values are compared between economies and a lower SVI value will lead to a better ranking. Step (4) thus seeks to make all standardised values of all practical indicators consistent for ranking purposes.

Step (6) determines the sub-environment rankings of each economy. The average RSVI of all the indicators in the sub-environment are calculated, restandardised across all the economies and compared to other economies. Economies with a higher average RSVI rank better in the sub-environment.

To arrive at the ranking for each environment, the RSVIs of the sub-environments are averaged and restandardised across all economies as detailed in Step (7). Finally, Step (8) requires the RSVI values of each environment to be averaged and restandardised across all economies to determine the overall ranking of the economy. Economies with a higher RSVI are ranked ahead of those with a lower RSVI.

Although the number of sub-environments and indicators may vary for each environment, the aggregate score for each environment is given an equal weight which is 25% of the

ASEAN-10 Overall Competitiveness Index. This method is repeated and applied consistently across all economies to ensure precision of the ranking. Mathematically, this can be illustrated as follows:

ASEAN-10 Overall Competitiveness Index:

= 25% × (Macroeconomic Stability)
+ 25% × (Government and Institutional Setting)
+ 25% × (Financial, Businesses and Manpower Conditions)
+ 25% × (Quality of Life and Infrastructure Development)

Appendix 6

Income Group-Specific Models of Growth Slowdown, Probit Specification

	Growth Slowdown Models		
Income Groups	**Low-Income**	**Lower-Middle-Income**	**Combined Group of Upper-Middle-Income and High-Income Economies**
GRDP Per Capita	0.0007**	0.0003***	0.0002***
	(0.0003)	(0.0001)	(0.00004)
Literacy Rate	–0.0171**	–0.0124*	–0.0937***
	(0.0069)	(0.0065)	(0.0364)
FDI Inflows as Percentage of GRDP	–0.2135**	–0.0997***	
	(0.1010)	(0.0266)	
Length of Road Per Capita	–0.0068*		
	(0.0039)		
Employment in Tertiary Industry as Percentage of Total Employment		–0.0165**	–0.0263**
		(0.0065)	(0.0103)
Old Dependency Ratio		0.0378**	
		(0.0164)	
Openness to Trade			–0.0057***
			(0.0018)
Secondary Industry Value-added Per Worker			–0.00001**
			($4.72e^{-6}$)
Constant	–0.5704	–0.4116	9.1347***
	(0.5692)	(0.6006)	(3.3867)
No. of observations	358	667	147
Pseudo R^2	0.0660	0.0857	0.1234

Note: Numbers in the parentheses are standard errors. *, ** and *** denote the coefficient is significant at 10 percent level, 5 percent level and 1 percent level, respectively.

Source: Asia Competitiveness Institute

Appendix 7

Predictive Probabilities of Growth Slowdown for ASEAN Economies for the Period 2012–2017 (Based on Probit Specification of the Income Group-Specific Growth Slowdown Models)

Economy	Income Group Which Economy Belongs to in 2012	Probability of Experiencing Growth Slowdown during 2012–2017
Cambodia	Lower-middle-income	0.08168
Indonesia	Lower-middle-income	0.26420
Malaysia	Upper-middle-income	0.21517
Myanmar	Lower-middle-income	0.21684
Philippines	Lower-middle-income	0.09903
Singapore	High-income	0.45531
Thailand	Upper-middle-income	0.29846
Vietnam	Lower-middle-income	0.05941
	Average	0.21126

Notes: (i) Average reported is simple average. (ii) Predictive probabilities for Brunei and Laos are not generated. This is because Brunei's GRDP per capita in 1990 PPP dollars is not available throughout the study period while Laos' GRDP per capita in 1990 PPP dollars is not available from 2009 onwards.

Source: Asia Competitiveness Institute

Asia Competitiveness Institute - World Scientific Series

(Continued from page vi)

2015 Estimation of Agricultural Productivity and Annual Update of Competitiveness Analysis for Greater China: Optimising Agricultural Productivity and Promoting Innovation Driven Growth
by Tan Khee Giap, Yuan Randong & Xie Teleixi (Lee Kuan Yew School of Public Policy, NUS, Singapore)

2015 Agricultural Total Factor Productivity and Competitiveness Analysis for States and Federal Territories and Five Regions of India: Annual Competitiveness Update and Evidence on the Agricultural Development Models for Selected Indian States
by Tan Khee Giap, Sasidaran Gopalan & Anuja Tandon (Lee Kuan Yew School of Public Policy, NUS, Singapore)

2015 Agricultural Productivity, Decentralisation, and Competitiveness Analysis for Provinces and Regions of Indonesia
by Tan Khee Giap, Nurina Merdikawati, Mulya Amri & Tan Kong Yam (Lee Kuan Yew School of Public Policy, NUS, Singapore)

2015 Annual Competitiveness Analysis and Development Strategies for Indonesian Provinces
by Tan Khee Giap, Mulya Amri, Nurina Merdikawati & Nursyahida Ahmad (Lee Kuan Yew School of Public Policy, NUS, Singapore)

2014

2014 Annual Competitiveness Ranking and Simulation Study for ASEAN-10 and Development Strategies to Enhance Asia Economic Connectivity
by Tan Khee Giap, Sangiita Yoong Wei Cher, Sasidaran Gopalan & Nguyen Le Phuong Anh (Lee Kuan Yew School of Public Policy, NUS, Singapore)

2014 Annual Provincial and Regional Competitiveness Analysis for Greater China Economies: Development Strategies under the New Normal
by Tan Khee Giap, Yuan Randong & Sangiita Yoong Wei Cher (Lee Kuan Yew School of Public Policy, NUS, Singapore)

2014 Regional Competitiveness Analysis and a Master Plan on Regional Development Strategies for India: Annual Competitiveness Update and Evidence on Economic Development Model for Selected States of India
by Tan Khee Giap, Linda Low, Kartik Rao & Tan Kong Yam (Lee Kuan Yew School of Public Policy, NUS, Singapore)

2014 Provincial and Inaugural Regional Competitiveness Analysis: Safeguarding Indonesia's Growth Momentum
by Tan Khee Giap, Nurina Merdikawati, Mulya Amri & Tan Kong Yam (Lee Kuan Yew School of Public Policy, NUS, Singapore)

2014 Annual Competitiveness Analysis and Development Strategies for Indonesian Provinces
by Tan Khee Giap, Nurina Merdikawati, Mulya Amri & Blake Harley Berger (Lee Kuan Yew School of Public Policy, NUS, Singapore)

2013

Annual Analysis of Competitiveness, Simulation Studies and Development Perspective for 34 Greater China Economies: 2000–2010
by Tan Khee Giap, Yuan Randong, Sangiita Yoong Wei Cher & Yang Mu (Lee Kuan Yew School of Public Policy, NUS, Singapore)

Annual Analysis of Competitiveness, Simulation Studies and Development Perspective for 35 States and Federal Territories of India: 2000–2010
by Tan Khee Giap, Linda Low, Tan Kong Yam & Kartik Rao (Lee Kuan Yew School of Public Policy, NUS, Singapore)

Competitiveness Analysis and Development Strategies for 33 Indonesian Provinces
by Tan Khee Giap, Mulya Amri, Linda Low & Tan Kong Yam (Lee Kuan Yew School of Public Policy, NUS, Singapore)